JONAH HEX
COUNTING CORPSES

JUSTIN GRAY
& JIMMY PALMIOTTI
WRITERS

THE HYDE HOUSE MASSACRE
PAUL GULACY ART
ROB SCHWAGER COLOR

THE GREAT SILENCE
DARWYN COOKE ART
DAVE STEWART COLOR

DIVINING ROD
DICK GIORDANO ART
ROB SCHWAGER COLOR

TOO MEAN TO DIE & SHOOTING STARS
JORDI BERNET ART
ROB SCHWAGER COLOR

"YOU'LL NEVER DANCE AGAIN"
BILLY TUCCI ART
PAUL MOUNTS COLOR

ROB LEIGH LETTERER

DARWYN COOKE
COLLECTION COVER ARTIST

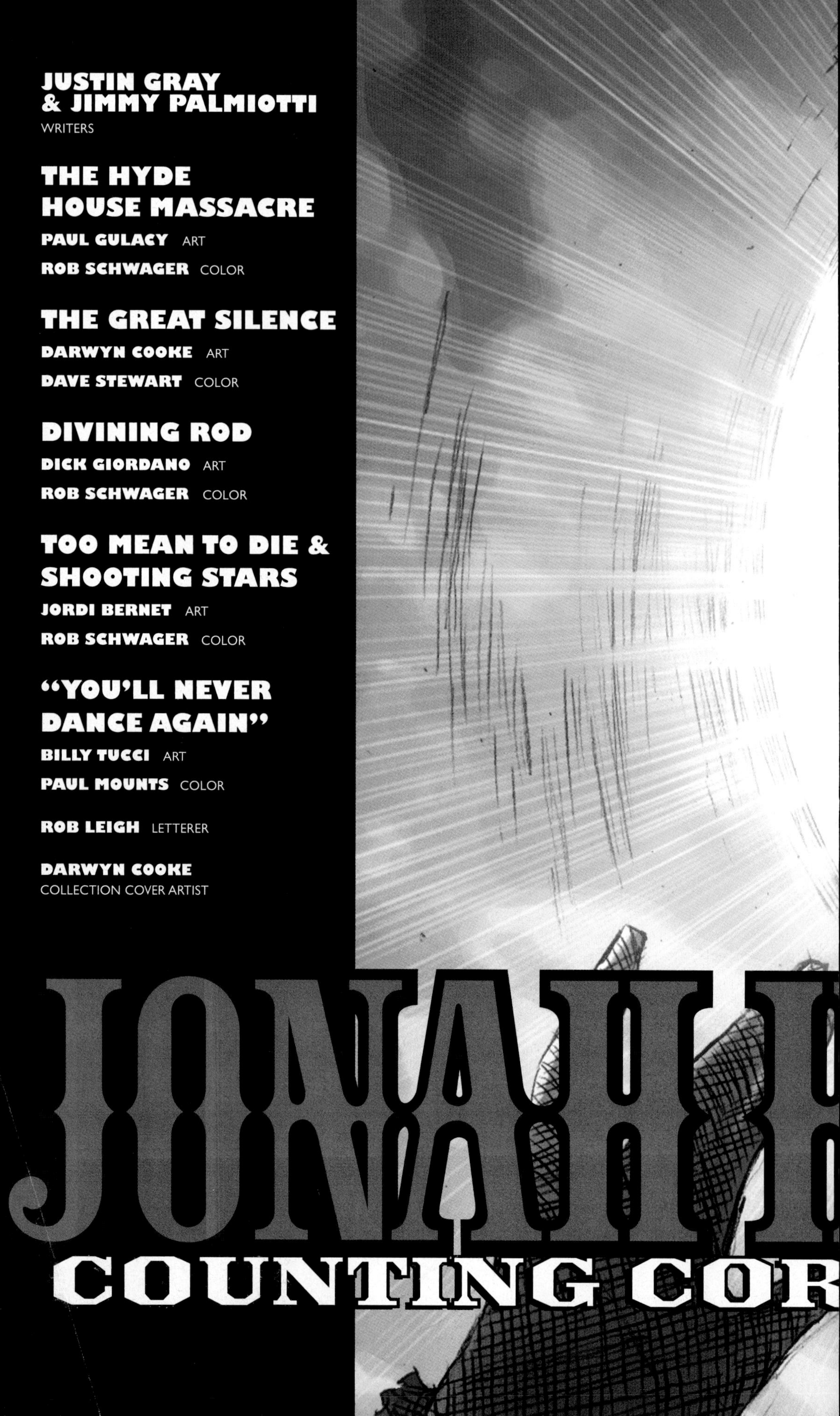
JONAH H
COUNTING COR

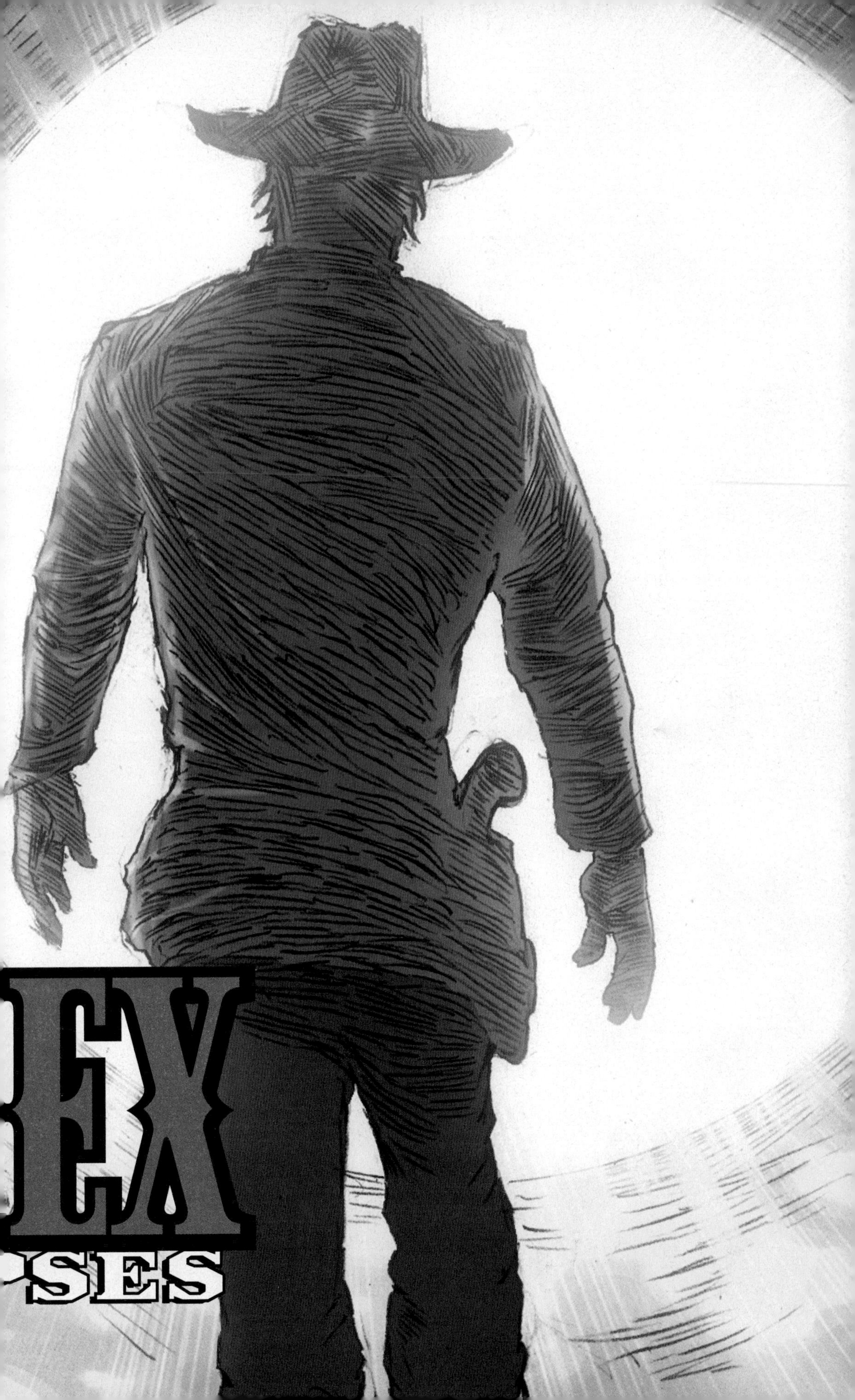

EX
SES

WIL MOSS
ELISABETH V. GEHRLEIN
Editors-original series
SEAN RYAN
Associate Editor-original series
BOB HARRAS
Group Editor-Collected Editions
SEAN MACKIEWICZ
Editor
ROBBIN BROSTERMAN
Design Director-Books

DC COMICS
DIANE NELSON
President
DAN DIDIO AND JIM LEE
Co-Publishers
GEOFF JOHNS
Chief Creative Officer
PATRICK CALDON
EVP-Finance and Administration
JOHN ROOD
EVP-Sales, Marketing and Business
Development
AMY GENKINS
SVP-Business and Legal Affairs
STEVE ROTTERDAM
SVP-Sales and Marketing
JOHN CUNNINGHAM
VP-Marketing

TERRI CUNNINGHAM
VP-Managing Editor
ALISON GILL
VP-Manufacturing
DAVID HYDE
VP-Publicity
SUE POHJA
VP-Book Trade Sales
ALYSSE SOLL
VP-Advertising and
Custom Publishing
BOB WAYNE
VP-Sales
MARK CHIARELLO
Art Director

JONAH HEX:
COUNTING CORPSES
Published by DC Comics.
Cover, text and compilation
Copyright © 2010 DC Comics.
All Rights Reserved.

DC Comics, 1700 Broadway,
New York, NY 10019 A Warner
Bros. Entertainment Company
Printed by Quad/Graphics,
Dubuque, IA, USA. 9/22/10.
First printing.
ISBN: 978-1-4012-2899-6

Cover by Paul Gulacy
with Rob Schwager

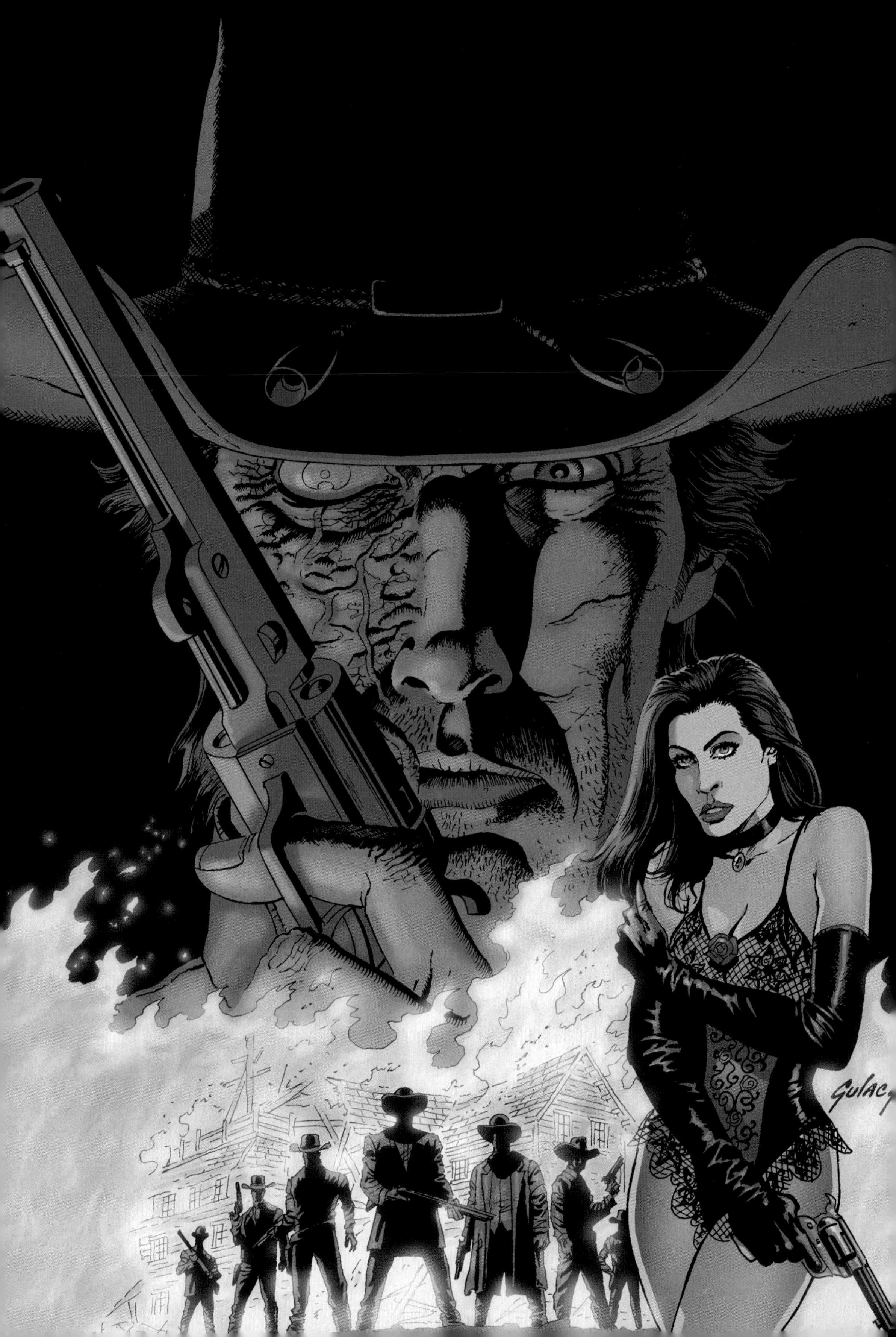

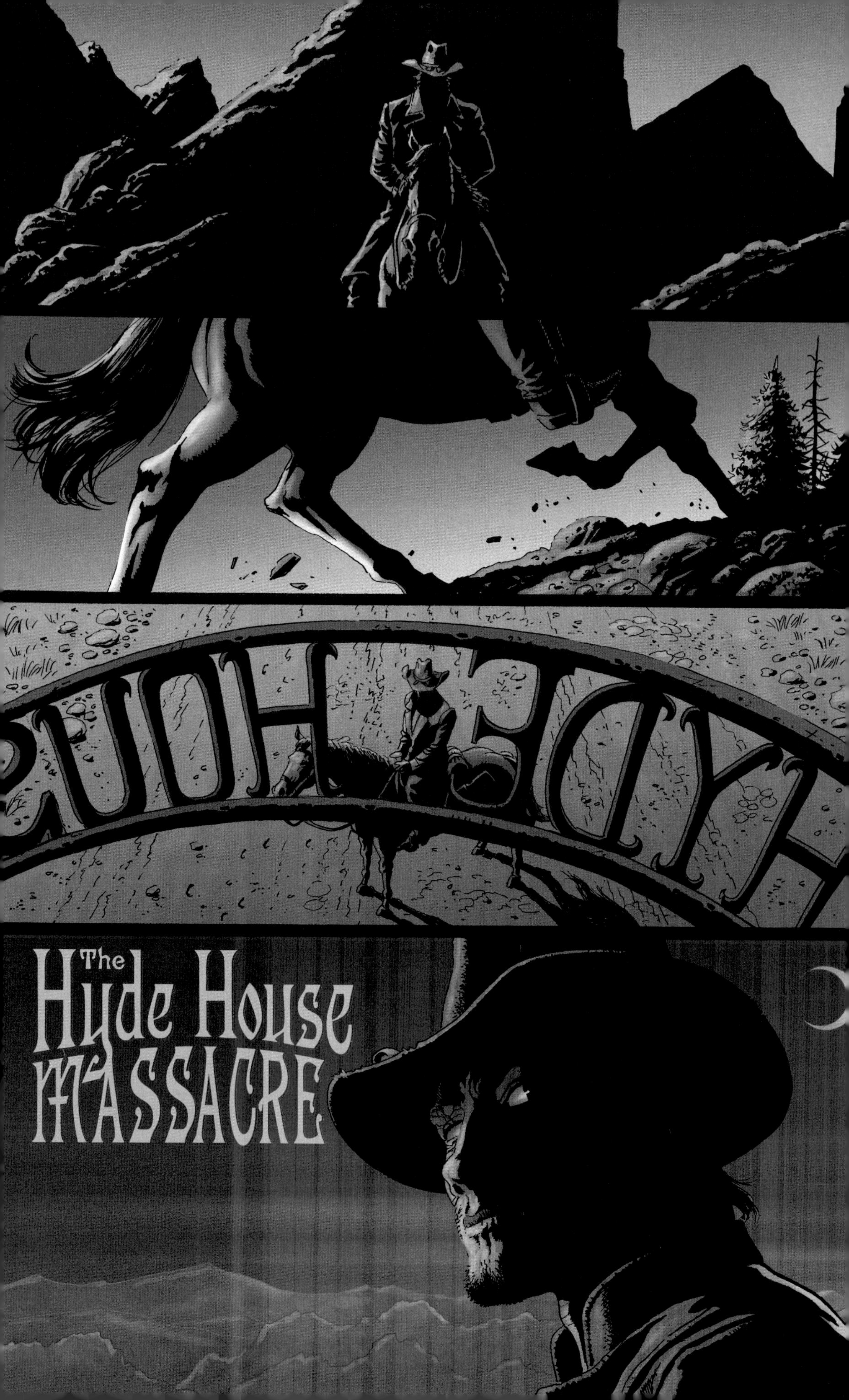
The Hyde House MASSACRE

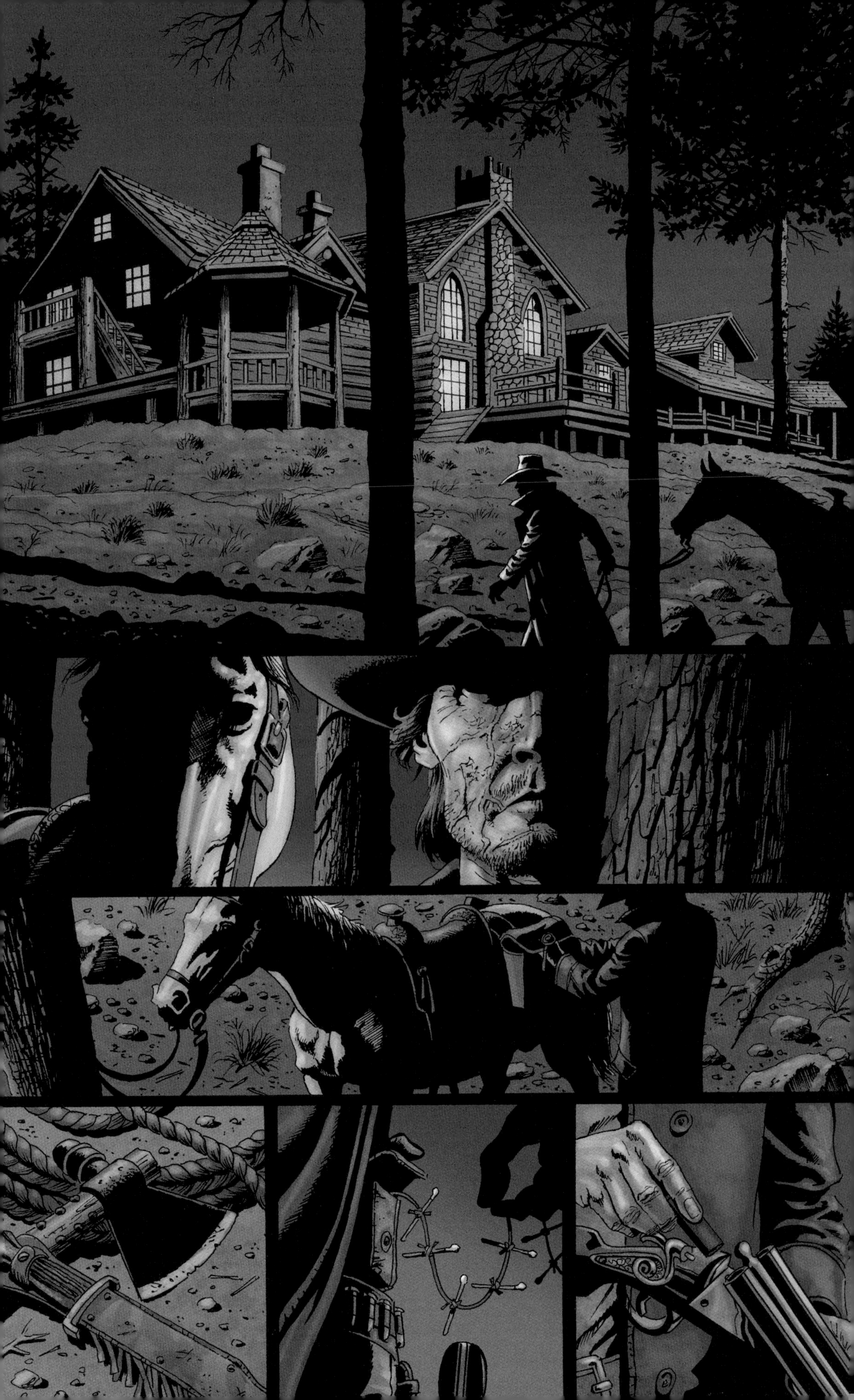

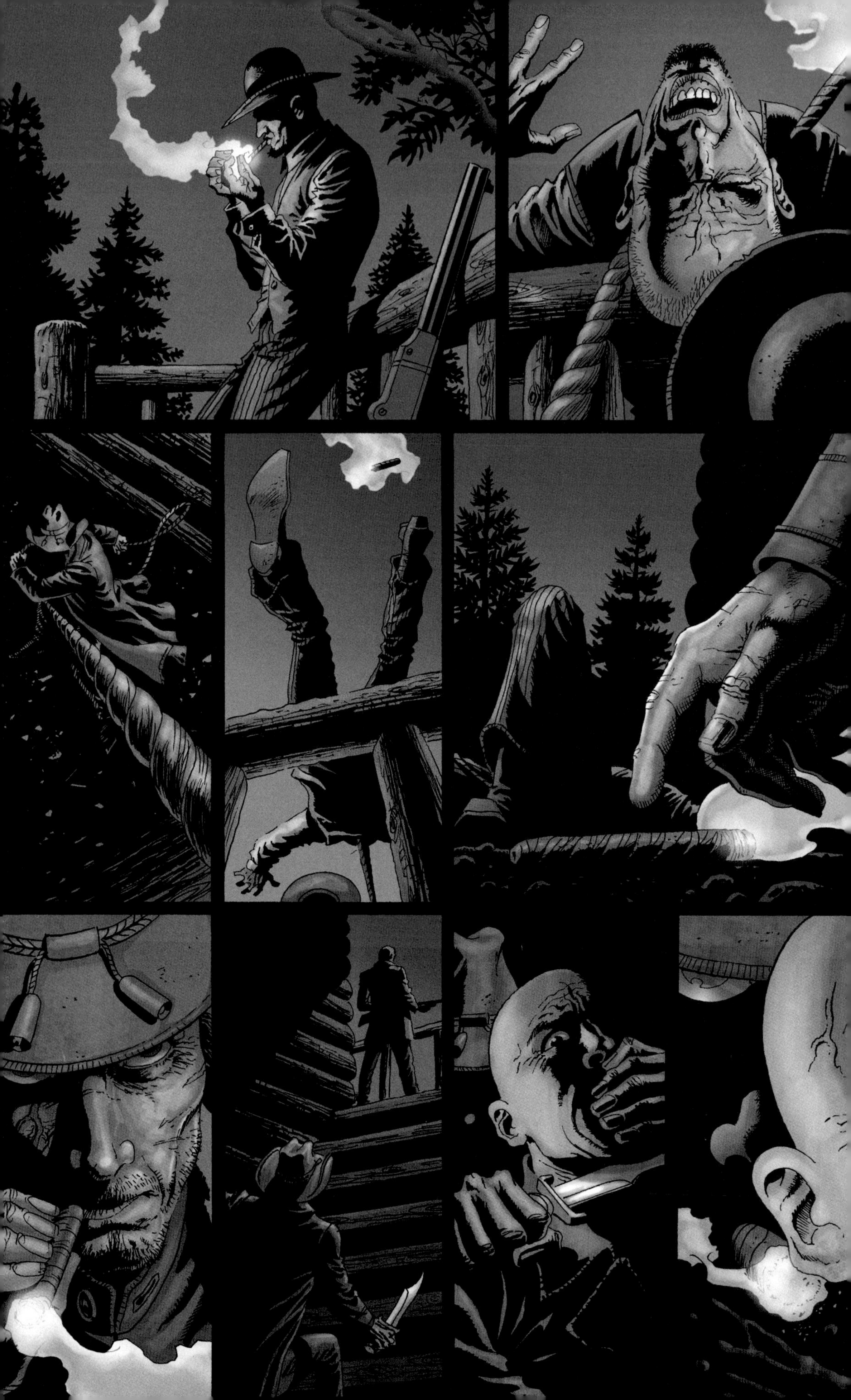

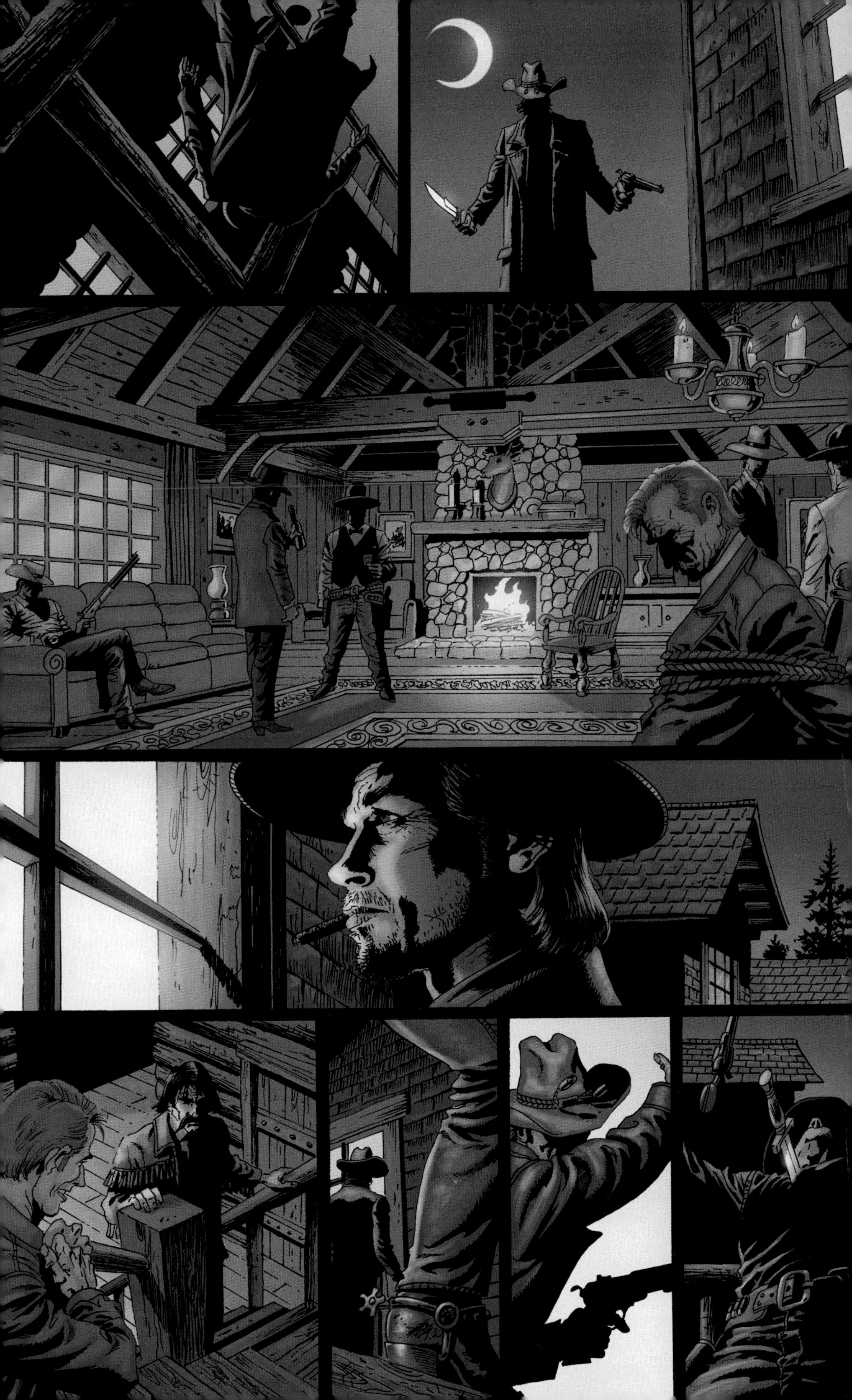

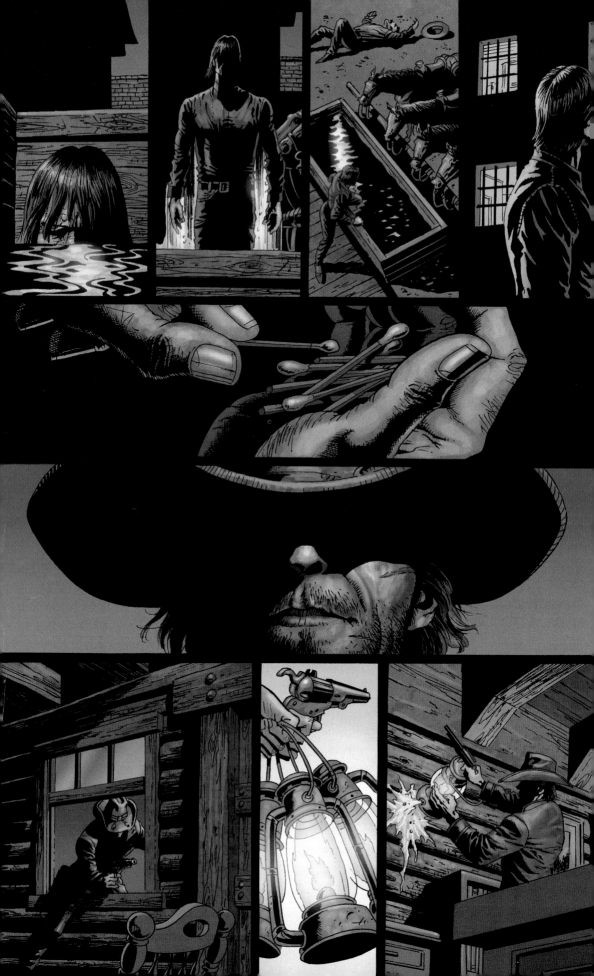

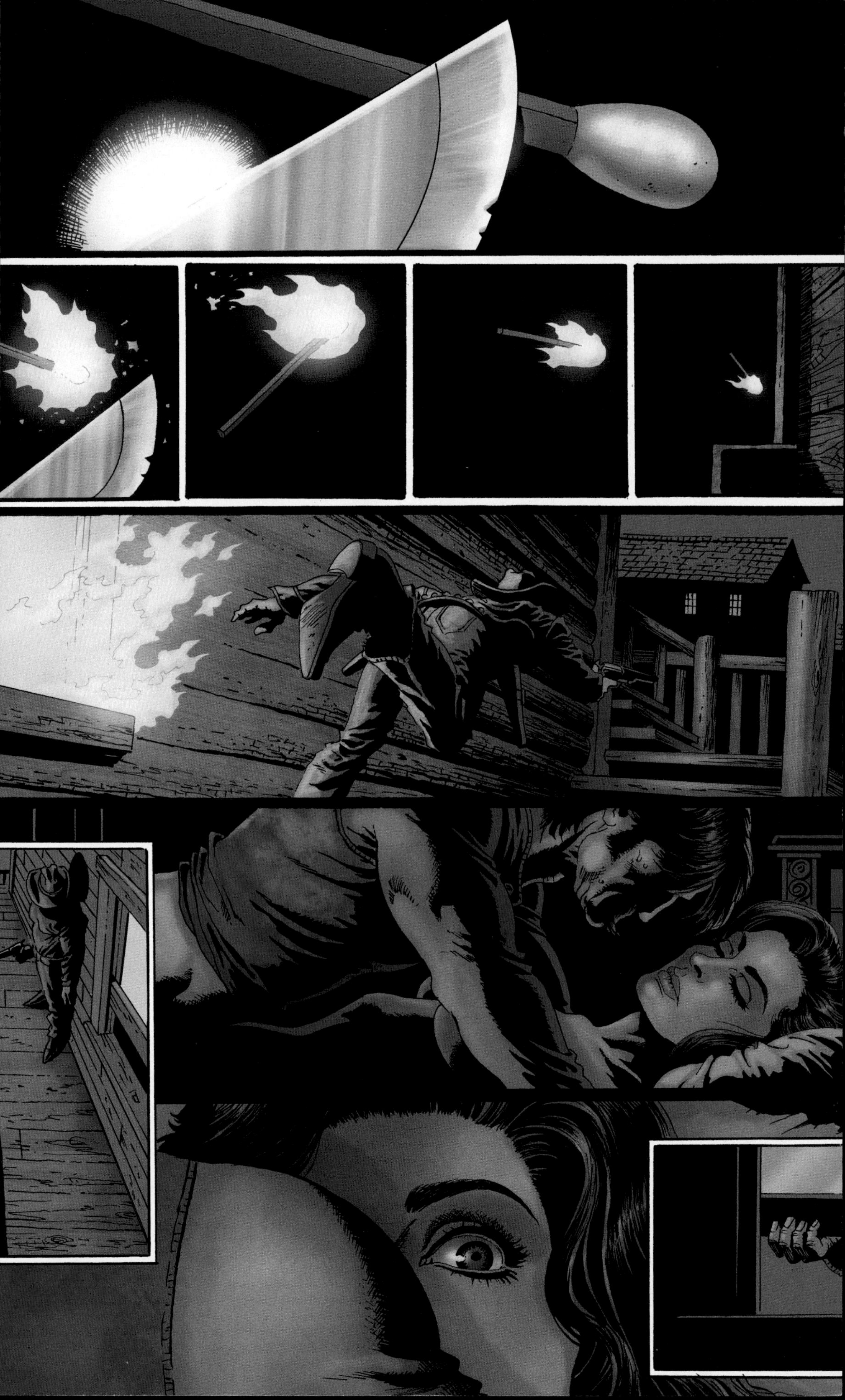

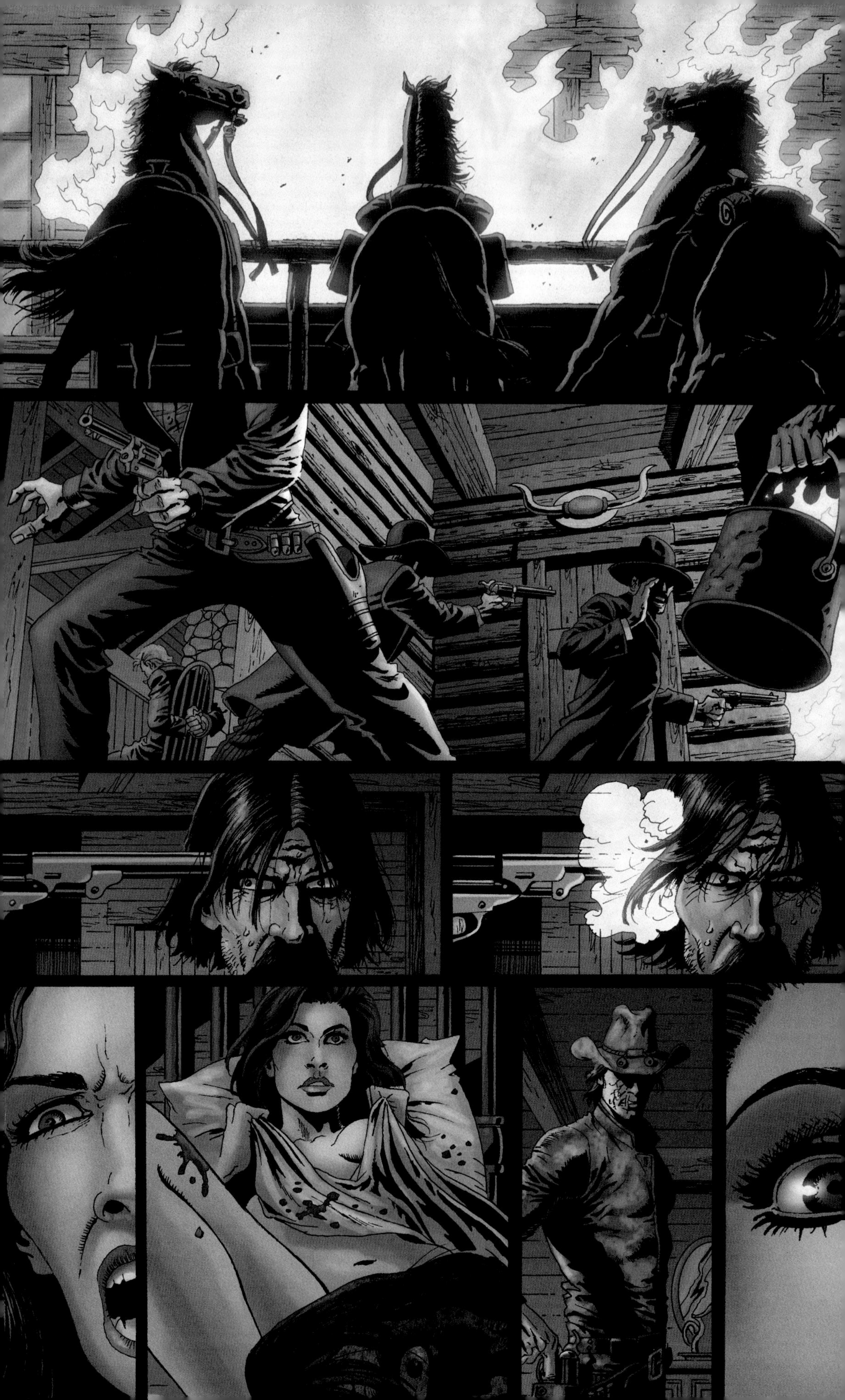

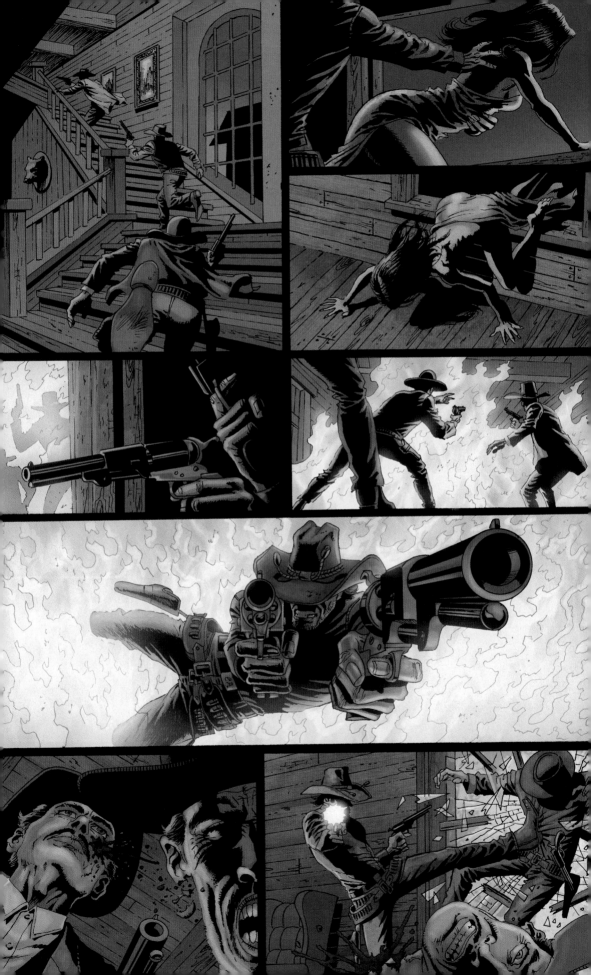

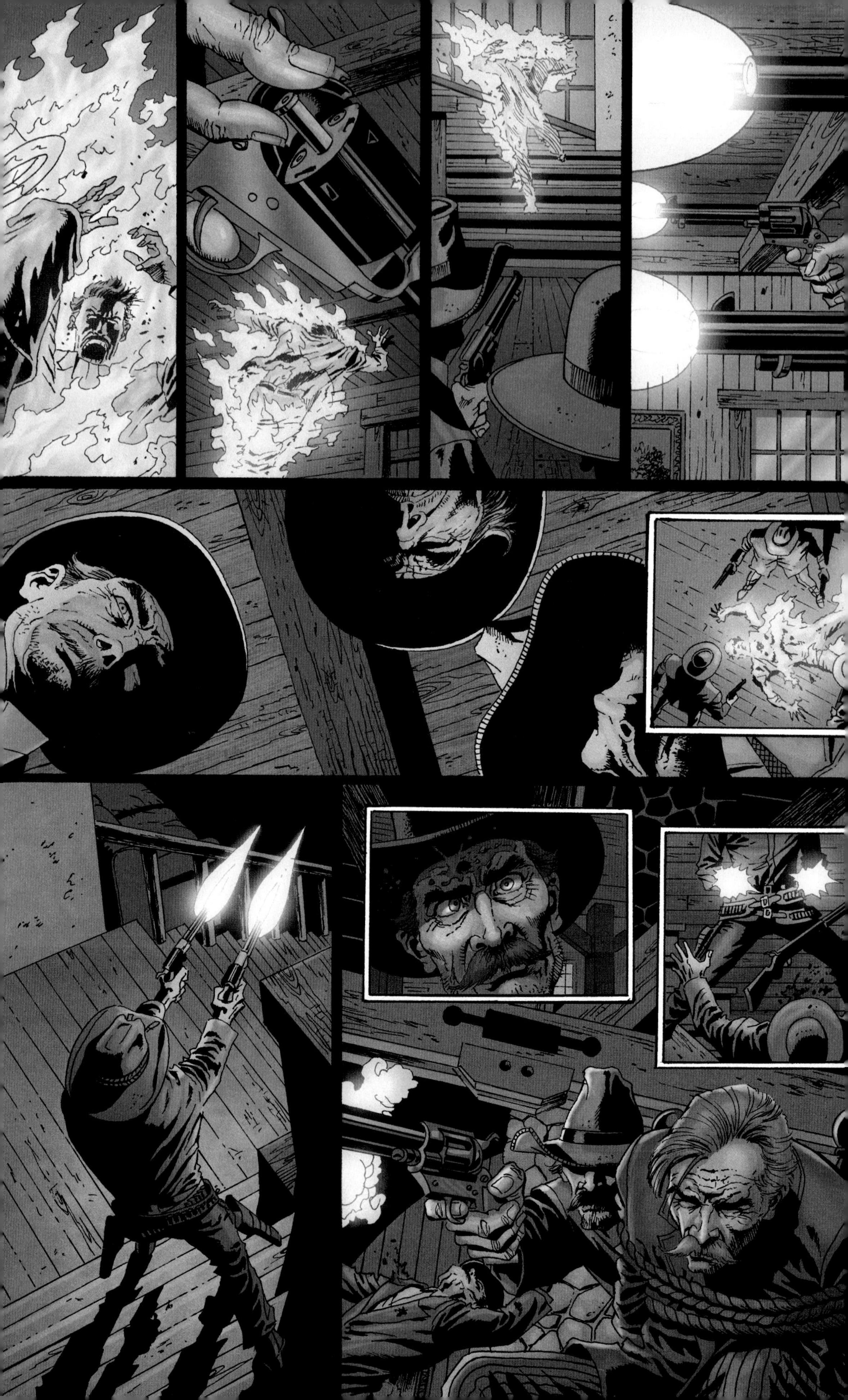

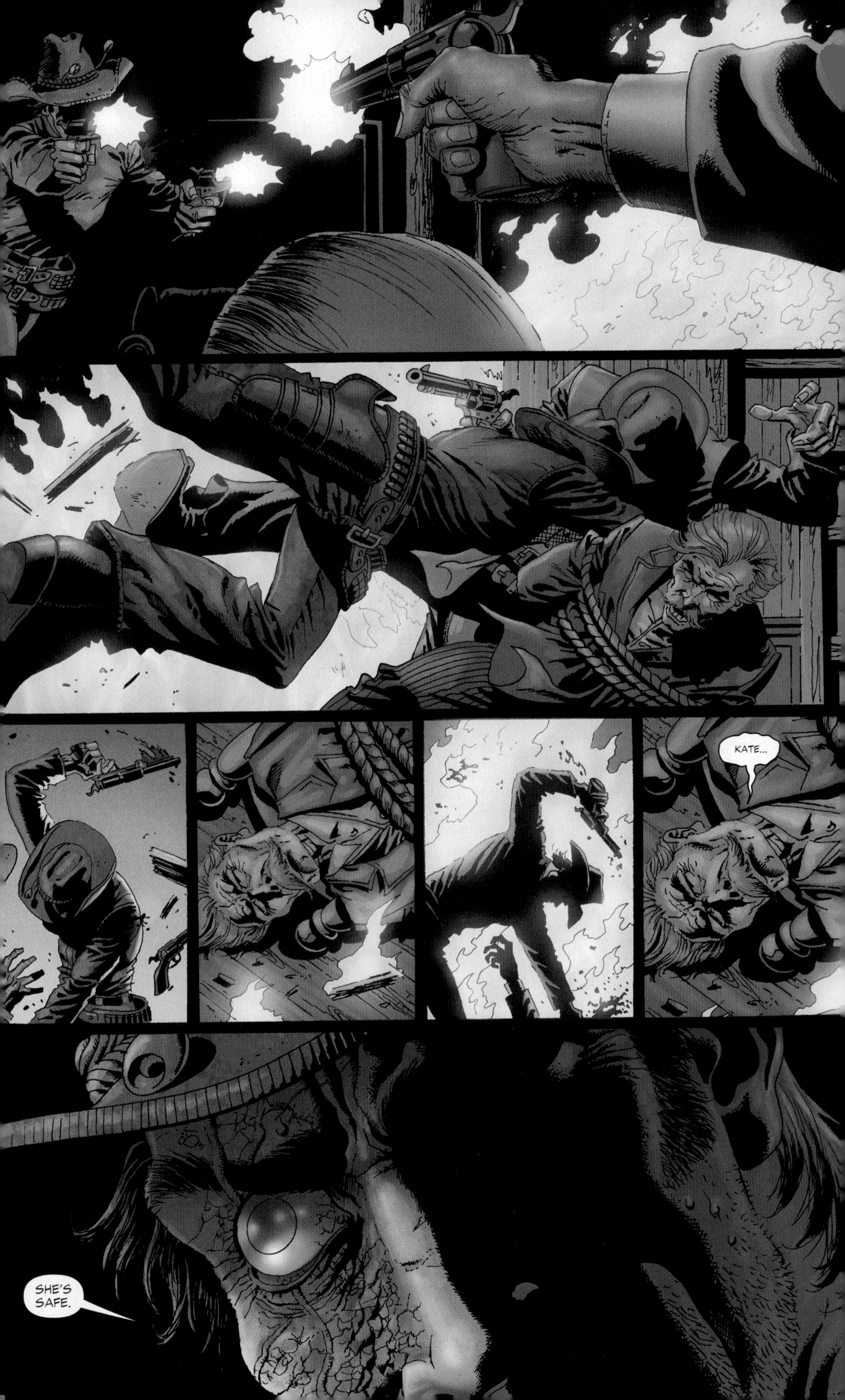
KATE...
SHE'S SAFE.

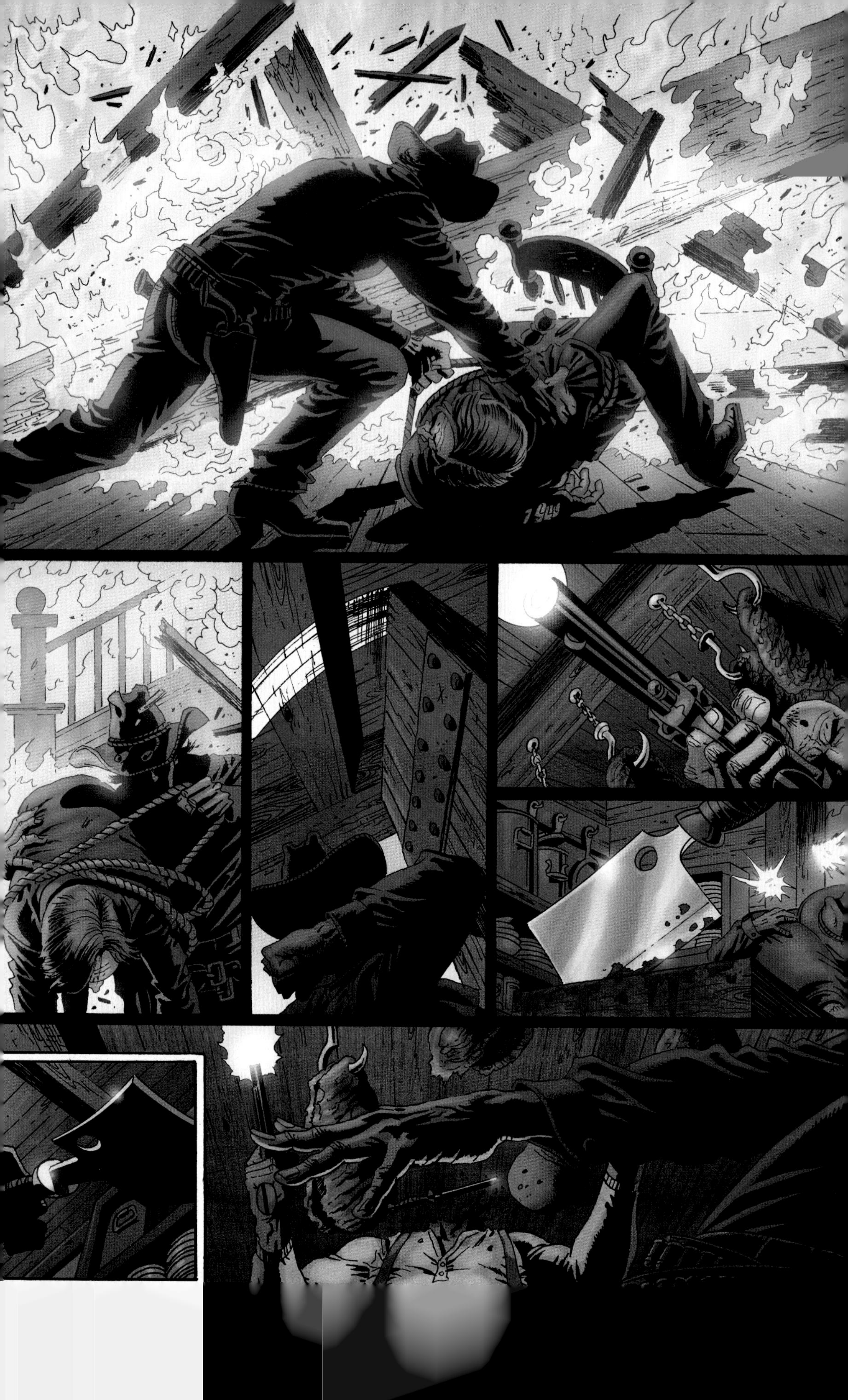

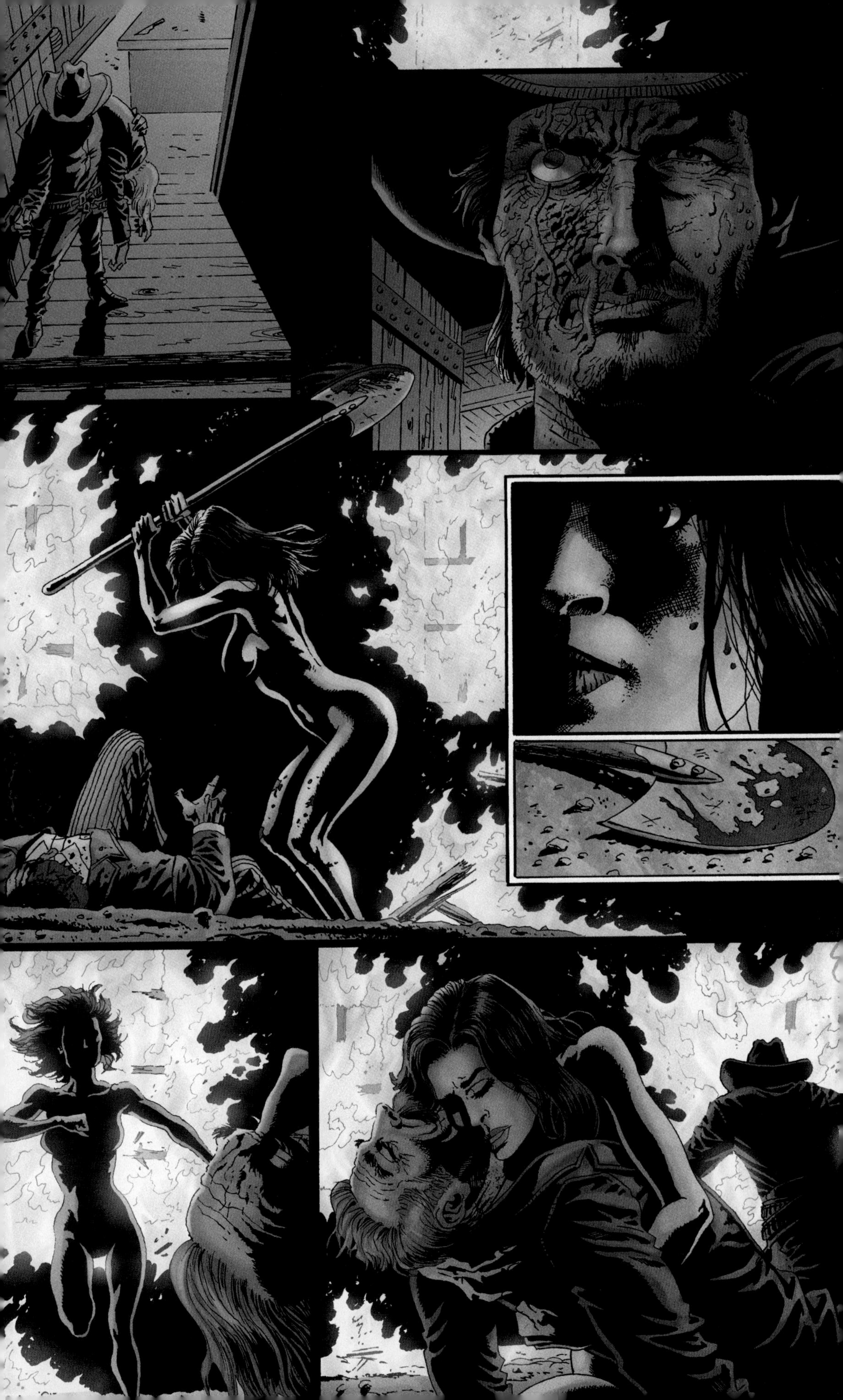

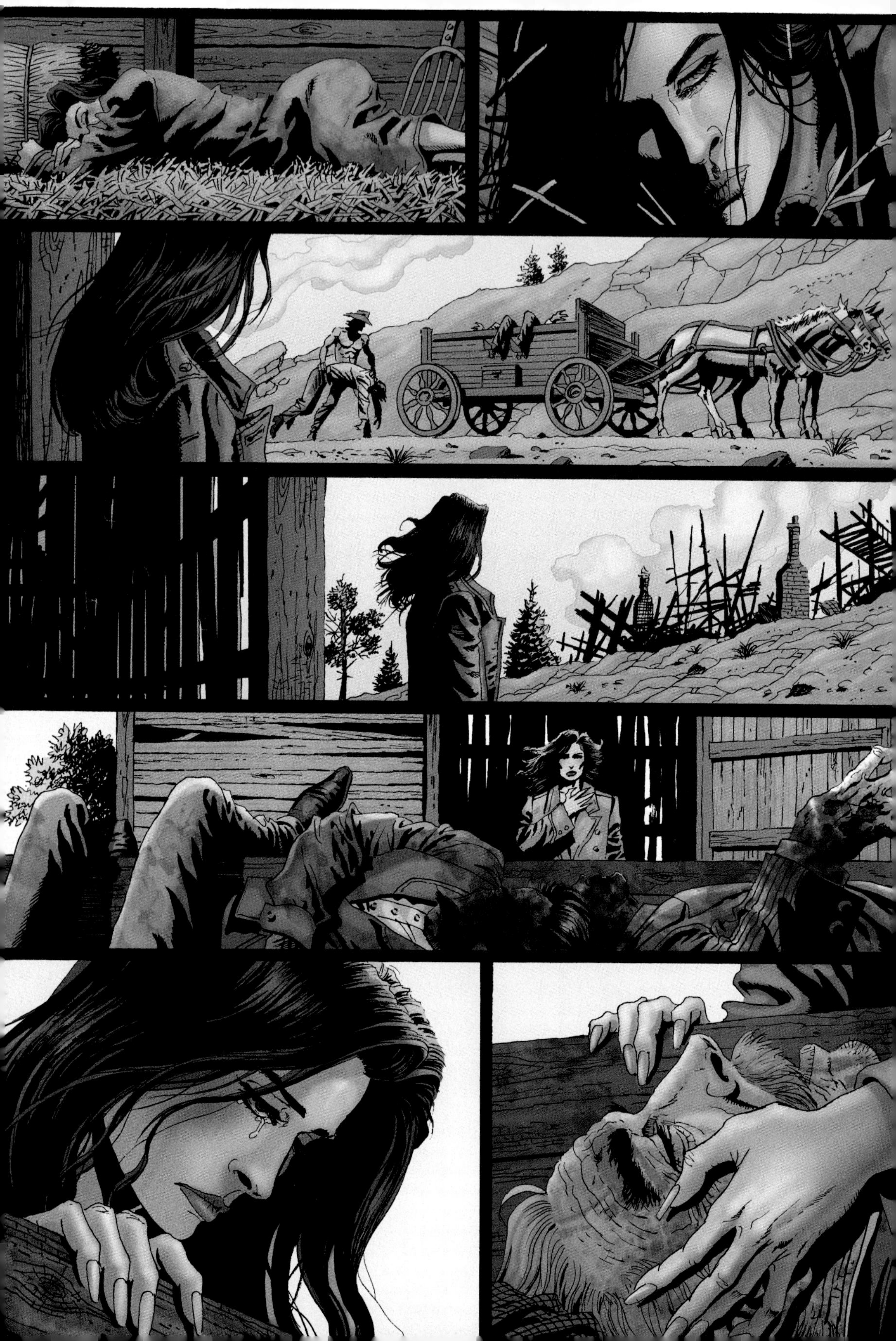

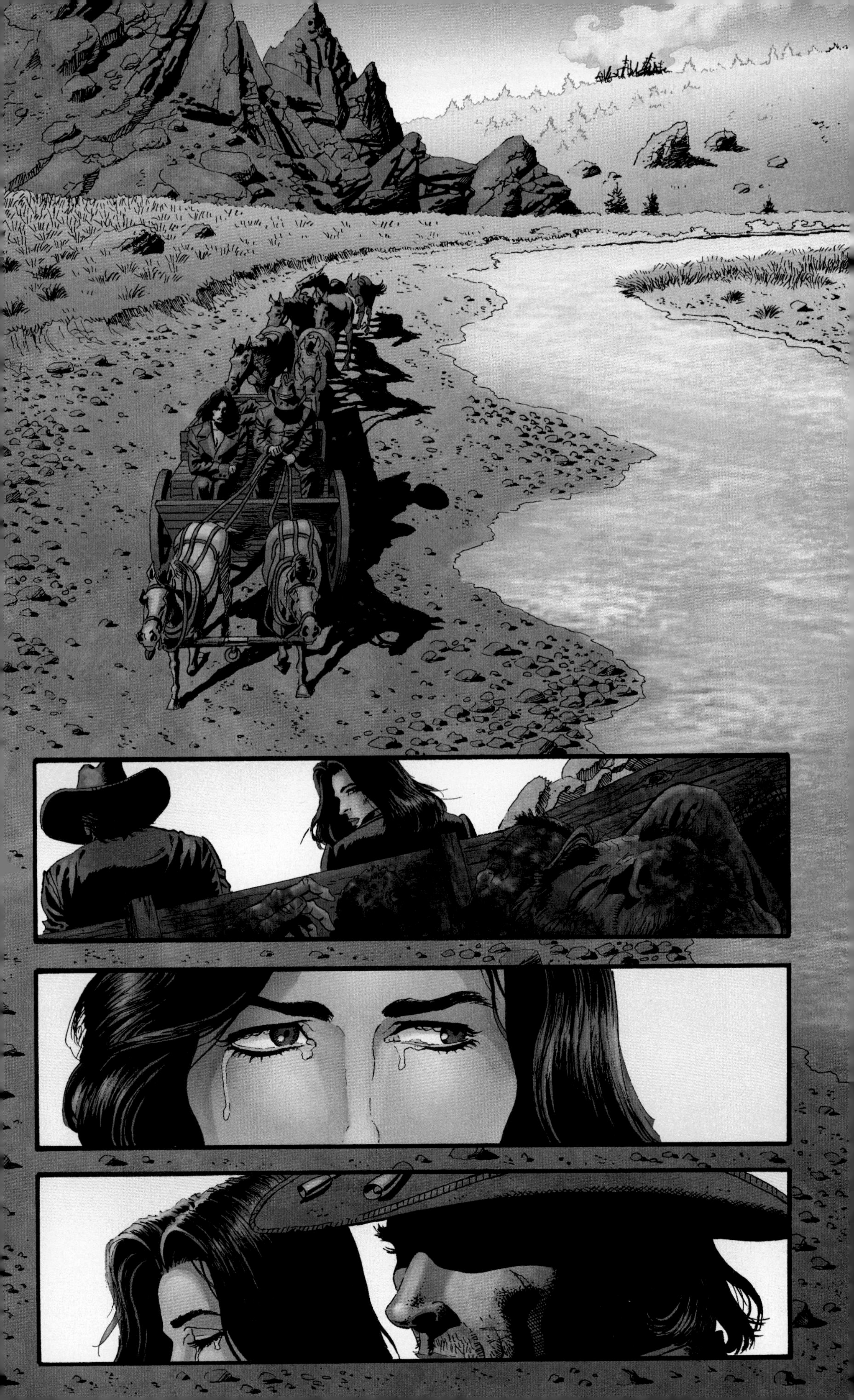

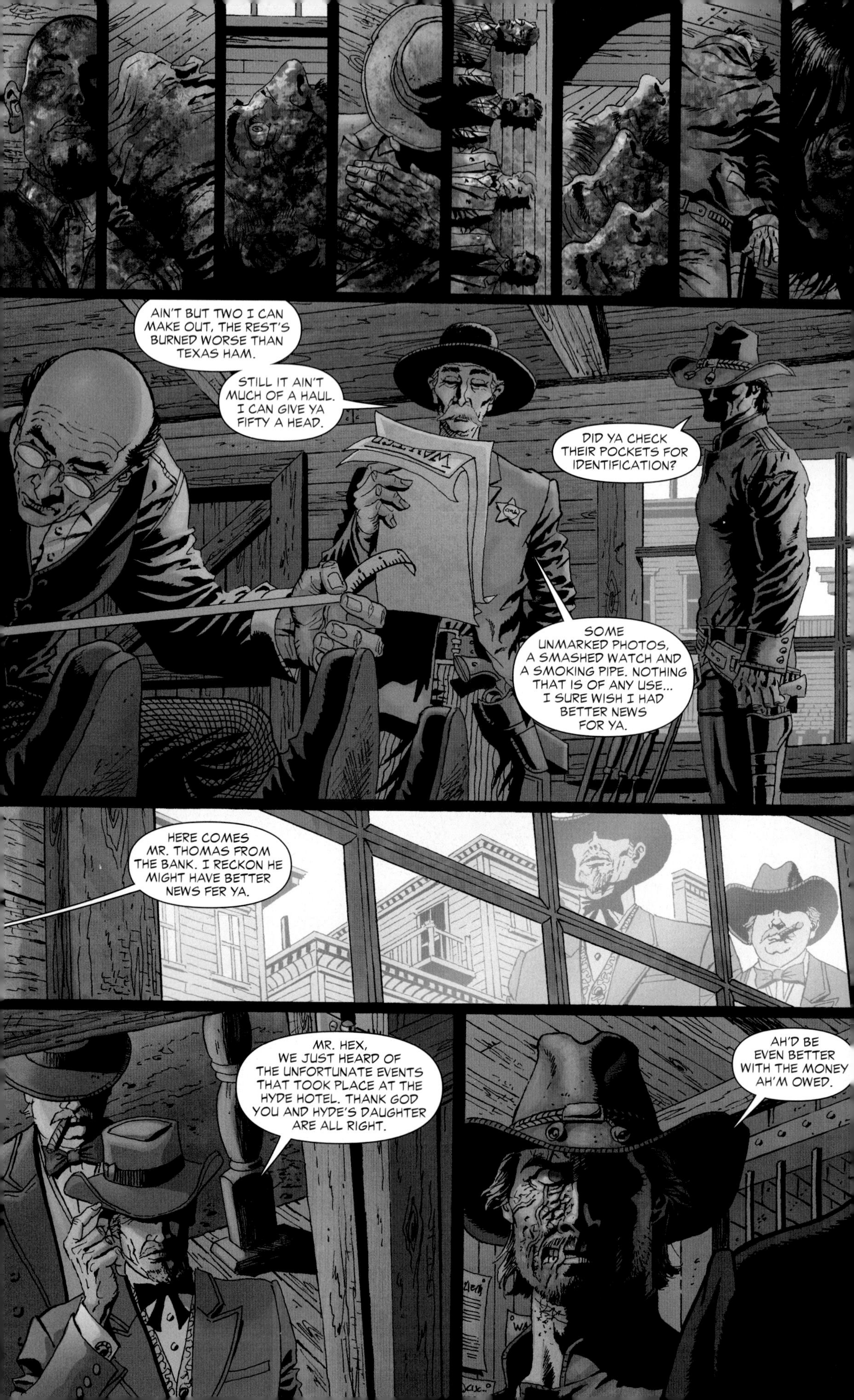
AIN'T BUT TWO I CAN MAKE OUT, THE REST'S BURNED WORSE THAN TEXAS HAM.
STILL IT AIN'T MUCH OF A HAUL. I CAN GIVE YA FIFTY A HEAD.
DID YA CHECK THEIR POCKETS FOR IDENTIFICATION?
SOME UNMARKED PHOTOS, A SMASHED WATCH AND A SMOKING PIPE. NOTHING THAT IS OF ANY USE... I SURE WISH I HAD BETTER NEWS FOR YA.
HERE COMES MR. THOMAS FROM THE BANK. I RECKON HE MIGHT HAVE BETTER NEWS FER YA.
MR. HEX, WE JUST HEARD OF THE UNFORTUNATE EVENTS THAT TOOK PLACE AT THE HYDE HOTEL. THANK GOD YOU AND HYDE'S DAUGHTER ARE ALL RIGHT.
AH'D BE EVEN BETTER WITH THE MONEY AH'M OWED.

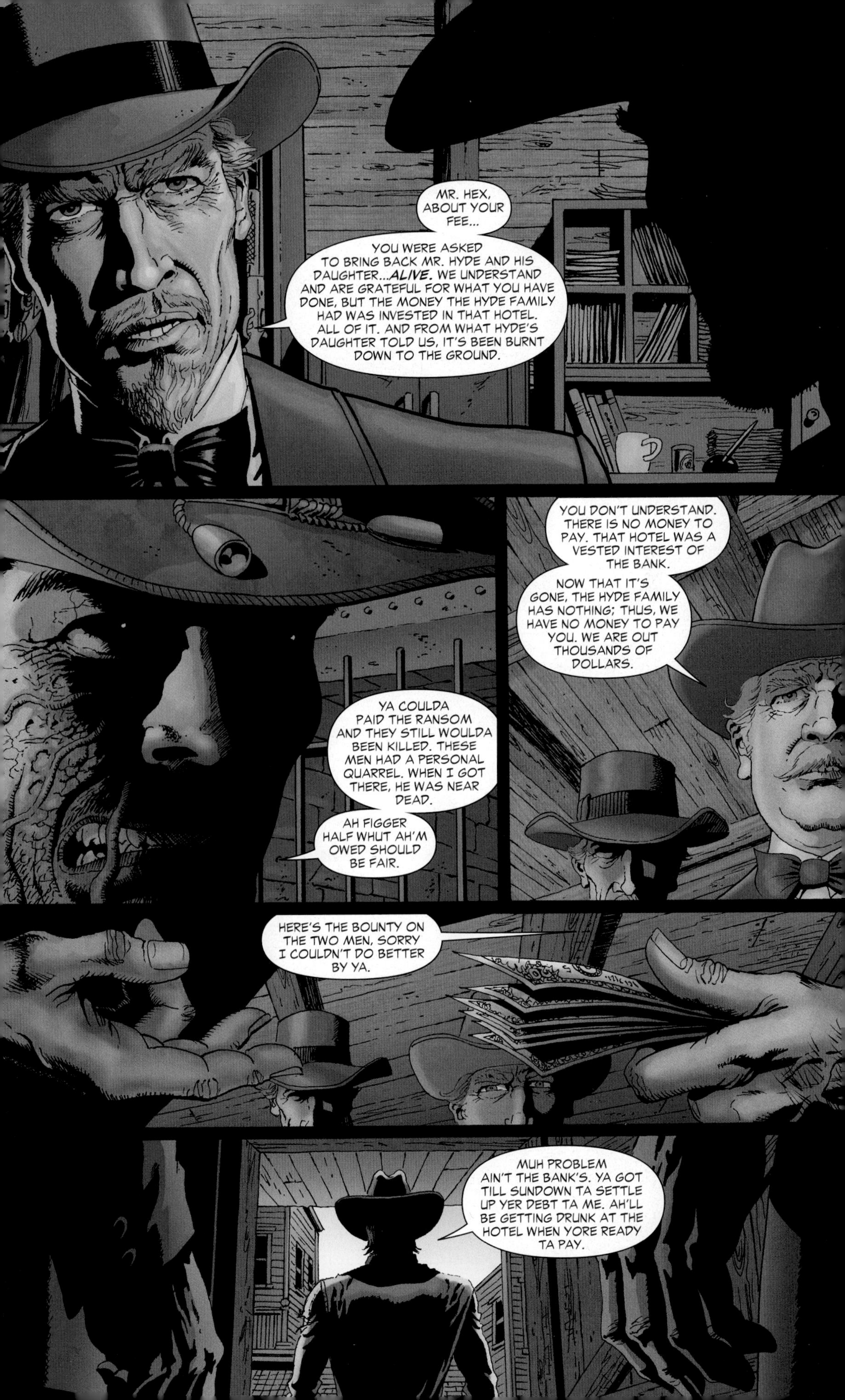
MR. HEX, ABOUT YOUR FEE...
YOU WERE ASKED TO BRING BACK MR. HYDE AND HIS DAUGHTER...ALIVE. WE UNDERSTAND AND ARE GRATEFUL FOR WHAT YOU HAVE DONE, BUT THE MONEY THE HYDE FAMILY HAD WAS INVESTED IN THAT HOTEL. ALL OF IT. AND FROM WHAT HYDE'S DAUGHTER TOLD US, IT'S BEEN BURNT DOWN TO THE GROUND.
YA COULDA PAID THE RANSOM AND THEY STILL WOULDA BEEN KILLED. THESE MEN HAD A PERSONAL QUARREL. WHEN I GOT THERE, HE WAS NEAR DEAD.
AH FIGGER HALF WHUT AH'M OWED SHOULD BE FAIR.
YOU DON'T UNDERSTAND. THERE IS NO MONEY TO PAY. THAT HOTEL WAS A VESTED INTEREST OF THE BANK.
NOW THAT IT'S GONE, THE HYDE FAMILY HAS NOTHING; THUS, WE HAVE NO MONEY TO PAY YOU. WE ARE OUT THOUSANDS OF DOLLARS.
HERE'S THE BOUNTY ON THE TWO MEN, SORRY I COULDN'T DO BETTER BY YA.
MUH PROBLEM AIN'T THE BANK'S. YA GOT TILL SUNDOWN TA SETTLE UP YER DEBT TA ME. AH'LL BE GETTING DRUNK AT THE HOTEL WHEN YORE READY TA PAY.

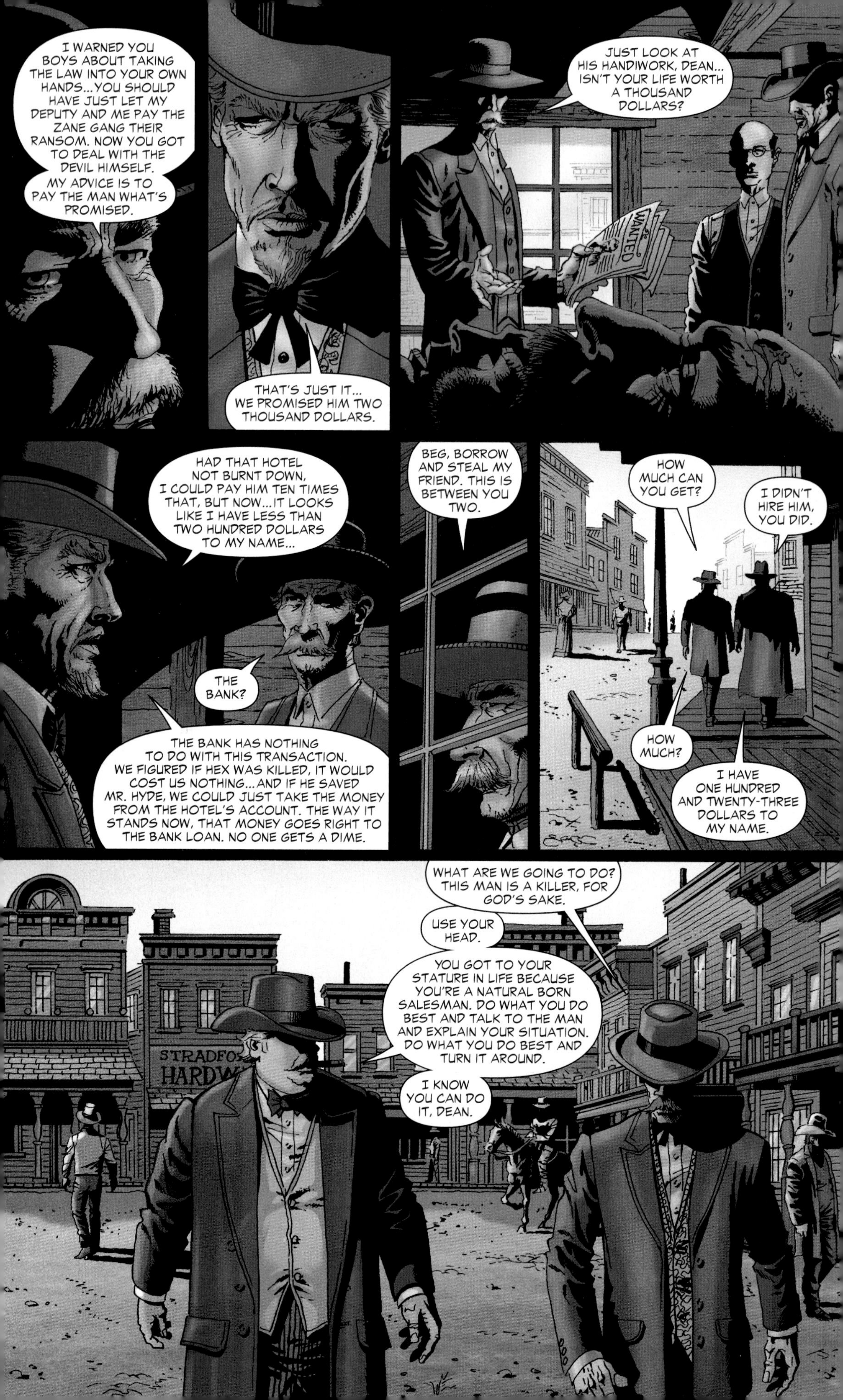
I WARNED YOU BOYS ABOUT TAKING THE LAW INTO YOUR OWN HANDS...YOU SHOULD HAVE JUST LET MY DEPUTY AND ME PAY THE ZANE GANG THEIR RANSOM. NOW YOU GOT TO DEAL WITH THE DEVIL HIMSELF.
MY ADVICE IS TO PAY THE MAN WHAT'S PROMISED.
THAT'S JUST IT... WE PROMISED HIM TWO THOUSAND DOLLARS.
JUST LOOK AT HIS HANDIWORK, DEAN... ISN'T YOUR LIFE WORTH A THOUSAND DOLLARS?
WANTED
HAD THAT HOTEL NOT BURNT DOWN, I COULD PAY HIM TEN TIMES THAT, BUT NOW...IT LOOKS LIKE I HAVE LESS THAN TWO HUNDRED DOLLARS TO MY NAME...
THE BANK?
THE BANK HAS NOTHING TO DO WITH THIS TRANSACTION. WE FIGURED IF HEX WAS KILLED, IT WOULD COST US NOTHING...AND IF HE SAVED MR. HYDE, WE COULD JUST TAKE THE MONEY FROM THE HOTEL'S ACCOUNT. THE WAY IT STANDS NOW, THAT MONEY GOES RIGHT TO THE BANK LOAN. NO ONE GETS A DIME.
BEG, BORROW AND STEAL MY FRIEND. THIS IS BETWEEN YOU TWO.
HOW MUCH CAN YOU GET?
I DIDN'T HIRE HIM, YOU DID.
HOW MUCH?
I HAVE ONE HUNDRED AND TWENTY-THREE DOLLARS TO MY NAME.
WHAT ARE WE GOING TO DO? THIS MAN IS A KILLER, FOR GOD'S SAKE.
USE YOUR HEAD.
YOU GOT TO YOUR STATURE IN LIFE BECAUSE YOU'RE A NATURAL BORN SALESMAN. DO WHAT YOU DO BEST AND TALK TO THE MAN AND EXPLAIN YOUR SITUATION. DO WHAT YOU DO BEST AND TURN IT AROUND.
I KNOW YOU CAN DO IT, DEAN.

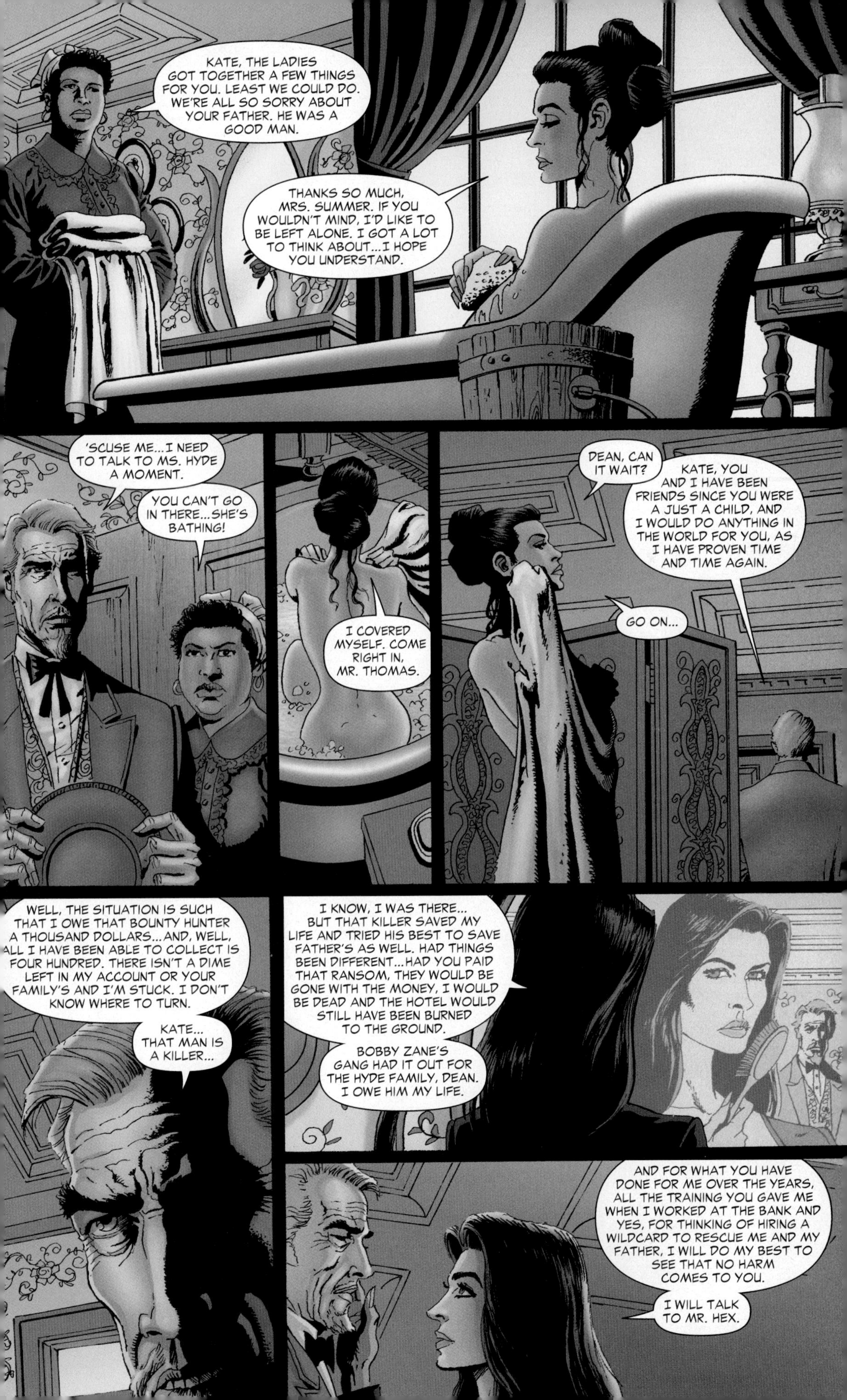
KATE, THE LADIES GOT TOGETHER A FEW THINGS FOR YOU. LEAST WE COULD DO. WE'RE ALL SO SORRY ABOUT YOUR FATHER. HE WAS A GOOD MAN.
THANKS SO MUCH, MRS. SUMMER. IF YOU WOULDN'T MIND, I'D LIKE TO BE LEFT ALONE. I GOT A LOT TO THINK ABOUT...I HOPE YOU UNDERSTAND.
'SCUSE ME...I NEED TO TALK TO MS. HYDE A MOMENT.
YOU CAN'T GO IN THERE...SHE'S BATHING!
I COVERED MYSELF. COME RIGHT IN, MR. THOMAS.
DEAN, CAN IT WAIT?
KATE, YOU AND I HAVE BEEN FRIENDS SINCE YOU WERE A JUST A CHILD, AND I WOULD DO ANYTHING IN THE WORLD FOR YOU, AS I HAVE PROVEN TIME AND TIME AGAIN.
GO ON...
WELL, THE SITUATION IS SUCH THAT I OWE THAT BOUNTY HUNTER A THOUSAND DOLLARS...AND, WELL, ALL I HAVE BEEN ABLE TO COLLECT IS FOUR HUNDRED. THERE ISN'T A DIME LEFT IN MY ACCOUNT OR YOUR FAMILY'S AND I'M STUCK. I DON'T KNOW WHERE TO TURN.
KATE... THAT MAN IS A KILLER...
I KNOW, I WAS THERE... BUT THAT KILLER SAVED MY LIFE AND TRIED HIS BEST TO SAVE FATHER'S AS WELL. HAD THINGS BEEN DIFFERENT...HAD YOU PAID THAT RANSOM, THEY WOULD BE GONE WITH THE MONEY, I WOULD BE DEAD AND THE HOTEL WOULD STILL HAVE BEEN BURNED TO THE GROUND.
BOBBY ZANE'S GANG HAD IT OUT FOR THE HYDE FAMILY, DEAN. I OWE HIM MY LIFE.
AND FOR WHAT YOU HAVE DONE FOR ME OVER THE YEARS, ALL THE TRAINING YOU GAVE ME WHEN I WORKED AT THE BANK AND YES, FOR THINKING OF HIRING A WILDCARD TO RESCUE ME AND MY FATHER, I WILL DO MY BEST TO SEE THAT NO HARM COMES TO YOU.
I WILL TALK TO MR. HEX.

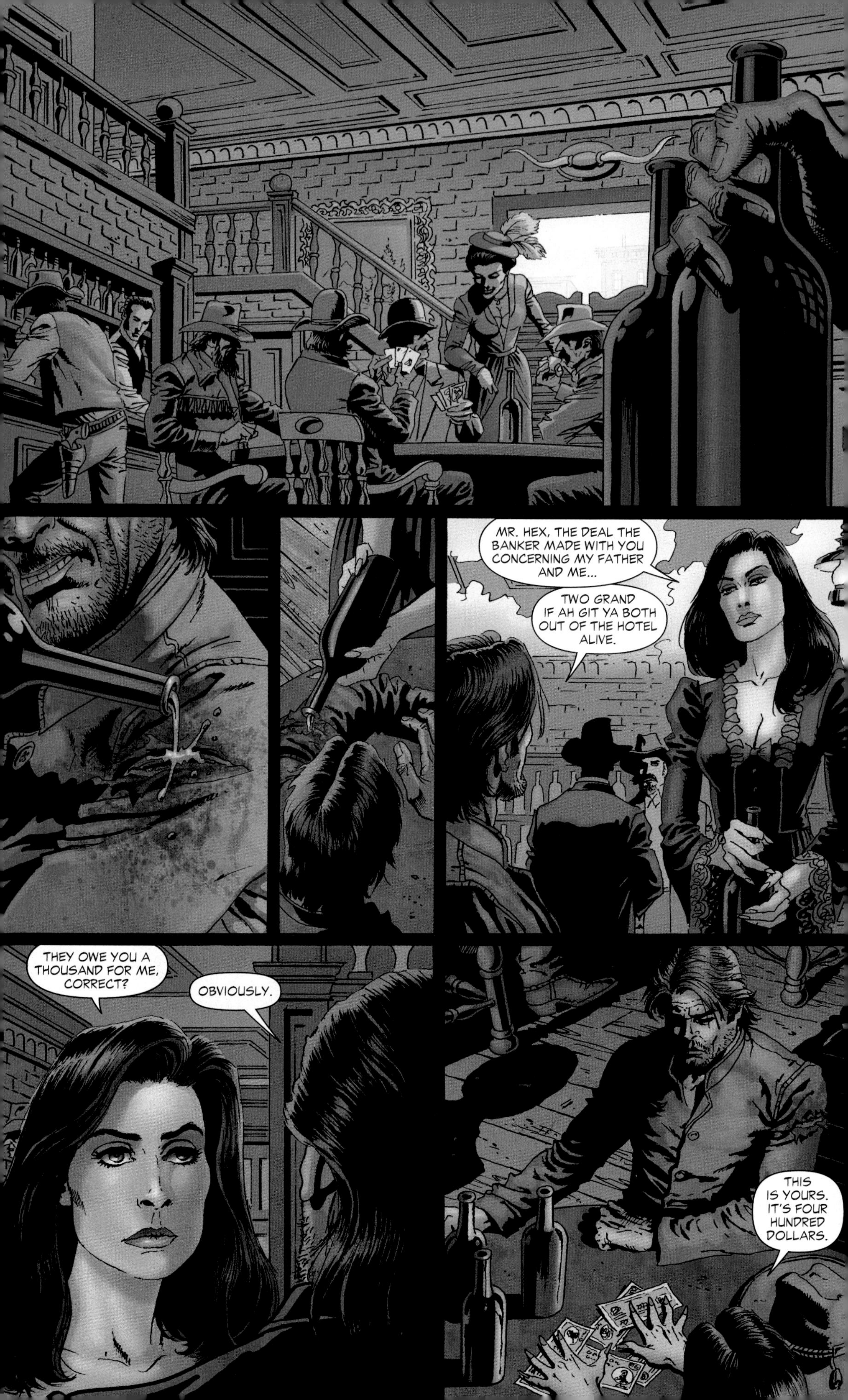

MR. HEX, THE DEAL THE BANKER MADE WITH YOU CONCERNING MY FATHER AND ME...
TWO GRAND IF AH GIT YA BOTH OUT OF THE HOTEL ALIVE.
THEY OWE YOU A THOUSAND FOR ME, CORRECT?
OBVIOUSLY.
THIS IS YOURS. IT'S FOUR HUNDRED DOLLARS.

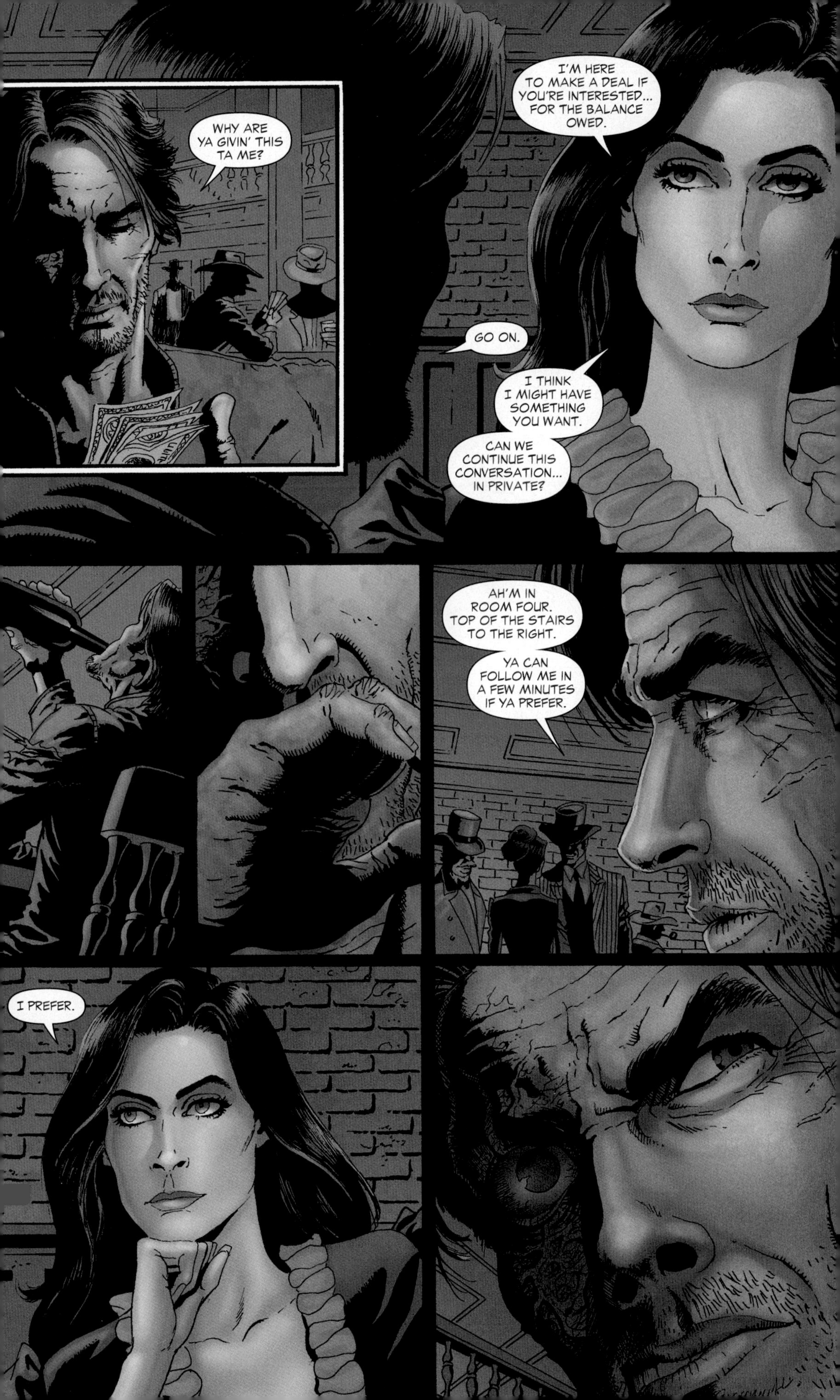
WHY ARE YA GIVIN' THIS TA ME?
I'M HERE TO MAKE A DEAL IF YOU'RE INTERESTED... FOR THE BALANCE OWED.
GO ON.
I THINK I MIGHT HAVE SOMETHING YOU WANT.
CAN WE CONTINUE THIS CONVERSATION... IN PRIVATE?
AH'M IN ROOM FOUR. TOP OF THE STAIRS TO THE RIGHT.
YA CAN FOLLOW ME IN A FEW MINUTES IF YA PREFER.
I PREFER.

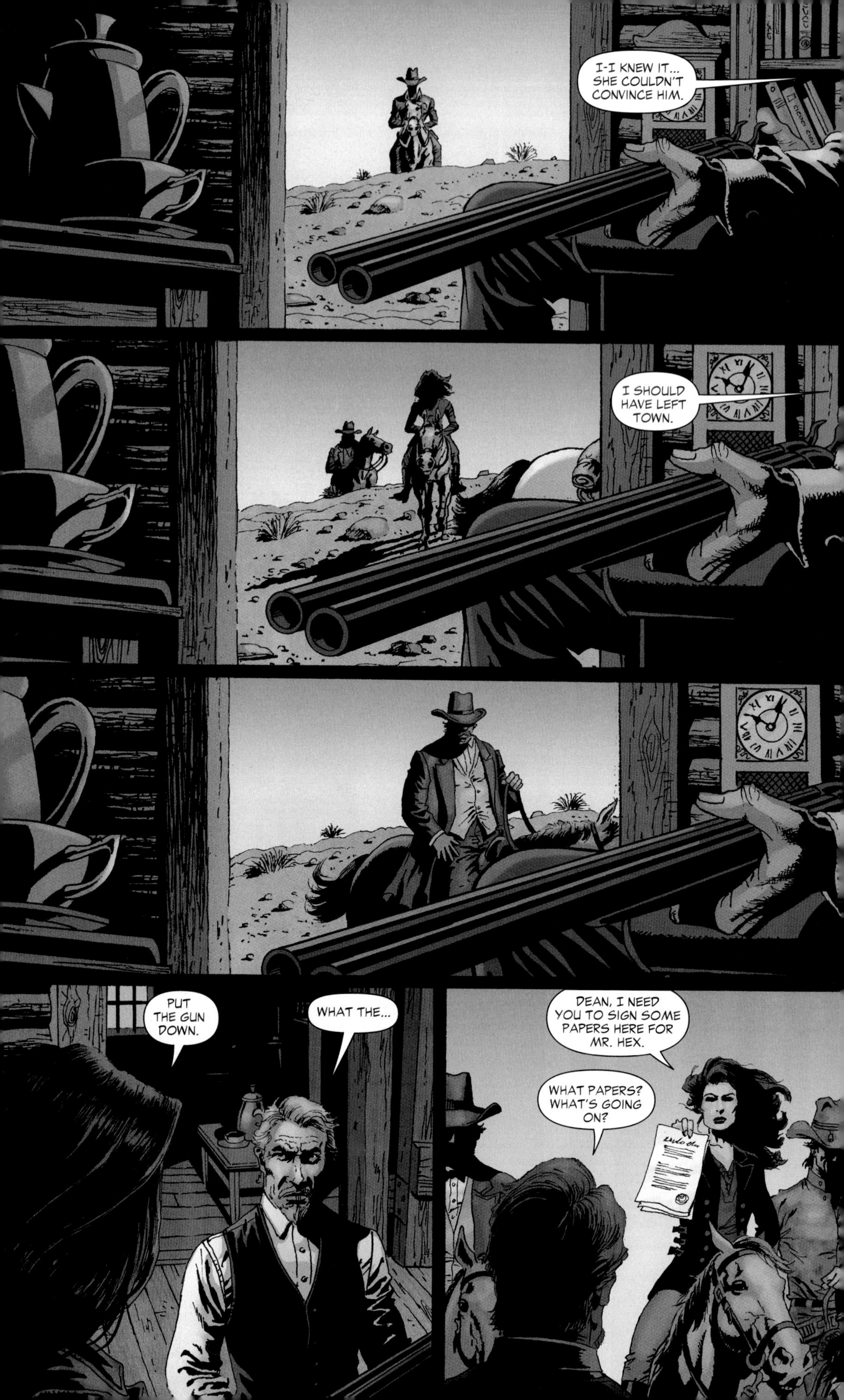
I-I KNEW IT... SHE COULDN'T CONVINCE HIM.
I SHOULD HAVE LEFT TOWN.
PUT THE GUN DOWN.
WHAT THE...
DEAN, I NEED YOU TO SIGN SOME PAPERS HERE FOR MR. HEX.
WHAT PAPERS? WHAT'S GOING ON?

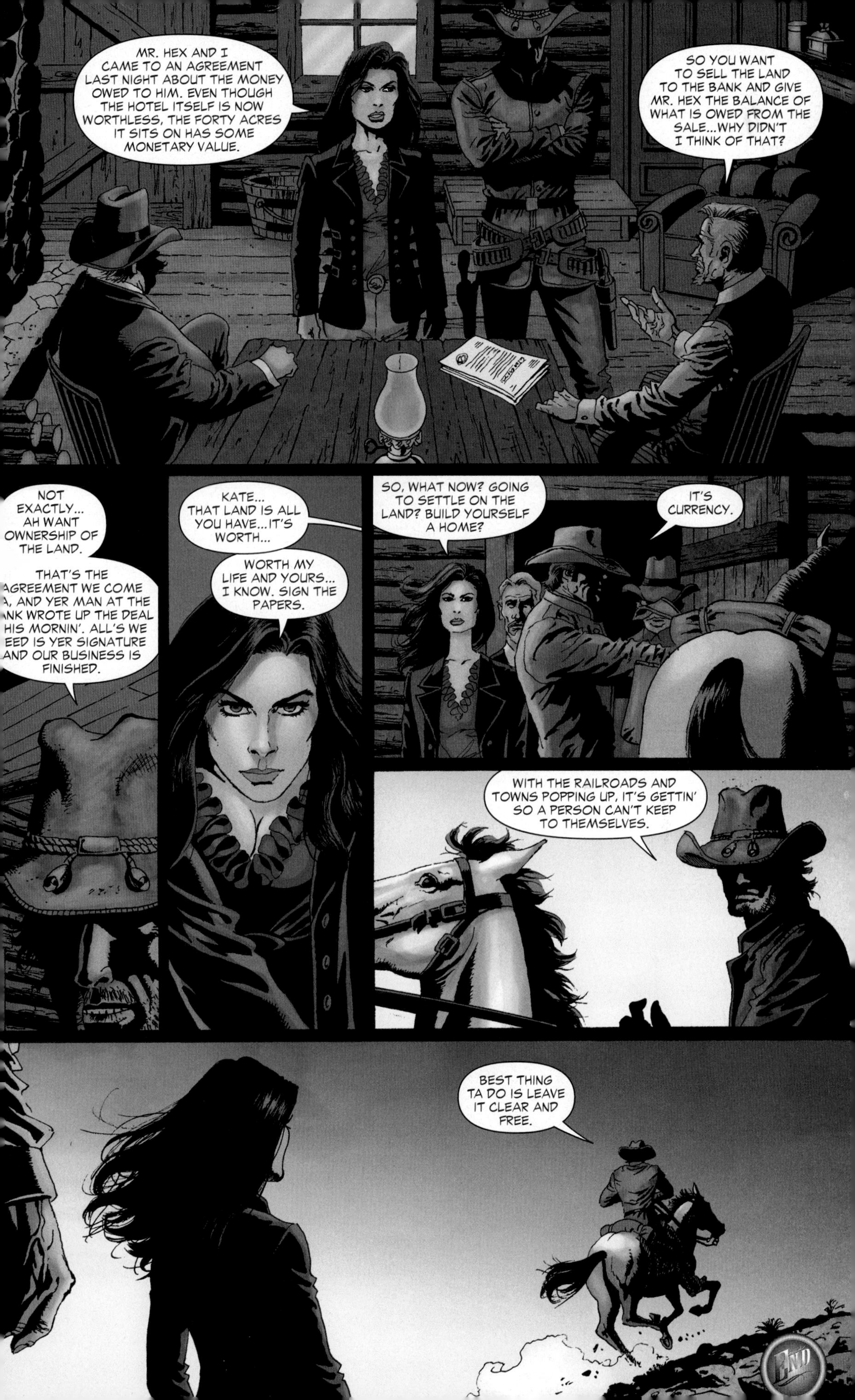
MR. HEX AND I CAME TO AN AGREEMENT LAST NIGHT ABOUT THE MONEY OWED TO HIM. EVEN THOUGH THE HOTEL ITSELF IS NOW WORTHLESS, THE FORTY ACRES IT SITS ON HAS SOME MONETARY VALUE.
SO YOU WANT TO SELL THE LAND TO THE BANK AND GIVE MR. HEX THE BALANCE OF WHAT IS OWED FROM THE SALE...WHY DIDN'T I THINK OF THAT?
NOT EXACTLY... AH WANT OWNERSHIP OF THE LAND.
THAT'S THE AGREEMENT WE COME A, AND YER MAN AT THE NK WROTE UP THE DEAL HIS MORNIN'. ALL'S WE EED IS YER SIGNATURE AND OUR BUSINESS IS FINISHED.
KATE... THAT LAND IS ALL YOU HAVE...IT'S WORTH...
WORTH MY LIFE AND YOURS... I KNOW. SIGN THE PAPERS.
SO, WHAT NOW? GOING TO SETTLE ON THE LAND? BUILD YOURSELF A HOME?
IT'S CURRENCY.
WITH THE RAILROADS AND TOWNS POPPING UP, IT'S GETTIN' SO A PERSON CAN'T KEEP TO THEMSELVES.
BEST THING TA DO IS LEAVE IT CLEAR AND FREE.
END

Cover by Darwyn Cooke

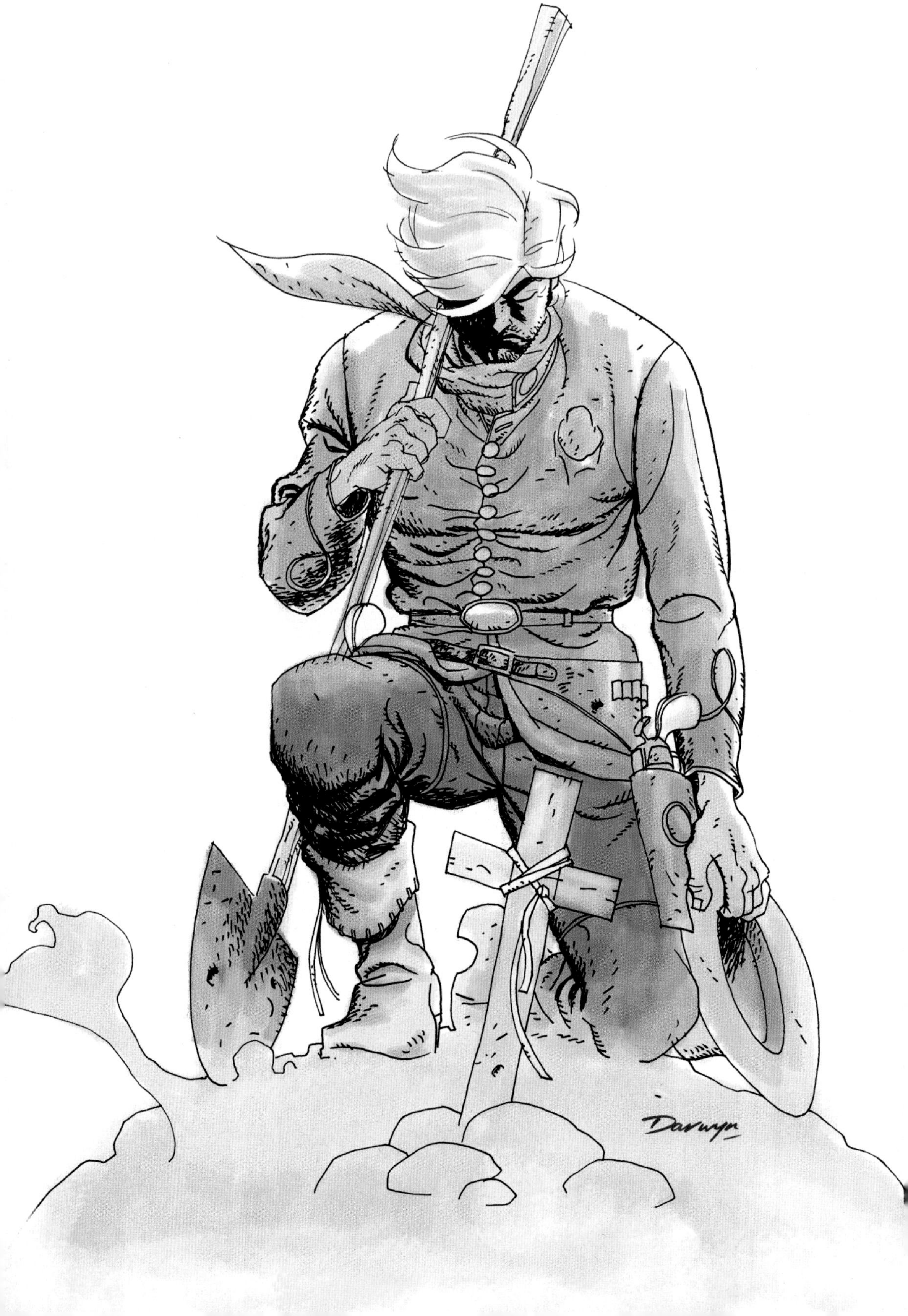
Darwyn

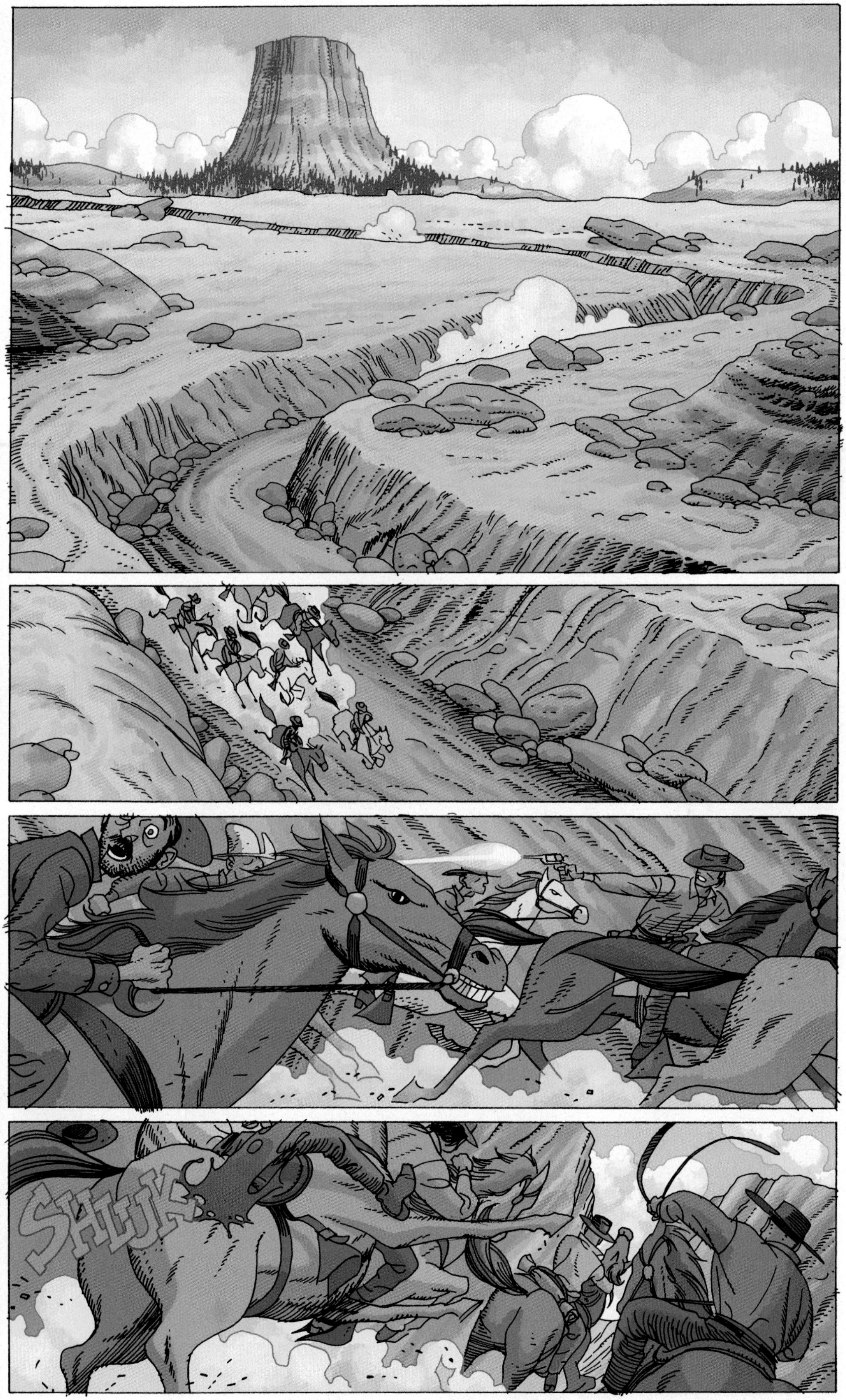
SHLUK

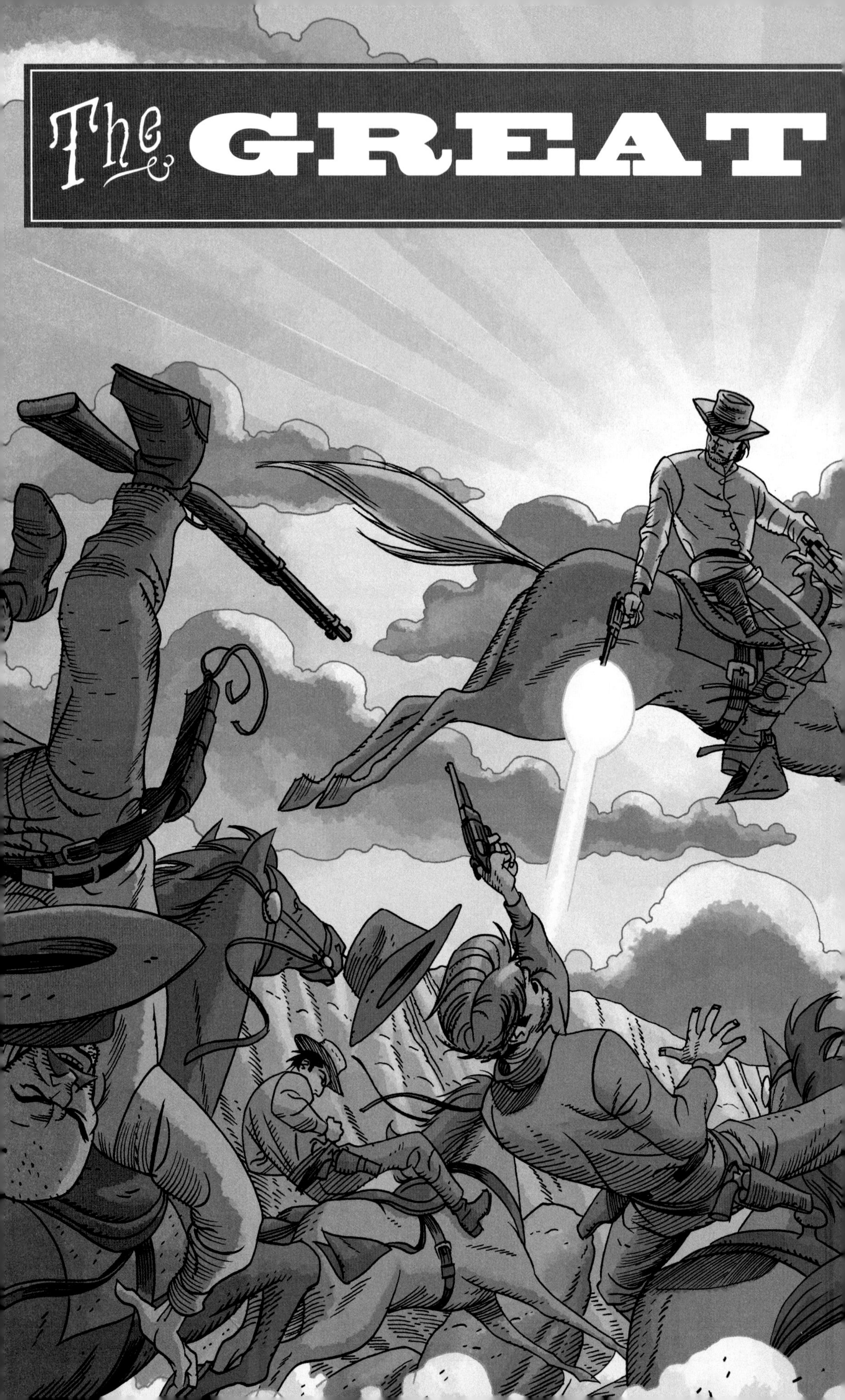
The GREAT

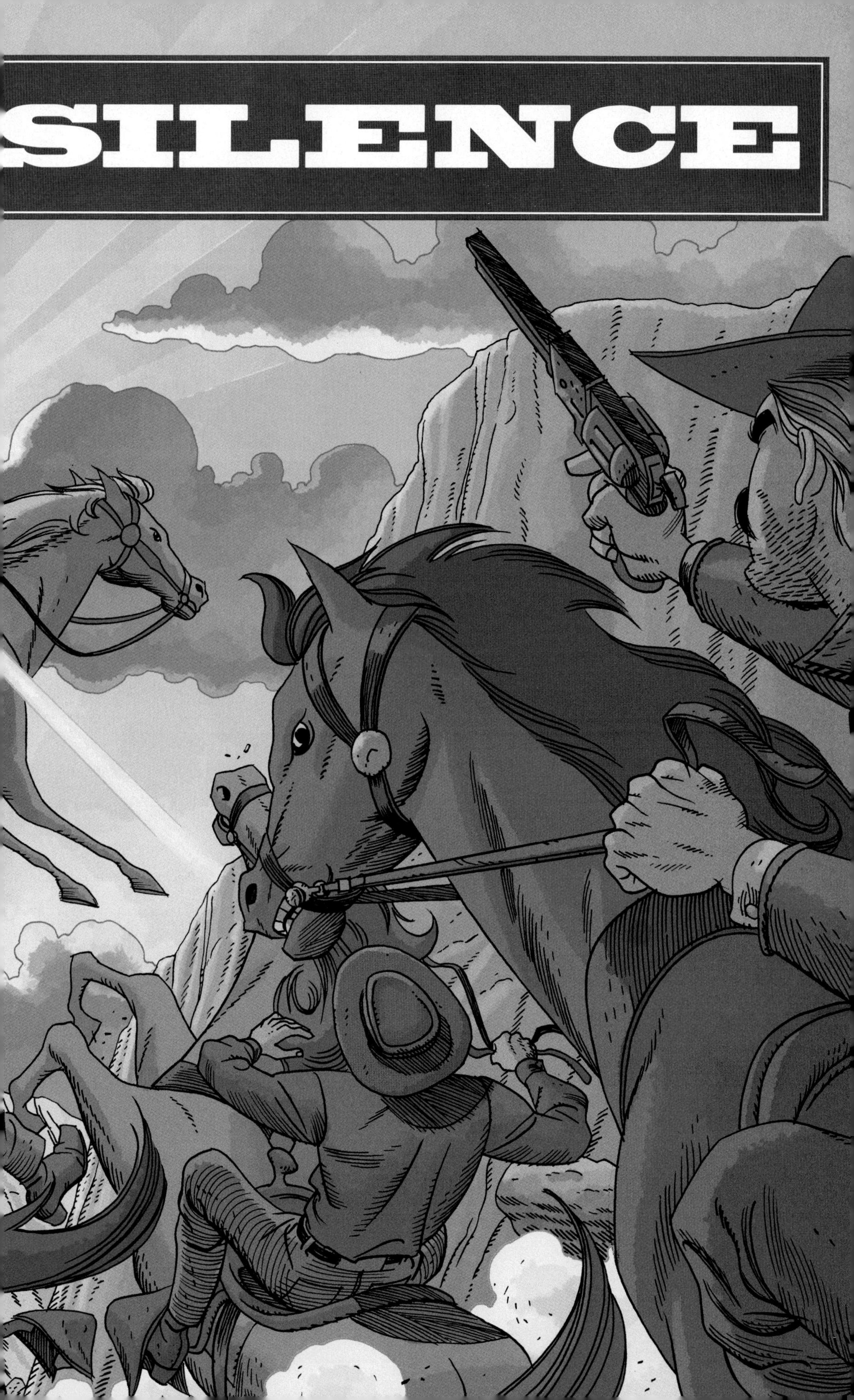
SILENCE

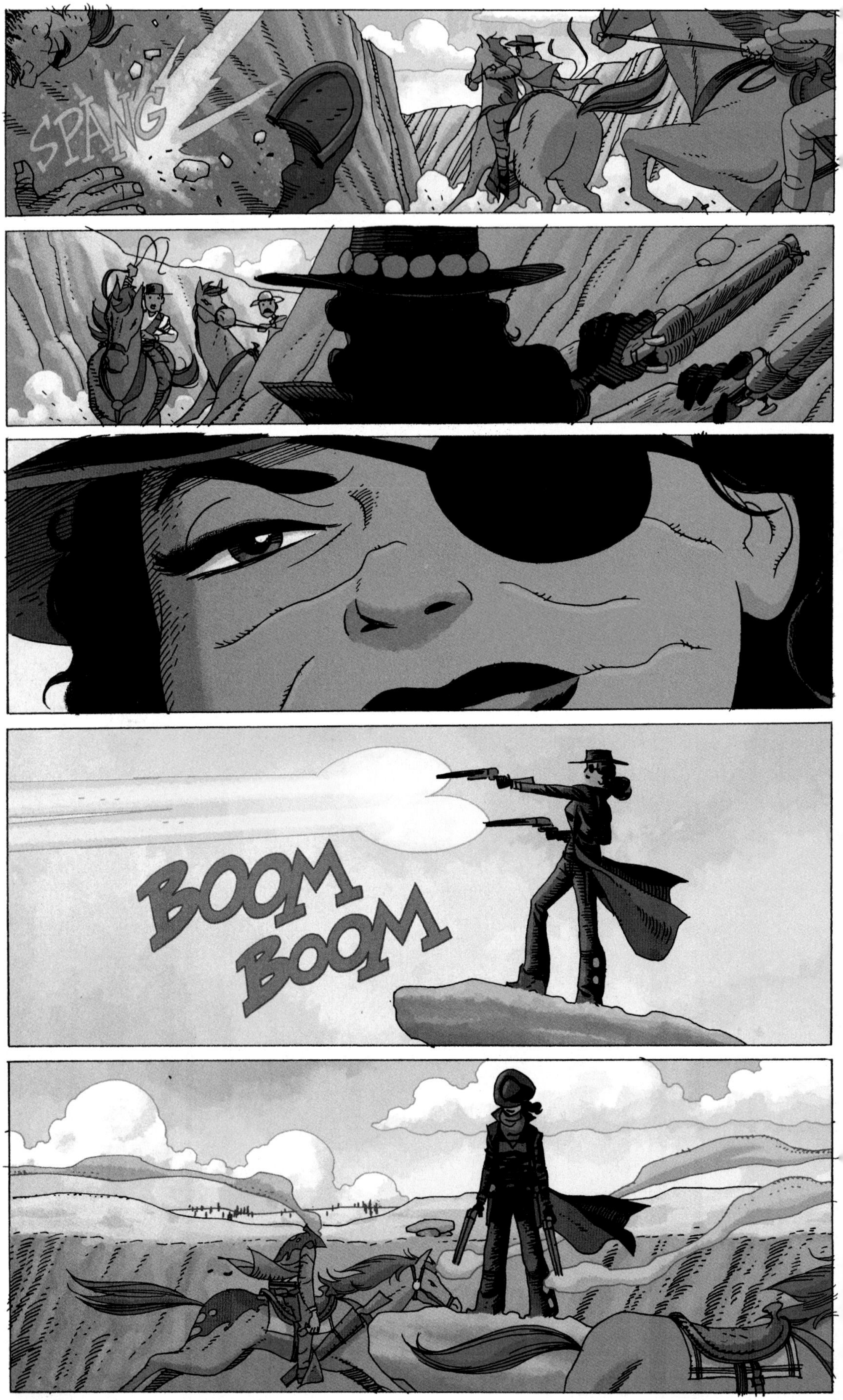
SPANG
BOOM
BOOM

BEFORE THE FALL

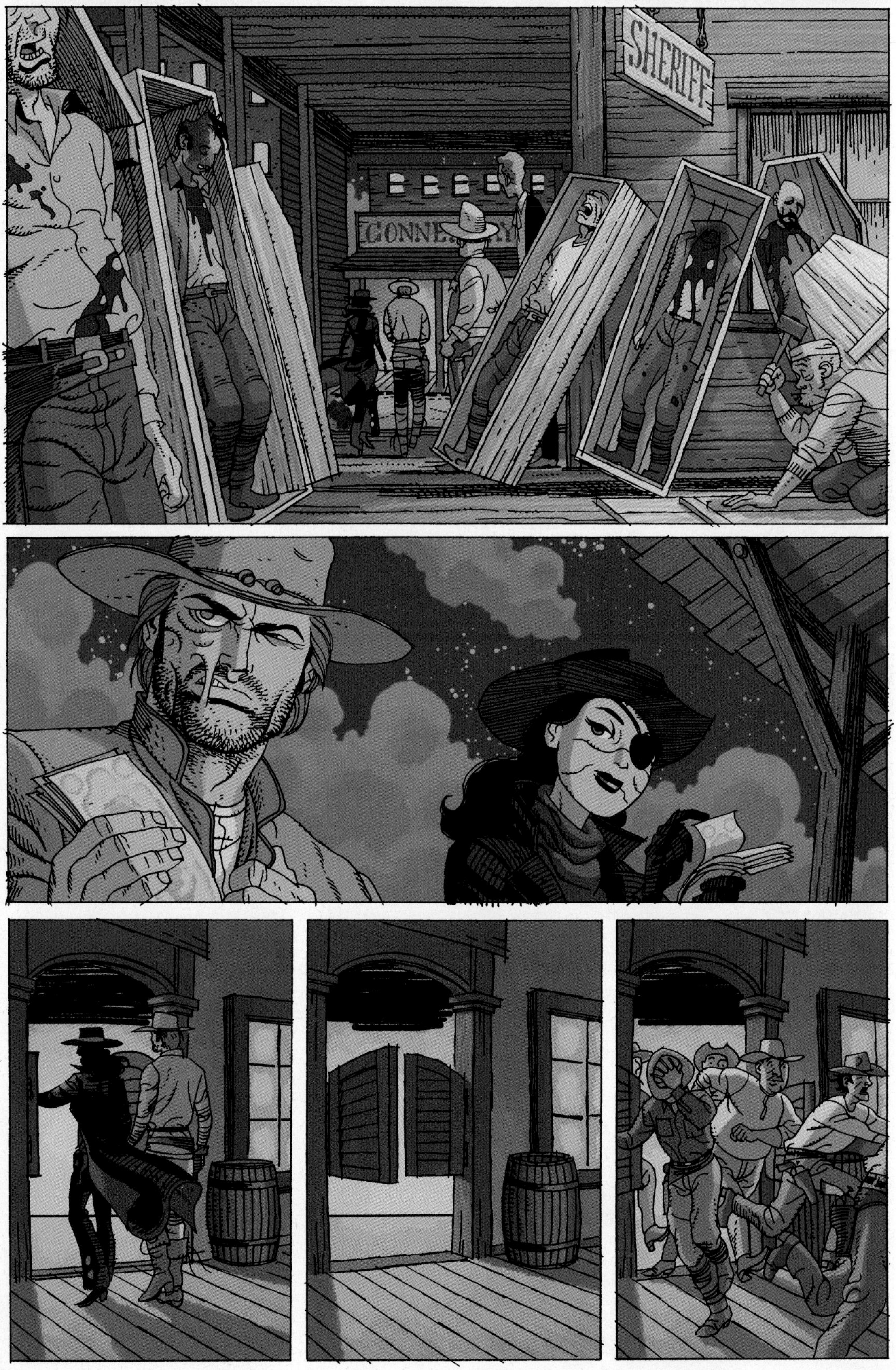
SHERIFF
CONNE

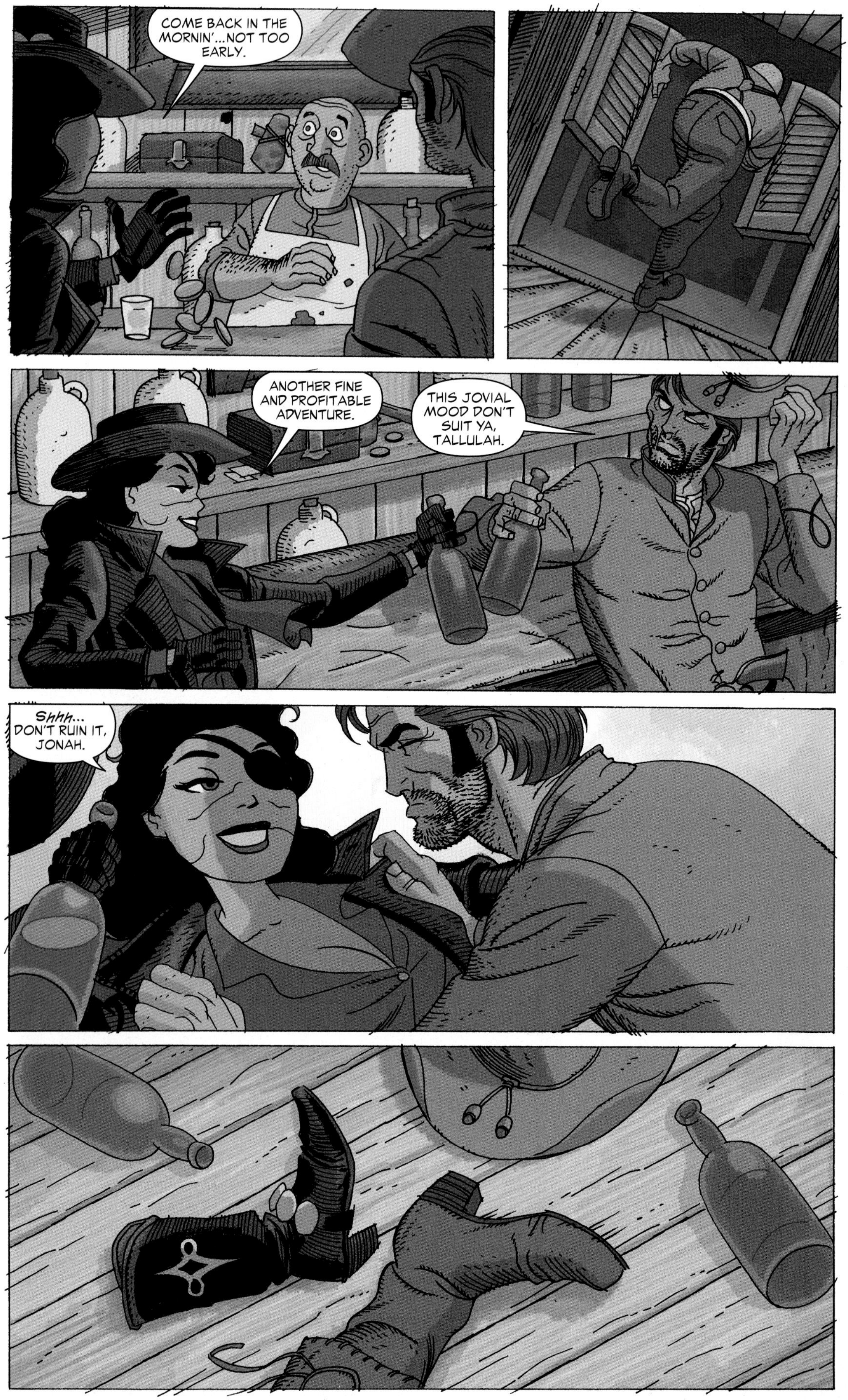
COME BACK IN THE MORNIN'...NOT TOO EARLY.
ANOTHER FINE AND PROFITABLE ADVENTURE.
THIS JOVIAL MOOD DON'T SUIT YA, TALLULAH.
Shhh... DON'T RUIN IT, JONAH.

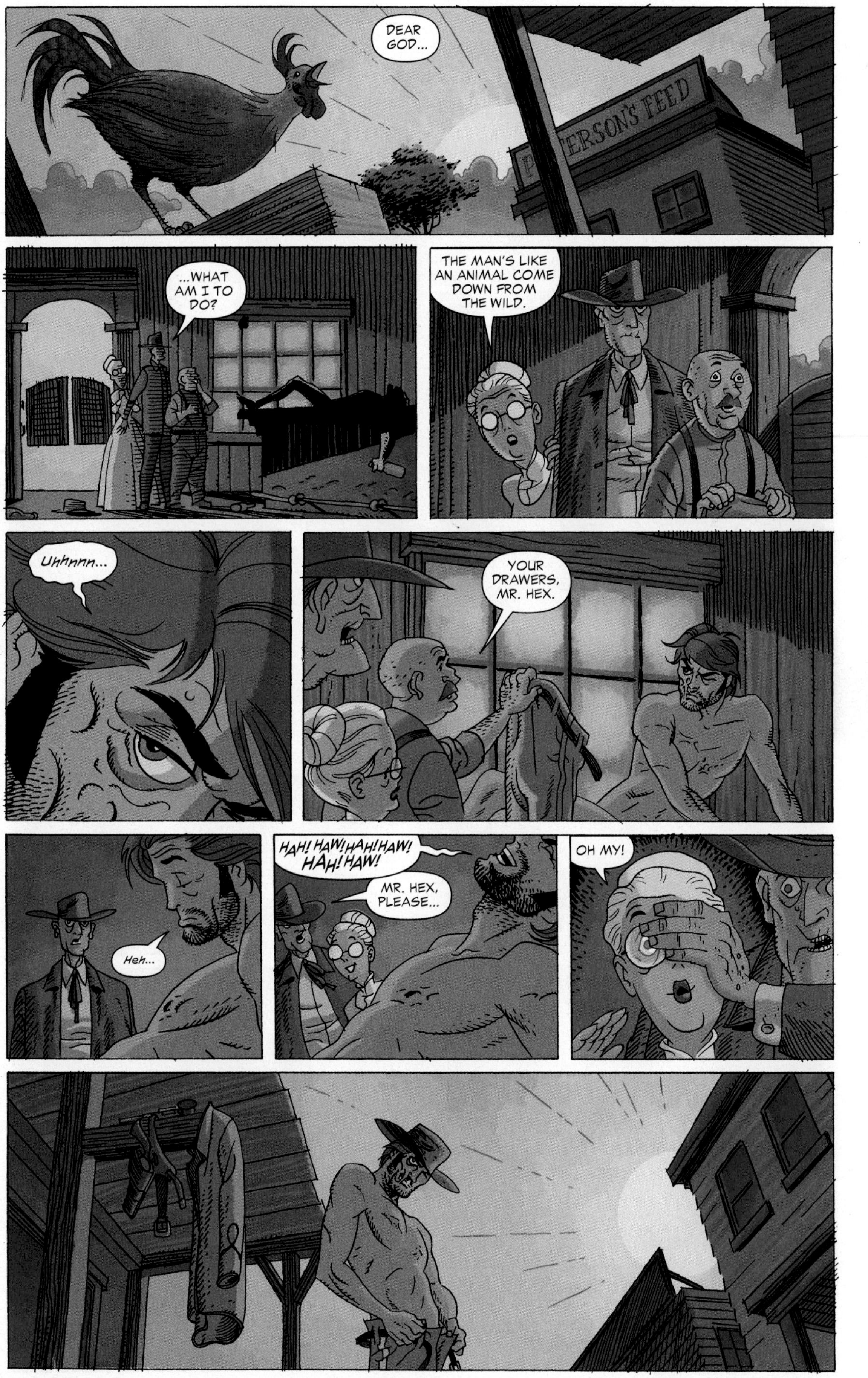
DEAR GOD...
PETERSON'S FEED
...WHAT AM I TO DO?
THE MAN'S LIKE AN ANIMAL COME DOWN FROM THE WILD.
Uhhnnn...
YOUR DRAWERS, MR. HEX.
Heh...
HAH! HAW! HAH! HAW! HAH! HAW!
MR. HEX, PLEASE...
OH MY!

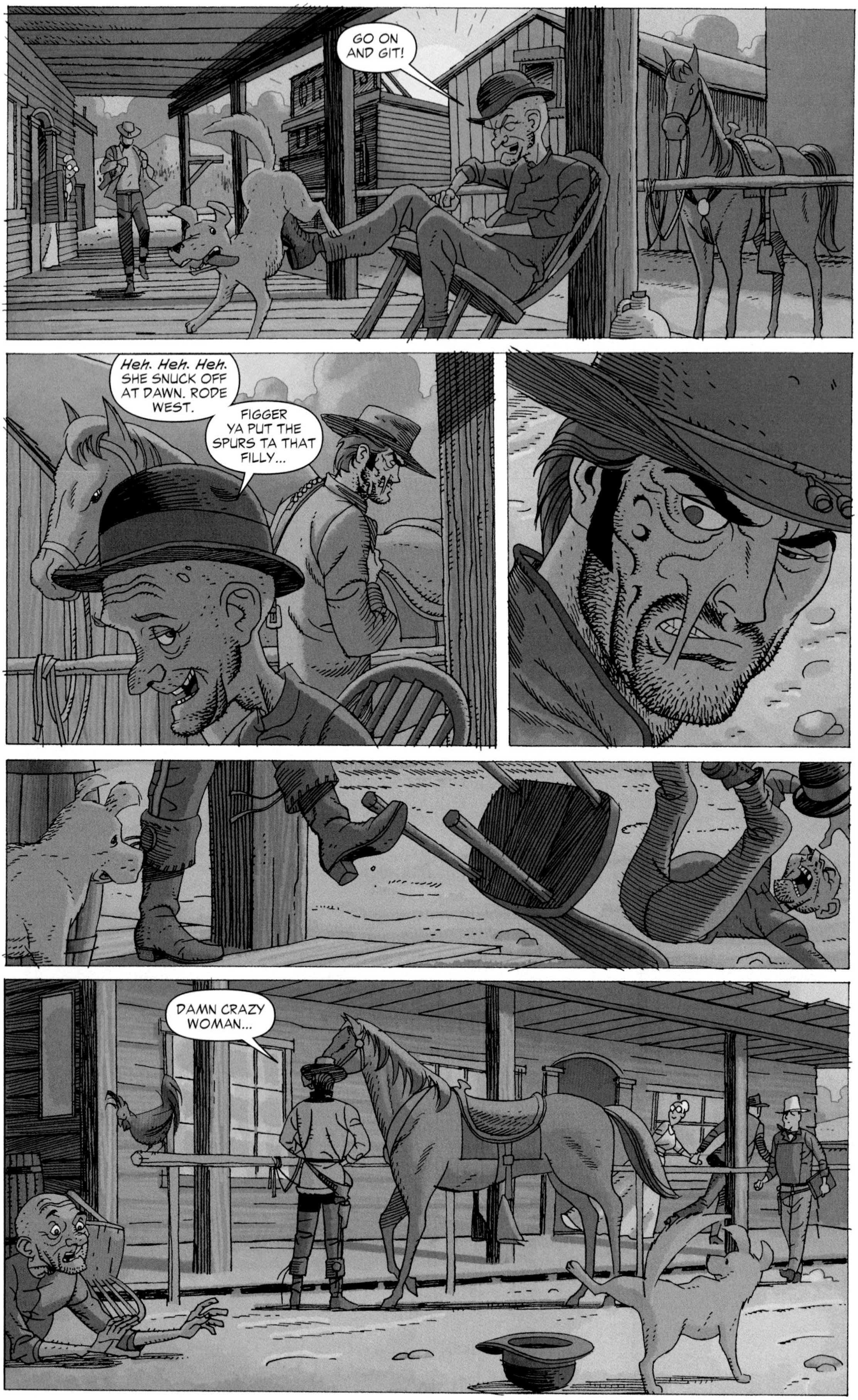
GO ON AND GIT!
Heh. Heh. Heh. SHE SNUCK OFF AT DAWN. RODE WEST.
FIGGER YA PUT THE SPURS TA THAT FILLY...
DAMN CRAZY WOMAN...

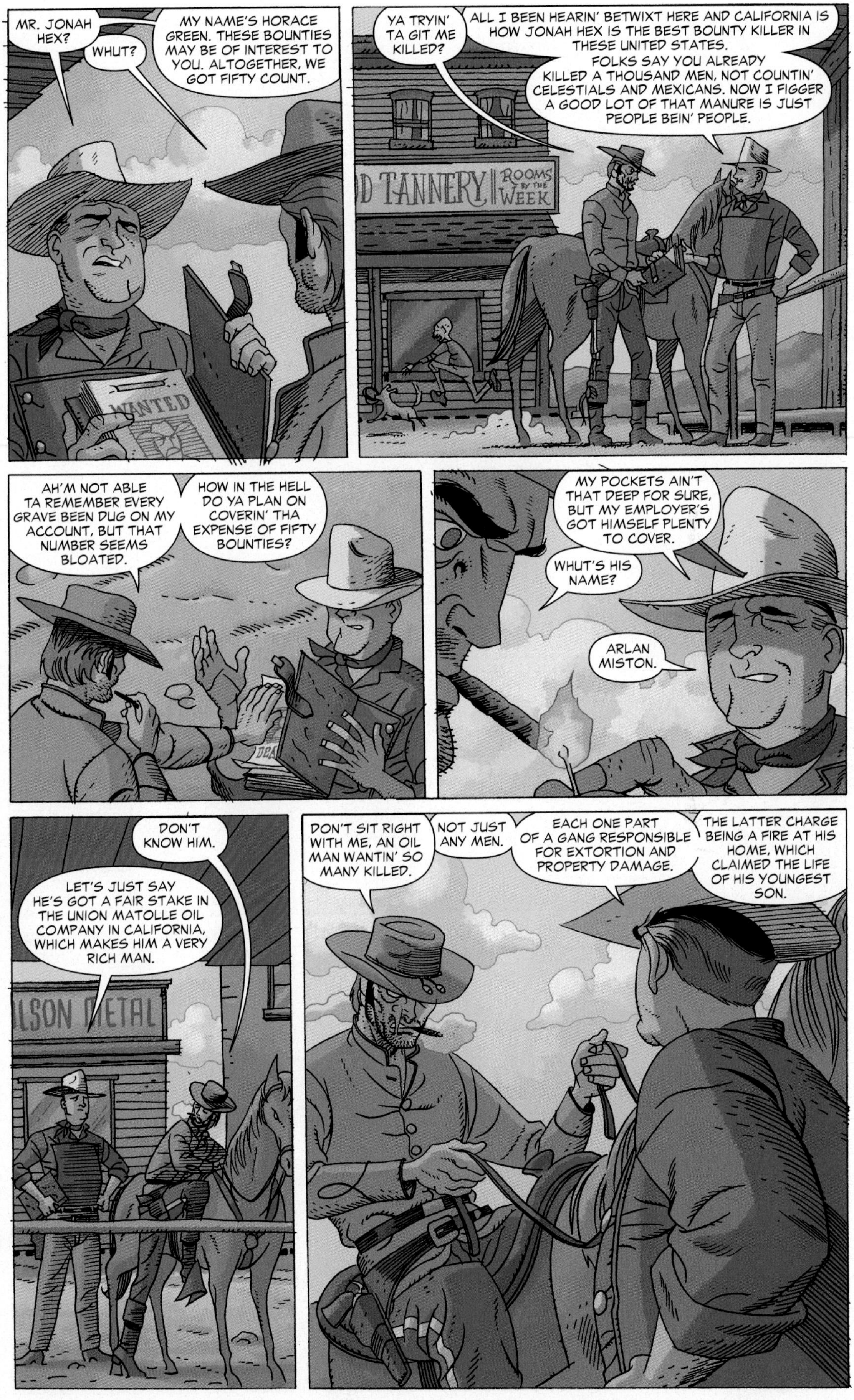
MR. JONAH HEX?
WHUT?
MY NAME'S HORACE GREEN. THESE BOUNTIES MAY BE OF INTEREST TO YOU. ALTOGETHER, WE GOT FIFTY COUNT.
WANTED
YA TRYIN' TA GIT ME KILLED?
ALL I BEEN HEARIN' BETWIXT HERE AND CALIFORNIA IS HOW JONAH HEX IS THE BEST BOUNTY KILLER IN THESE UNITED STATES.
FOLKS SAY YOU ALREADY KILLED A THOUSAND MEN, NOT COUNTIN' CELESTIALS AND MEXICANS. NOW I FIGGER A GOOD LOT OF THAT MANURE IS JUST PEOPLE BEIN' PEOPLE.
D TANNERY, ROOMS BY THE WEEK
AH'M NOT ABLE TA REMEMBER EVERY GRAVE BEEN DUG ON MY ACCOUNT, BUT THAT NUMBER SEEMS BLOATED.
HOW IN THE HELL DO YA PLAN ON COVERIN' THA EXPENSE OF FIFTY BOUNTIES?
MY POCKETS AIN'T THAT DEEP FOR SURE, BUT MY EMPLOYER'S GOT HIMSELF PLENTY TO COVER.
WHUT'S HIS NAME?
ARLAN MISTON.
DON'T KNOW HIM.
LET'S JUST SAY HE'S GOT A FAIR STAKE IN THE UNION MATOLLE OIL COMPANY IN CALIFORNIA, WHICH MAKES HIM A VERY RICH MAN.
LSON METAL
DON'T SIT RIGHT WITH ME, AN OIL MAN WANTIN' SO MANY KILLED.
NOT JUST ANY MEN.
EACH ONE PART OF A GANG RESPONSIBLE FOR EXTORTION AND PROPERTY DAMAGE.
THE LATTER CHARGE BEING A FIRE AT HIS HOME, WHICH CLAIMED THE LIFE OF HIS YOUNGEST SON.

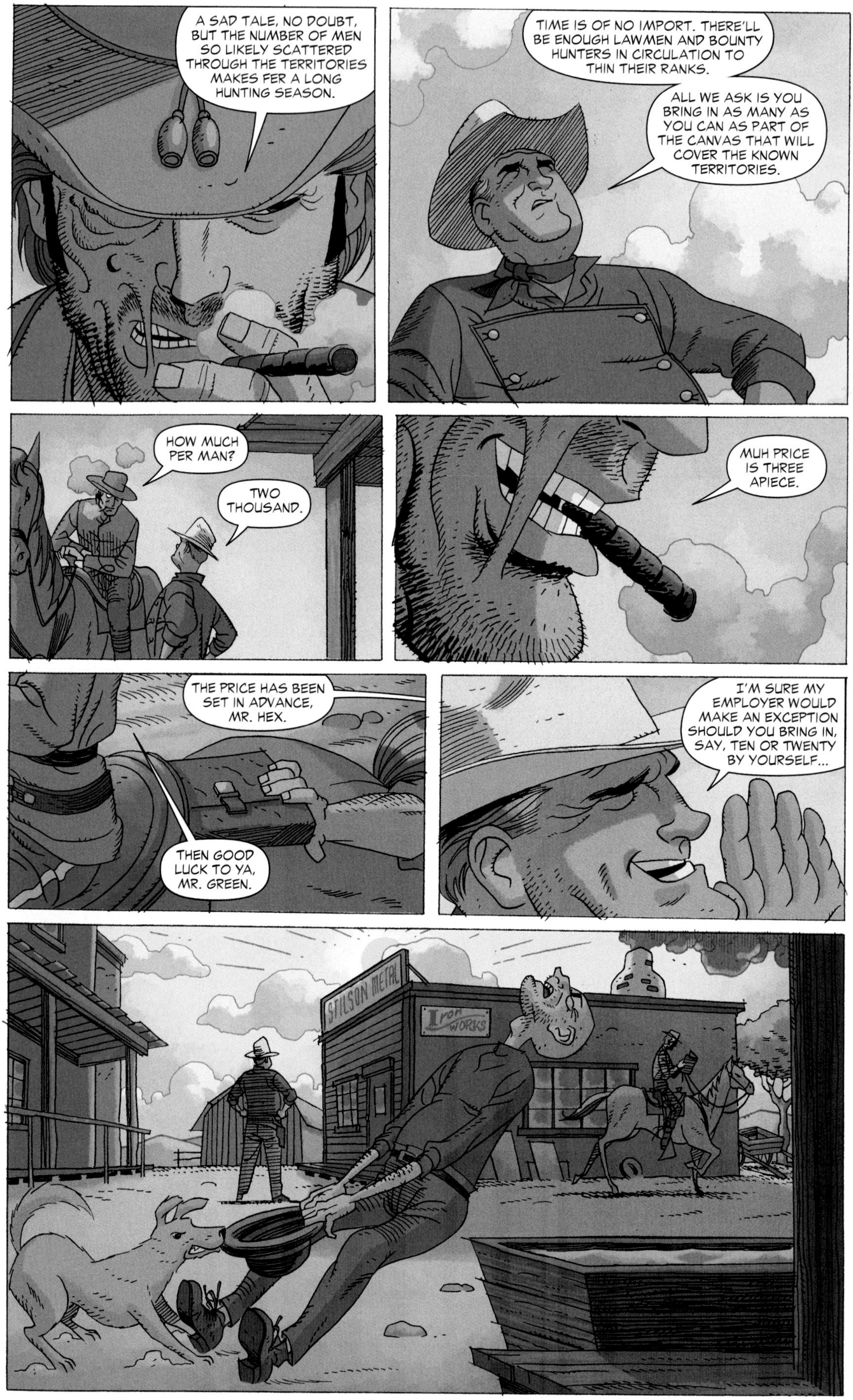
A SAD TALE, NO DOUBT, BUT THE NUMBER OF MEN SO LIKELY SCATTERED THROUGH THE TERRITORIES MAKES FER A LONG HUNTING SEASON.
TIME IS OF NO IMPORT. THERE'LL BE ENOUGH LAWMEN AND BOUNTY HUNTERS IN CIRCULATION TO THIN THEIR RANKS.
ALL WE ASK IS YOU BRING IN AS MANY AS YOU CAN AS PART OF THE CANVAS THAT WILL COVER THE KNOWN TERRITORIES.
HOW MUCH PER MAN?
TWO THOUSAND.
MUH PRICE IS THREE APIECE.
THE PRICE HAS BEEN SET IN ADVANCE, MR. HEX.
THEN GOOD LUCK TO YA, MR. GREEN.
I'M SURE MY EMPLOYER WOULD MAKE AN EXCEPTION SHOULD YOU BRING IN, SAY, TEN OR TWENTY BY YOURSELF...
STILSON METAL
Iron WORKS

THE HUNTER UNLEASHED

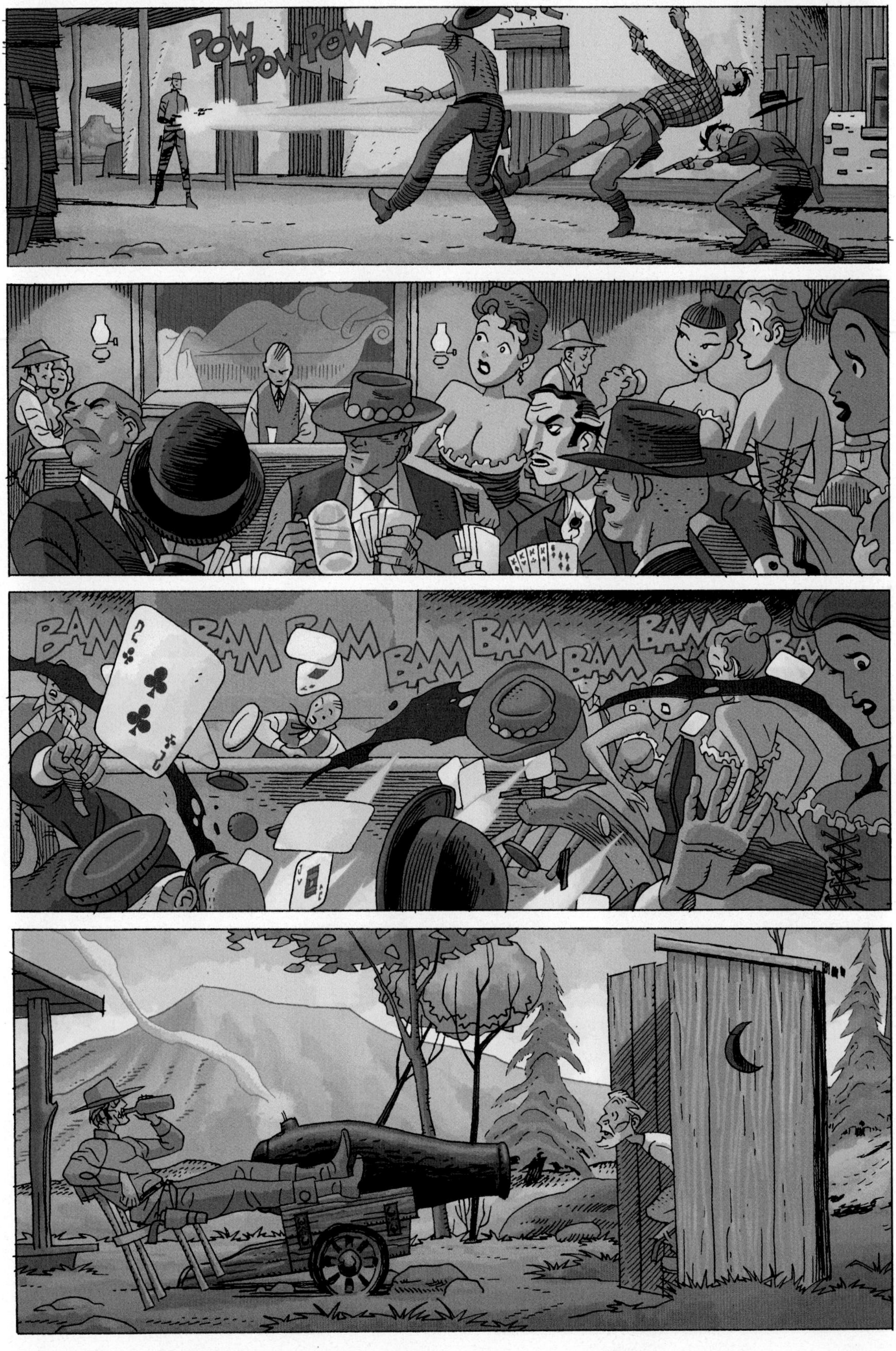
POW
POW
POW
BAM
BAM
BAM
BAM
BAM
BAM

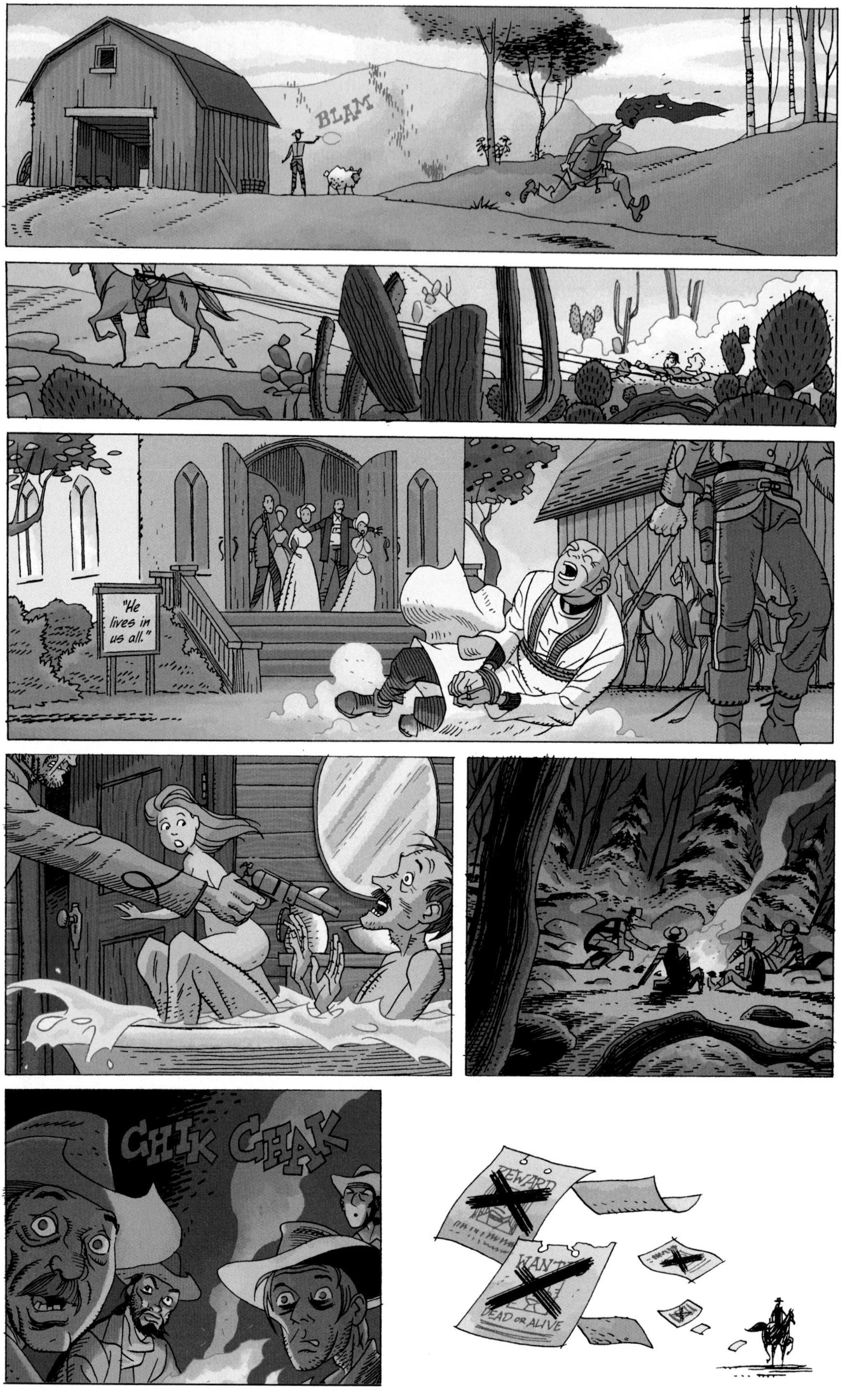
BLAM
"He lives in us all."
CHIK CHAK
REWARD
WANT
DEAD OR ALIVE

THE PROSPECT OF A FRESH START

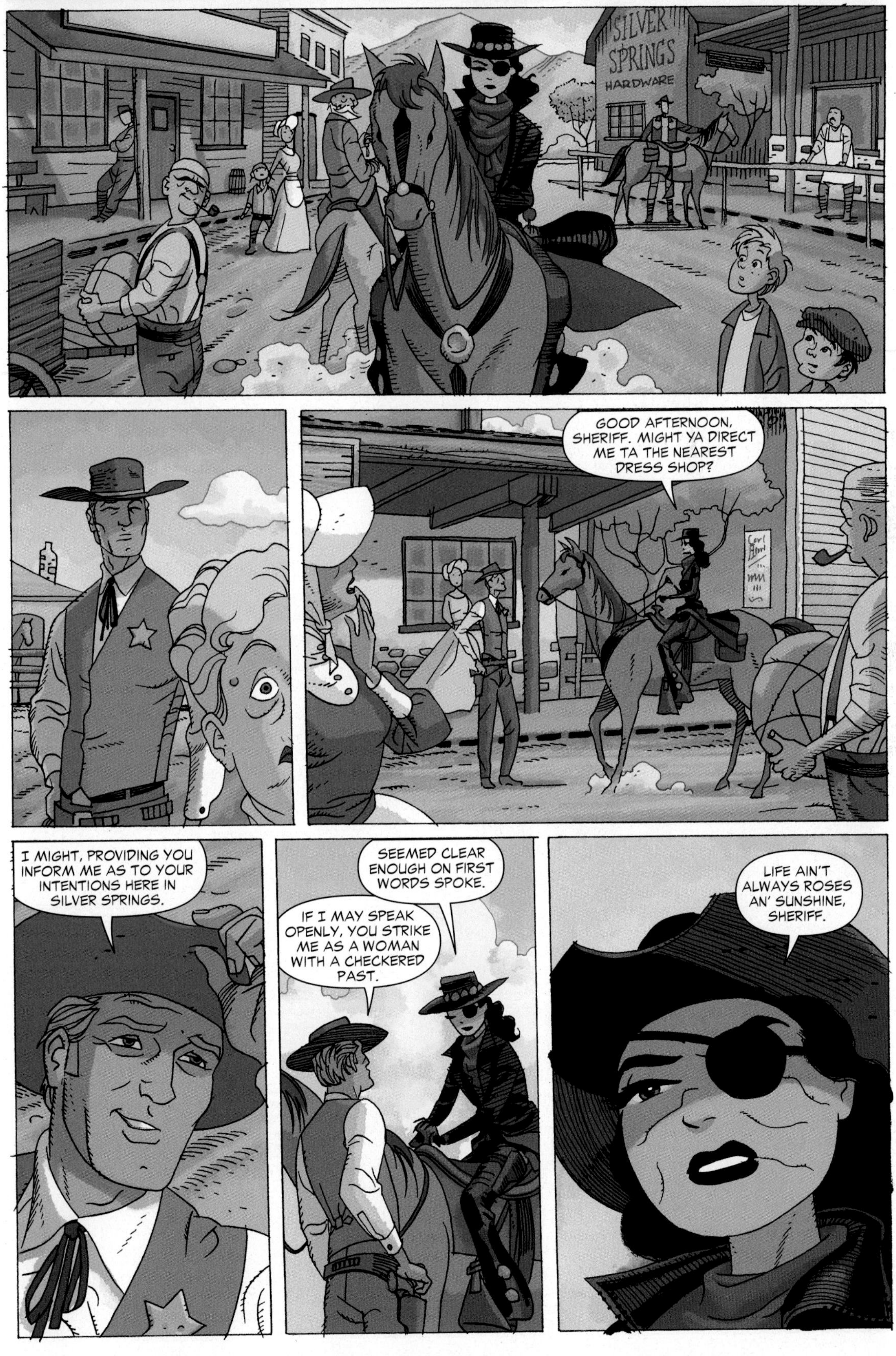
SILVER SPRINGS HARDWARE
GOOD AFTERNOON, SHERIFF. MIGHT YA DIRECT ME TA THE NEAREST DRESS SHOP?
I MIGHT, PROVIDING YOU INFORM ME AS TO YOUR INTENTIONS HERE IN SILVER SPRINGS.
SEEMED CLEAR ENOUGH ON FIRST WORDS SPOKE.
IF I MAY SPEAK OPENLY, YOU STRIKE ME AS A WOMAN WITH A CHECKERED PAST.
LIFE AIN'T ALWAYS ROSES AN' SUNSHINE, SHERIFF.

BE THAT AS IT MAY, THIS IS MY TOWN TO WATCH OVER.

I'LL BE SURE TO SLEEP SOUND IN THE KNOWLEDGE THAT YER LOOKIN' OUT FER ME.

SOMEHOW I HAVE THE FEELING YOU'RE QUITE CAPABLE OF LOOKING OUT FOR YOURSELF.

WE GONNA DANCE 'ROUND THE CAMPFIRE OR ARE YA GONNA COME OUT WITH IT?

THIS IS A GOOD TOWN WITH GOOD PEOPLE TRYING TO LIVE THEIR LIVES IN PEACE. I DON'T WANT TROUBLE, MISS.

THAT MAKES TWO OF US.

RIGHT. PROBLEM IS, YOU LOOK LIKE TROUBLE.

HENCE MY INTEREST IN LOCATIN' A PROPER DRESS SHOP, FROM WHICH I'LL EMERGE TRANSFORMED AND SMELLING OF LILAC.

YOU ARE A PECULIAR WOMAN.

WORSE TERMS HAVE BEEN APPLIED.

WHAT'S YOUR NAME?

YOU WON'T FIND IT ON A WANTED POSTER.

JUST THE SAME, I LIKE TO KNOW WHOM I AM SPEAKING WITH.

MISS ABIGA FABRIC and NOTIO

TALLULAH BLACK, AN' I'LL SAVE YA THE TELEGRAM: I AM, OR RATHER I WAS, A BOUNTY HUNTER. I'VE KILLED A HELL OF A LOT OF MEN, 'AN ALL OF 'EM HAD IT COMIN'.

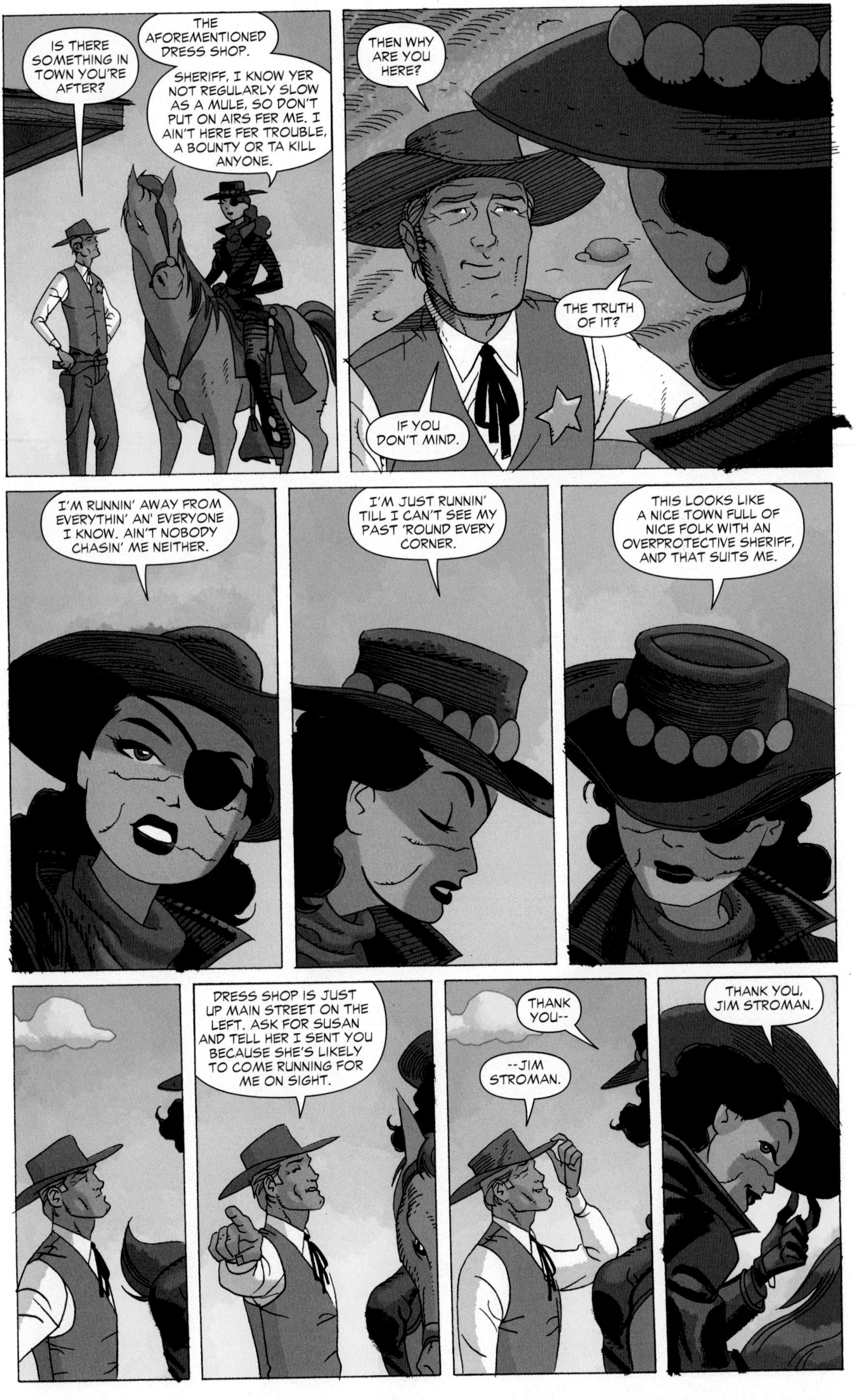
IS THERE SOMETHING IN TOWN YOU'RE AFTER?
THE AFOREMENTIONED DRESS SHOP.
SHERIFF, I KNOW YER NOT REGULARLY SLOW AS A MULE, SO DON'T PUT ON AIRS FER ME. I AIN'T HERE FER TROUBLE, A BOUNTY OR TA KILL ANYONE.
THEN WHY ARE YOU HERE?
THE TRUTH OF IT?
IF YOU DON'T MIND.
I'M RUNNIN' AWAY FROM EVERYTHIN' AN' EVERYONE I KNOW. AIN'T NOBODY CHASIN' ME NEITHER.
I'M JUST RUNNIN' TILL I CAN'T SEE MY PAST 'ROUND EVERY CORNER.
THIS LOOKS LIKE A NICE TOWN FULL OF NICE FOLK WITH AN OVERPROTECTIVE SHERIFF, AND THAT SUITS ME.
DRESS SHOP IS JUST UP MAIN STREET ON THE LEFT. ASK FOR SUSAN AND TELL HER I SENT YOU BECAUSE SHE'S LIKELY TO COME RUNNING FOR ME ON SIGHT.
THANK YOU--
--JIM STROMAN.
THANK YOU, JIM STROMAN.

THE FALL OF MANY MEN

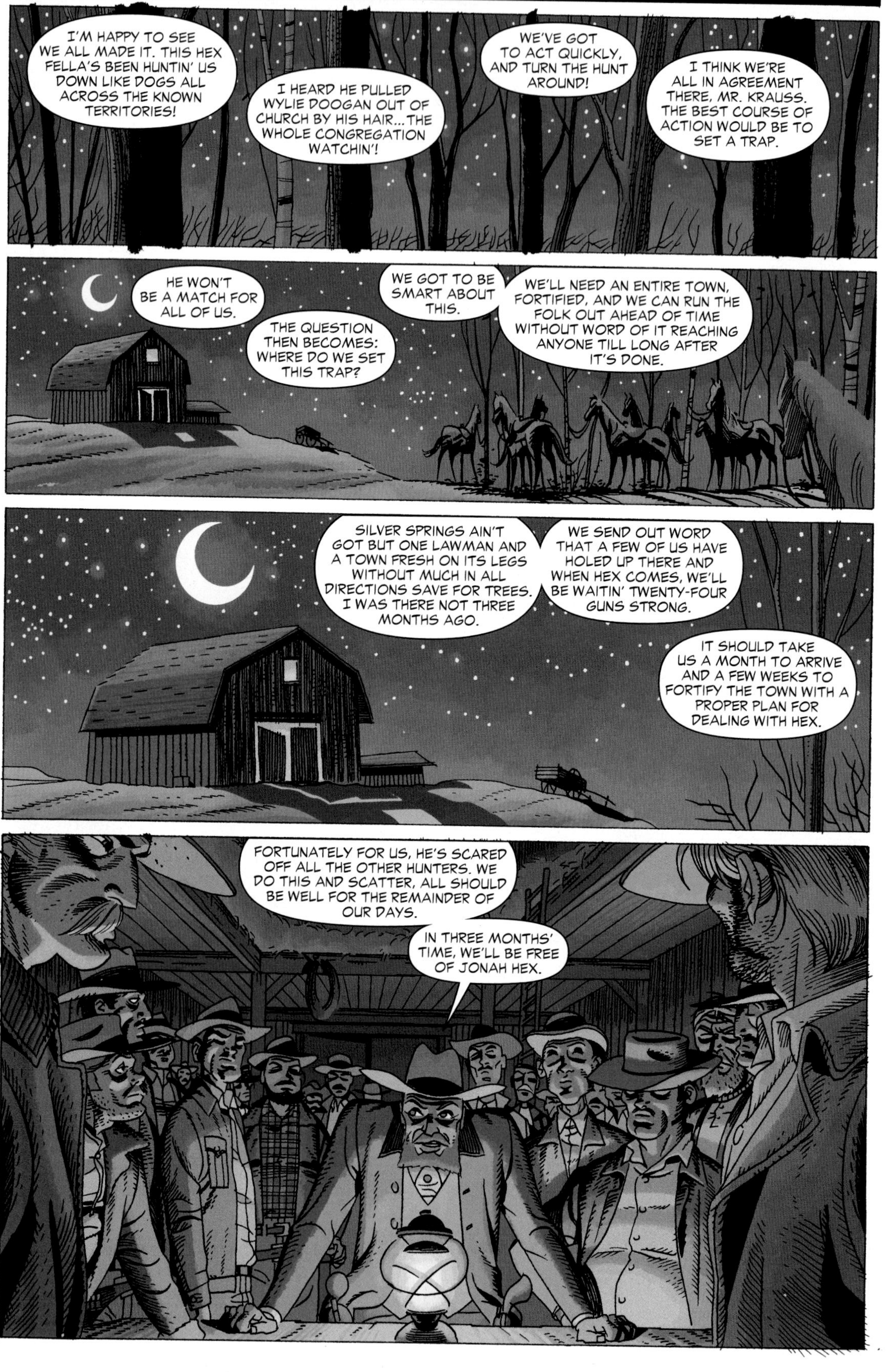

I'M HAPPY TO SEE WE ALL MADE IT. THIS HEX FELLA'S BEEN HUNTIN' US DOWN LIKE DOGS ALL ACROSS THE KNOWN TERRITORIES!
I HEARD HE PULLED WYLIE DOOGAN OUT OF CHURCH BY HIS HAIR...THE WHOLE CONGREGATION WATCHIN'!
WE'VE GOT TO ACT QUICKLY, AND TURN THE HUNT AROUND!
I THINK WE'RE ALL IN AGREEMENT THERE, MR. KRAUSS. THE BEST COURSE OF ACTION WOULD BE TO SET A TRAP.
HE WON'T BE A MATCH FOR ALL OF US.
THE QUESTION THEN BECOMES: WHERE DO WE SET THIS TRAP?
WE GOT TO BE SMART ABOUT THIS.
WE'LL NEED AN ENTIRE TOWN, FORTIFIED, AND WE CAN RUN THE FOLK OUT AHEAD OF TIME WITHOUT WORD OF IT REACHING ANYONE TILL LONG AFTER IT'S DONE.
SILVER SPRINGS AIN'T GOT BUT ONE LAWMAN AND A TOWN FRESH ON ITS LEGS WITHOUT MUCH IN ALL DIRECTIONS SAVE FOR TREES. I WAS THERE NOT THREE MONTHS AGO.
WE SEND OUT WORD THAT A FEW OF US HAVE HOLED UP THERE AND WHEN HEX COMES, WE'LL BE WAITIN' TWENTY-FOUR GUNS STRONG.
IT SHOULD TAKE US A MONTH TO ARRIVE AND A FEW WEEKS TO FORTIFY THE TOWN WITH A PROPER PLAN FOR DEALING WITH HEX.
FORTUNATELY FOR US, HE'S SCARED OFF ALL THE OTHER HUNTERS. WE DO THIS AND SCATTER, ALL SHOULD BE WELL FOR THE REMAINDER OF OUR DAYS.
IN THREE MONTHS' TIME, WE'LL BE FREE OF JONAH HEX.

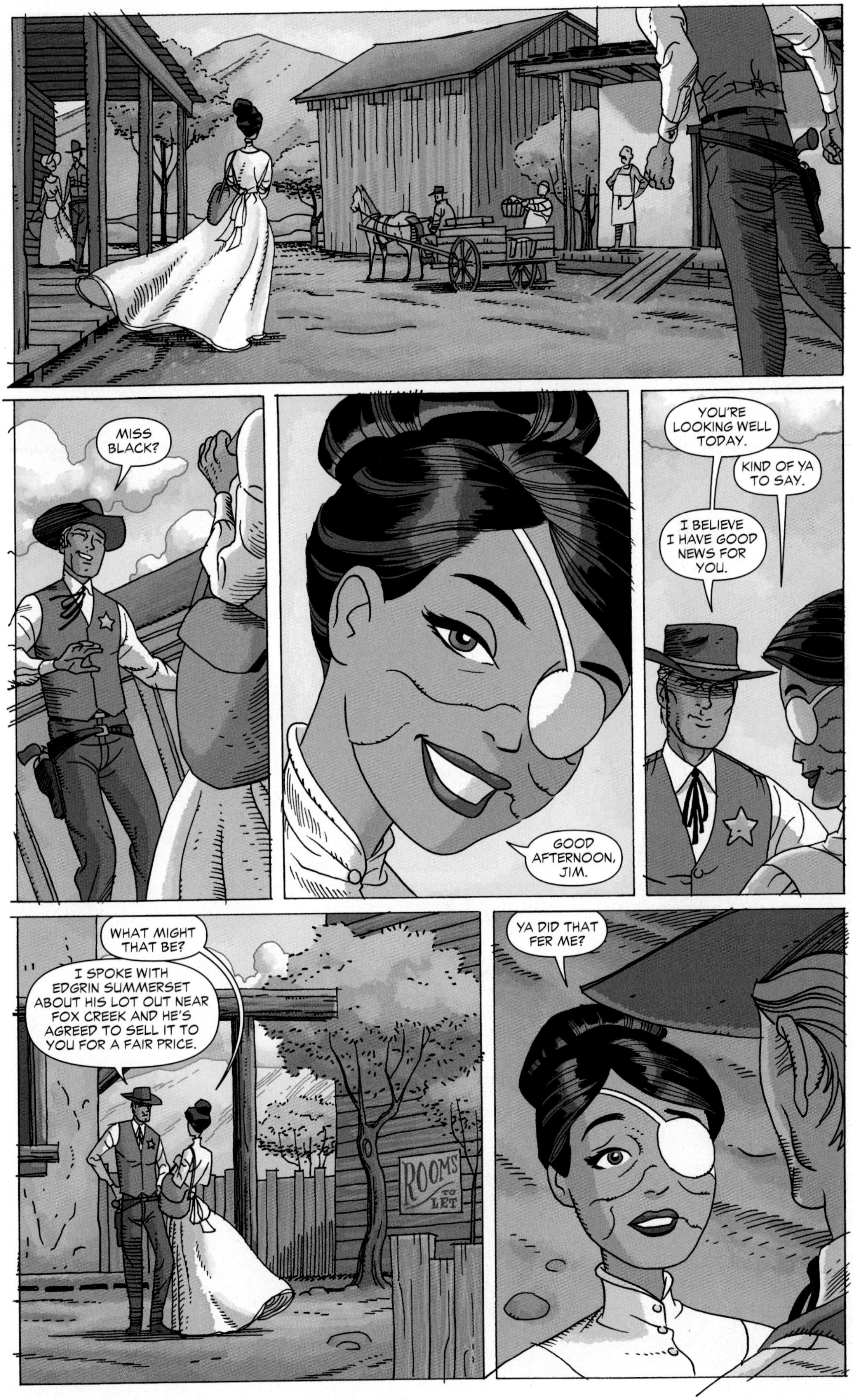
MISS BLACK?
GOOD AFTERNOON, JIM.
YOU'RE LOOKING WELL TODAY.
KIND OF YA TO SAY.
I BELIEVE I HAVE GOOD NEWS FOR YOU.
WHAT MIGHT THAT BE?
I SPOKE WITH EDGRIN SUMMERSET ABOUT HIS LOT OUT NEAR FOX CREEK AND HE'S AGREED TO SELL IT TO YOU FOR A FAIR PRICE.
ROOMS TO LET
YA DID THAT FER ME?

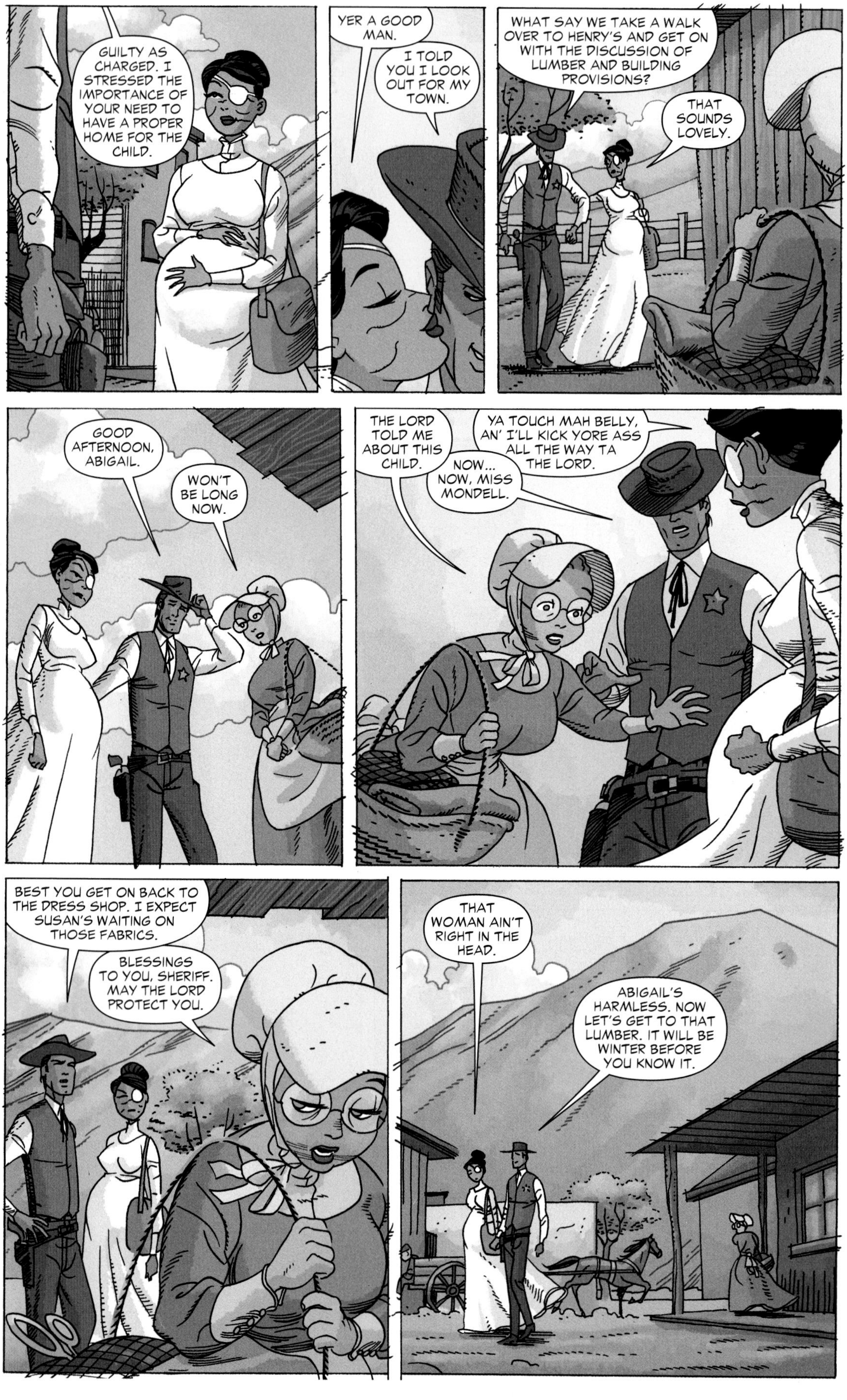
GUILTY AS CHARGED. I STRESSED THE IMPORTANCE OF YOUR NEED TO HAVE A PROPER HOME FOR THE CHILD.
YER A GOOD MAN.
I TOLD YOU I LOOK OUT FOR MY TOWN.
WHAT SAY WE TAKE A WALK OVER TO HENRY'S AND GET ON WITH THE DISCUSSION OF LUMBER AND BUILDING PROVISIONS?
THAT SOUNDS LOVELY.
GOOD AFTERNOON, ABIGAIL.
WON'T BE LONG NOW.
THE LORD TOLD ME ABOUT THIS CHILD.
YA TOUCH MAH BELLY, AN' I'LL KICK YORE ASS ALL THE WAY TA THE LORD.
NOW... NOW, MISS MONDELL.
BEST YOU GET ON BACK TO THE DRESS SHOP. I EXPECT SUSAN'S WAITING ON THOSE FABRICS.
BLESSINGS TO YOU, SHERIFF. MAY THE LORD PROTECT YOU.
THAT WOMAN AIN'T RIGHT IN THE HEAD.
ABIGAIL'S HARMLESS. NOW LET'S GET TO THAT LUMBER. IT WILL BE WINTER BEFORE YOU KNOW IT.

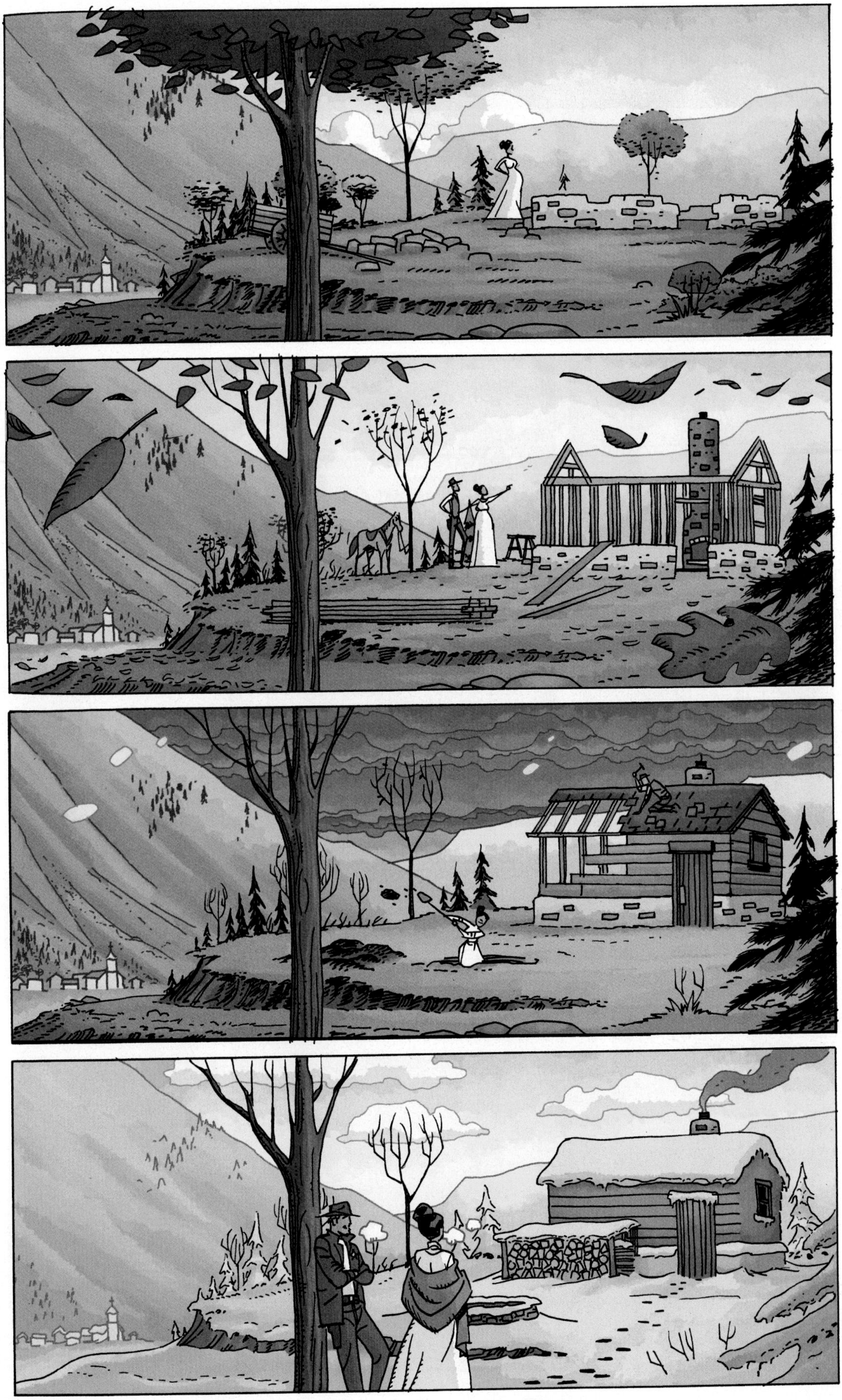

THE WINTER OF DISCONTENT

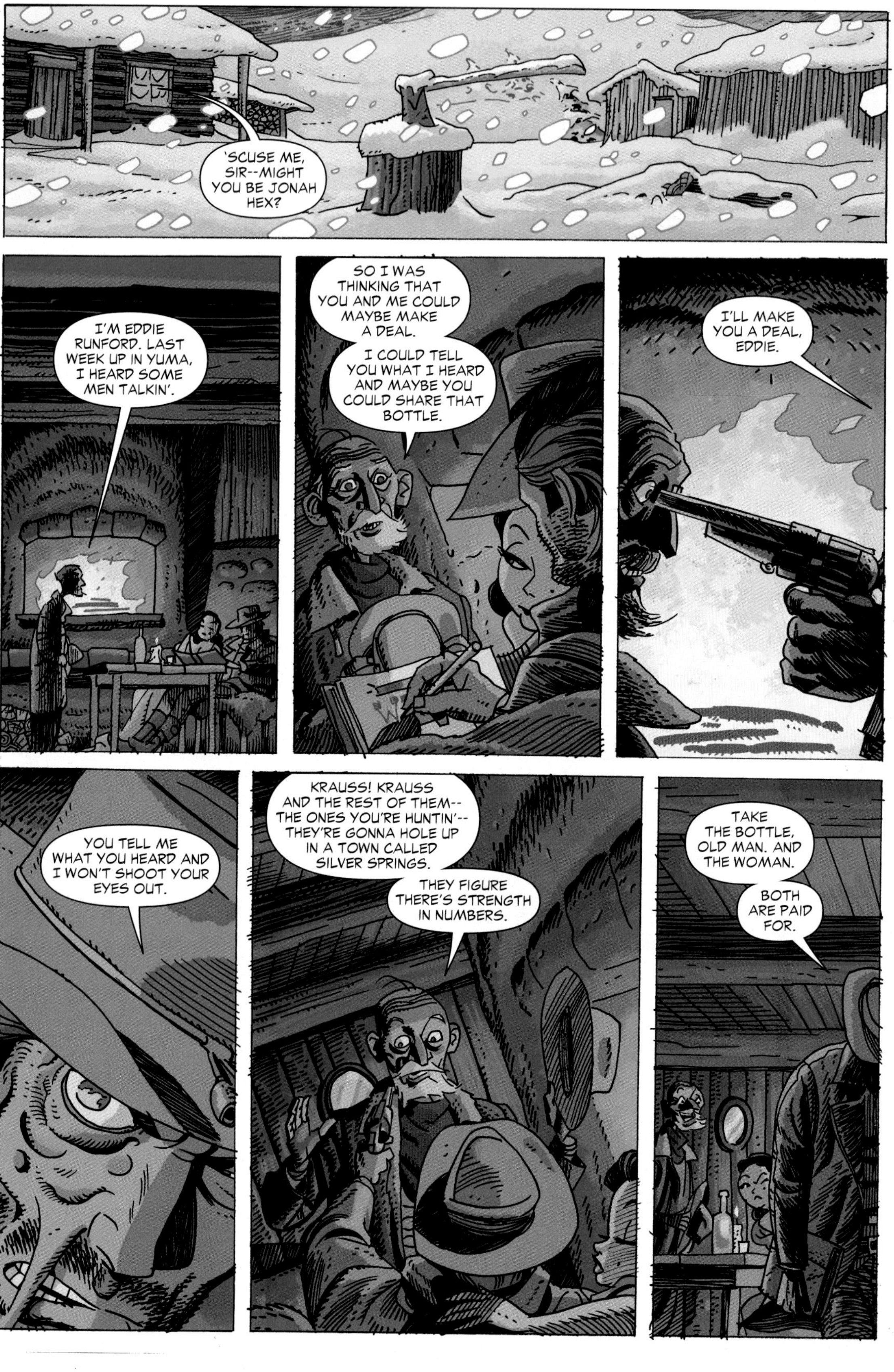
'SCUSE ME, SIR--MIGHT YOU BE JONAH HEX?
I'M EDDIE RUNFORD. LAST WEEK UP IN YUMA, I HEARD SOME MEN TALKIN'.
SO I WAS THINKING THAT YOU AND ME COULD MAYBE MAKE A DEAL.
I COULD TELL YOU WHAT I HEARD AND MAYBE YOU COULD SHARE THAT BOTTLE.
I'LL MAKE YOU A DEAL, EDDIE.
YOU TELL ME WHAT YOU HEARD AND I WON'T SHOOT YOUR EYES OUT.
KRAUSS! KRAUSS AND THE REST OF THEM-- THE ONES YOU'RE HUNTIN'-- THEY'RE GONNA HOLE UP IN A TOWN CALLED SILVER SPRINGS.
THEY FIGURE THERE'S STRENGTH IN NUMBERS.
TAKE THE BOTTLE, OLD MAN. AND THE WOMAN.
BOTH ARE PAID FOR.

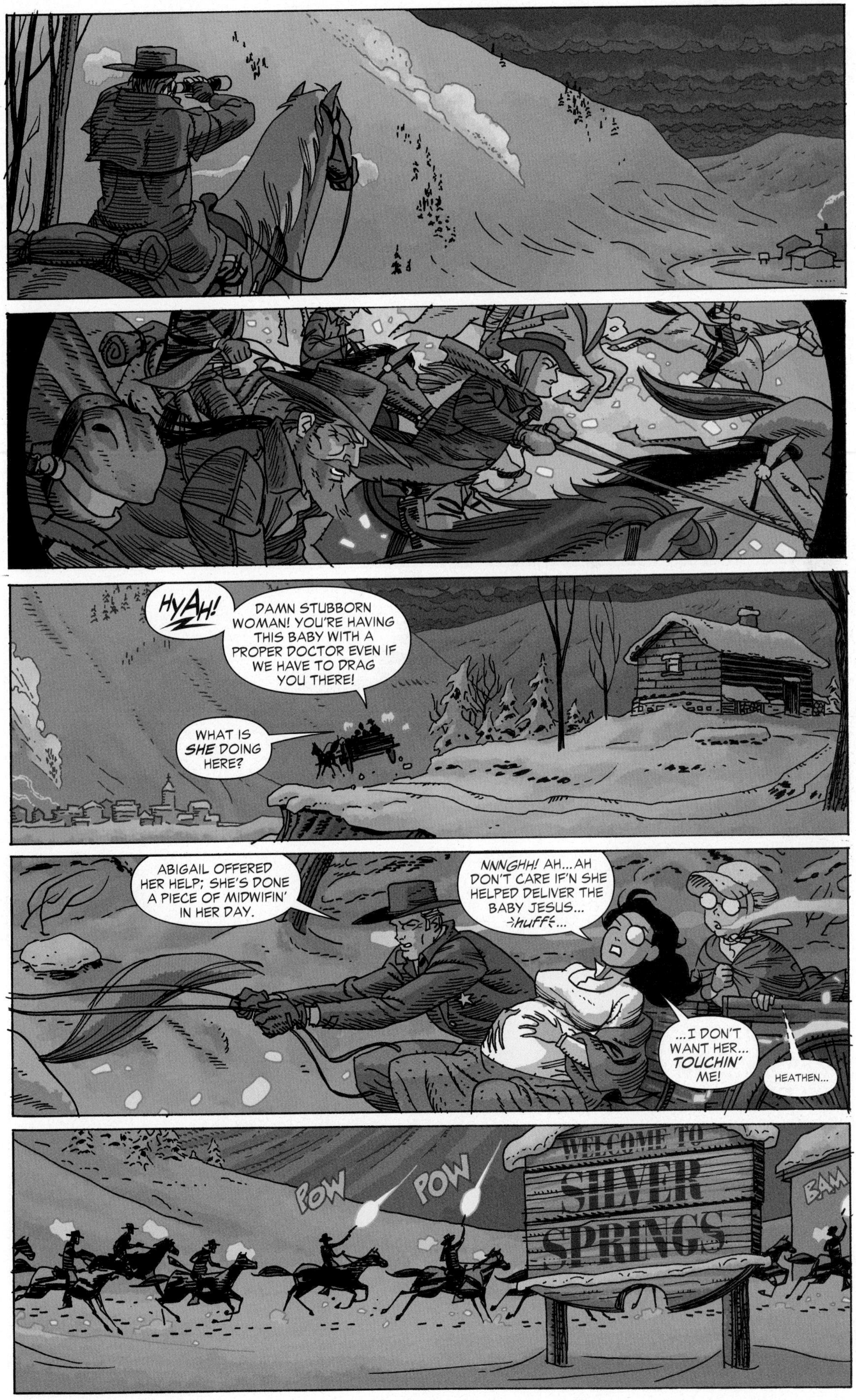
HYAH!
DAMN STUBBORN WOMAN! YOU'RE HAVING THIS BABY WITH A PROPER DOCTOR EVEN IF WE HAVE TO DRAG YOU THERE!
WHAT IS *SHE* DOING HERE?
ABIGAIL OFFERED HER HELP; SHE'S DONE A PIECE OF MIDWIFIN' IN HER DAY.
NNNGHH! AH...AH DON'T CARE IF'N SHE HELPED DELIVER THE BABY JESUS... *huff*...
...I DON'T WANT HER... *TOUCHIN'* ME!
HEATHEN...
POW
POW
WELCOME TO
SILVER SPRINGS
BAM

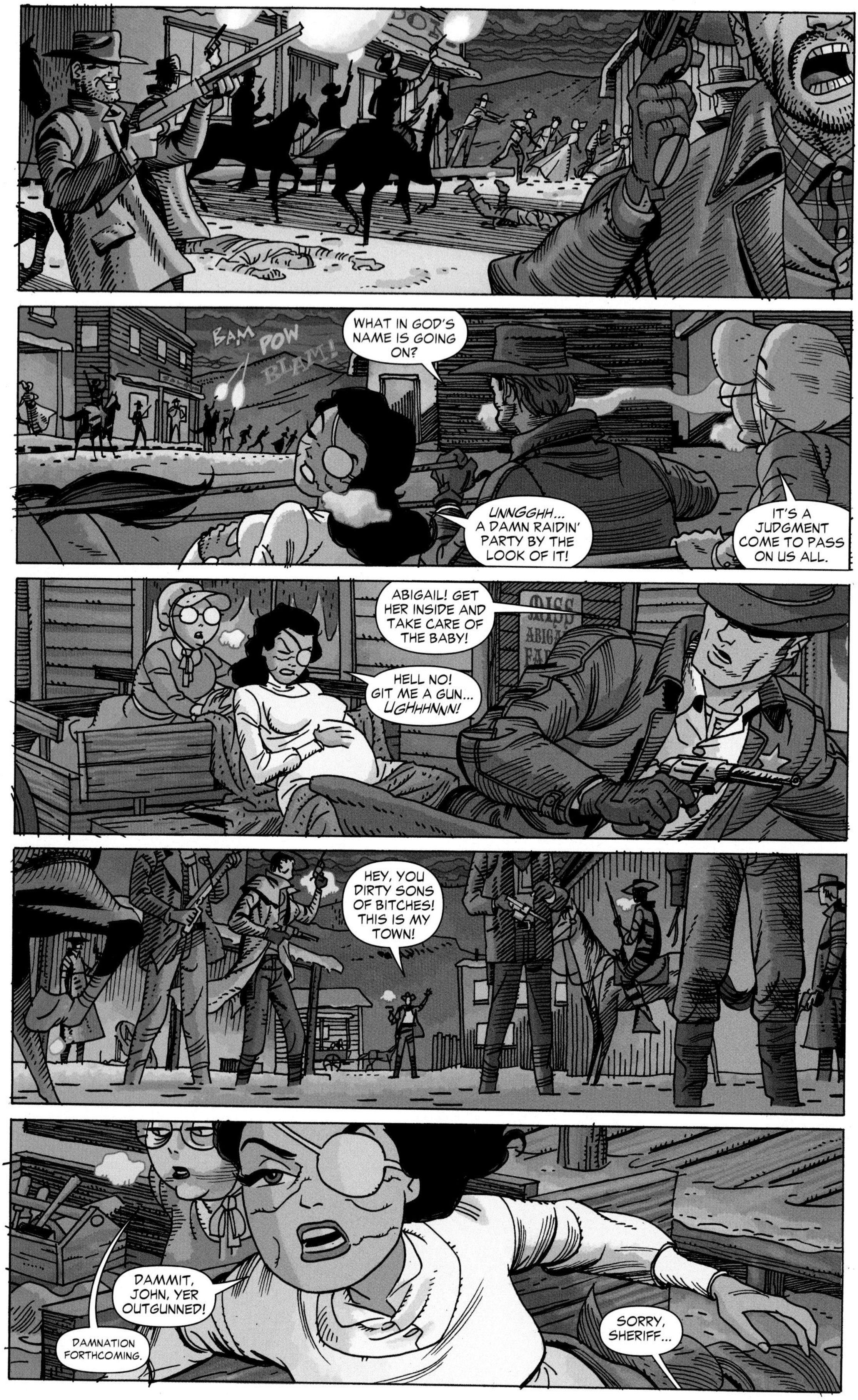
BAM
POW
BLAM!
WHAT IN GOD'S NAME IS GOING ON?
UNNGGHH... A DAMN RAIDIN' PARTY BY THE LOOK OF IT!
IT'S A JUDGMENT COME TO PASS ON US ALL.
ABIGAIL! GET HER INSIDE AND TAKE CARE OF THE BABY!
HELL NO! GIT ME A GUN... UGHHHNNN!
HEY, YOU DIRTY SONS OF BITCHES! THIS IS MY TOWN!
DAMMIT, JOHN, YER OUTGUNNED!
DAMNATION FORTHCOMING.
SORRY, SHERIFF...

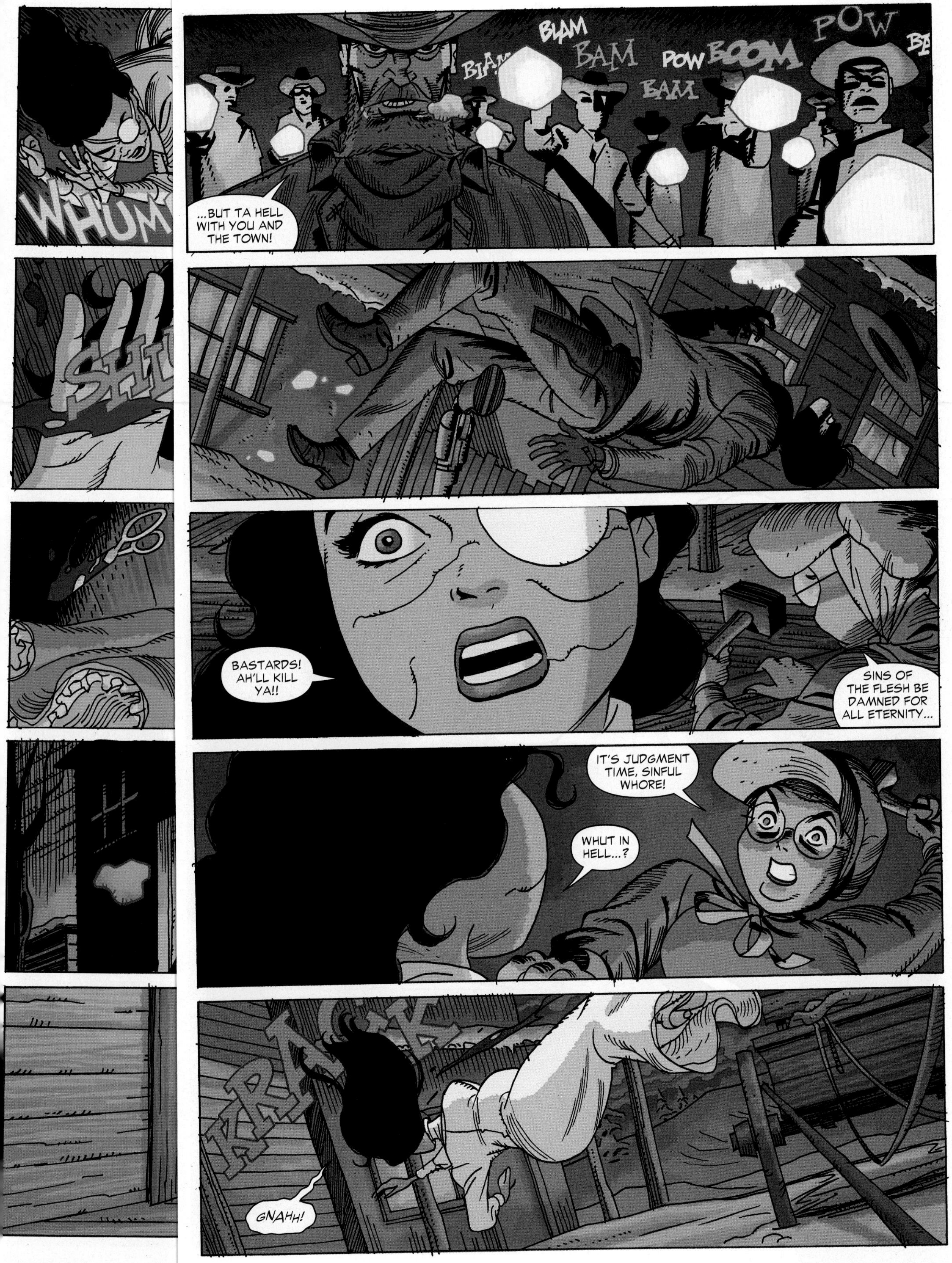
WHUM
BLAM
BLAM
BAM
POW
BOOM
BAM
POW
...BUT TA HELL WITH YOU AND THE TOWN!
BASTARDS! AH'LL KILL YA!!
SINS OF THE FLESH BE DAMNED FOR ALL ETERNITY...
IT'S JUDGMENT TIME, SINFUL WHORE!
WHUT IN HELL...?
GNAHH!

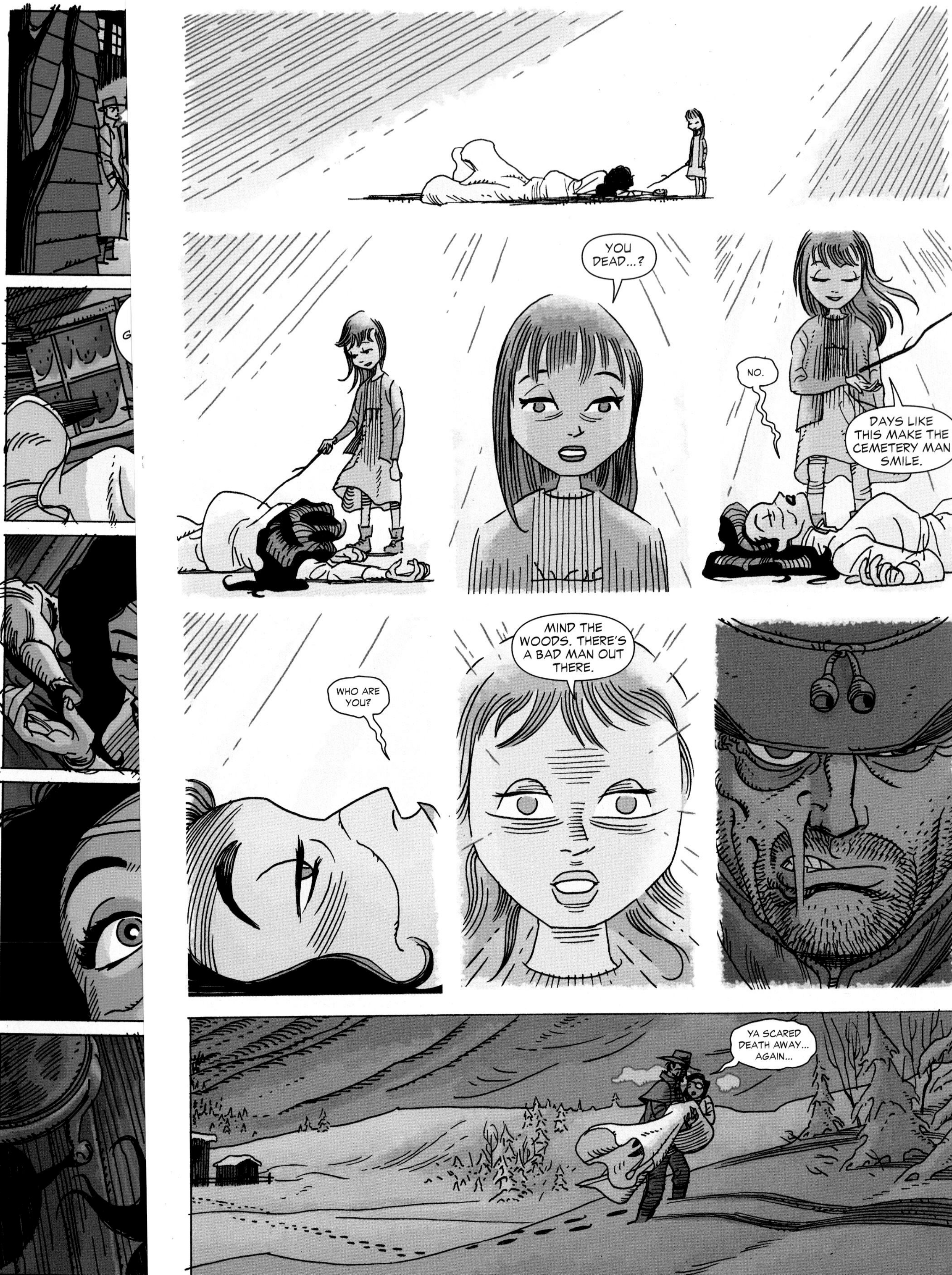
YOU DEAD...?
NO.
DAYS LIKE THIS MAKE THE CEMETERY MAN SMILE.
WHO ARE YOU?
MIND THE WOODS. THERE'S A BAD MAN OUT THERE.
YA SCARED DEATH AWAY... AGAIN...

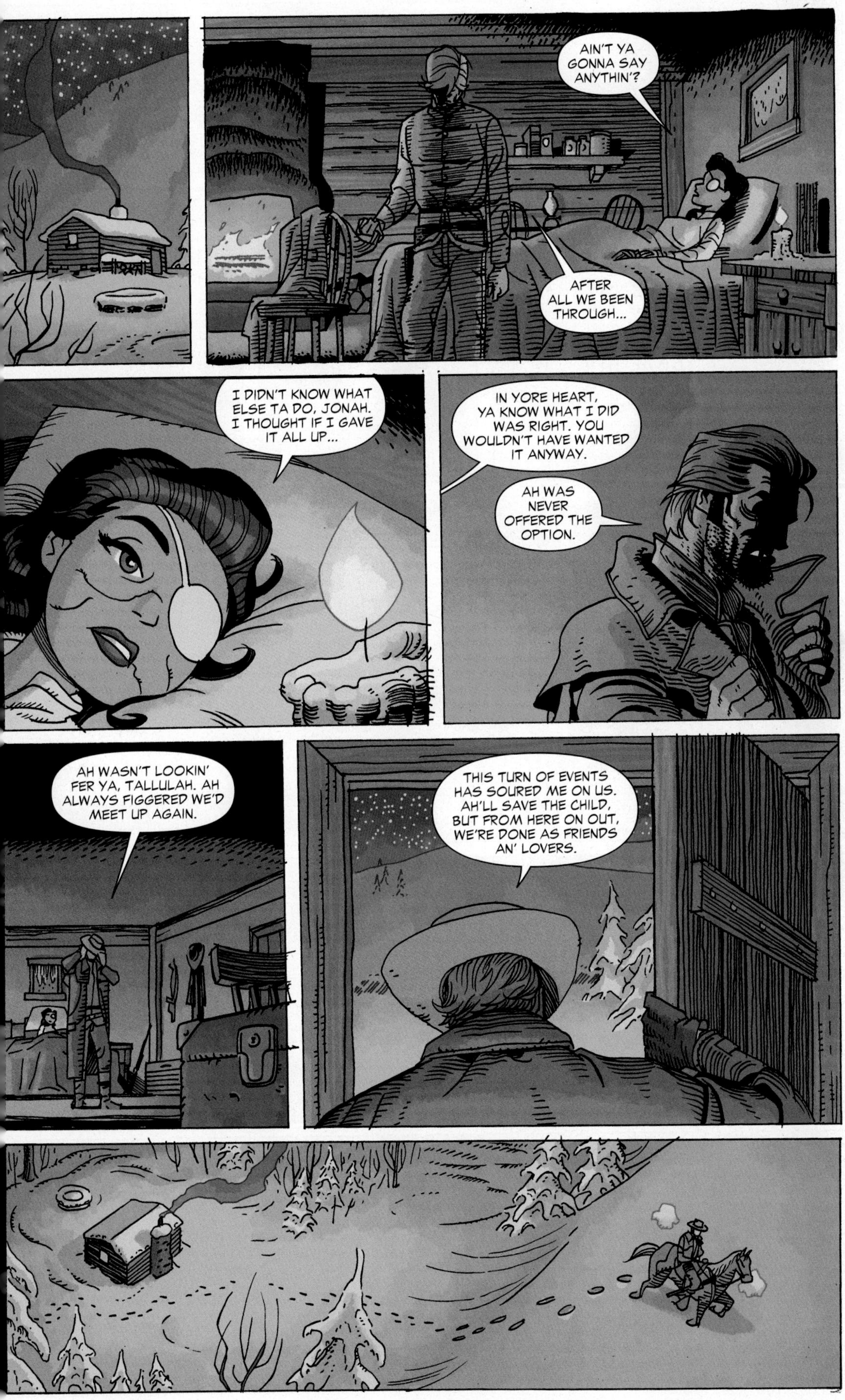
AIN'T YA GONNA SAY ANYTHIN'?
AFTER ALL WE BEEN THROUGH...
I DIDN'T KNOW WHAT ELSE TA DO, JONAH. I THOUGHT IF I GAVE IT ALL UP...
IN YORE HEART, YA KNOW WHAT I DID WAS RIGHT. YOU WOULDN'T HAVE WANTED IT ANYWAY.
AH WAS NEVER OFFERED THE OPTION.
AH WASN'T LOOKIN' FER YA, TALLULAH. AH ALWAYS FIGGERED WE'D MEET UP AGAIN.
THIS TURN OF EVENTS HAS SOURED ME ON US. AH'LL SAVE THE CHILD, BUT FROM HERE ON OUT, WE'RE DONE AS FRIENDS AN' LOVERS.

AH'M ONLY GONNA ASK THIS ONCE.

AH'M LOOKIN' FER A WOMAN WITH A STOLEN INFANT. HER NAME'S ABIGAIL.

STOLEN...?

FROM THE BELLY. YA SEEN HER?

SHE TOLD ME TALLULAH WAS DEAD...KILLED OUTRIGHT BY THE GANG AFTER DELIVERY.

JESUS HELP ME, I LET HER GO WITH THE CHILD...

WHERE'S THE TRAIN HEADED?

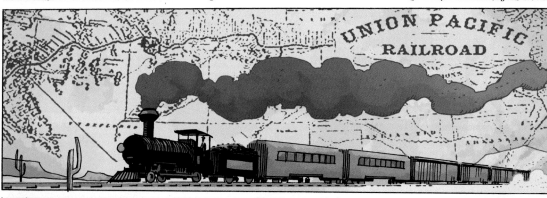

UNION PACIFIC RAILROAD

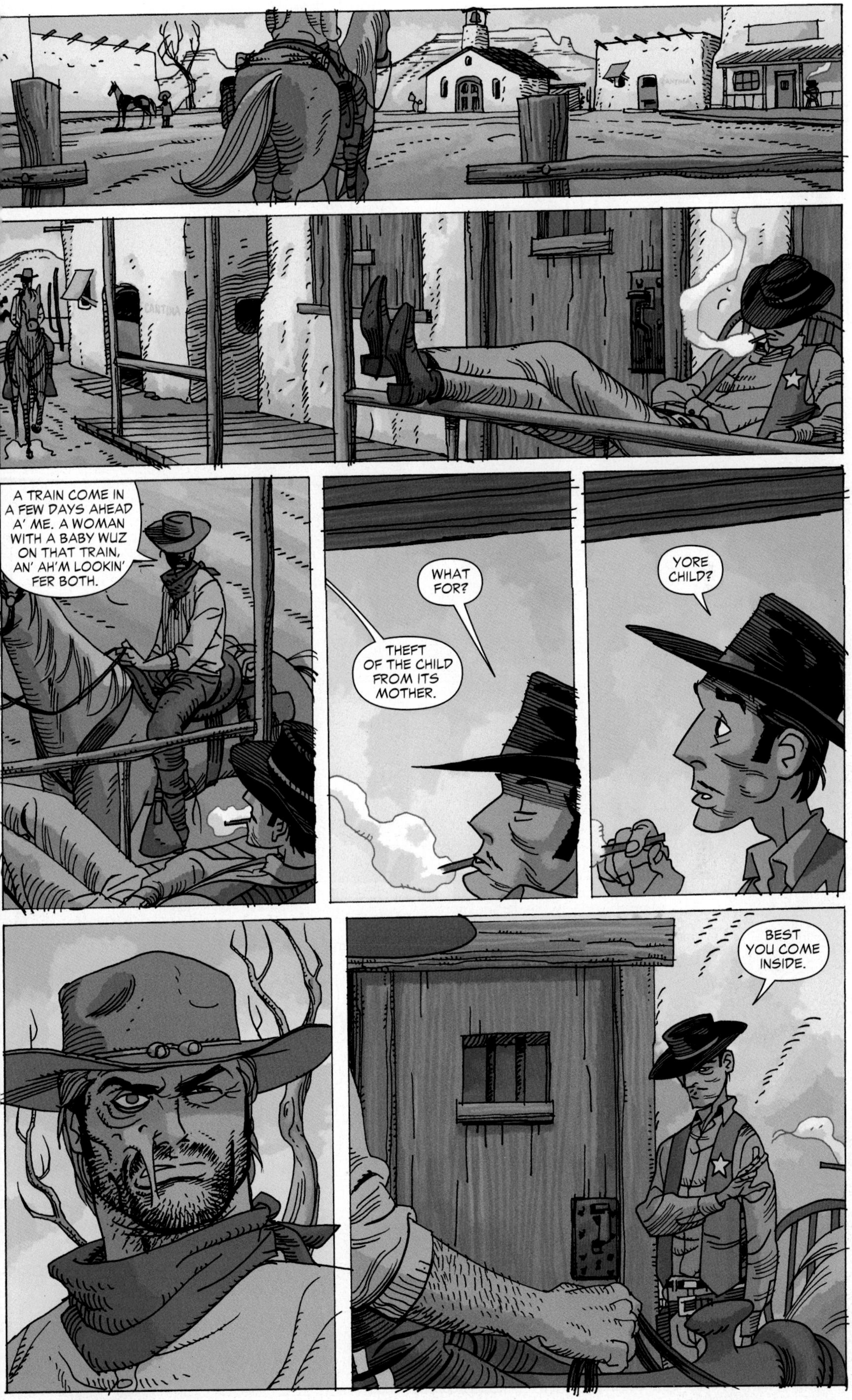
A TRAIN COME IN A FEW DAYS AHEAD A' ME. A WOMAN WITH A BABY WUZ ON THAT TRAIN, AN' AH'M LOOKIN' FER BOTH.
WHAT FOR?
THEFT OF THE CHILD FROM ITS MOTHER.
YORE CHILD?
BEST YOU COME INSIDE.

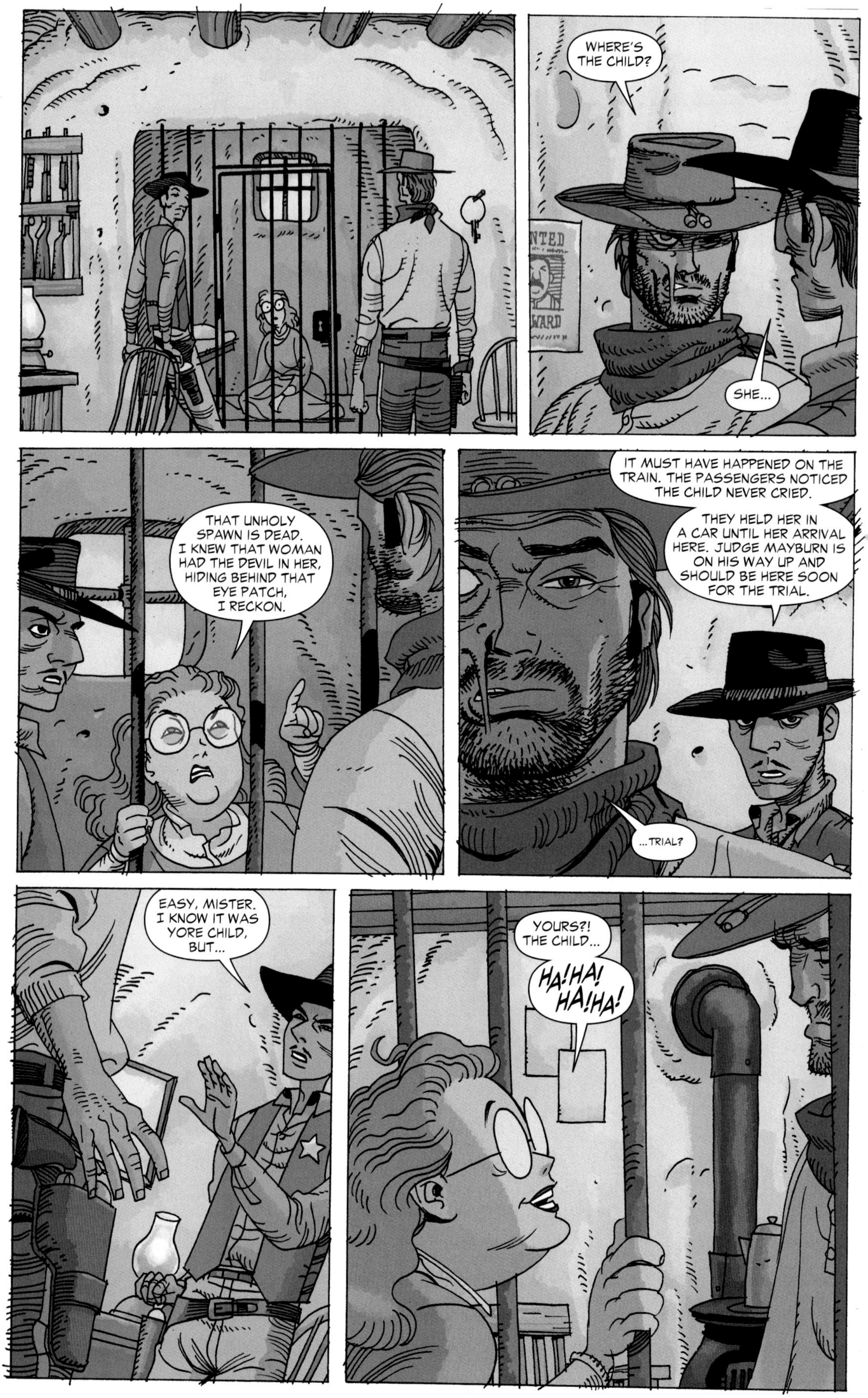
WHERE'S THE CHILD?
SHE...
THAT UNHOLY SPAWN IS DEAD. I KNEW THAT WOMAN HAD THE DEVIL IN HER, HIDING BEHIND THAT EYE PATCH, I RECKON.
IT MUST HAVE HAPPENED ON THE TRAIN. THE PASSENGERS NOTICED THE CHILD NEVER CRIED.
THEY HELD HER IN A CAR UNTIL HER ARRIVAL HERE. JUDGE MAYBURN IS ON HIS WAY UP AND SHOULD BE HERE SOON FOR THE TRIAL.
...TRIAL?
EASY, MISTER. I KNOW IT WAS YORE CHILD, BUT...
YOURS?! THE CHILD...
HA!HA! HA!HA!

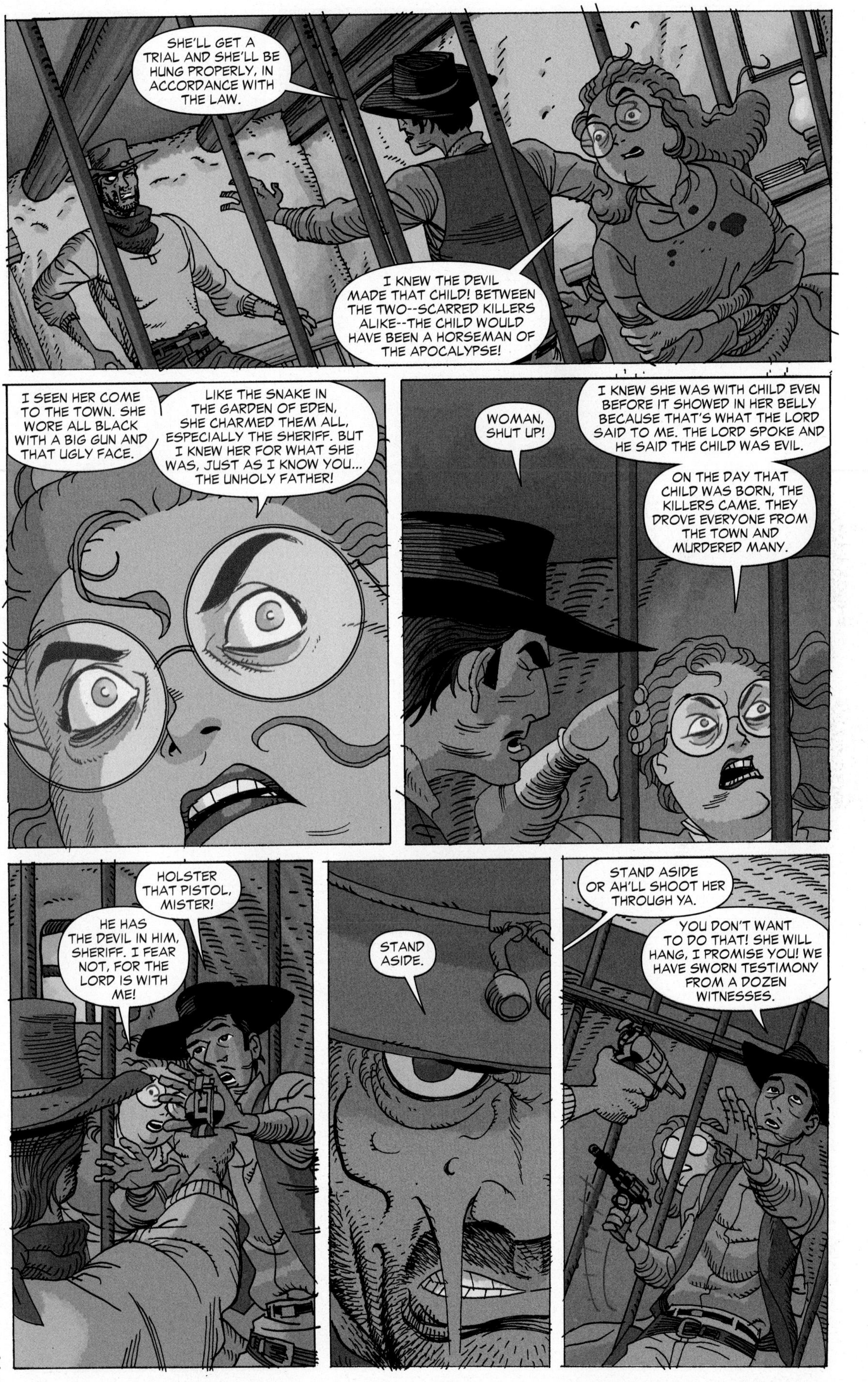
SHE'LL GET A TRIAL AND SHE'LL BE HUNG PROPERLY, IN ACCORDANCE WITH THE LAW.
I KNEW THE DEVIL MADE THAT CHILD! BETWEEN THE TWO--SCARRED KILLERS ALIKE--THE CHILD WOULD HAVE BEEN A HORSEMAN OF THE APOCALYPSE!
I SEEN HER COME TO THE TOWN. SHE WORE ALL BLACK WITH A BIG GUN AND THAT UGLY FACE.
LIKE THE SNAKE IN THE GARDEN OF EDEN, SHE CHARMED THEM ALL, ESPECIALLY THE SHERIFF. BUT I KNEW HER FOR WHAT SHE WAS, JUST AS I KNOW YOU... THE UNHOLY FATHER!
WOMAN, SHUT UP!
I KNEW SHE WAS WITH CHILD EVEN BEFORE IT SHOWED IN HER BELLY BECAUSE THAT'S WHAT THE LORD SAID TO ME. THE LORD SPOKE AND HE SAID THE CHILD WAS EVIL.
ON THE DAY THAT CHILD WAS BORN, THE KILLERS CAME. THEY DROVE EVERYONE FROM THE TOWN AND MURDERED MANY.
HOLSTER THAT PISTOL, MISTER!
HE HAS THE DEVIL IN HIM, SHERIFF. I FEAR NOT, FOR THE LORD IS WITH ME!
STAND ASIDE.
STAND ASIDE OR AH'LL SHOOT HER THROUGH YA.
YOU DON'T WANT TO DO THAT! SHE WILL HANG, I PROMISE YOU! WE HAVE SWORN TESTIMONY FROM A DOZEN WITNESSES.

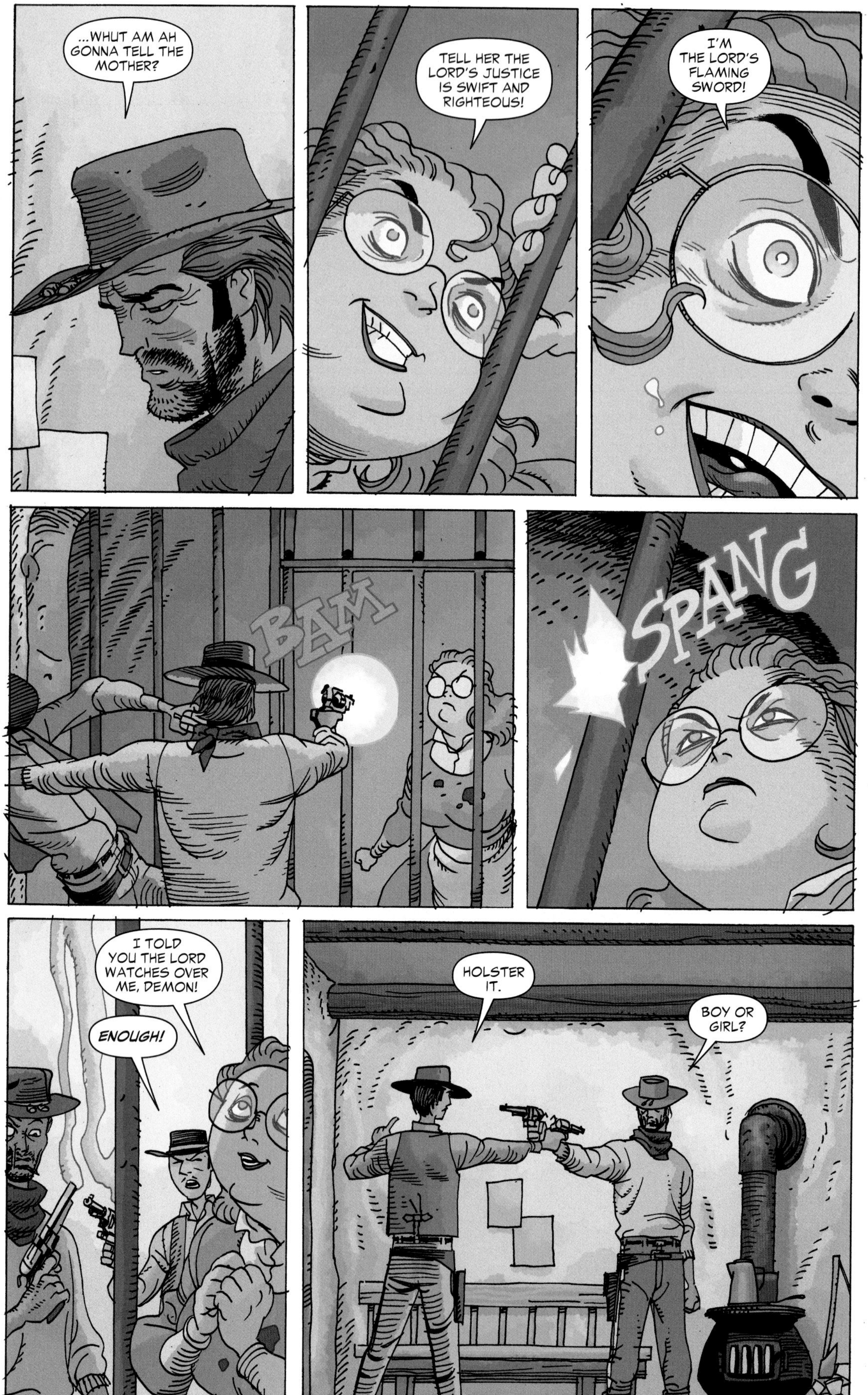
...WHUT AM AH GONNA TELL THE MOTHER?
TELL HER THE LORD'S JUSTICE IS SWIFT AND RIGHTEOUS!
I'M THE LORD'S FLAMING SWORD!
BAM
SPANG
I TOLD YOU THE LORD WATCHES OVER ME, DEMON!
ENOUGH!
HOLSTER IT.
BOY OR GIRL?

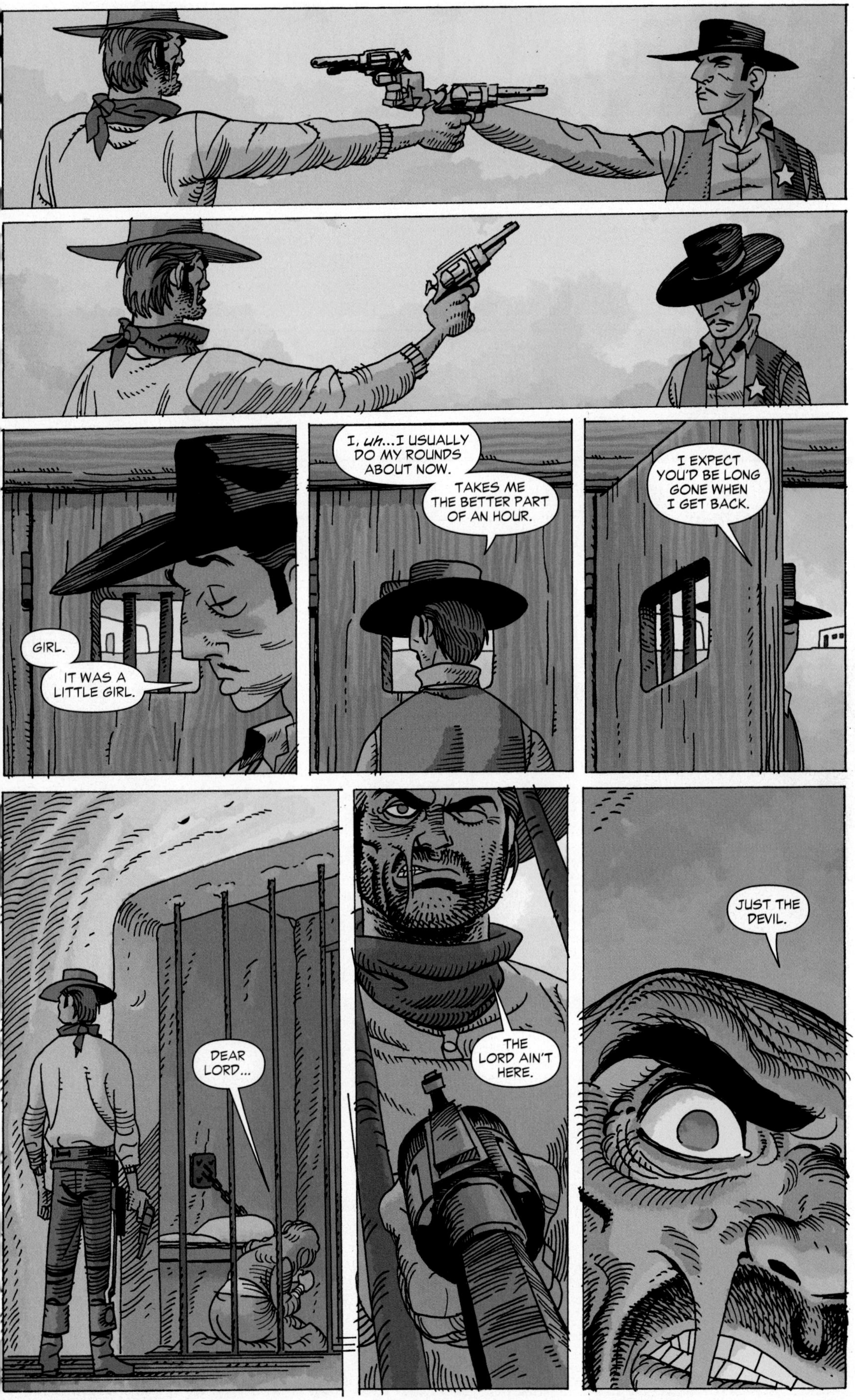
GIRL.
IT WAS A LITTLE GIRL.
I, *uh*...I USUALLY DO MY ROUNDS ABOUT NOW.
TAKES ME THE BETTER PART OF AN HOUR.
I EXPECT YOU'D BE LONG GONE WHEN I GET BACK.
DEAR LORD...
THE LORD AIN'T HERE.
JUST THE DEVIL.

SPRING SHOWERS AND CEMETERY FLOWERS

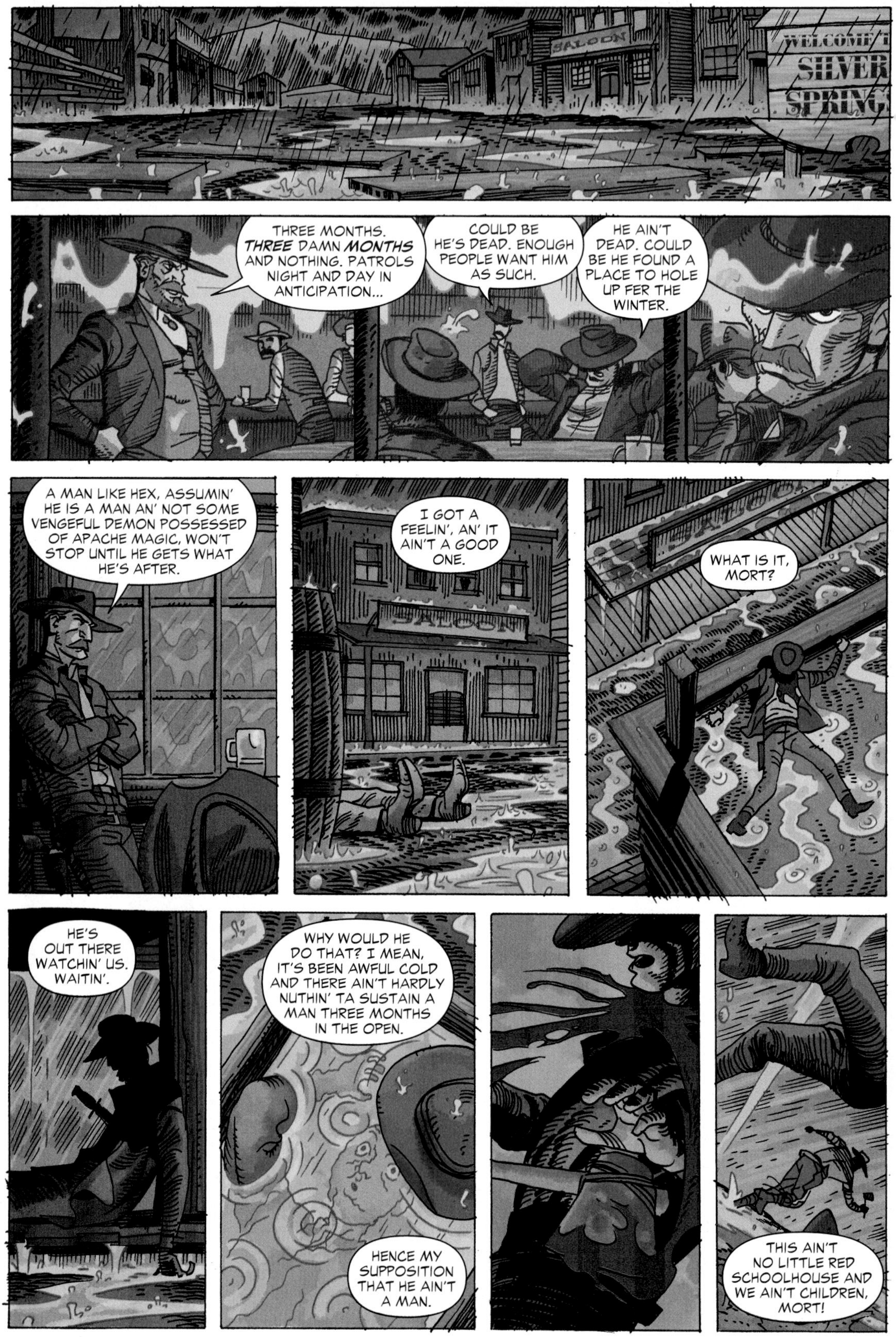

SALOON
WELCOME TO SILVER SPRINGS
THREE MONTHS. THREE DAMN MONTHS AND NOTHING. PATROLS NIGHT AND DAY IN ANTICIPATION...
COULD BE HE'S DEAD. ENOUGH PEOPLE WANT HIM AS SUCH.
HE AIN'T DEAD. COULD BE HE FOUND A PLACE TO HOLE UP FER THE WINTER.
A MAN LIKE HEX, ASSUMIN' HE IS A MAN AN' NOT SOME VENGEFUL DEMON POSSESSED OF APACHE MAGIC, WON'T STOP UNTIL HE GETS WHAT HE'S AFTER.
I GOT A FEELIN', AN' IT AIN'T A GOOD ONE.
SALOON
WHAT IS IT, MORT?
HE'S OUT THERE WATCHIN' US. WAITIN'.
WHY WOULD HE DO THAT? I MEAN, IT'S BEEN AWFUL COLD AND THERE AIN'T HARDLY NUTHIN' TA SUSTAIN A MAN THREE MONTHS IN THE OPEN.
HENCE MY SUPPOSITION THAT HE AIN'T A MAN.
THIS AIN'T NO LITTLE RED SCHOOLHOUSE AND WE AIN'T CHILDREN, MORT!

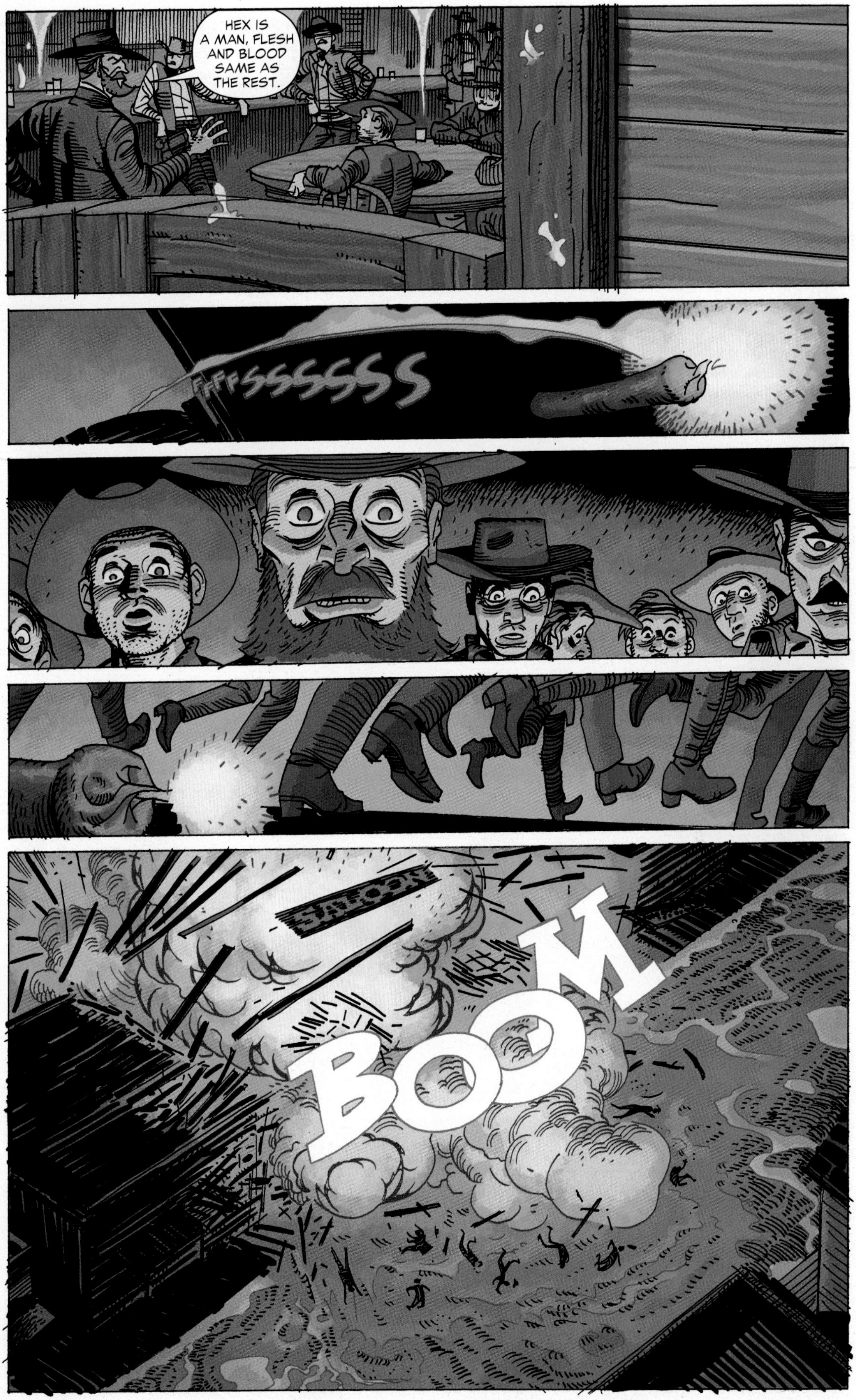
HEX IS A MAN, FLESH AND BLOOD SAME AS THE REST.
FFFSSSSSSS
BOOM

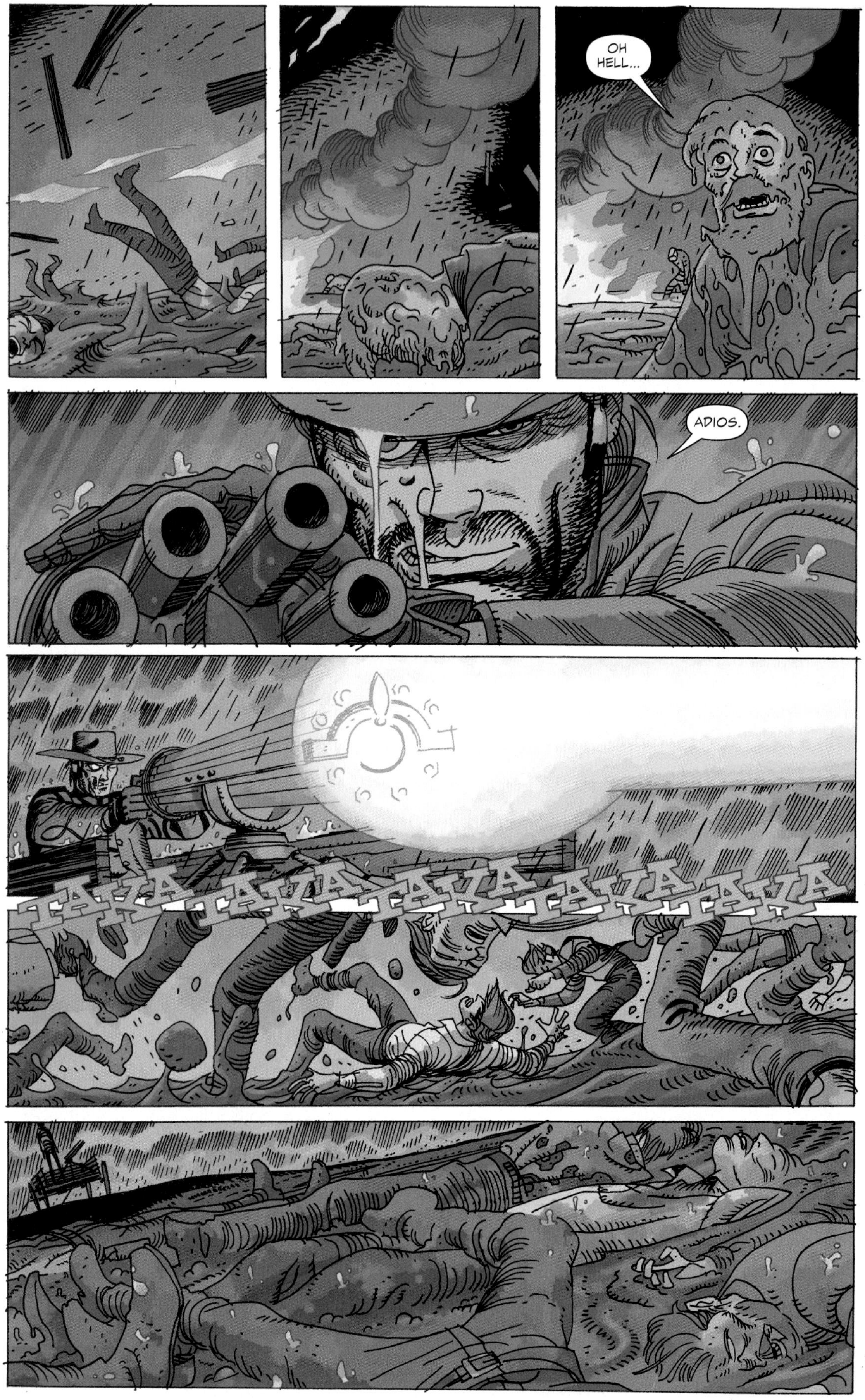
OH HELL...
ADIOS.
TAKATAKATAKATAKATAKA

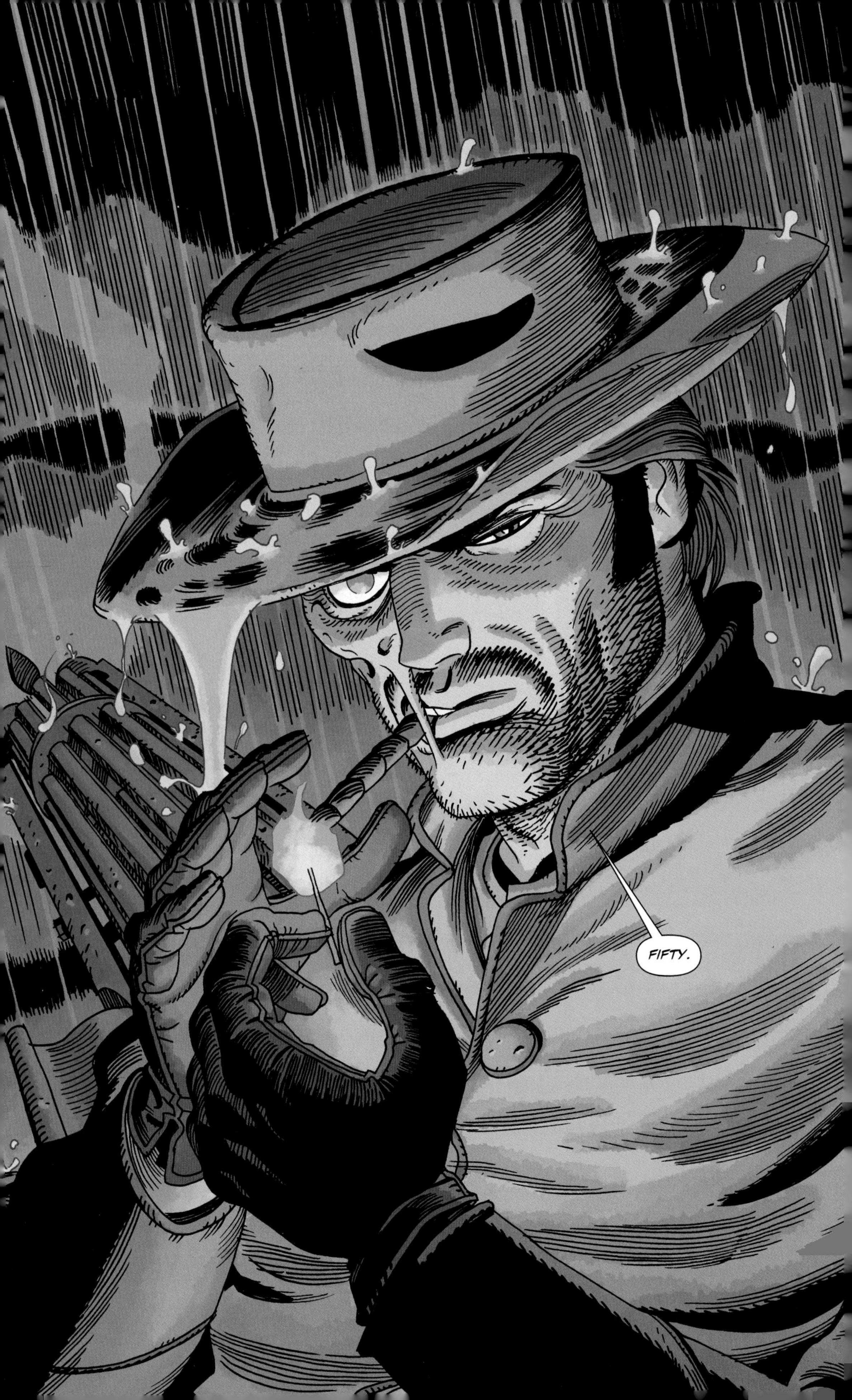
FIFTY.

YOU NEVER KNOW WHAT YOU'LL GET

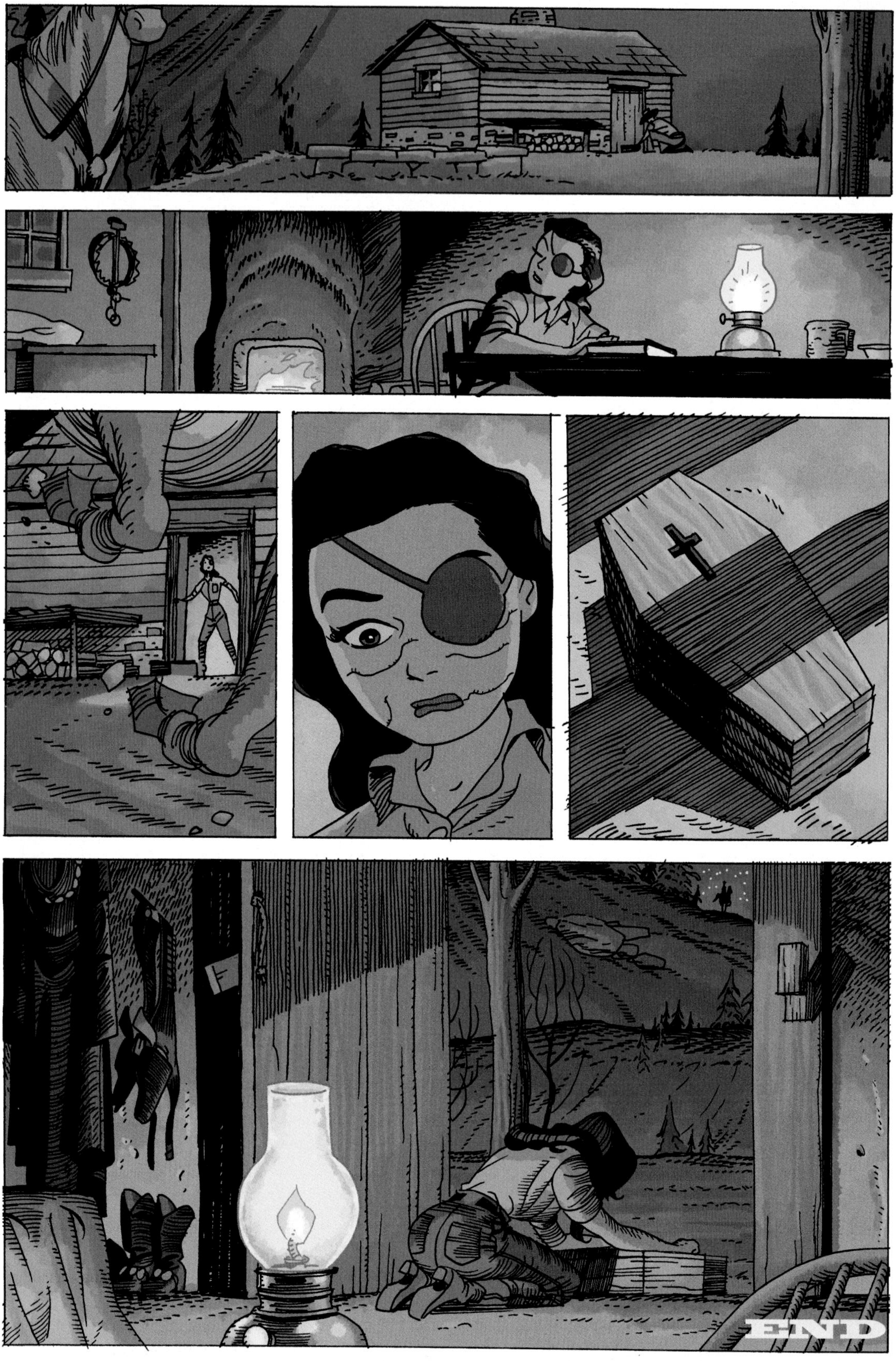
END

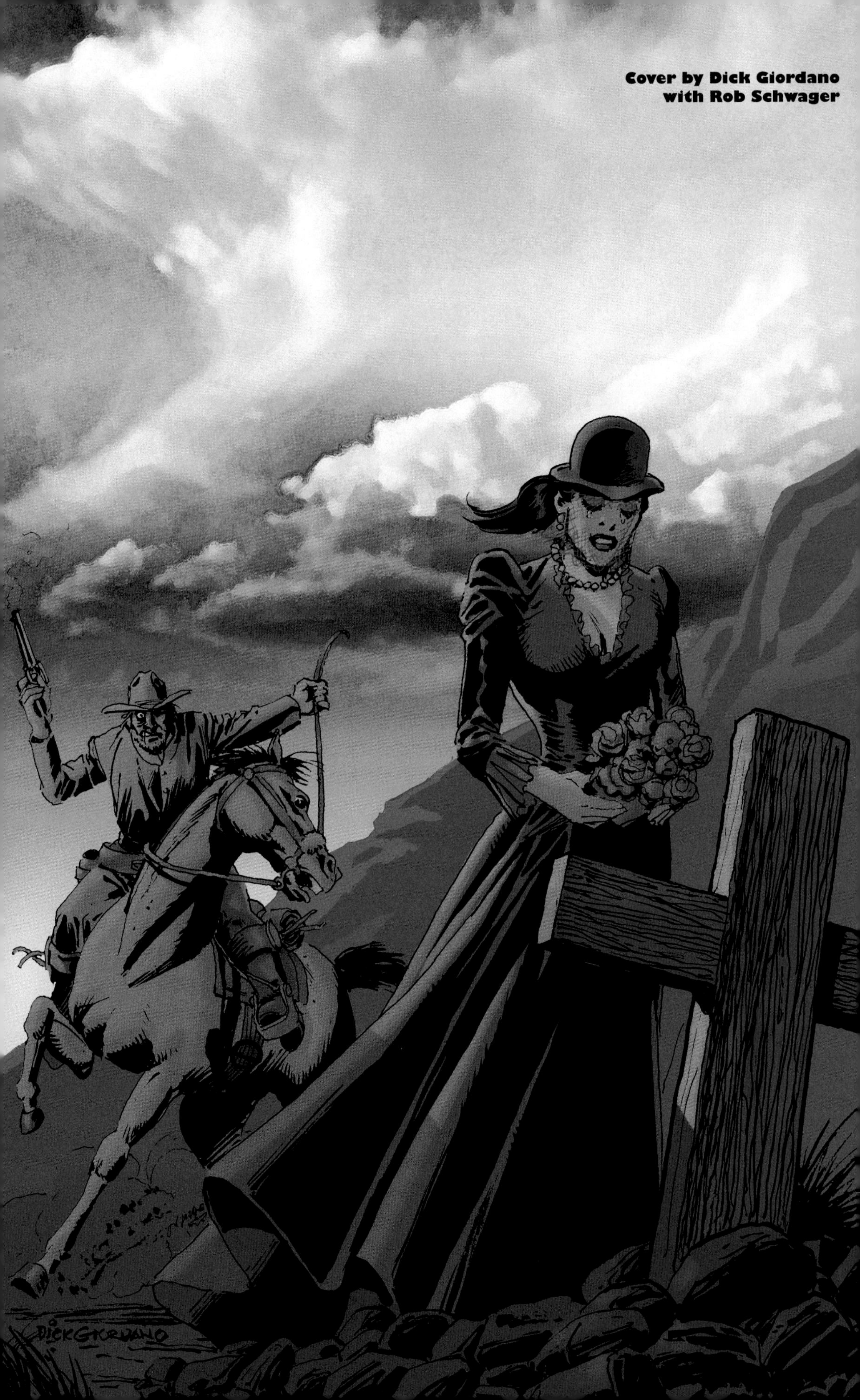
DICK GIORDANO

Cover by Dick Giordano
with Rob Schwager

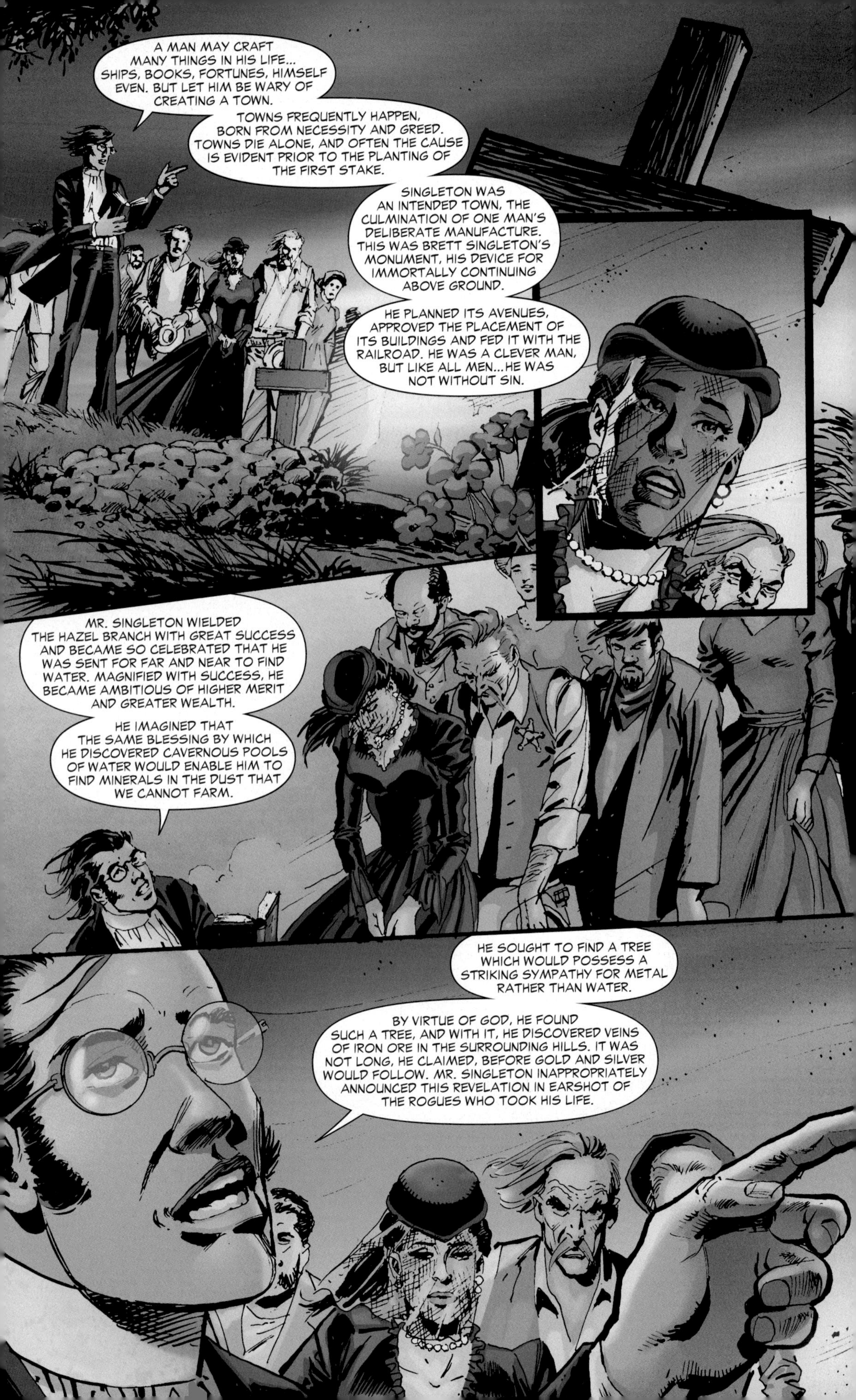
A MAN MAY CRAFT MANY THINGS IN HIS LIFE... SHIPS, BOOKS, FORTUNES, HIMSELF EVEN. BUT LET HIM BE WARY OF CREATING A TOWN.
TOWNS FREQUENTLY HAPPEN, BORN FROM NECESSITY AND GREED. TOWNS DIE ALONE, AND OFTEN THE CAUSE IS EVIDENT PRIOR TO THE PLANTING OF THE FIRST STAKE.
SINGLETON WAS AN INTENDED TOWN, THE CULMINATION OF ONE MAN'S DELIBERATE MANUFACTURE. THIS WAS BRETT SINGLETON'S MONUMENT, HIS DEVICE FOR IMMORTALLY CONTINUING ABOVE GROUND.
HE PLANNED ITS AVENUES, APPROVED THE PLACEMENT OF ITS BUILDINGS AND FED IT WITH THE RAILROAD. HE WAS A CLEVER MAN, BUT LIKE ALL MEN...HE WAS NOT WITHOUT SIN.
MR. SINGLETON WIELDED THE HAZEL BRANCH WITH GREAT SUCCESS AND BECAME SO CELEBRATED THAT HE WAS SENT FOR FAR AND NEAR TO FIND WATER. MAGNIFIED WITH SUCCESS, HE BECAME AMBITIOUS OF HIGHER MERIT AND GREATER WEALTH.
HE IMAGINED THAT THE SAME BLESSING BY WHICH HE DISCOVERED CAVERNOUS POOLS OF WATER WOULD ENABLE HIM TO FIND MINERALS IN THE DUST THAT WE CANNOT FARM.
HE SOUGHT TO FIND A TREE WHICH WOULD POSSESS A STRIKING SYMPATHY FOR METAL RATHER THAN WATER.
BY VIRTUE OF GOD, HE FOUND SUCH A TREE, AND WITH IT, HE DISCOVERED VEINS OF IRON ORE IN THE SURROUNDING HILLS. IT WAS NOT LONG, HE CLAIMED, BEFORE GOLD AND SILVER WOULD FOLLOW. MR. SINGLETON INAPPROPRIATELY ANNOUNCED THIS REVELATION IN EARSHOT OF THE ROGUES WHO TOOK HIS LIFE.

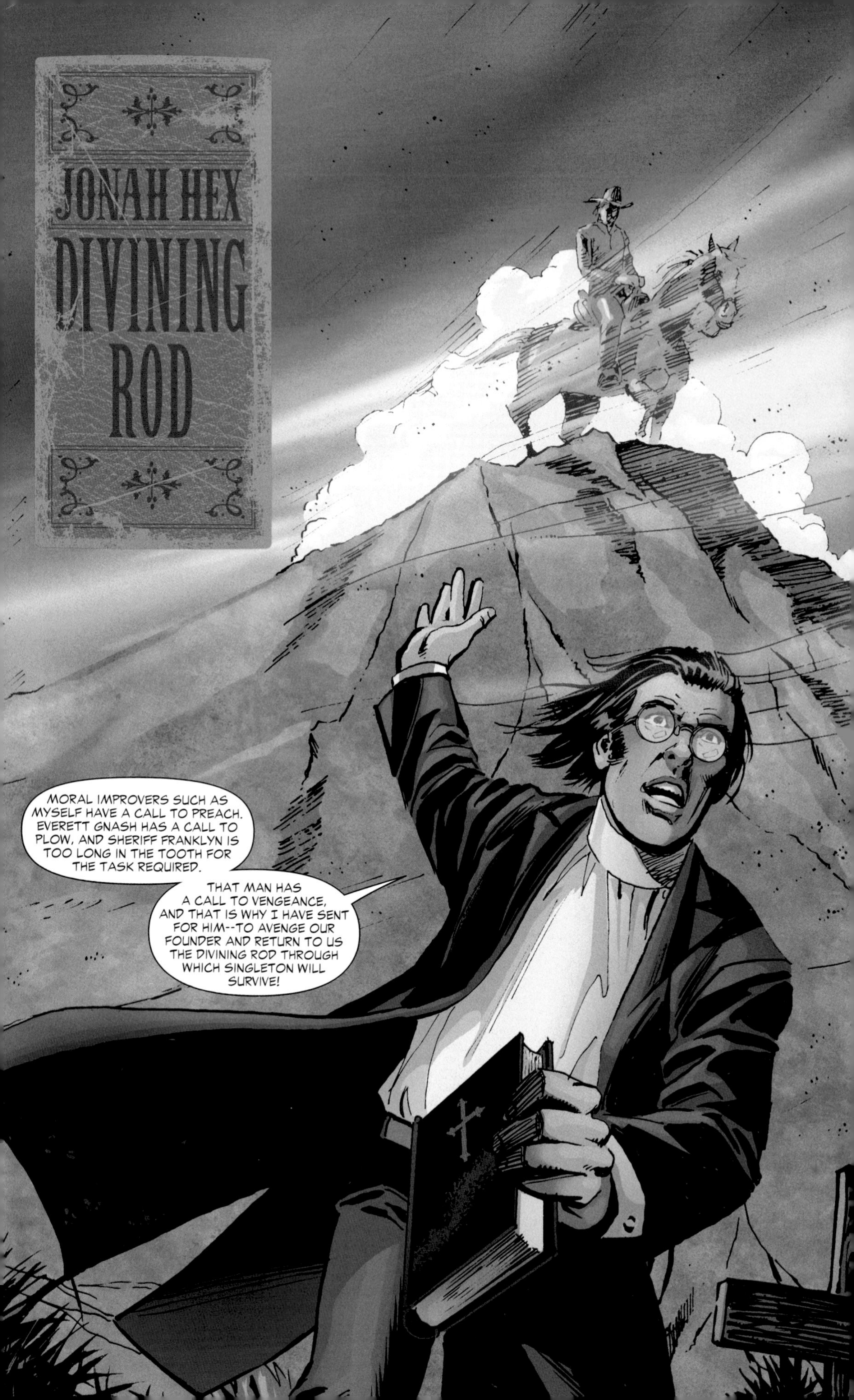
JONAH HEX
DIVINING ROD
MORAL IMPROVERS SUCH AS MYSELF HAVE A CALL TO PREACH. EVERETT GNASH HAS A CALL TO PLOW, AND SHERIFF FRANKLYN IS TOO LONG IN THE TOOTH FOR THE TASK REQUIRED.
THAT MAN HAS A CALL TO VENGEANCE, AND THAT IS WHY I HAVE SENT FOR HIM--TO AVENGE OUR FOUNDER AND RETURN TO US THE DIVINING ROD THROUGH WHICH SINGLETON WILL SURVIVE!

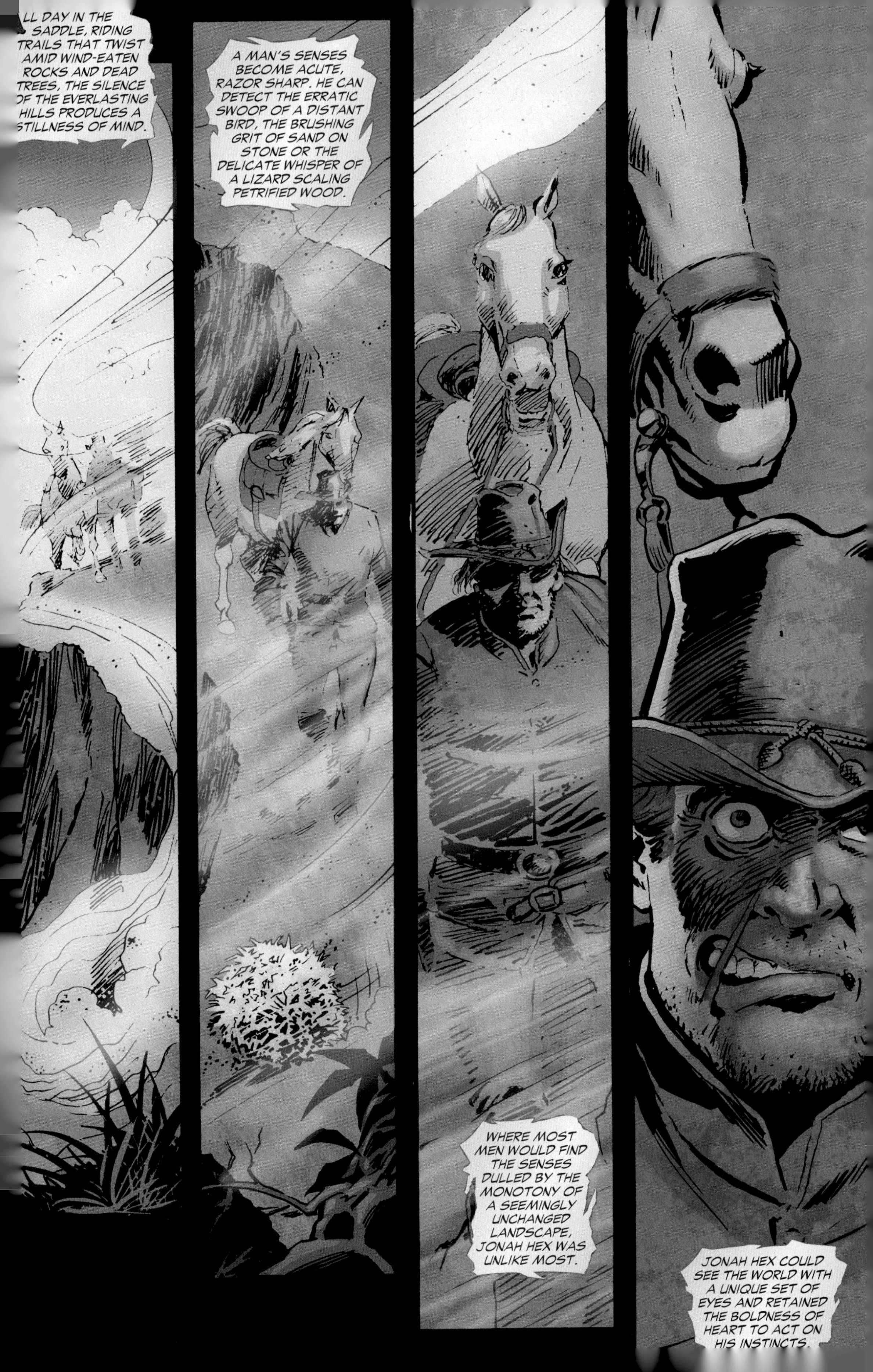
LL DAY IN THE SADDLE, RIDING TRAILS THAT TWIST AMID WIND-EATEN ROCKS AND DEAD TREES, THE SILENCE OF THE EVERLASTING HILLS PRODUCES A STILLNESS OF MIND.
A MAN'S SENSES BECOME ACUTE, RAZOR SHARP. HE CAN DETECT THE ERRATIC SWOOP OF A DISTANT BIRD, THE BRUSHING GRIT OF SAND ON STONE OR THE DELICATE WHISPER OF A LIZARD SCALING PETRIFIED WOOD.
WHERE MOST MEN WOULD FIND THE SENSES DULLED BY THE MONOTONY OF A SEEMINGLY UNCHANGED LANDSCAPE, JONAH HEX WAS UNLIKE MOST.
JONAH HEX COULD SEE THE WORLD WITH A UNIQUE SET OF EYES AND RETAINED THE BOLDNESS OF HEART TO ACT ON HIS INSTINCTS.

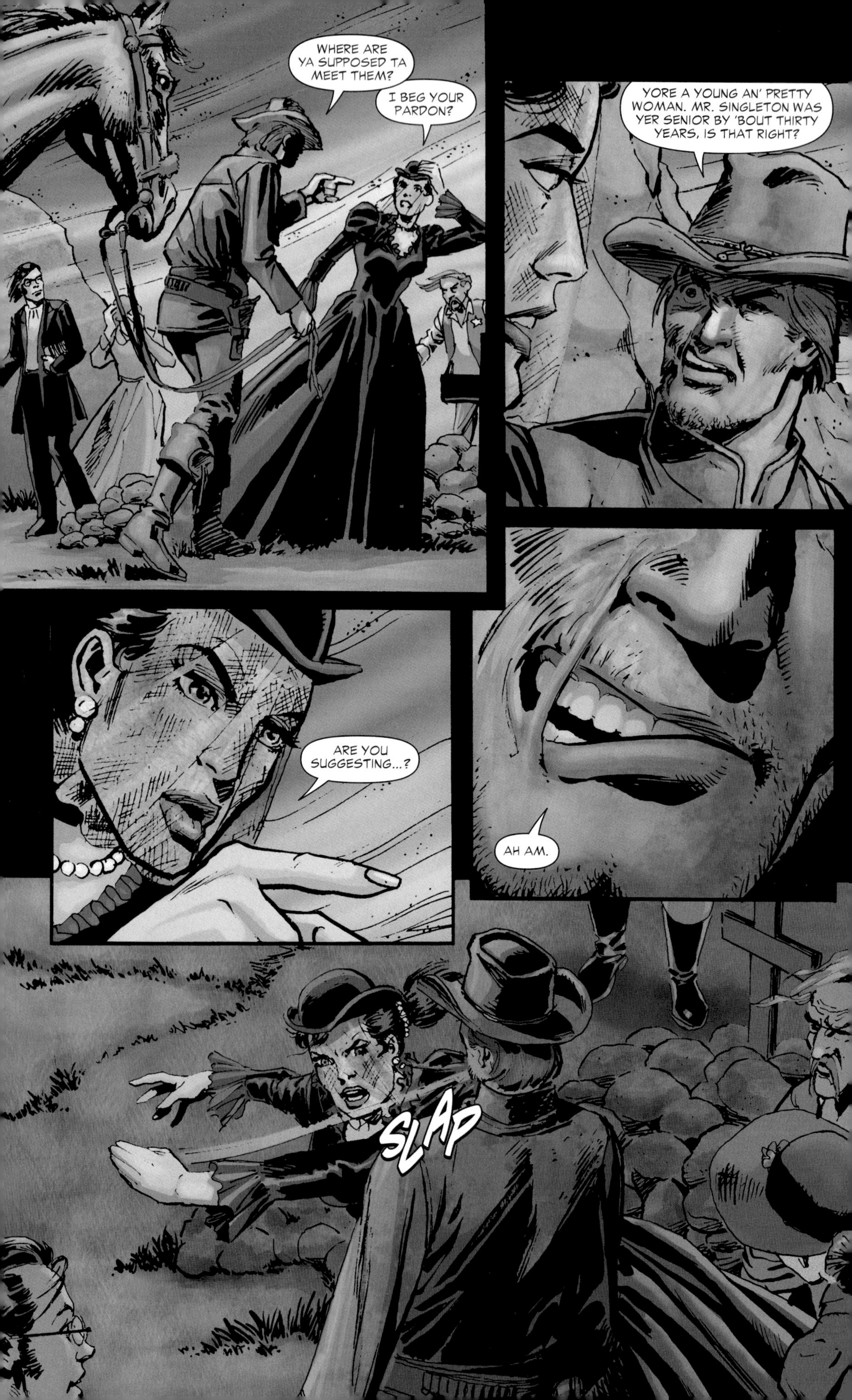
WHERE ARE YA SUPPOSED TA MEET THEM?
I BEG YOUR PARDON?
YORE A YOUNG AN' PRETTY WOMAN. MR. SINGLETON WAS YER SENIOR BY 'BOUT THIRTY YEARS, IS THAT RIGHT?
ARE YOU SUGGESTING...?
AH AM.
SLAP

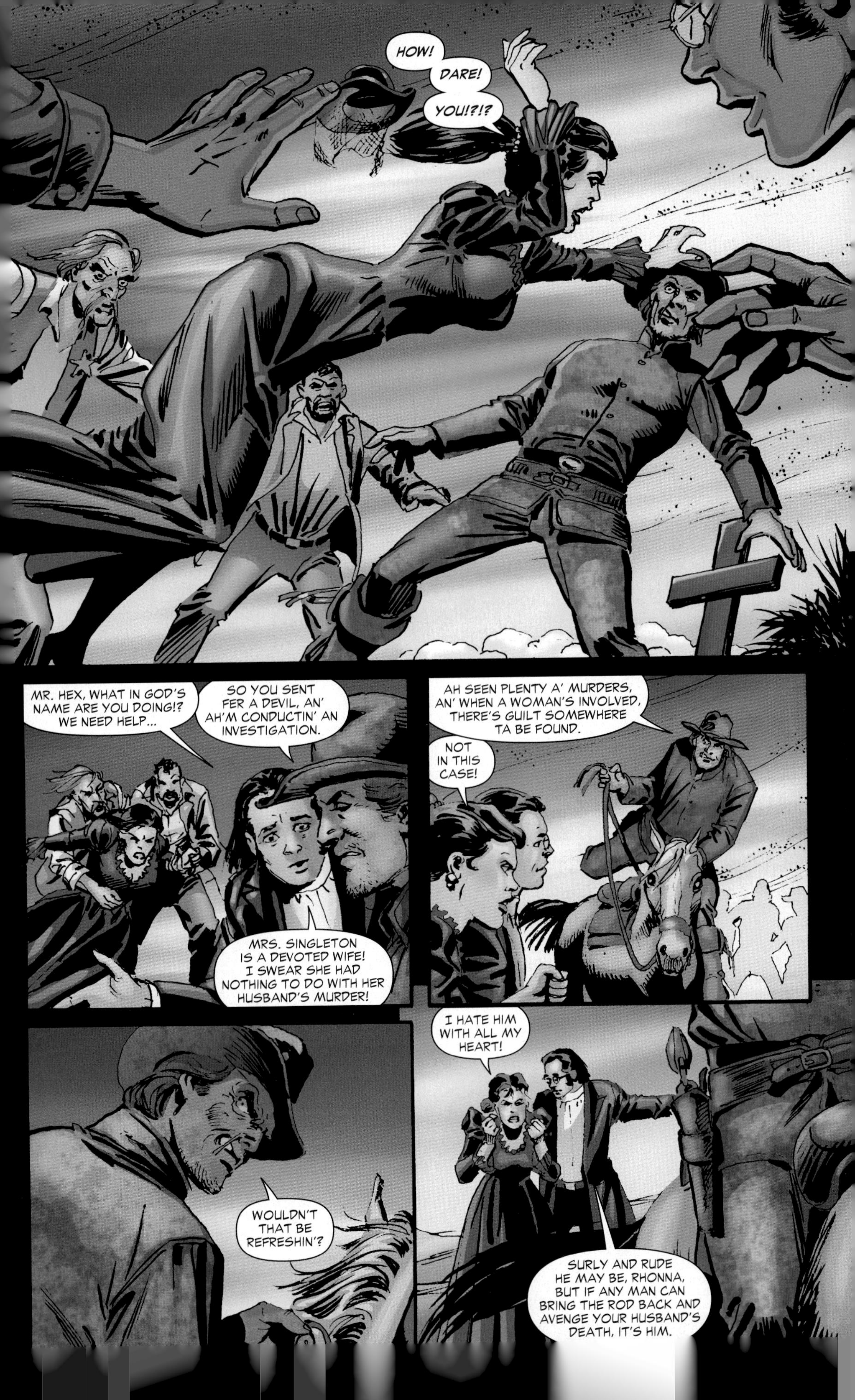
HOW!
DARE!
YOU!?!?
MR. HEX, WHAT IN GOD'S NAME ARE YOU DOING!? WE NEED HELP...
SO YOU SENT FER A DEVIL, AN' AH'M CONDUCTIN' AN INVESTIGATION.
MRS. SINGLETON IS A DEVOTED WIFE! I SWEAR SHE HAD NOTHING TO DO WITH HER HUSBAND'S MURDER!
AH SEEN PLENTY A' MURDERS, AN' WHEN A WOMAN'S INVOLVED, THERE'S GUILT SOMEWHERE TA BE FOUND.
NOT IN THIS CASE!
WOULDN'T THAT BE REFRESHIN'?
I HATE HIM WITH ALL MY HEART!
SURLY AND RUDE HE MAY BE, RHONNA, BUT IF ANY MAN CAN BRING THE ROD BACK AND AVENGE YOUR HUSBAND'S DEATH, IT'S HIM.

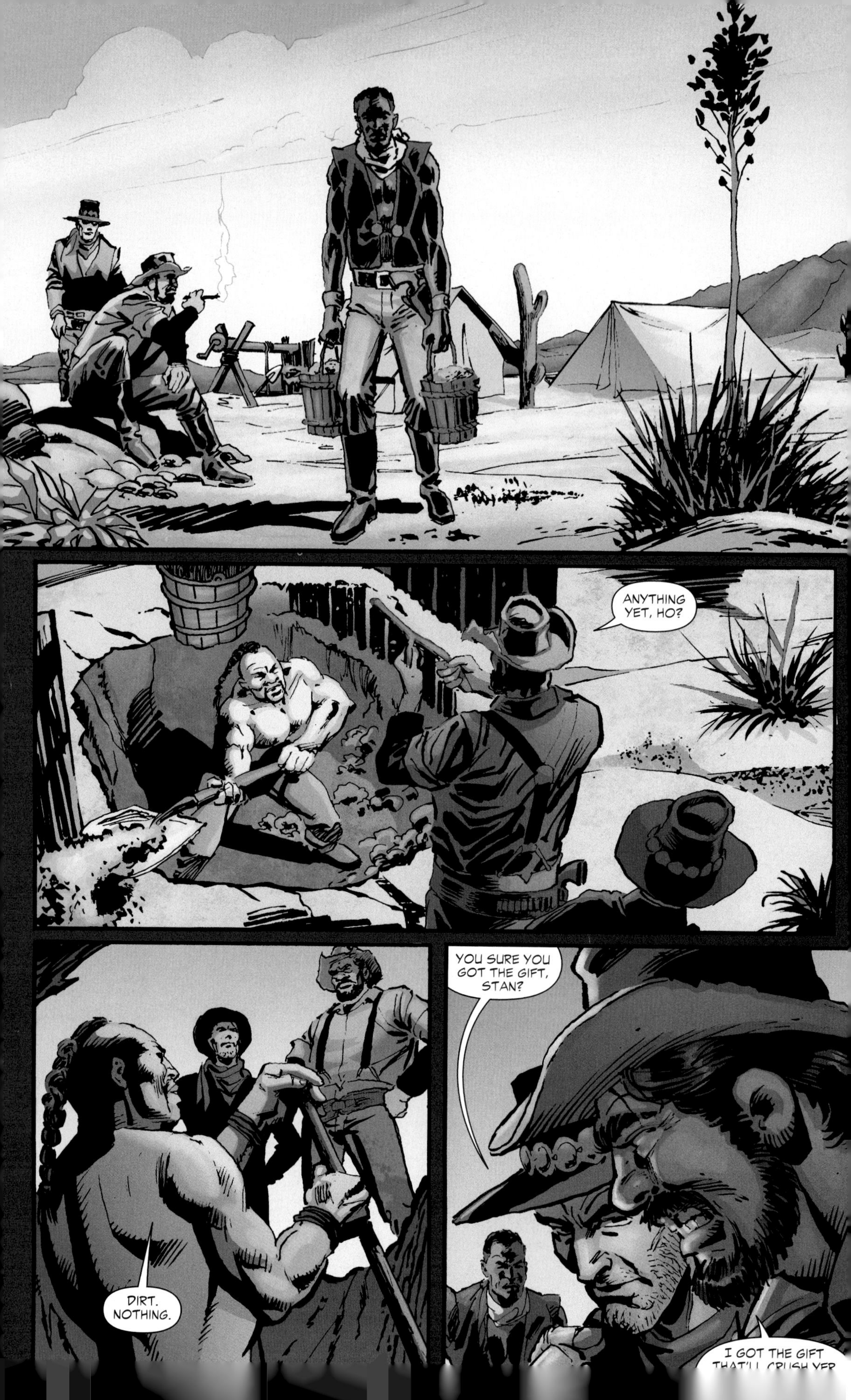
ANYTHING YET, HO?
DIRT. NOTHING.
YOU SURE YOU GOT THE GIFT, STAN?
I GOT THE GIFT

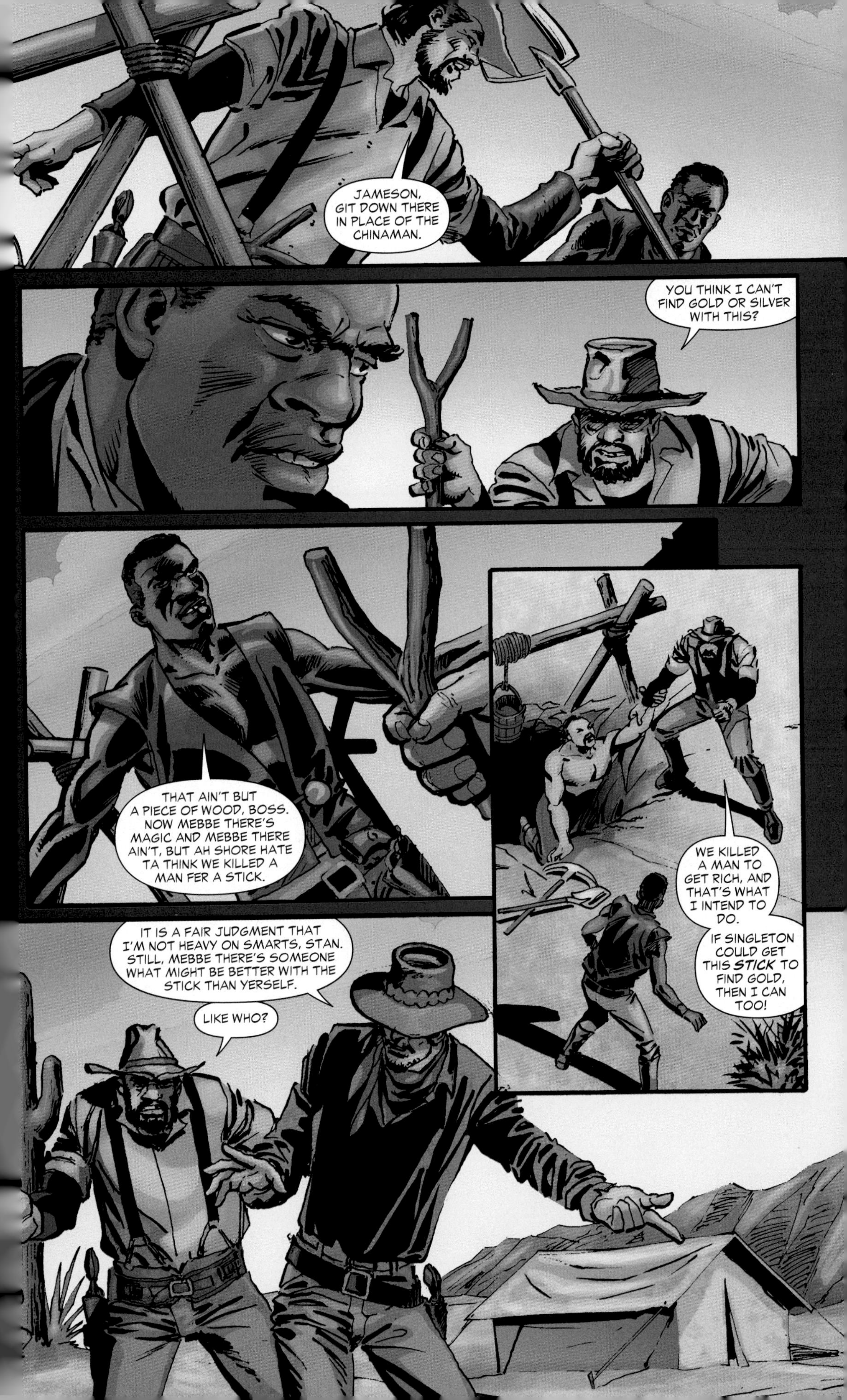
JAMESON, GIT DOWN THERE IN PLACE OF THE CHINAMAN.
YOU THINK I CAN'T FIND GOLD OR SILVER WITH THIS?
THAT AIN'T BUT A PIECE OF WOOD, BOSS. NOW MEBBE THERE'S MAGIC AND MEBBE THERE AIN'T, BUT AH SHORE HATE TA THINK WE KILLED A MAN FER A STICK.
WE KILLED A MAN TO GET RICH, AND THAT'S WHAT I INTEND TO DO.
IF SINGLETON COULD GET THIS STICK TO FIND GOLD, THEN I CAN TOO!
IT IS A FAIR JUDGMENT THAT I'M NOT HEAVY ON SMARTS, STAN. STILL, MEBBE THERE'S SOMEONE WHAT MIGHT BE BETTER WITH THE STICK THAN YERSELF.
LIKE WHO?

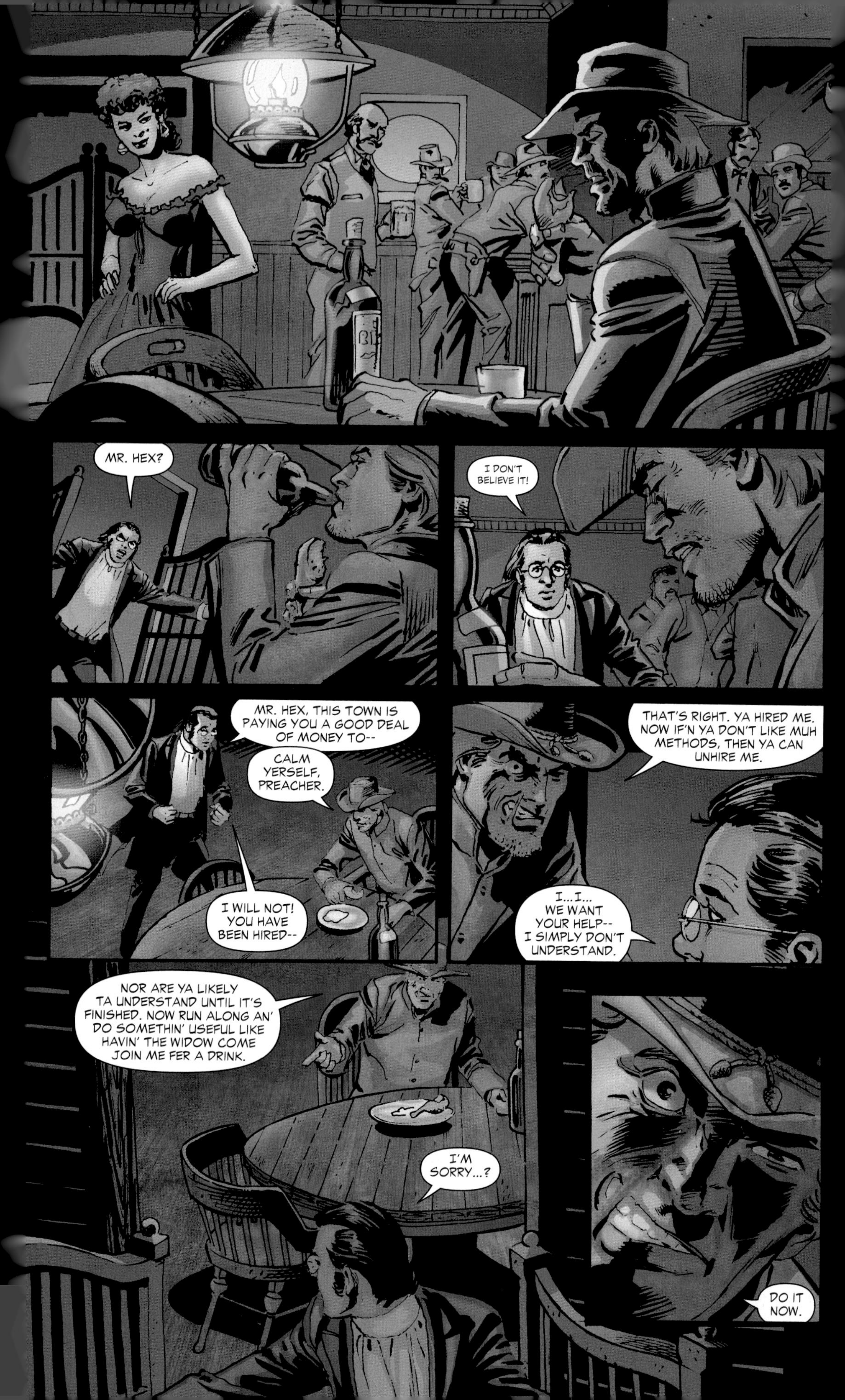
MR. HEX?
I DON'T BELIEVE IT!
MR. HEX, THIS TOWN IS PAYING YOU A GOOD DEAL OF MONEY TO--
CALM YERSELF, PREACHER.
I WILL NOT! YOU HAVE BEEN HIRED--
THAT'S RIGHT. YA HIRED ME. NOW IF'N YA DON'T LIKE MUH METHODS, THEN YA CAN UNHIRE ME.
I...I... WE WANT YOUR HELP-- I SIMPLY DON'T UNDERSTAND.
NOR ARE YA LIKELY TA UNDERSTAND UNTIL IT'S FINISHED. NOW RUN ALONG AN' DO SOMETHIN' USEFUL LIKE HAVIN' THE WIDOW COME JOIN ME FER A DRINK.
I'M SORRY...?
DO IT NOW.

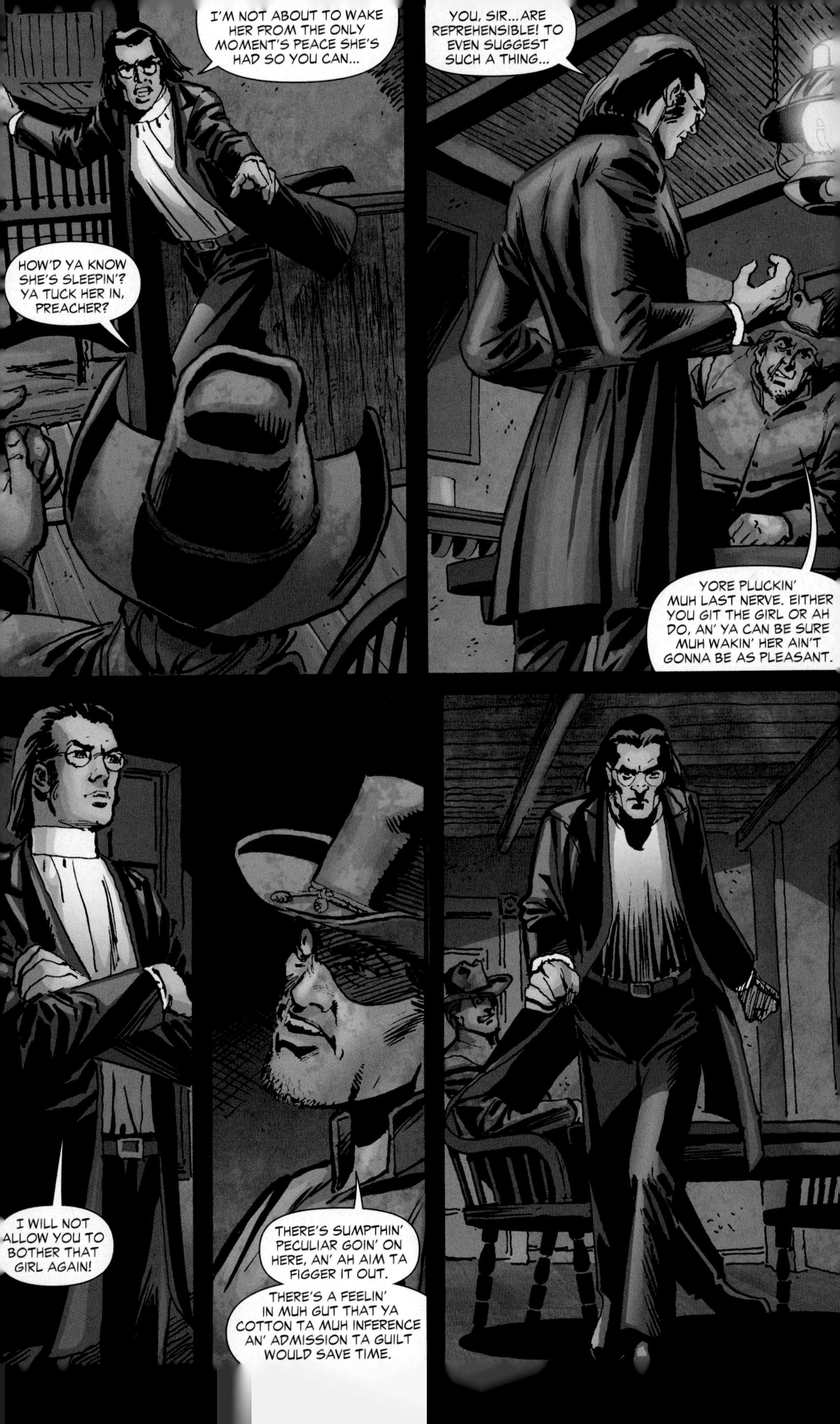
I'M NOT ABOUT TO WAKE HER FROM THE ONLY MOMENT'S PEACE SHE'S HAD SO YOU CAN...
HOW'D YA KNOW SHE'S SLEEPIN'? YA TUCK HER IN, PREACHER?
YOU, SIR...ARE REPREHENSIBLE! TO EVEN SUGGEST SUCH A THING...
YORE PLUCKIN' MUH LAST NERVE. EITHER YOU GIT THE GIRL OR AH DO, AN' YA CAN BE SURE MUH WAKIN' HER AIN'T GONNA BE AS PLEASANT.
I WILL NOT ALLOW YOU TO BOTHER THAT GIRL AGAIN!
THERE'S SUMPTHIN' PECULIAR GOIN' ON HERE, AN' AH AIM TA FIGGER IT OUT.
THERE'S A FEELIN' IN MUH GUT THAT YA COTTON TA MUH INFERENCE AN' ADMISSION TA GUILT WOULD SAVE TIME.

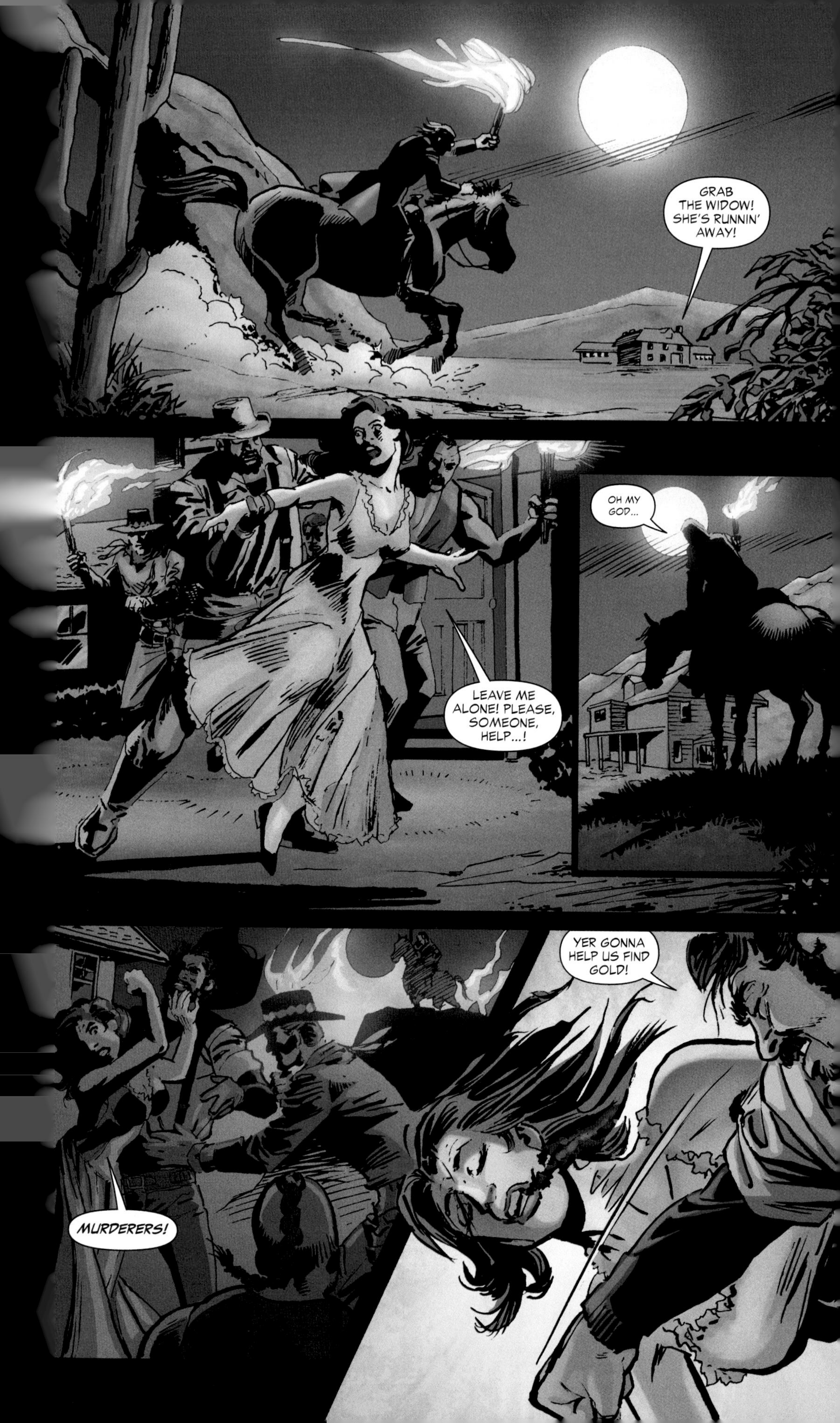
GRAB THE WIDOW! SHE'S RUNNIN' AWAY!
LEAVE ME ALONE! PLEASE, SOMEONE, HELP...!
OH MY GOD...
YER GONNA HELP US FIND GOLD!
MURDERERS!

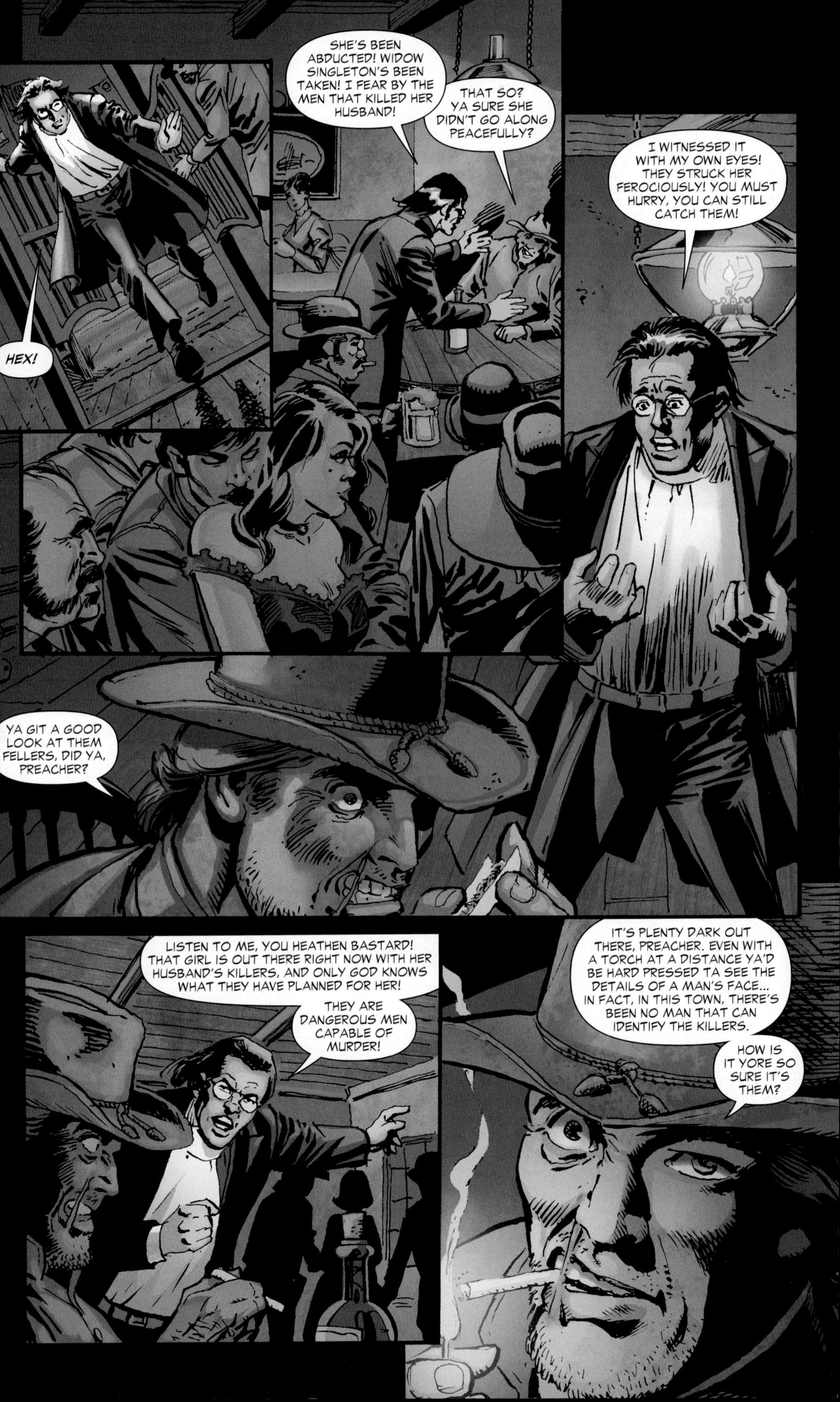
HEX!
SHE'S BEEN ABDUCTED! WIDOW SINGLETON'S BEEN TAKEN! I FEAR BY THE MEN THAT KILLED HER HUSBAND!
THAT SO? YA SURE SHE DIDN'T GO ALONG PEACEFULLY?
I WITNESSED IT WITH MY OWN EYES! THEY STRUCK HER FEROCIOUSLY! YOU MUST HURRY, YOU CAN STILL CATCH THEM!
YA GIT A GOOD LOOK AT THEM FELLERS, DID YA, PREACHER?
LISTEN TO ME, YOU HEATHEN BASTARD! THAT GIRL IS OUT THERE RIGHT NOW WITH HER HUSBAND'S KILLERS, AND ONLY GOD KNOWS WHAT THEY HAVE PLANNED FOR HER!
THEY ARE DANGEROUS MEN CAPABLE OF MURDER!
IT'S PLENTY DARK OUT THERE, PREACHER. EVEN WITH A TORCH AT A DISTANCE YA'D BE HARD PRESSED TA SEE THE DETAILS OF A MAN'S FACE... IN FACT, IN THIS TOWN, THERE'S BEEN NO MAN THAT CAN IDENTIFY THE KILLERS.
HOW IS IT YORE SO SURE IT'S THEM?

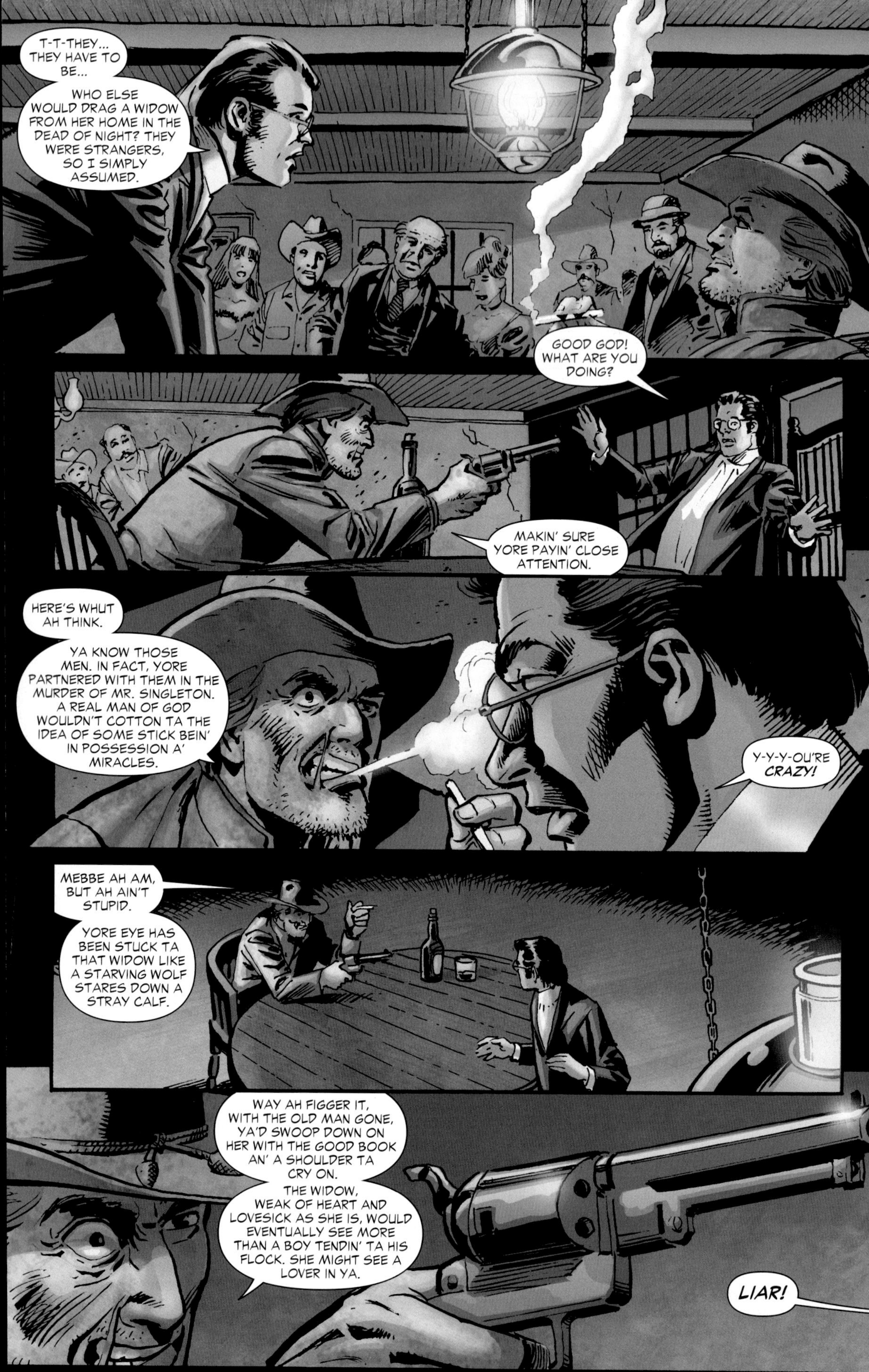

T-T-THEY... THEY HAVE TO BE...
WHO ELSE WOULD DRAG A WIDOW FROM HER HOME IN THE DEAD OF NIGHT? THEY WERE STRANGERS, SO I SIMPLY ASSUMED.
GOOD GOD! WHAT ARE YOU DOING?
MAKIN' SURE YORE PAYIN' CLOSE ATTENTION.
HERE'S WHUT AH THINK.
YA KNOW THOSE MEN. IN FACT, YORE PARTNERED WITH THEM IN THE MURDER OF MR. SINGLETON. A REAL MAN OF GOD WOULDN'T COTTON TA THE IDEA OF SOME STICK BEIN' IN POSSESSION A' MIRACLES.
Y-Y-Y-OU'RE *CRAZY!*
MEBBE AH AM, BUT AH AIN'T STUPID.
YORE EYE HAS BEEN STUCK TA THAT WIDOW LIKE A STARVING WOLF STARES DOWN A STRAY CALF.
WAY AH FIGGER IT, WITH THE OLD MAN GONE, YA'D SWOOP DOWN ON HER WITH THE GOOD BOOK AN' A SHOULDER TA CRY ON.
THE WIDOW, WEAK OF HEART AND LOVESICK AS SHE IS, WOULD EVENTUALLY SEE MORE THAN A BOY TENDIN' TA HIS FLOCK. SHE MIGHT SEE A LOVER IN YA.
LIAR!

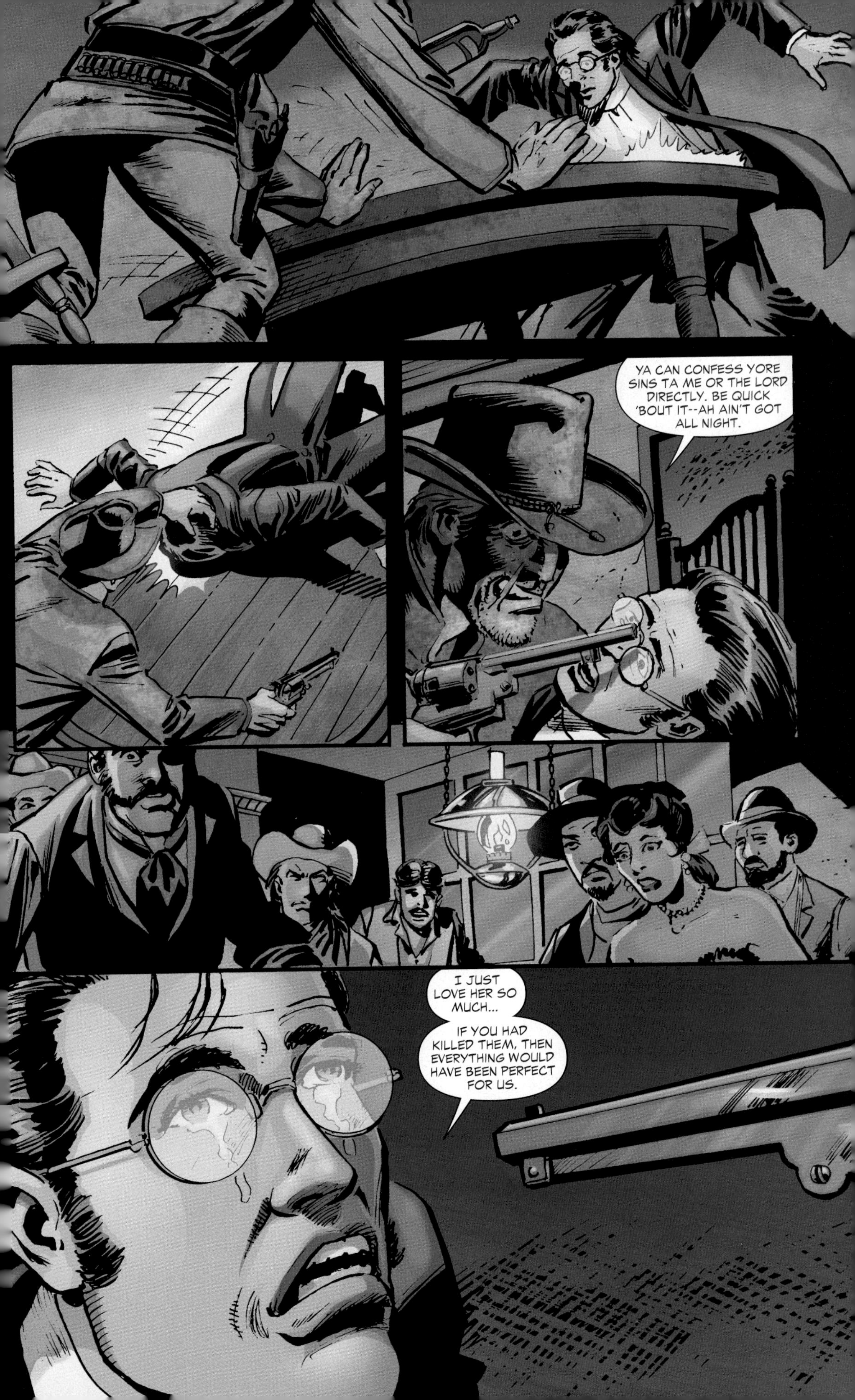
YA CAN CONFESS YORE SINS TA ME OR THE LORD DIRECTLY. BE QUICK 'BOUT IT--AH AIN'T GOT ALL NIGHT.
I JUST LOVE HER SO MUCH...
IF YOU HAD KILLED THEM, THEN EVERYTHING WOULD HAVE BEEN PERFECT FOR US.

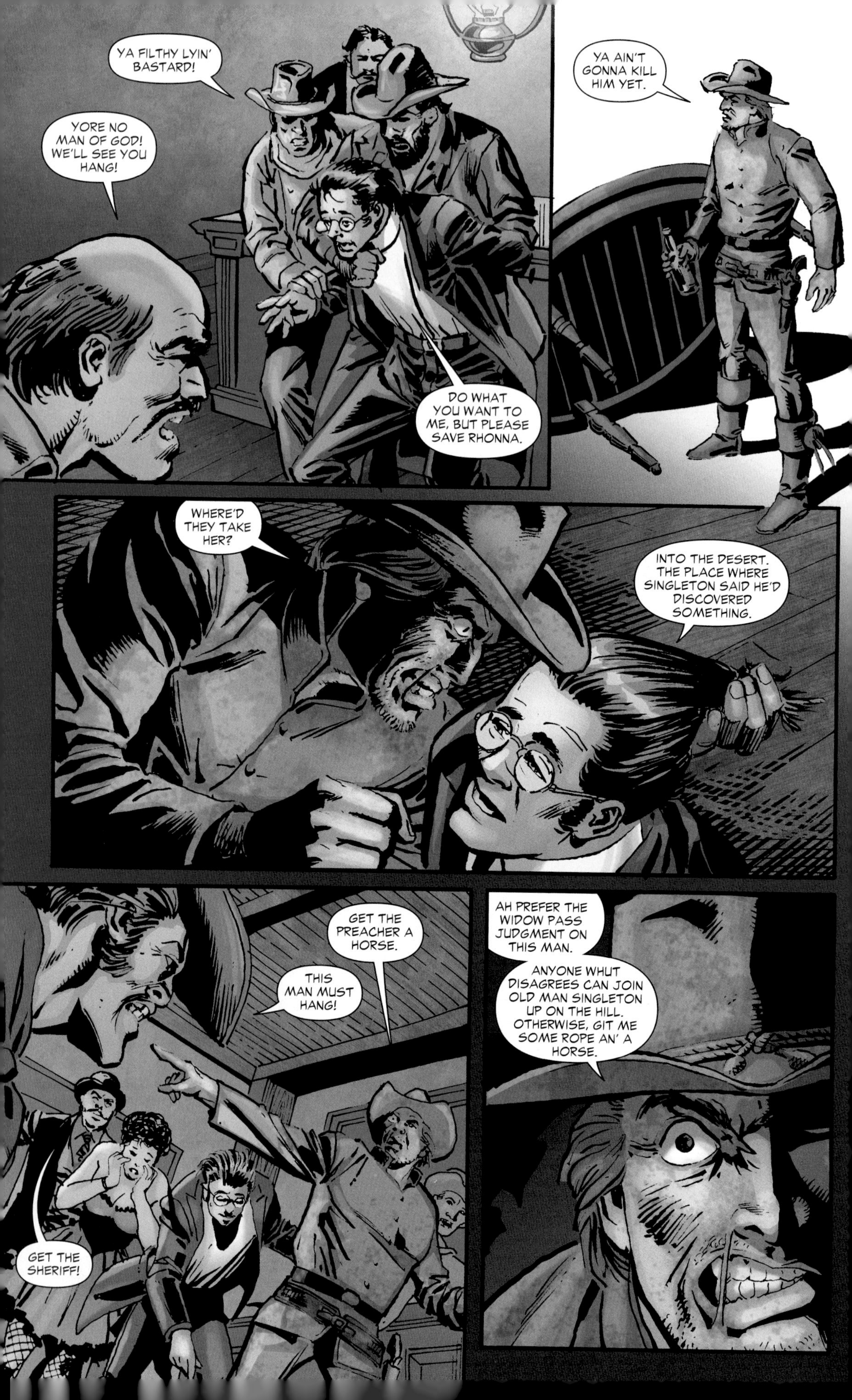

YA FILTHY LYIN' BASTARD!
YORE NO MAN OF GOD! WE'LL SEE YOU HANG!
DO WHAT YOU WANT TO ME, BUT PLEASE SAVE RHONNA.
YA AIN'T GONNA KILL HIM YET.
WHERE'D THEY TAKE HER?
INTO THE DESERT. THE PLACE WHERE SINGLETON SAID HE'D DISCOVERED SOMETHING.
GET THE PREACHER A HORSE.
THIS MAN MUST HANG!
GET THE SHERIFF!
AH PREFER THE WIDOW PASS JUDGMENT ON THIS MAN.
ANYONE WHUT DISAGREES CAN JOIN OLD MAN SINGLETON UP ON THE HILL. OTHERWISE, GIT ME SOME ROPE AN' A HORSE.

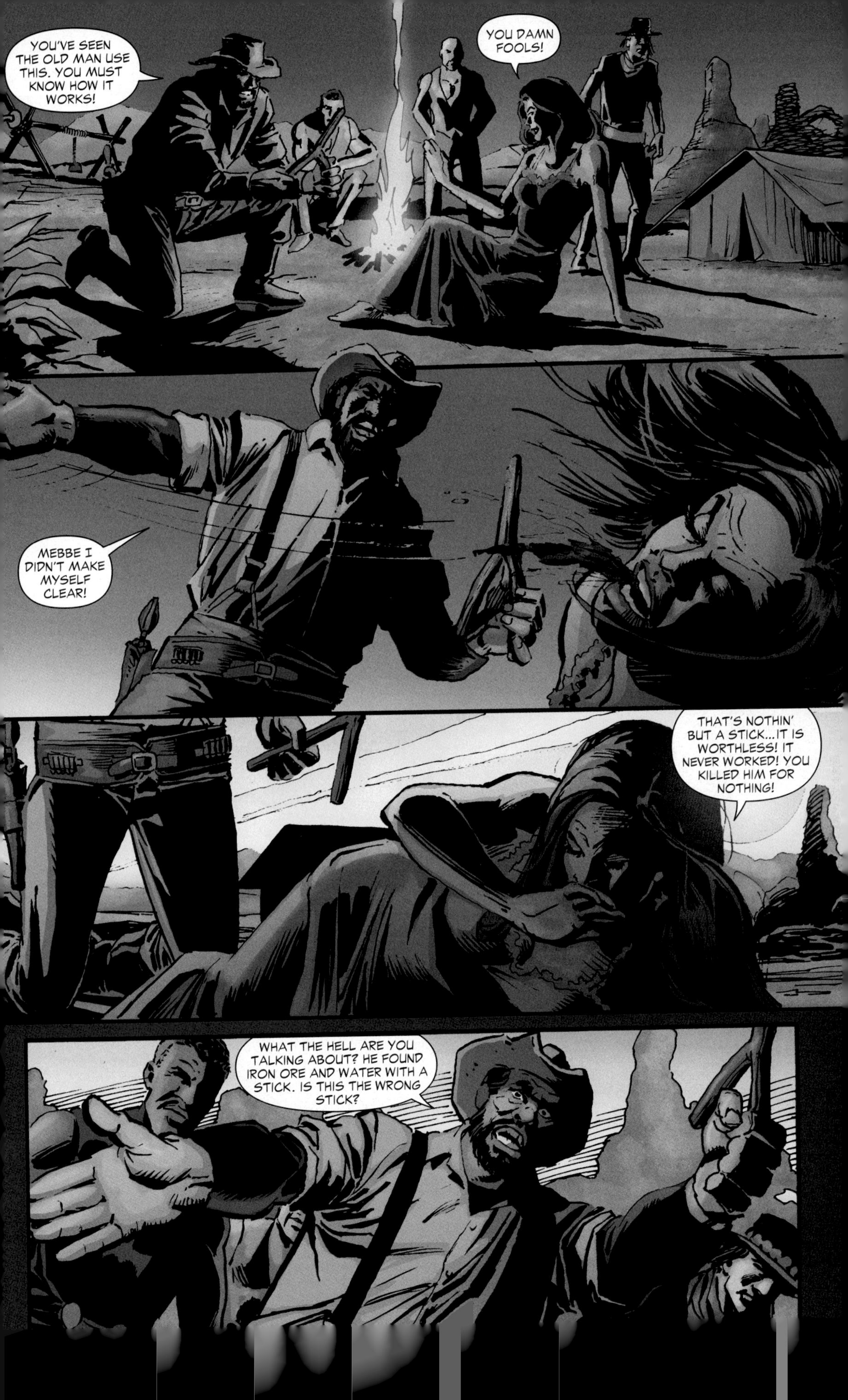
YOU'VE SEEN THE OLD MAN USE THIS. YOU MUST KNOW HOW IT WORKS!
YOU DAMN FOOLS!
MEBBE I DIDN'T MAKE MYSELF CLEAR!
THAT'S NOTHIN' BUT A STICK...IT IS WORTHLESS! IT NEVER WORKED! YOU KILLED HIM FOR NOTHING!
WHAT THE HELL ARE YOU TALKING ABOUT? HE FOUND IRON ORE AND WATER WITH A STICK. IS THIS THE WRONG STICK?

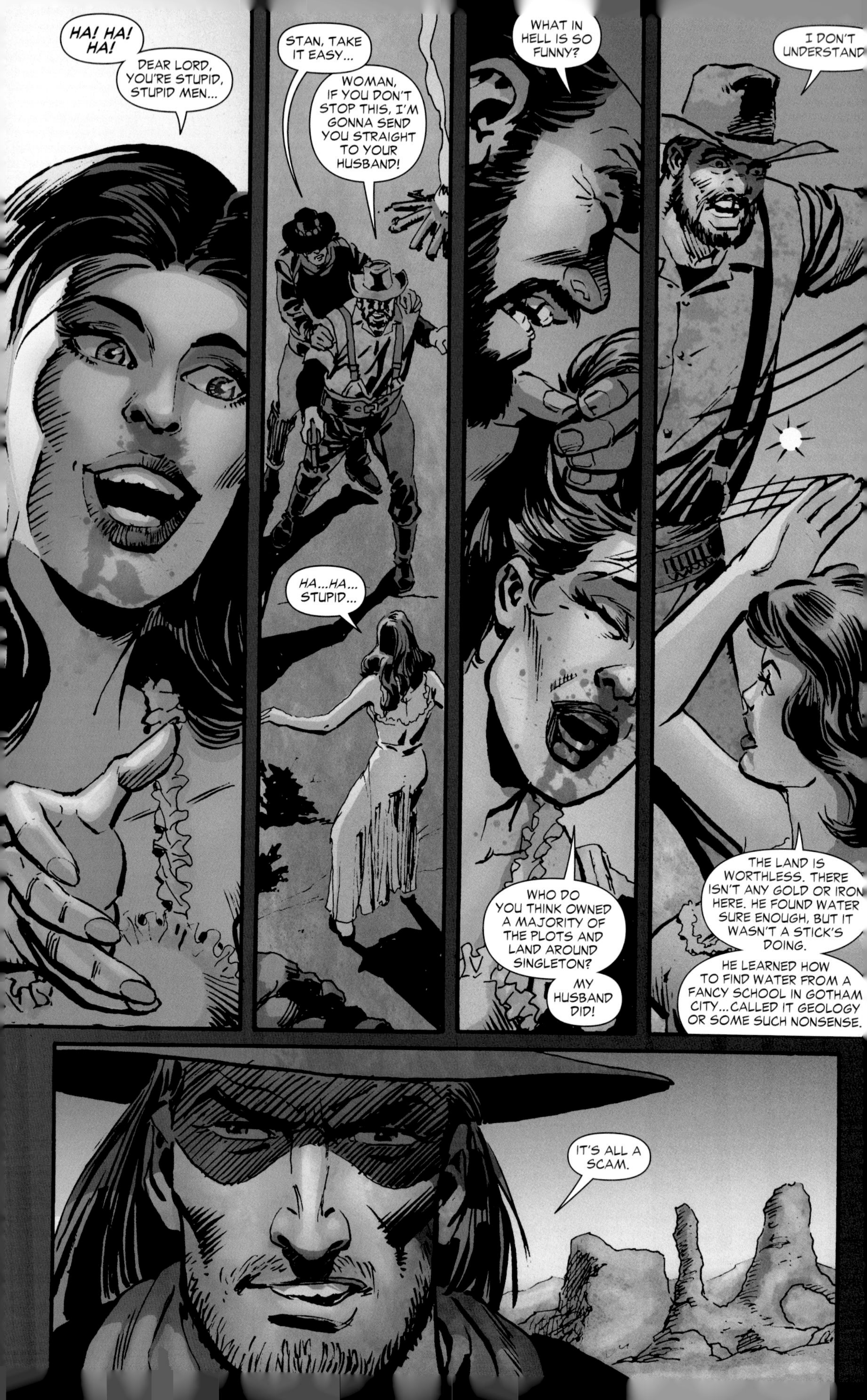
HA! HA! HA!
DEAR LORD, YOU'RE STUPID, STUPID MEN...
STAN, TAKE IT EASY...
WOMAN, IF YOU DON'T STOP THIS, I'M GONNA SEND YOU STRAIGHT TO YOUR HUSBAND!
HA...HA... STUPID...
WHAT IN HELL IS SO FUNNY?
WHO DO YOU THINK OWNED A MAJORITY OF THE PLOTS AND LAND AROUND SINGLETON?
MY HUSBAND DID!
I DON'T UNDERSTAND
THE LAND IS WORTHLESS. THERE ISN'T ANY GOLD OR IRON HERE. HE FOUND WATER SURE ENOUGH, BUT IT WASN'T A STICK'S DOING.
HE LEARNED HOW TO FIND WATER FROM A FANCY SCHOOL IN GOTHAM CITY...CALLED IT GEOLOGY OR SOME SUCH NONSENSE.
IT'S ALL A SCAM.

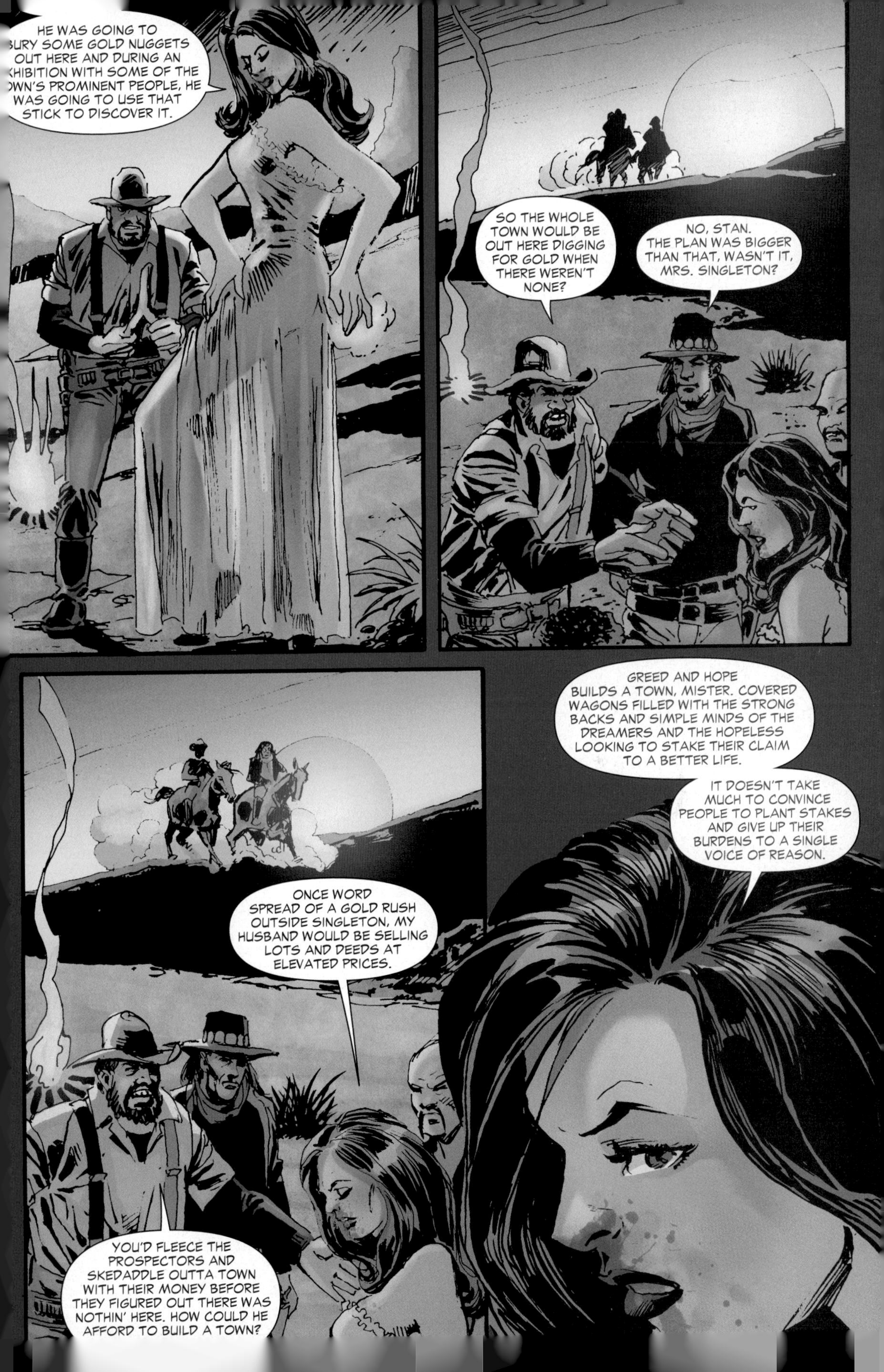
HE WAS GOING TO BURY SOME GOLD NUGGETS OUT HERE AND DURING AN XHIBITION WITH SOME OF THE WN'S PROMINENT PEOPLE, HE WAS GOING TO USE THAT STICK TO DISCOVER IT.
SO THE WHOLE TOWN WOULD BE OUT HERE DIGGING FOR GOLD WHEN THERE WEREN'T NONE?
NO, STAN. THE PLAN WAS BIGGER THAN THAT, WASN'T IT, MRS. SINGLETON?
ONCE WORD SPREAD OF A GOLD RUSH OUTSIDE SINGLETON, MY HUSBAND WOULD BE SELLING LOTS AND DEEDS AT ELEVATED PRICES.
YOU'D FLEECE THE PROSPECTORS AND SKEDADDLE OUTTA TOWN WITH THEIR MONEY BEFORE THEY FIGURED OUT THERE WAS NOTHIN' HERE. HOW COULD HE AFFORD TO BUILD A TOWN?
GREED AND HOPE BUILDS A TOWN, MISTER. COVERED WAGONS FILLED WITH THE STRONG BACKS AND SIMPLE MINDS OF THE DREAMERS AND THE HOPELESS LOOKING TO STAKE THEIR CLAIM TO A BETTER LIFE.
IT DOESN'T TAKE MUCH TO CONVINCE PEOPLE TO PLANT STAKES AND GIVE UP THEIR BURDENS TO A SINGLE VOICE OF REASON.

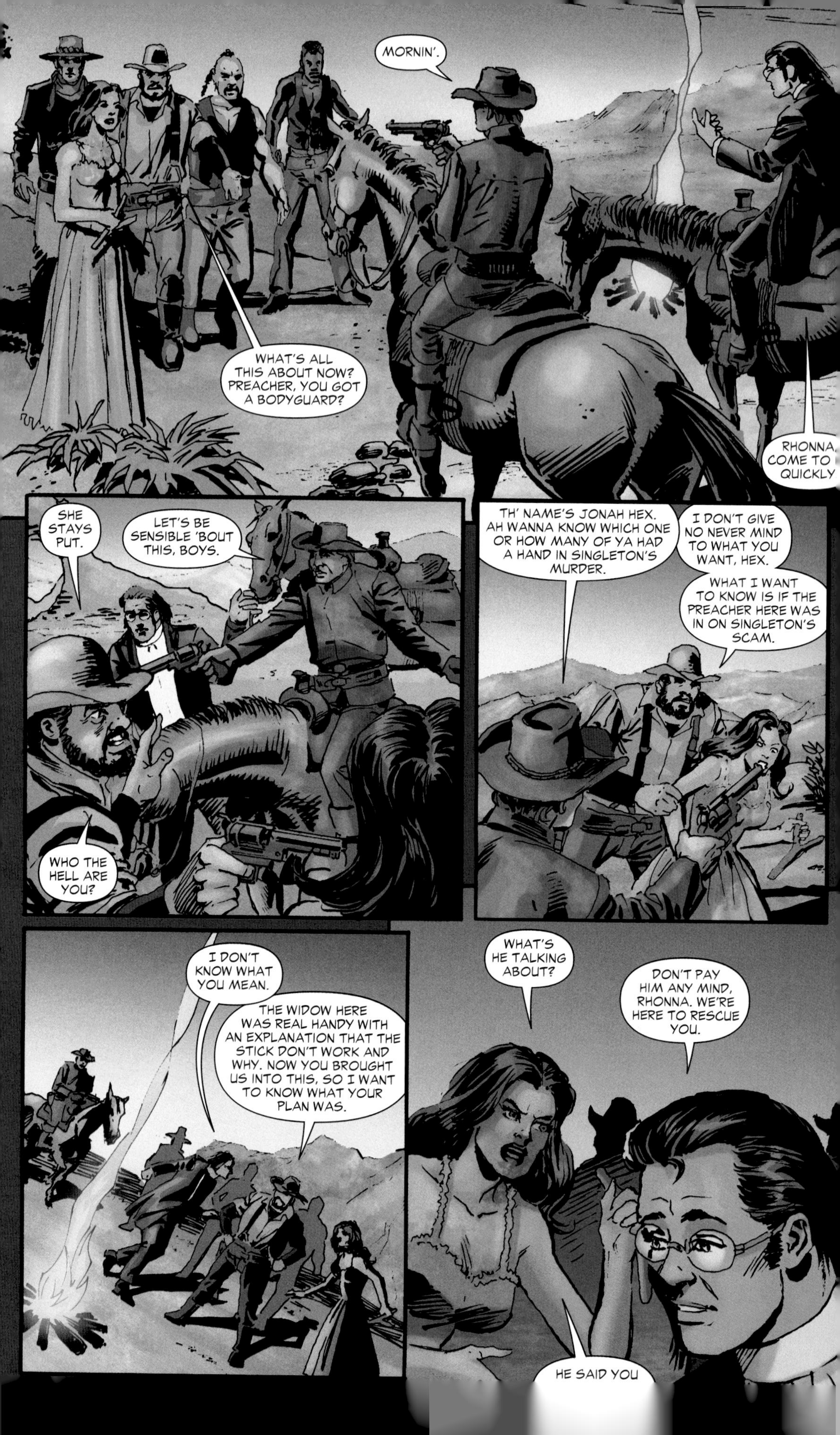
MORNIN'.
WHAT'S ALL THIS ABOUT NOW? PREACHER, YOU GOT A BODYGUARD?
RHONNA, COME TO QUICKLY
SHE STAYS PUT.
LET'S BE SENSIBLE 'BOUT THIS, BOYS.
WHO THE HELL ARE YOU?
TH' NAME'S JONAH HEX. AH WANNA KNOW WHICH ONE OR HOW MANY OF YA HAD A HAND IN SINGLETON'S MURDER.
I DON'T GIVE NO NEVER MIND TO WHAT YOU WANT, HEX.
WHAT I WANT TO KNOW IS IF THE PREACHER HERE WAS IN ON SINGLETON'S SCAM.
I DON'T KNOW WHAT YOU MEAN.
THE WIDOW HERE WAS REAL HANDY WITH AN EXPLANATION THAT THE STICK DON'T WORK AND WHY. NOW YOU BROUGHT US INTO THIS, SO I WANT TO KNOW WHAT YOUR PLAN WAS.
WHAT'S HE TALKING ABOUT?
DON'T PAY HIM ANY MIND, RHONNA. WE'RE HERE TO RESCUE YOU.
HE SAID YOU

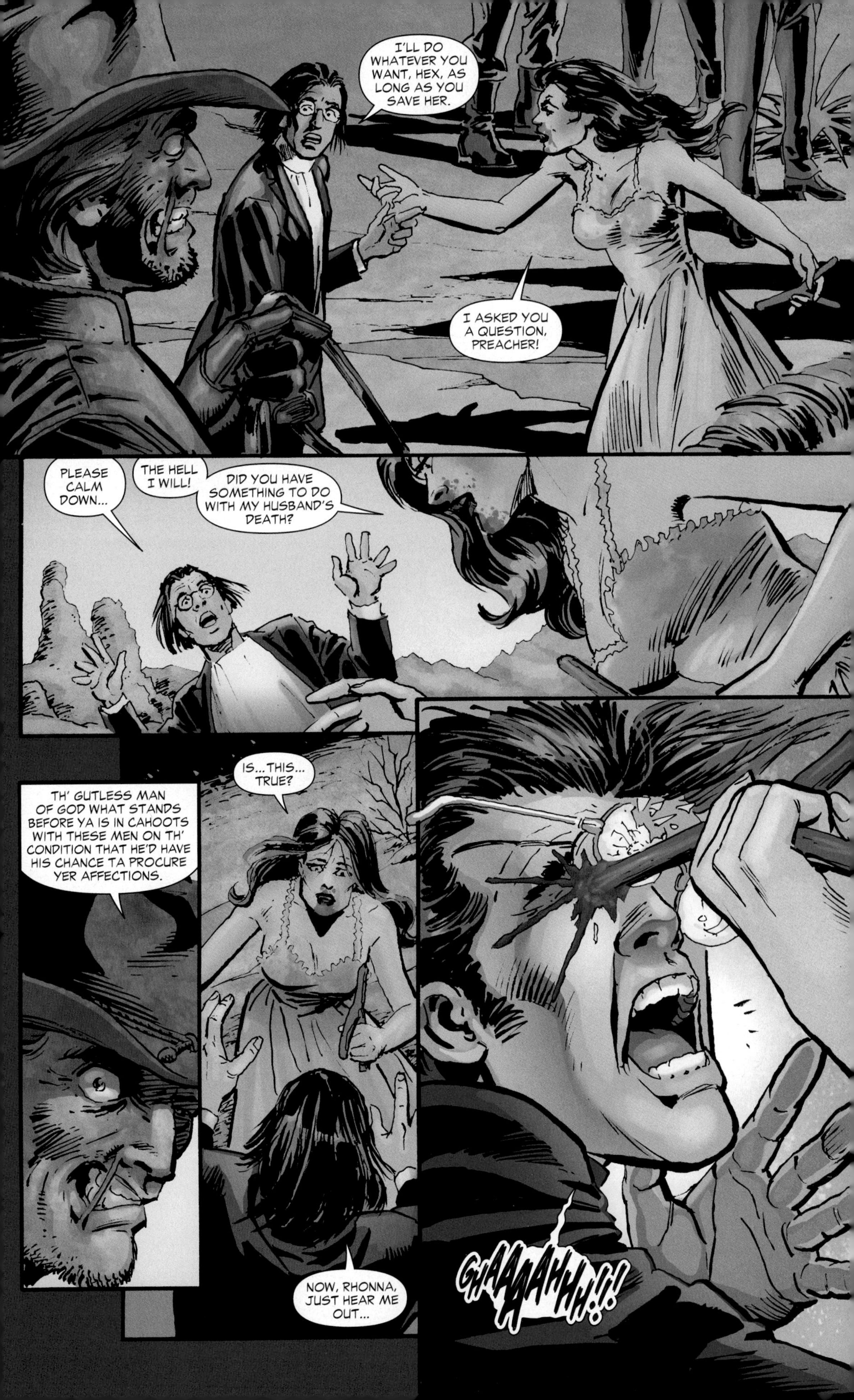
I'LL DO WHATEVER YOU WANT, HEX, AS LONG AS YOU SAVE HER.
I ASKED YOU A QUESTION, PREACHER!
PLEASE CALM DOWN...
THE HELL I WILL!
DID YOU HAVE SOMETHING TO DO WITH MY HUSBAND'S DEATH?
TH' GUTLESS MAN OF GOD WHAT STANDS BEFORE YA IS IN CAHOOTS WITH THESE MEN ON TH' CONDITION THAT HE'D HAVE HIS CHANCE TA PROCURE YER AFFECTIONS.
IS...THIS... TRUE?
NOW, RHONNA, JUST HEAR ME OUT...
GHAAAAHHH!!!

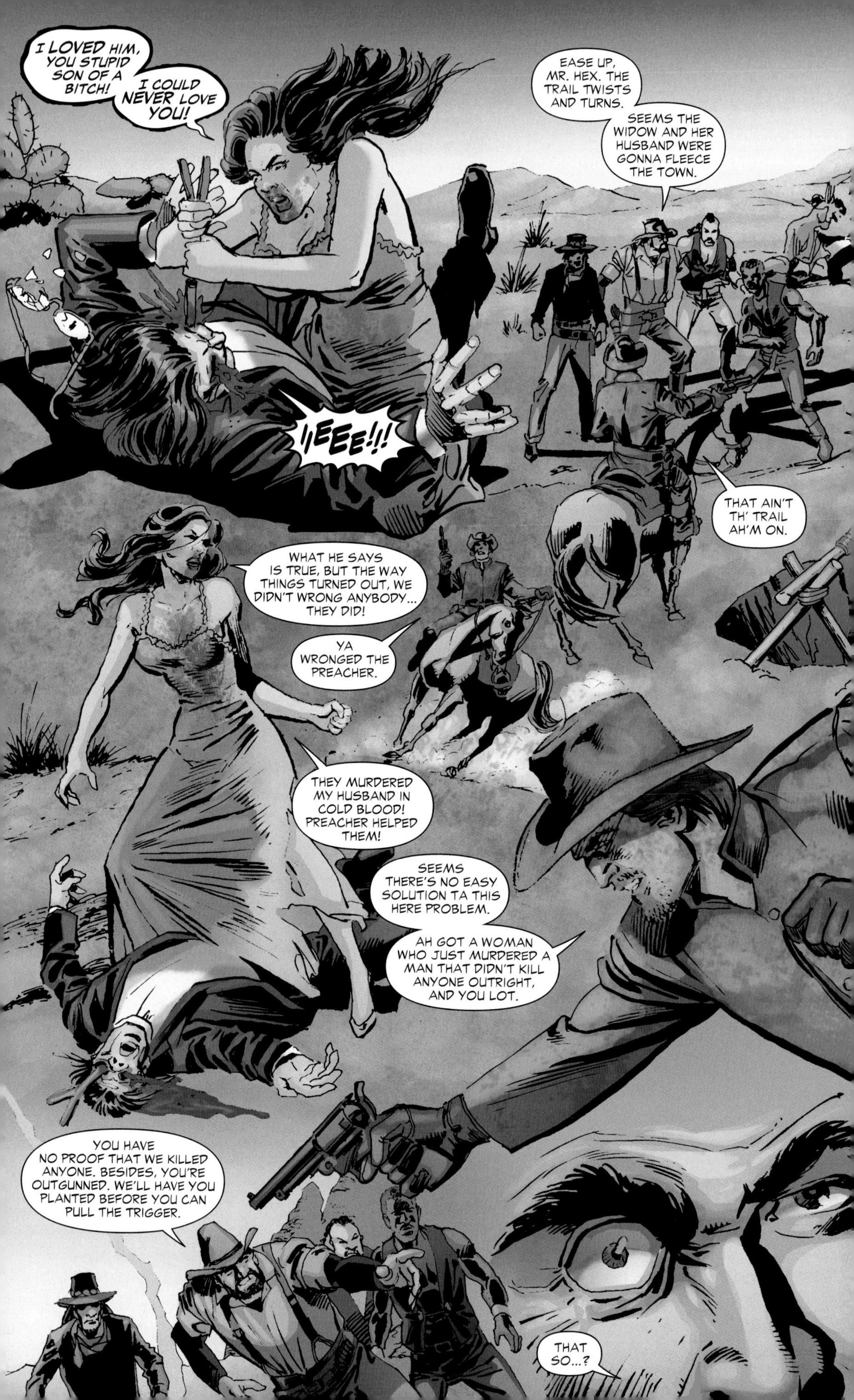
I LOVED HIM, YOU STUPID SON OF A BITCH!
I COULD NEVER LOVE YOU!
EASE UP, MR. HEX. THE TRAIL TWISTS AND TURNS.
SEEMS THE WIDOW AND HER HUSBAND WERE GONNA FLEECE THE TOWN.
IIEEE!!!
THAT AIN'T TH' TRAIL AH'M ON.
WHAT HE SAYS IS TRUE, BUT THE WAY THINGS TURNED OUT, WE DIDN'T WRONG ANYBODY... THEY DID!
YA WRONGED THE PREACHER.
THEY MURDERED MY HUSBAND IN COLD BLOOD! PREACHER HELPED THEM!
SEEMS THERE'S NO EASY SOLUTION TA THIS HERE PROBLEM.
AH GOT A WOMAN WHO JUST MURDERED A MAN THAT DIDN'T KILL ANYONE OUTRIGHT, AND YOU LOT.
YOU HAVE NO PROOF THAT WE KILLED ANYONE. BESIDES, YOU'RE OUTGUNNED. WE'LL HAVE YOU PLANTED BEFORE YOU CAN PULL THE TRIGGER.
THAT SO...?

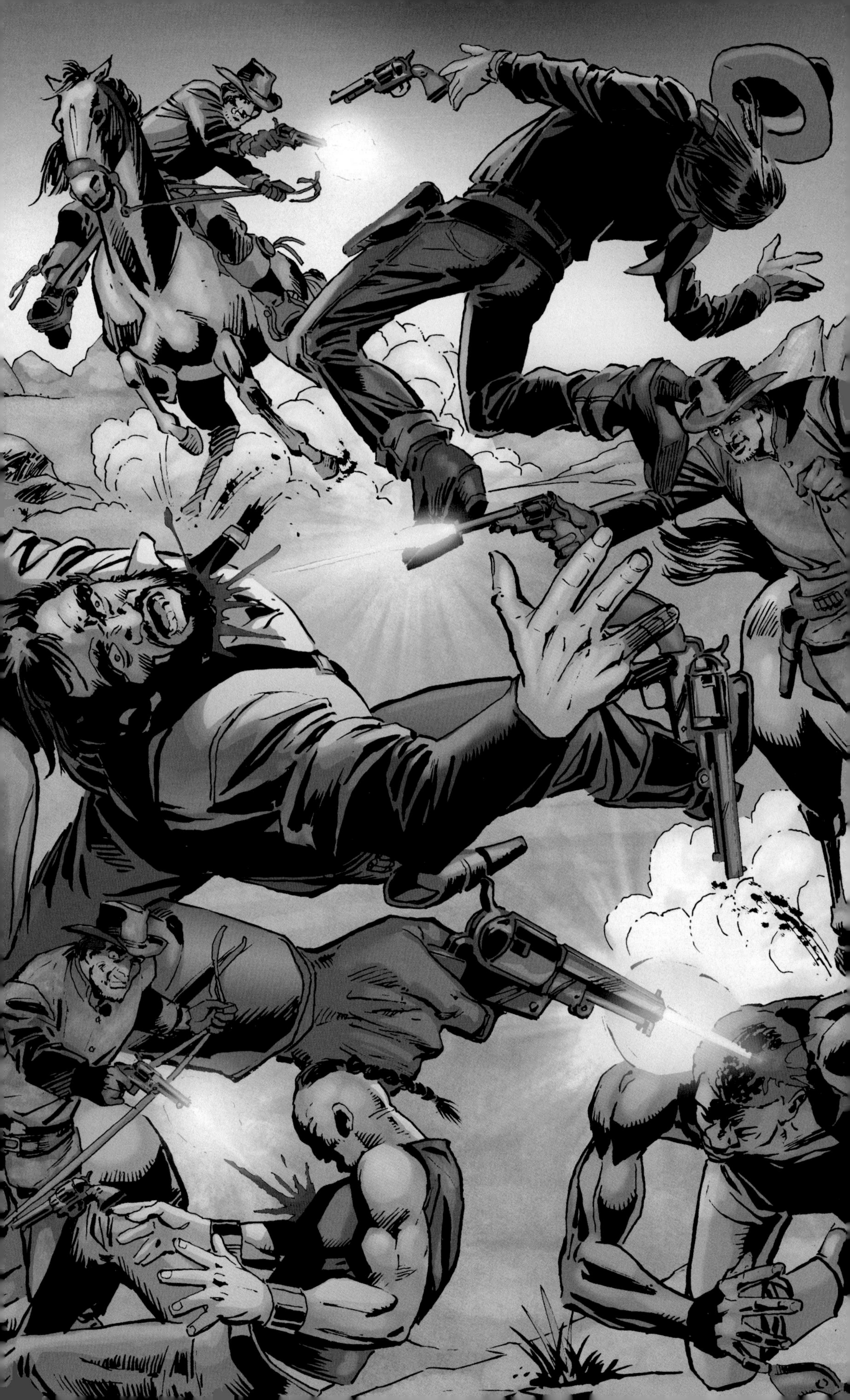

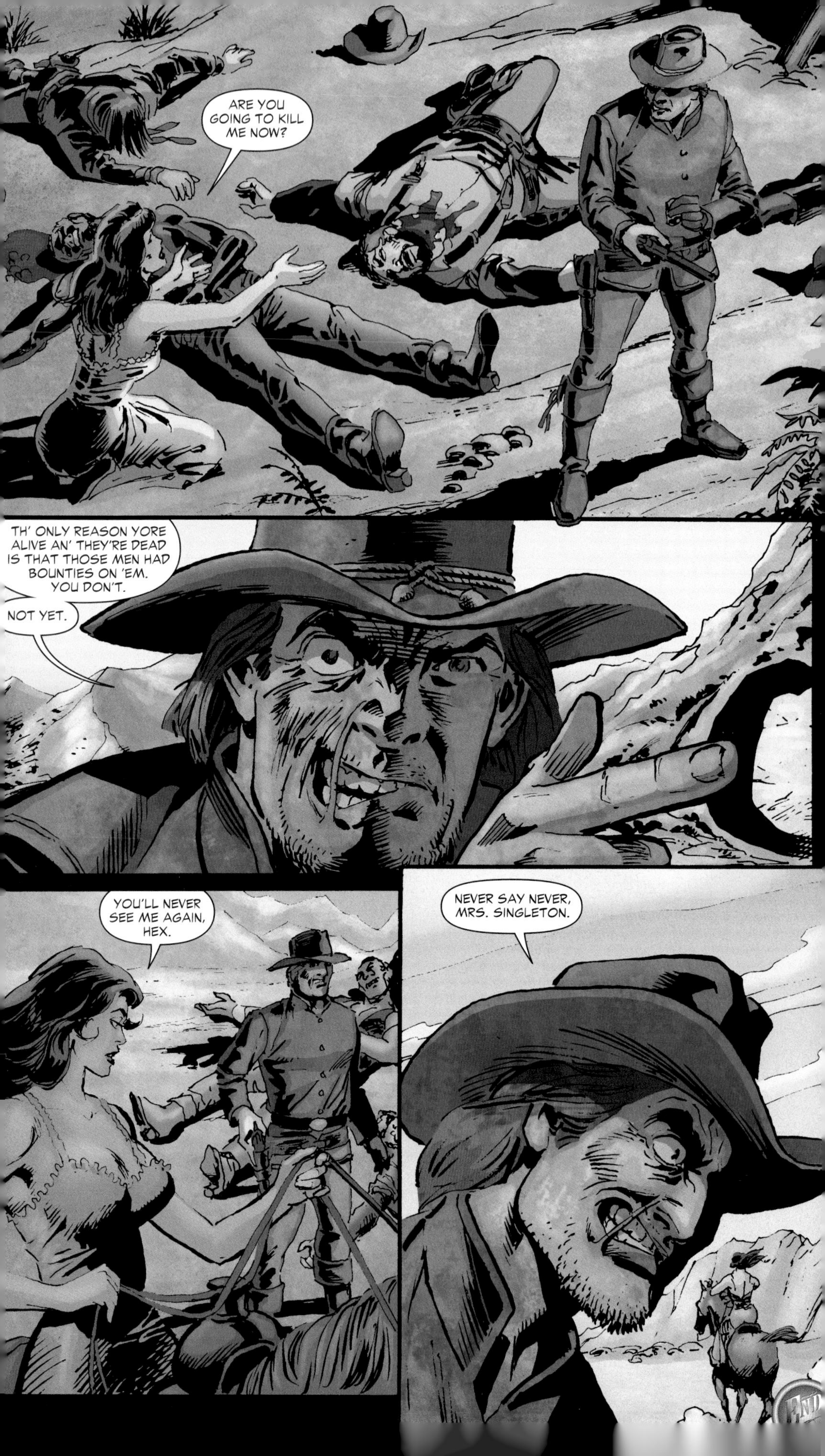
ARE YOU GOING TO KILL ME NOW?
TH' ONLY REASON YORE ALIVE AN' THEY'RE DEAD IS THAT THOSE MEN HAD BOUNTIES ON 'EM. YOU DON'T.
NOT YET.
YOU'LL NEVER SEE ME AGAIN, HEX.
NEVER SAY NEVER, MRS. SINGLETON.
END

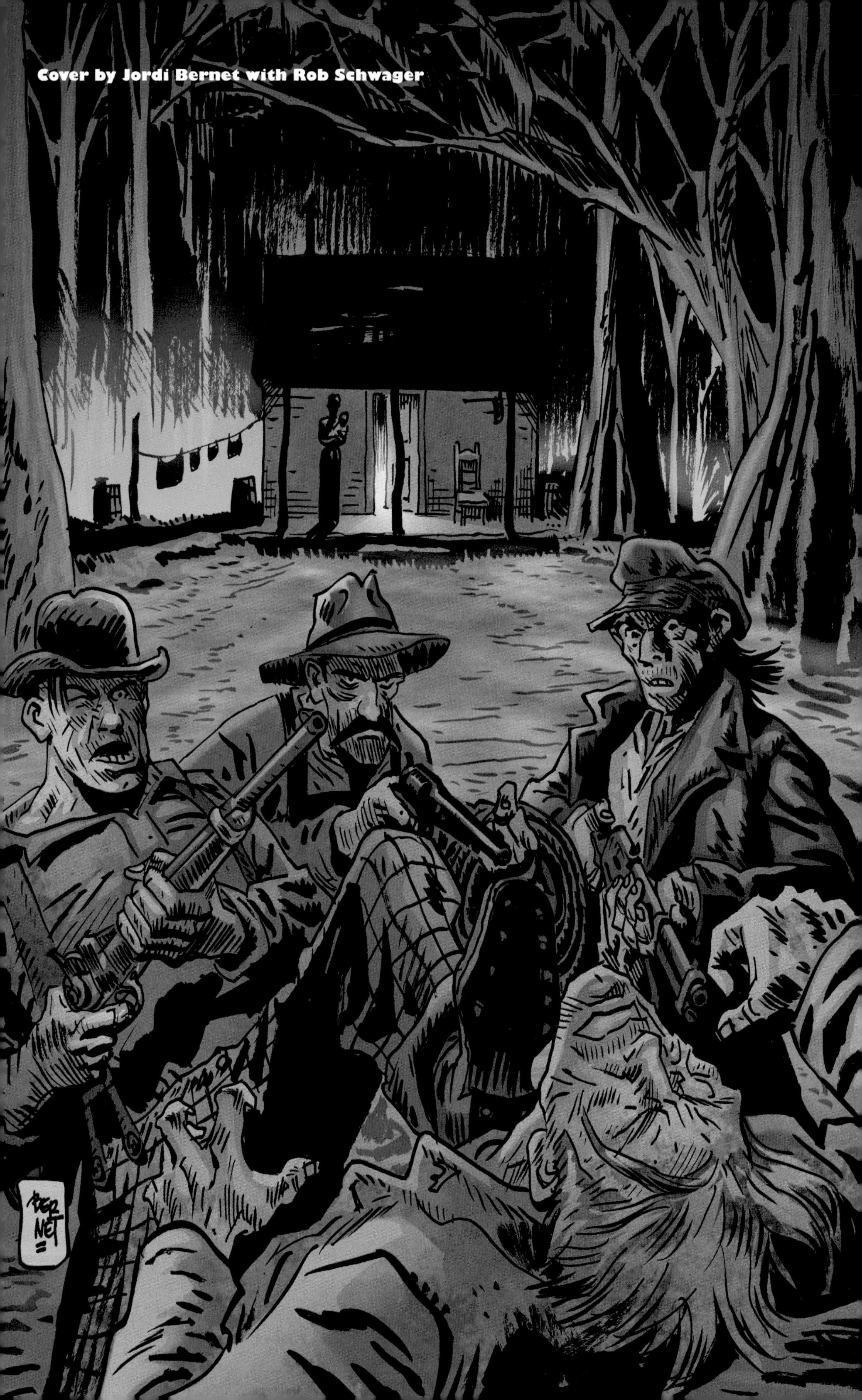

Cover by Jordi Bernet with Rob Schwager

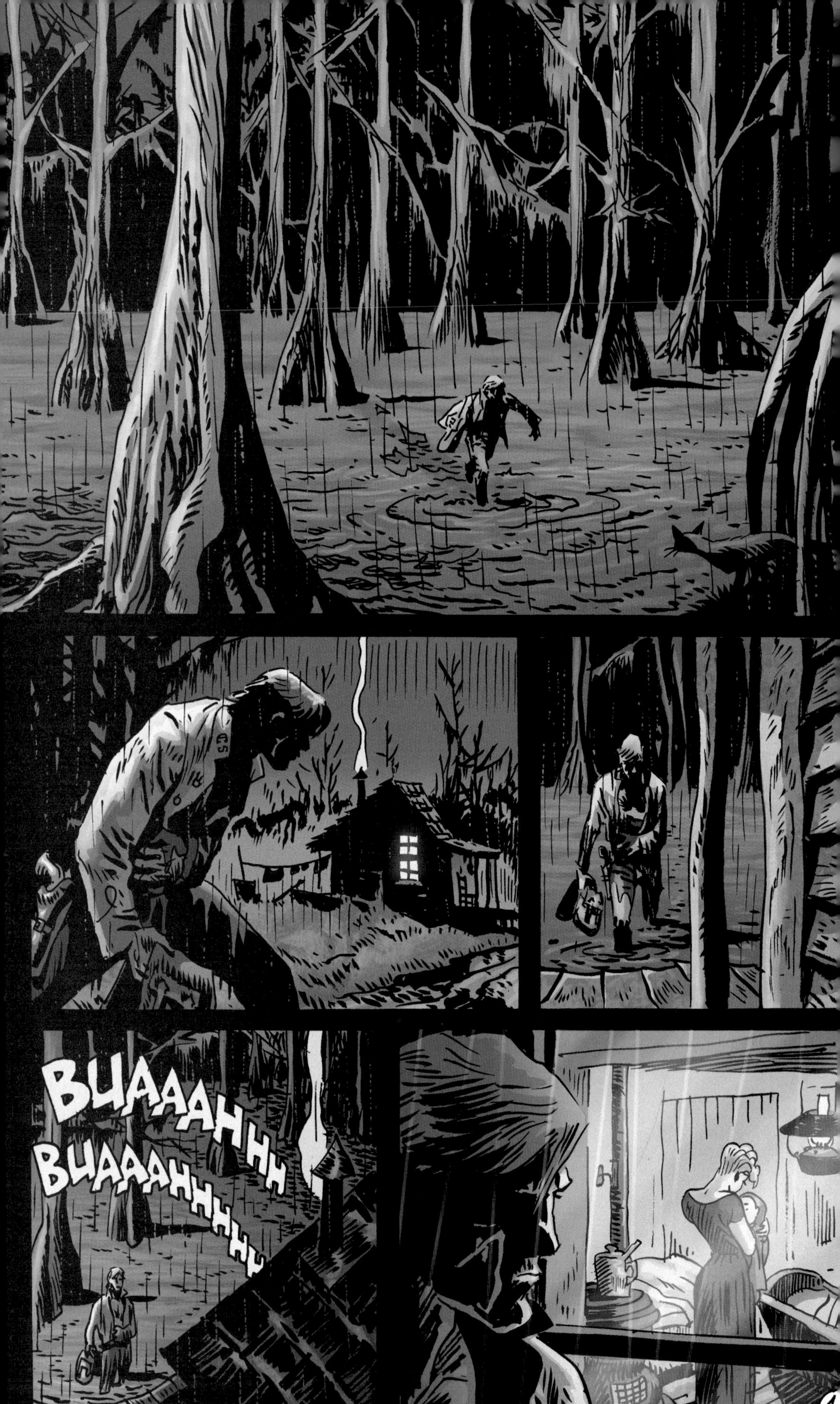
BUAAAHHH
BUAAAHHHHHH

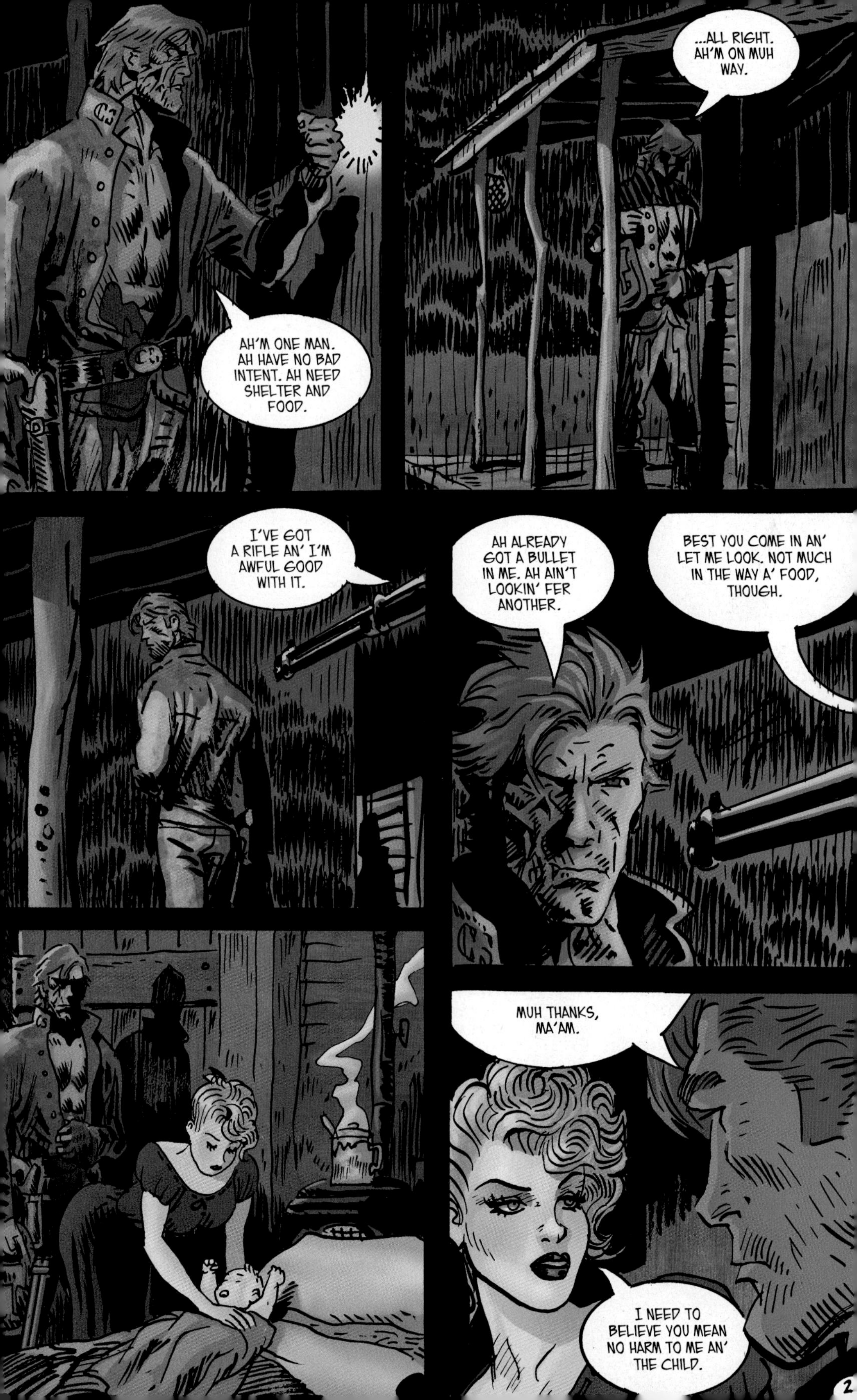
AH'M ONE MAN. AH HAVE NO BAD INTENT. AH NEED SHELTER AND FOOD.
...ALL RIGHT. AH'M ON MUH WAY.
I'VE GOT A RIFLE AN' I'M AWFUL GOOD WITH IT.
AH ALREADY GOT A BULLET IN ME. AH AIN'T LOOKIN' FER ANOTHER.
BEST YOU COME IN AN' LET ME LOOK. NOT MUCH IN THE WAY A' FOOD, THOUGH.
MUH THANKS, MA'AM.
I NEED TO BELIEVE YOU MEAN NO HARM TO ME AN' THE CHILD.

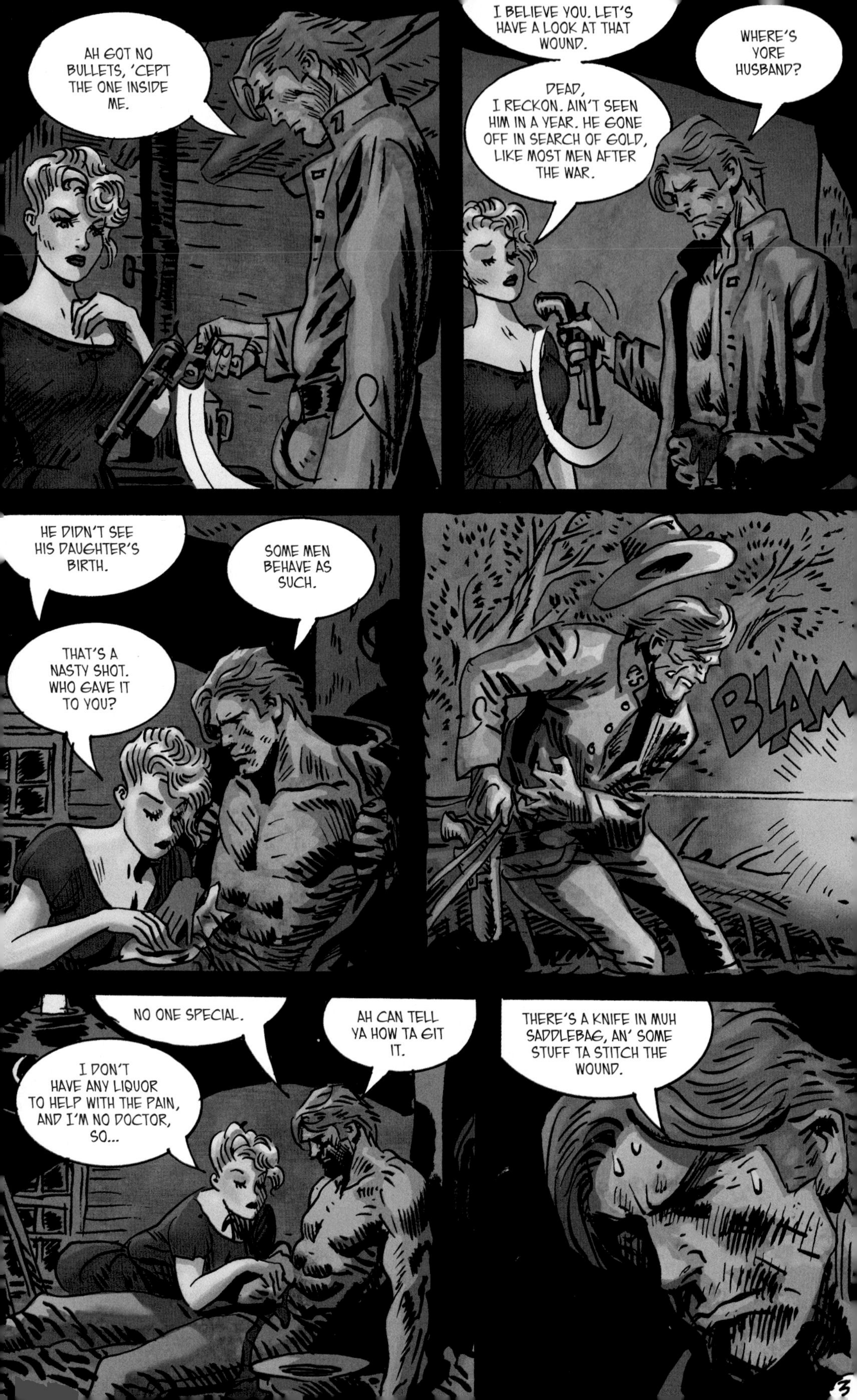
AH GOT NO BULLETS, 'CEPT THE ONE INSIDE ME.
I BELIEVE YOU. LET'S HAVE A LOOK AT THAT WOUND.
WHERE'S YORE HUSBAND?
DEAD, I RECKON. AIN'T SEEN HIM IN A YEAR. HE GONE OFF IN SEARCH OF GOLD, LIKE MOST MEN AFTER THE WAR.
HE DIDN'T SEE HIS DAUGHTER'S BIRTH.
SOME MEN BEHAVE AS SUCH.
THAT'S A NASTY SHOT. WHO GAVE IT TO YOU?
BLAM
NO ONE SPECIAL.
I DON'T HAVE ANY LIQUOR TO HELP WITH THE PAIN, AND I'M NO DOCTOR, SO...
AH CAN TELL YA HOW TA GIT IT.
THERE'S A KNIFE IN MUH SADDLEBAG, AN' SOME STUFF TA STITCH THE WOUND.
3

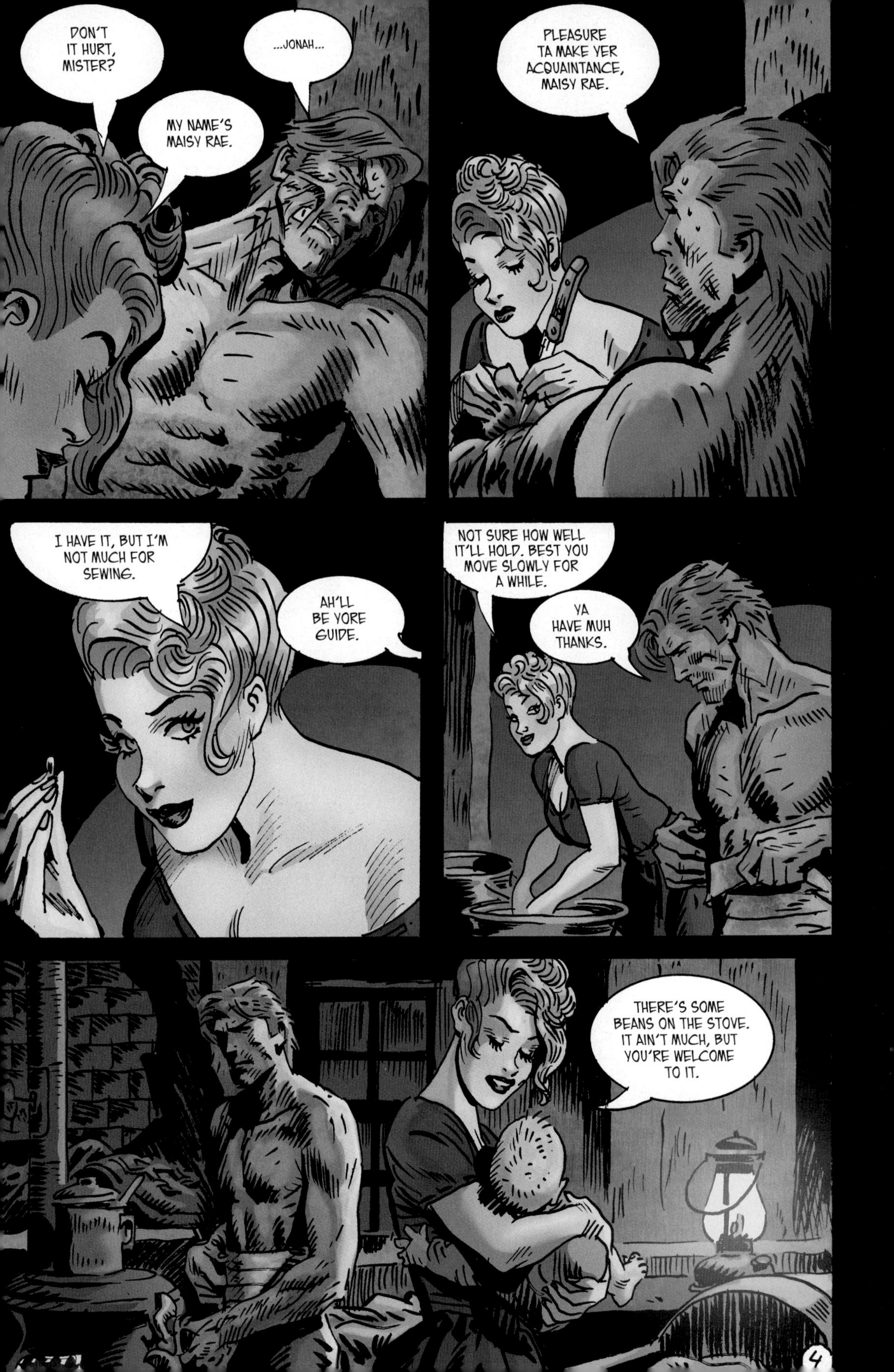
DON'T IT HURT, MISTER?
MY NAME'S MAISY RAE.
...JONAH...
PLEASURE TA MAKE YER ACQUAINTANCE, MAISY RAE.
I HAVE IT, BUT I'M NOT MUCH FOR SEWING.
AH'LL BE YORE GUIDE.
NOT SURE HOW WELL IT'LL HOLD. BEST YOU MOVE SLOWLY FOR A WHILE.
YA HAVE MUH THANKS.
THERE'S SOME BEANS ON THE STOVE. IT AIN'T MUCH, BUT YOU'RE WELCOME TO IT.

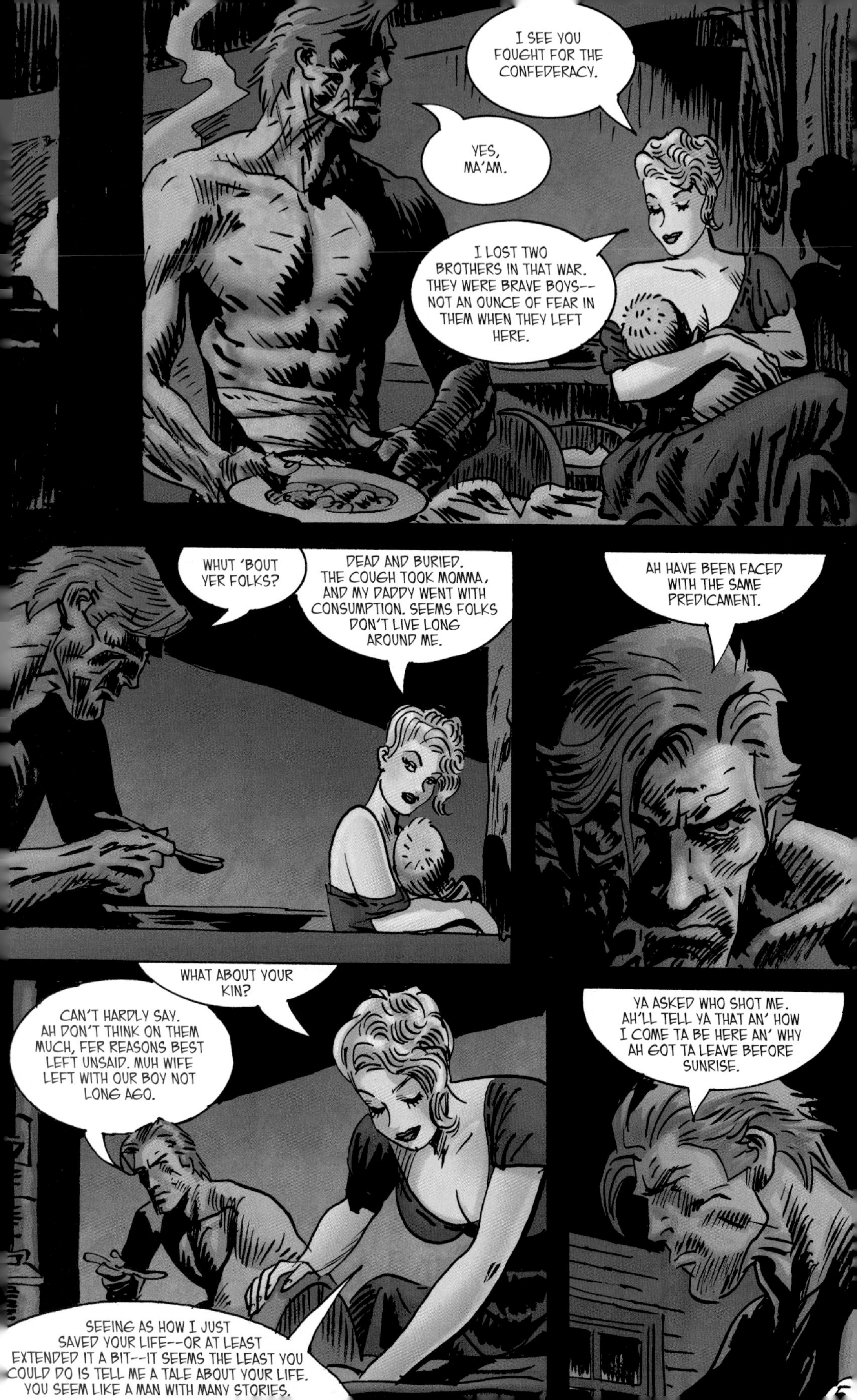

I SEE YOU FOUGHT FOR THE CONFEDERACY.
YES, MA'AM.
I LOST TWO BROTHERS IN THAT WAR. THEY WERE BRAVE BOYS-- NOT AN OUNCE OF FEAR IN THEM WHEN THEY LEFT HERE.
WHUT 'BOUT YER FOLKS?
DEAD AND BURIED. THE COUGH TOOK MOMMA, AND MY DADDY WENT WITH CONSUMPTION. SEEMS FOLKS DON'T LIVE LONG AROUND ME.
AH HAVE BEEN FACED WITH THE SAME PREDICAMENT.
WHAT ABOUT YOUR KIN?
CAN'T HARDLY SAY. AH DON'T THINK ON THEM MUCH, FER REASONS BEST LEFT UNSAID. MUH WIFE LEFT WITH OUR BOY NOT LONG AGO.
SEEING AS HOW I JUST SAVED YOUR LIFE--OR AT LEAST EXTENDED IT A BIT--IT SEEMS THE LEAST YOU COULD DO IS TELL ME A TALE ABOUT YOUR LIFE. YOU SEEM LIKE A MAN WITH MANY STORIES.
YA ASKED WHO SHOT ME. AH'LL TELL YA THAT AN' HOW I COME TA BE HERE AN' WHY AH GOT TA LEAVE BEFORE SUNRISE.

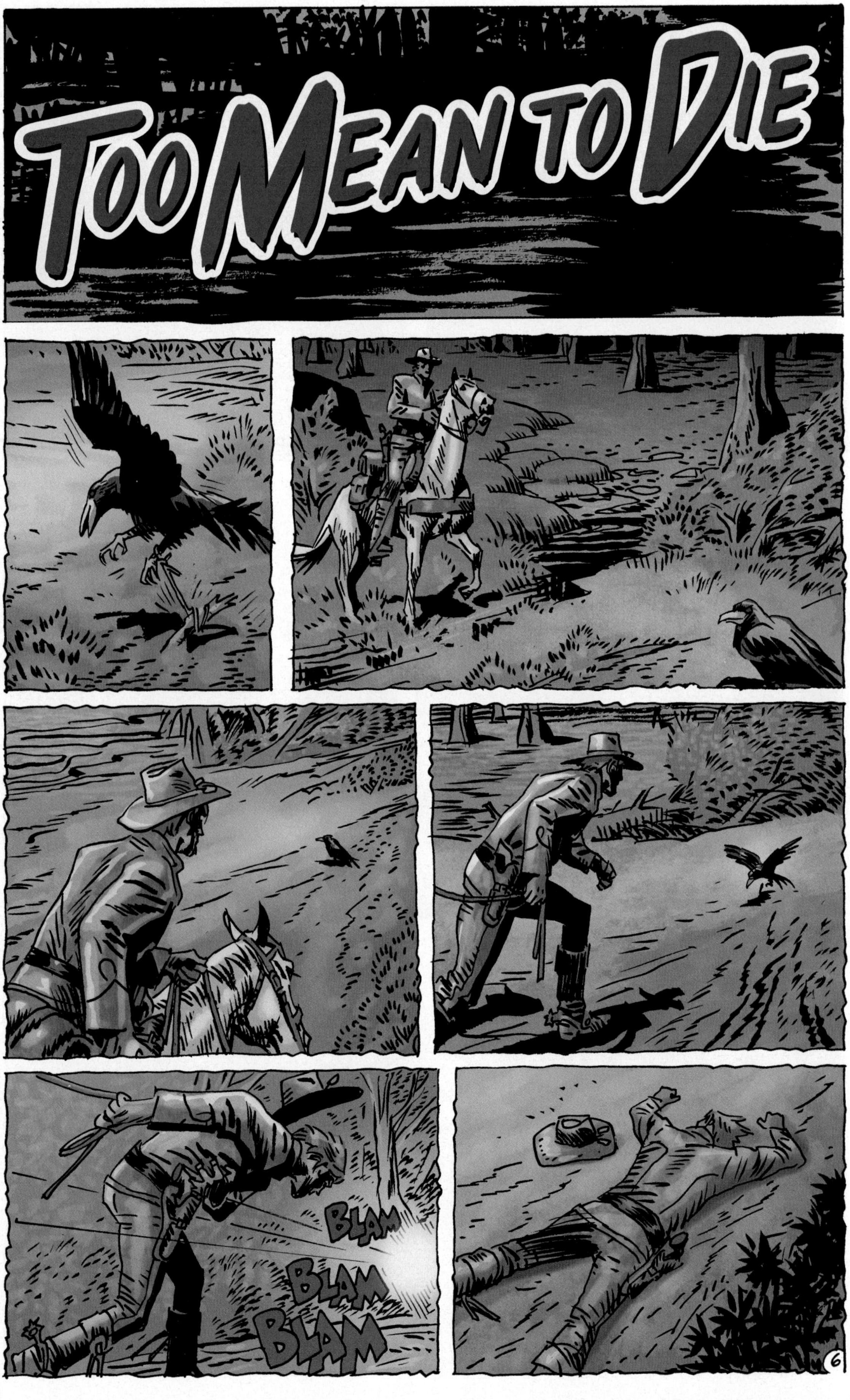
TOO MEAN TO DIE
BLAM
BLAM
BLAM

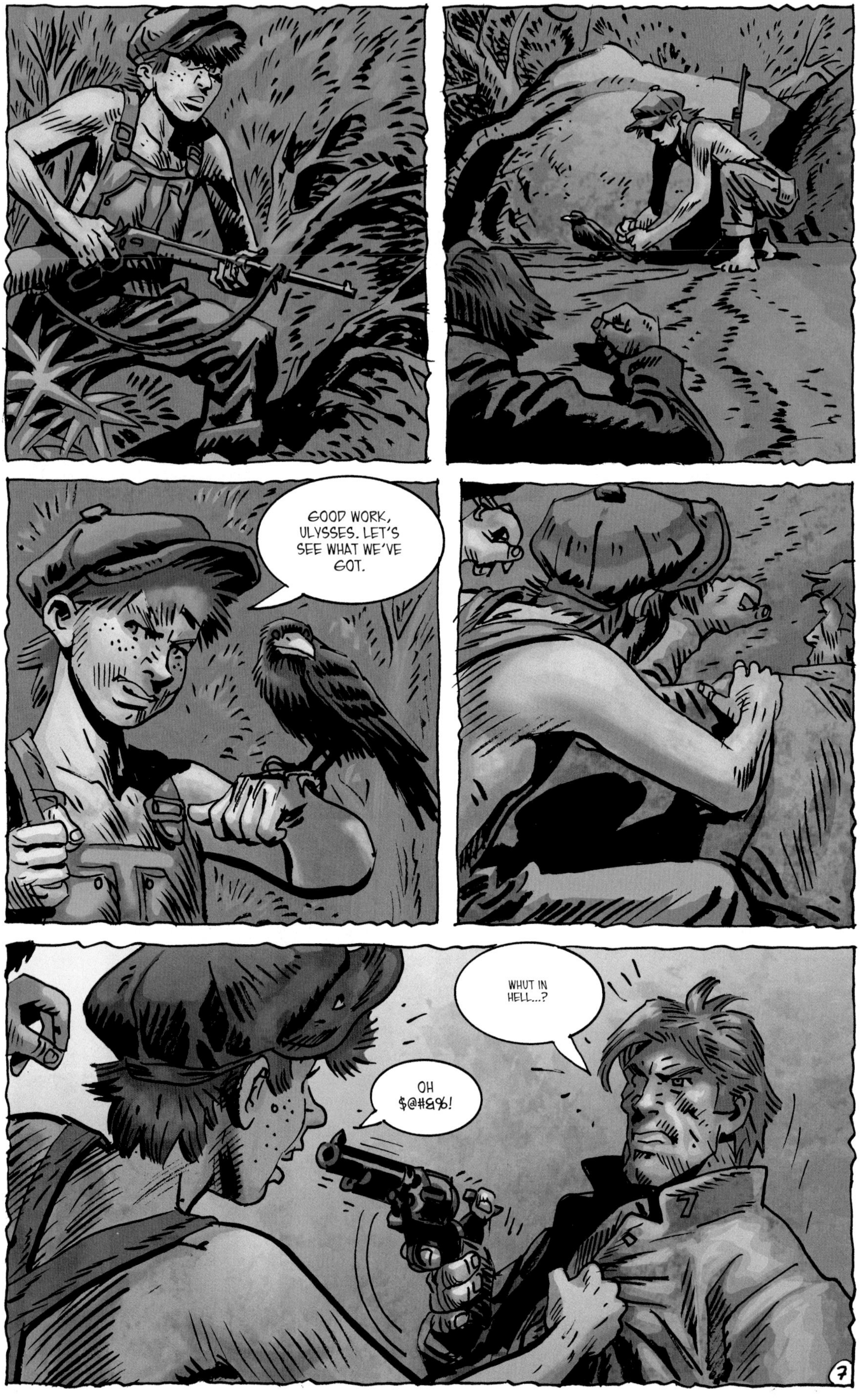
GOOD WORK, ULYSSES. LET'S SEE WHAT WE'VE GOT.
WHUT IN HELL...?
OH $@#&%!
7

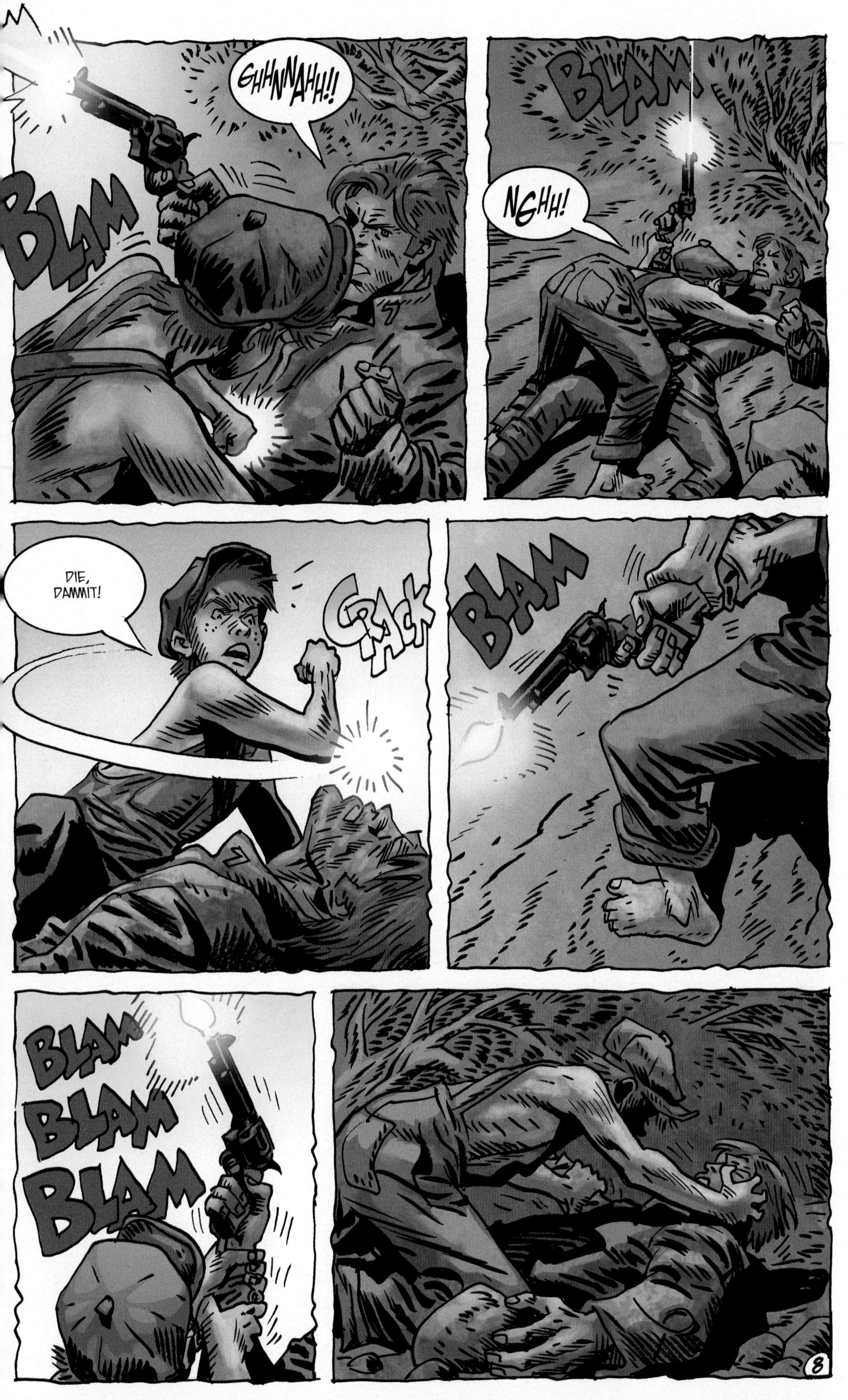
BLAM
GHHNNAHH!!
BLAM
NGHH!
DIE, DAMMIT!
CRACK
BLAM
BLAM
BLAM
BLAM

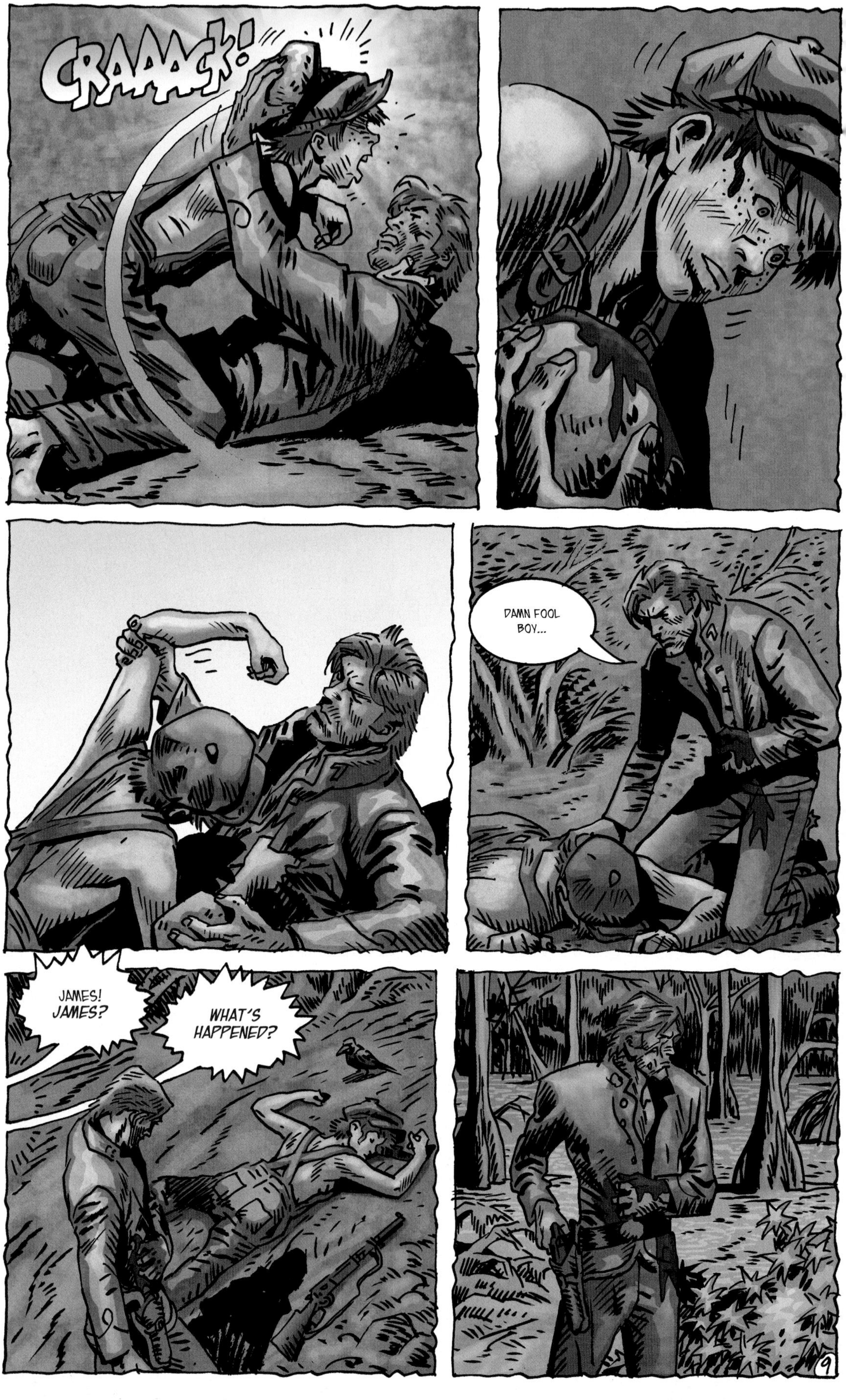
CRAAACK!
DAMN FOOL BOY...
JAMES! JAMES?
WHAT'S HAPPENED?

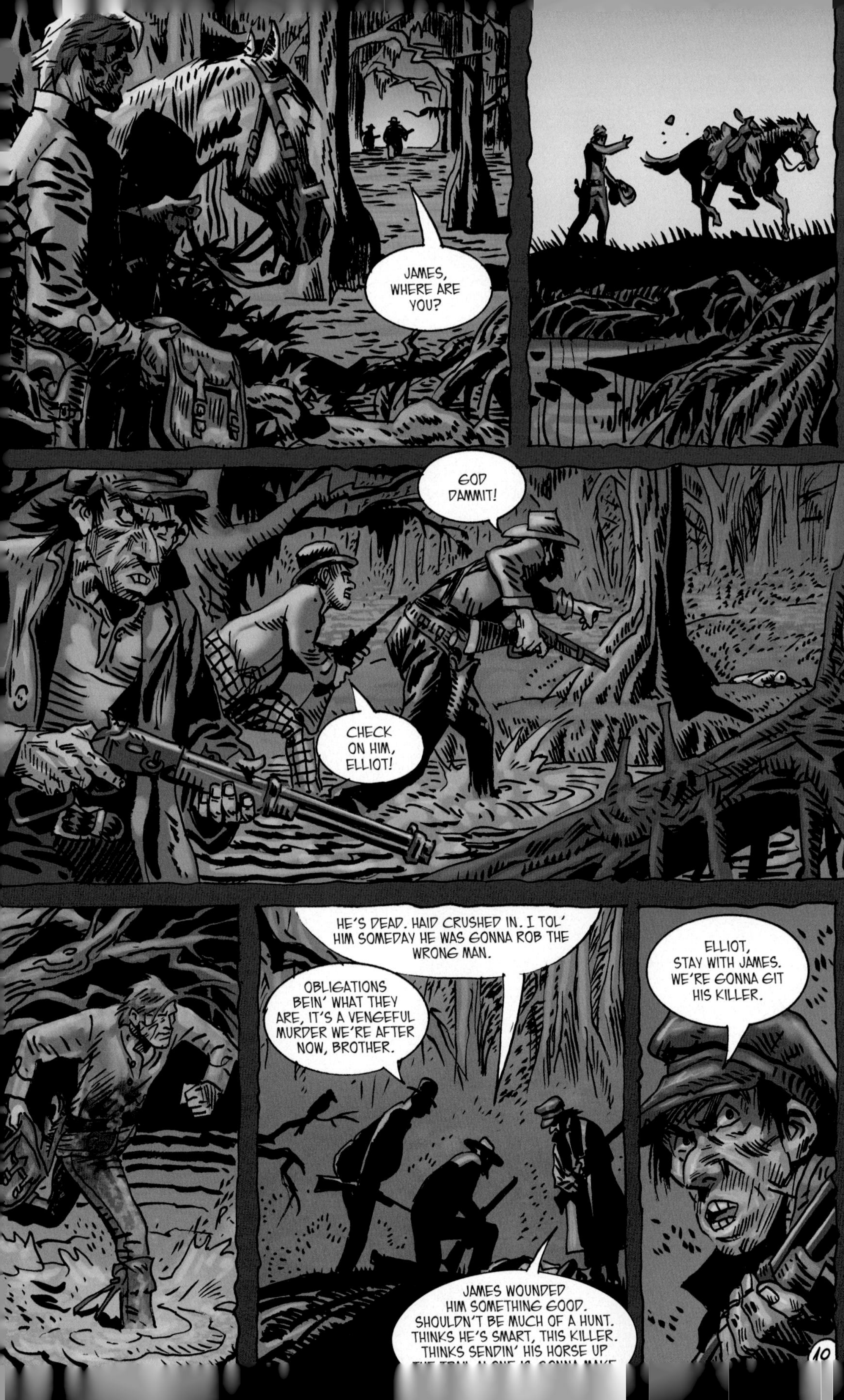
JAMES, WHERE ARE YOU?
GOD DAMMIT!
CHECK ON HIM, ELLIOT!
HE'S DEAD. HAID CRUSHED IN. I TOL' HIM SOMEDAY HE WAS GONNA ROB THE WRONG MAN.
OBLIGATIONS BEIN' WHAT THEY ARE, IT'S A VENGEFUL MURDER WE'RE AFTER NOW, BROTHER.
ELLIOT, STAY WITH JAMES. WE'RE GONNA GIT HIS KILLER.
JAMES WOUNDED HIM SOMETHING GOOD. SHOULDN'T BE MUCH OF A HUNT. THINKS HE'S SMART, THIS KILLER. THINKS SENDIN' HIS HORSE UP
10

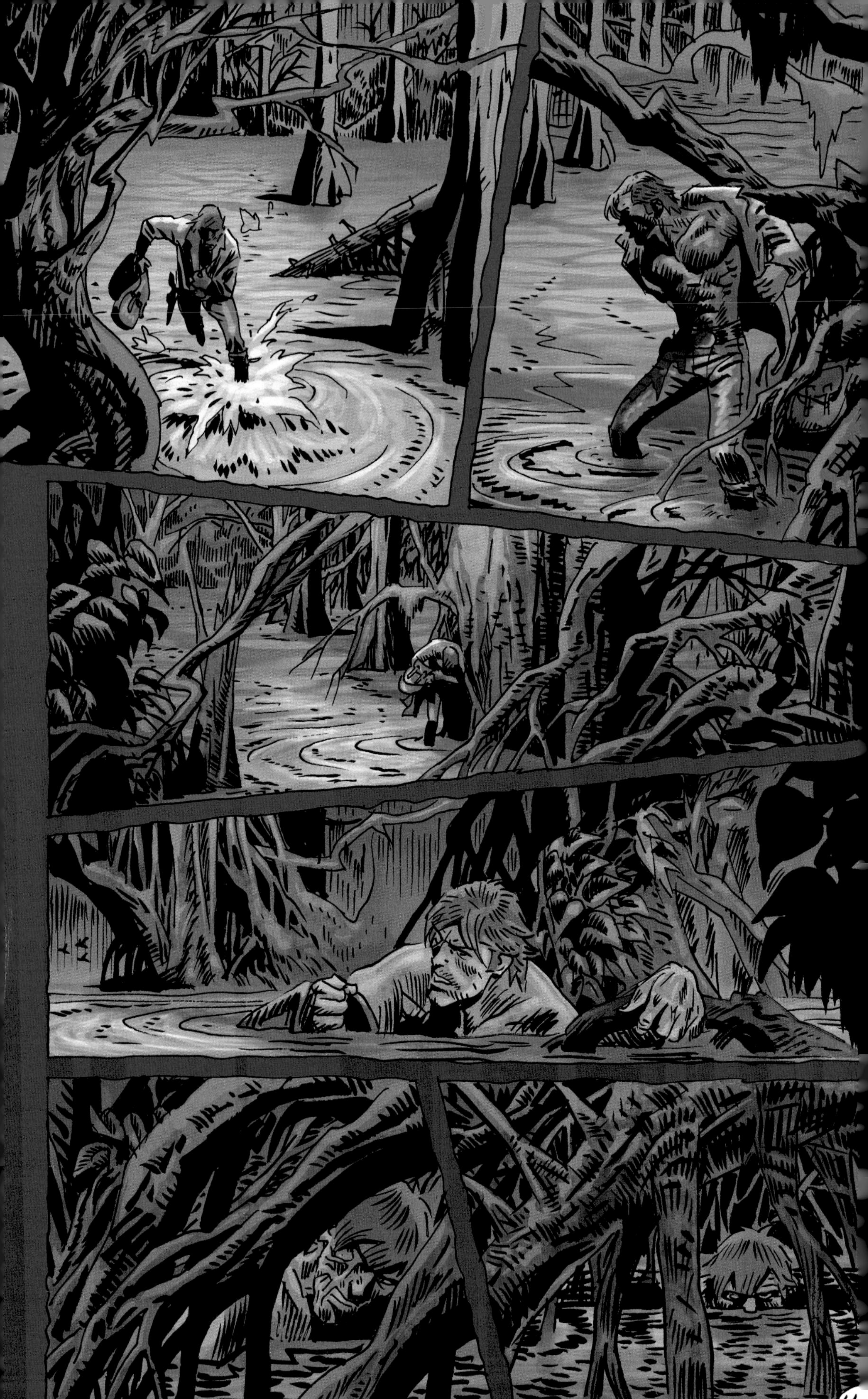

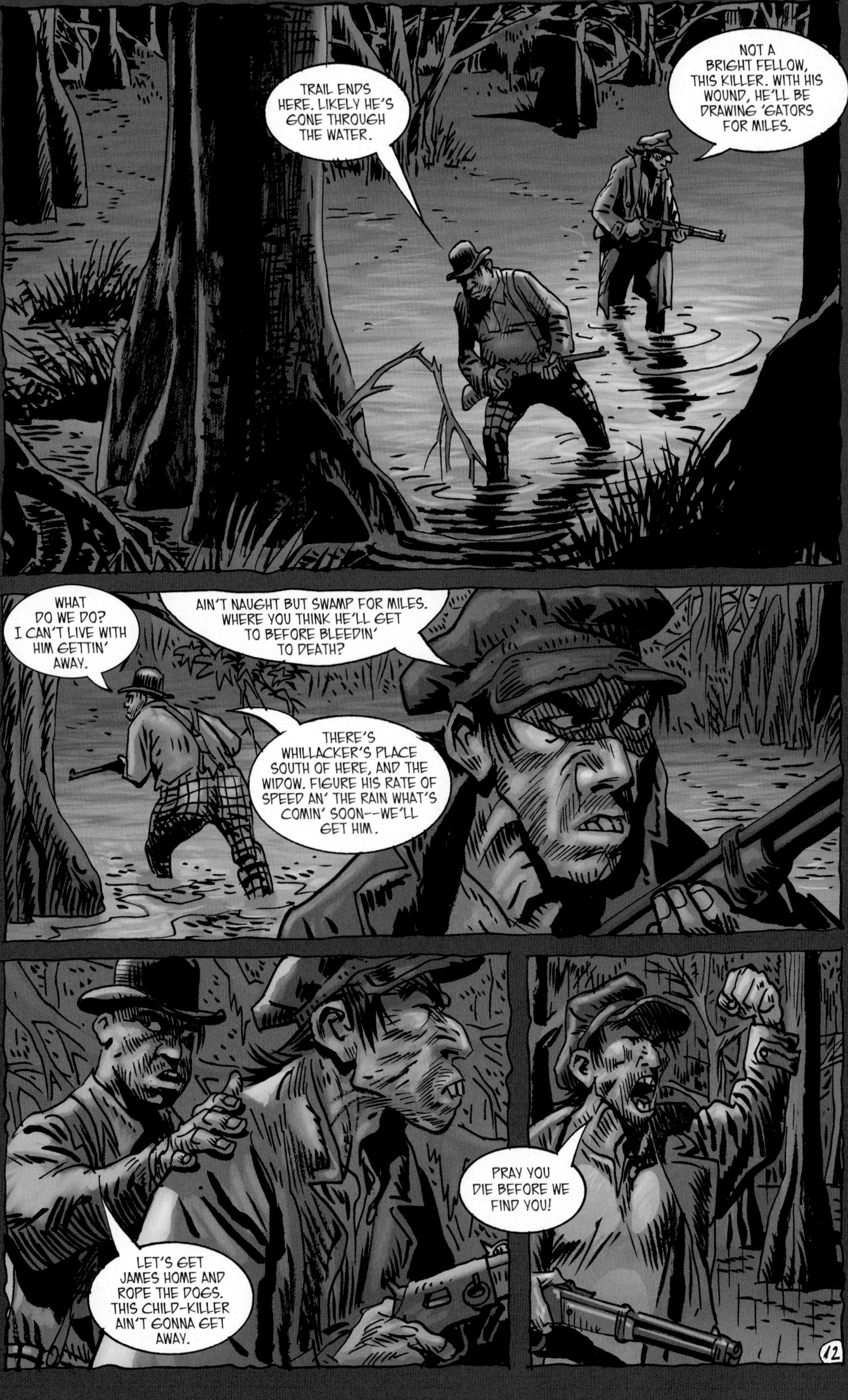
TRAIL ENDS HERE. LIKELY HE'S GONE THROUGH THE WATER.
NOT A BRIGHT FELLOW, THIS KILLER. WITH HIS WOUND, HE'LL BE DRAWING 'GATORS FOR MILES.
WHAT DO WE DO? I CAN'T LIVE WITH HIM GETTIN' AWAY.
AIN'T NAUGHT BUT SWAMP FOR MILES. WHERE YOU THINK HE'LL GET TO BEFORE BLEEDIN' TO DEATH?
THERE'S WHILLACKER'S PLACE SOUTH OF HERE, AND THE WIDOW. FIGURE HIS RATE OF SPEED AN' THE RAIN WHAT'S COMIN' SOON--WE'LL GET HIM.
LET'S GET JAMES HOME AND ROPE THE DOGS. THIS CHILD-KILLER AIN'T GONNA GET AWAY.
PRAY YOU DIE BEFORE WE FIND YOU!

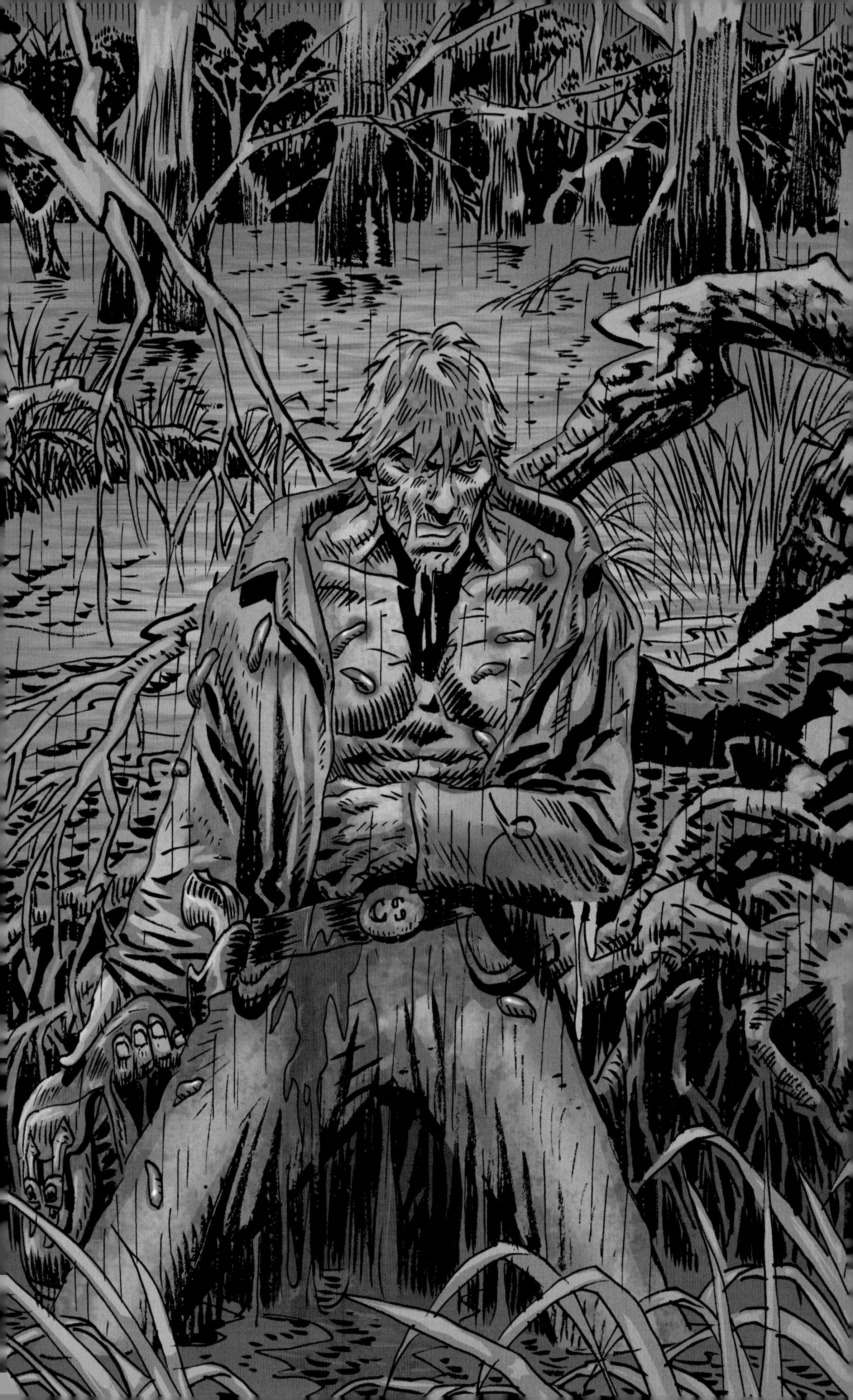

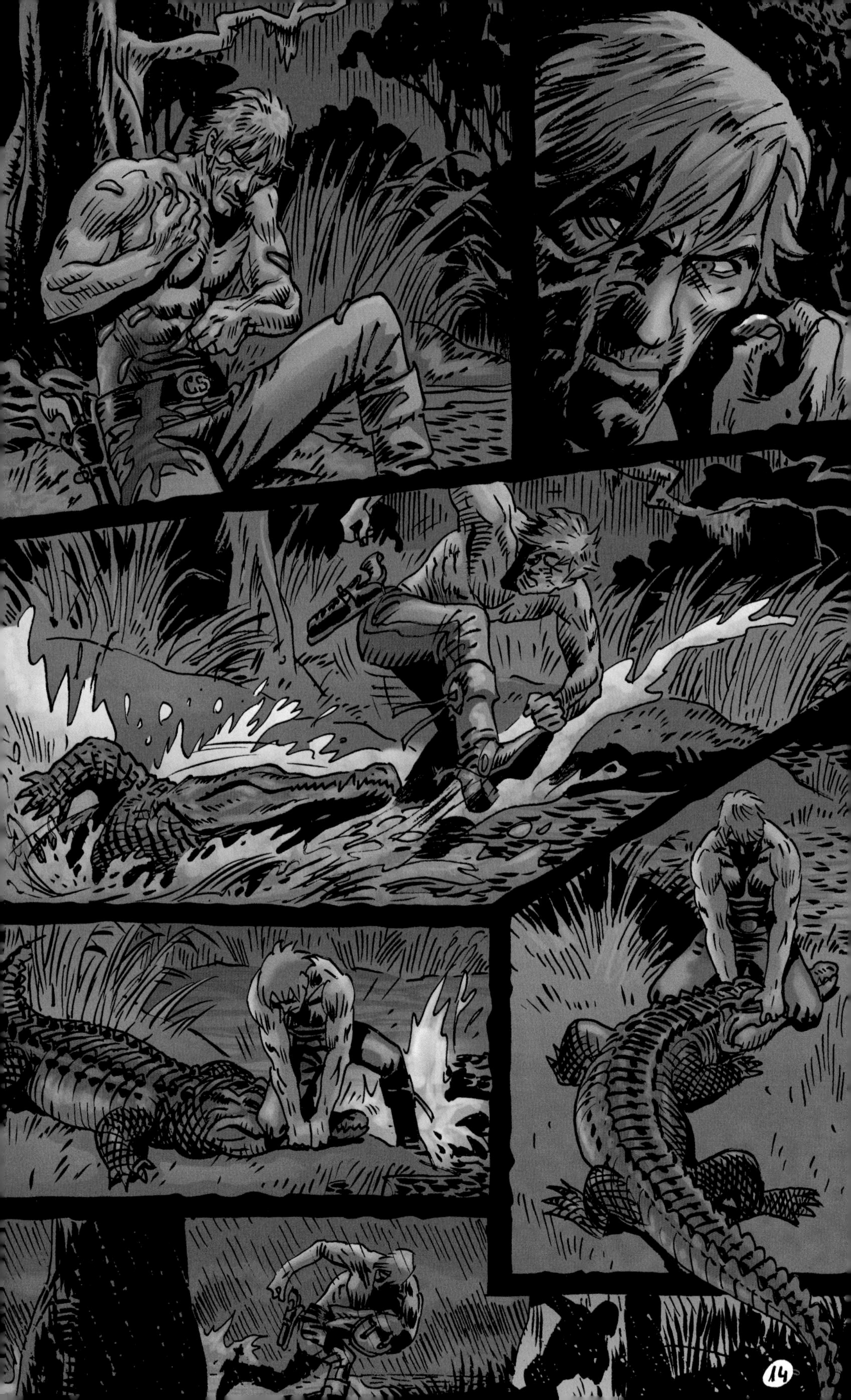
CS

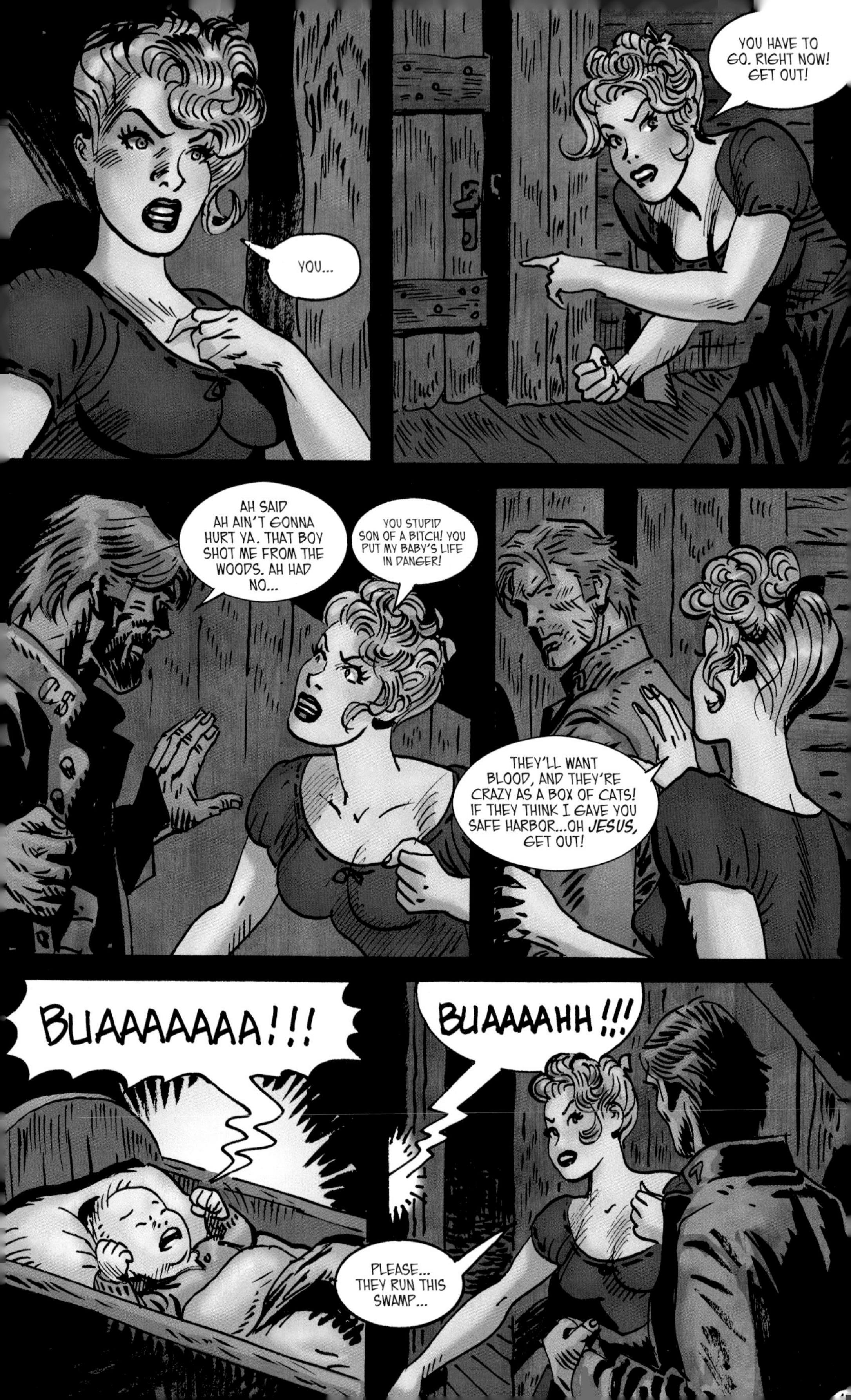
YOU...
YOU HAVE TO GO. RIGHT NOW! GET OUT!
AH SAID AH AIN'T GONNA HURT YA. THAT BOY SHOT ME FROM THE WOODS. AH HAD NO...
YOU STUPID SON OF A BITCH! YOU PUT MY BABY'S LIFE IN DANGER!
THEY'LL WANT BLOOD, AND THEY'RE CRAZY AS A BOX OF CATS! IF THEY THINK I GAVE YOU SAFE HARBOR...OH JESUS, GET OUT!
BUAAAAAAA!!!
BUAAAAHH!!!
PLEASE... THEY RUN THIS SWAMP...

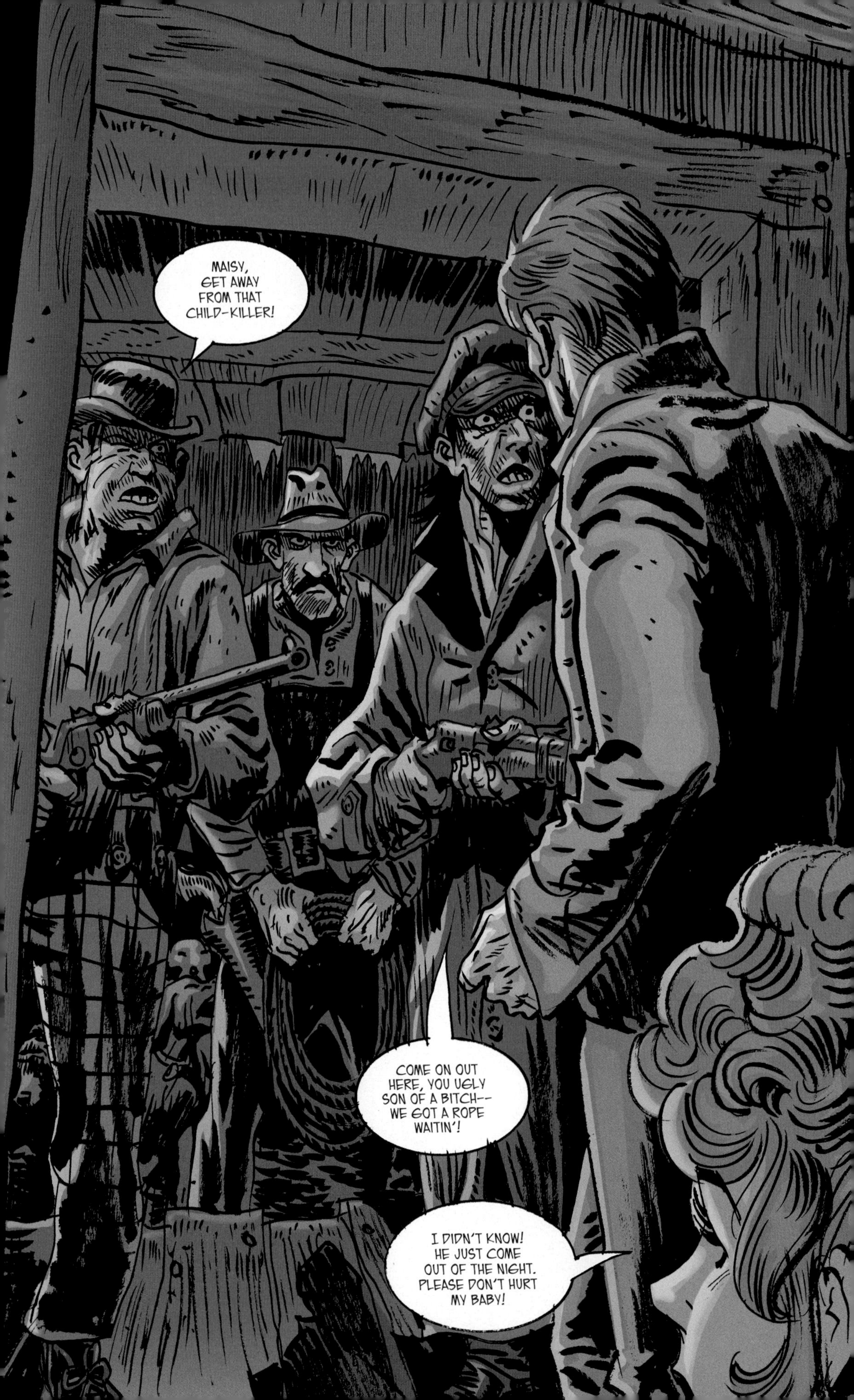
MAISY, GET AWAY FROM THAT CHILD-KILLER!
COME ON OUT HERE, YOU UGLY SON OF A BITCH-- WE GOT A ROPE WAITIN'!
I DIDN'T KNOW! HE JUST COME OUT OF THE NIGHT. PLEASE DON'T HURT MY BABY!

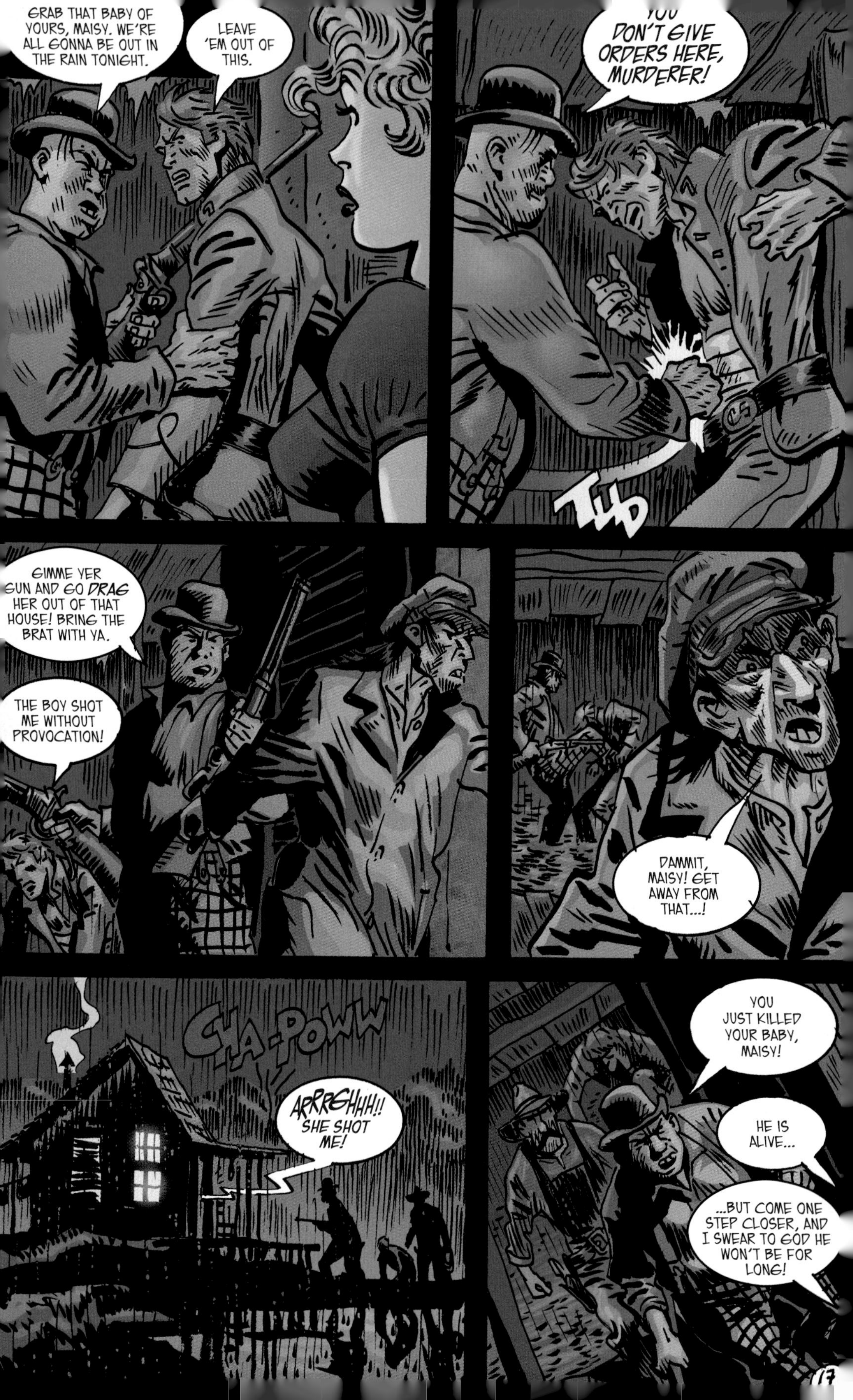
GRAB THAT BABY OF YOURS, MAISY. WE'RE ALL GONNA BE OUT IN THE RAIN TONIGHT.
LEAVE 'EM OUT OF THIS.
YOU DON'T GIVE ORDERS HERE, MURDERER!
TUD
GIMME YER GUN AND GO DRAG HER OUT OF THAT HOUSE! BRING THE BRAT WITH YA.
THE BOY SHOT ME WITHOUT PROVOCATION!
DAMMIT, MAISY! GET AWAY FROM THAT...!
CHA-POWW
ARRRGHHH!! SHE SHOT ME!
YOU JUST KILLED YOUR BABY, MAISY!
HE IS ALIVE...
...BUT COME ONE STEP CLOSER, AND I SWEAR TO GOD HE WON'T BE FOR LONG!

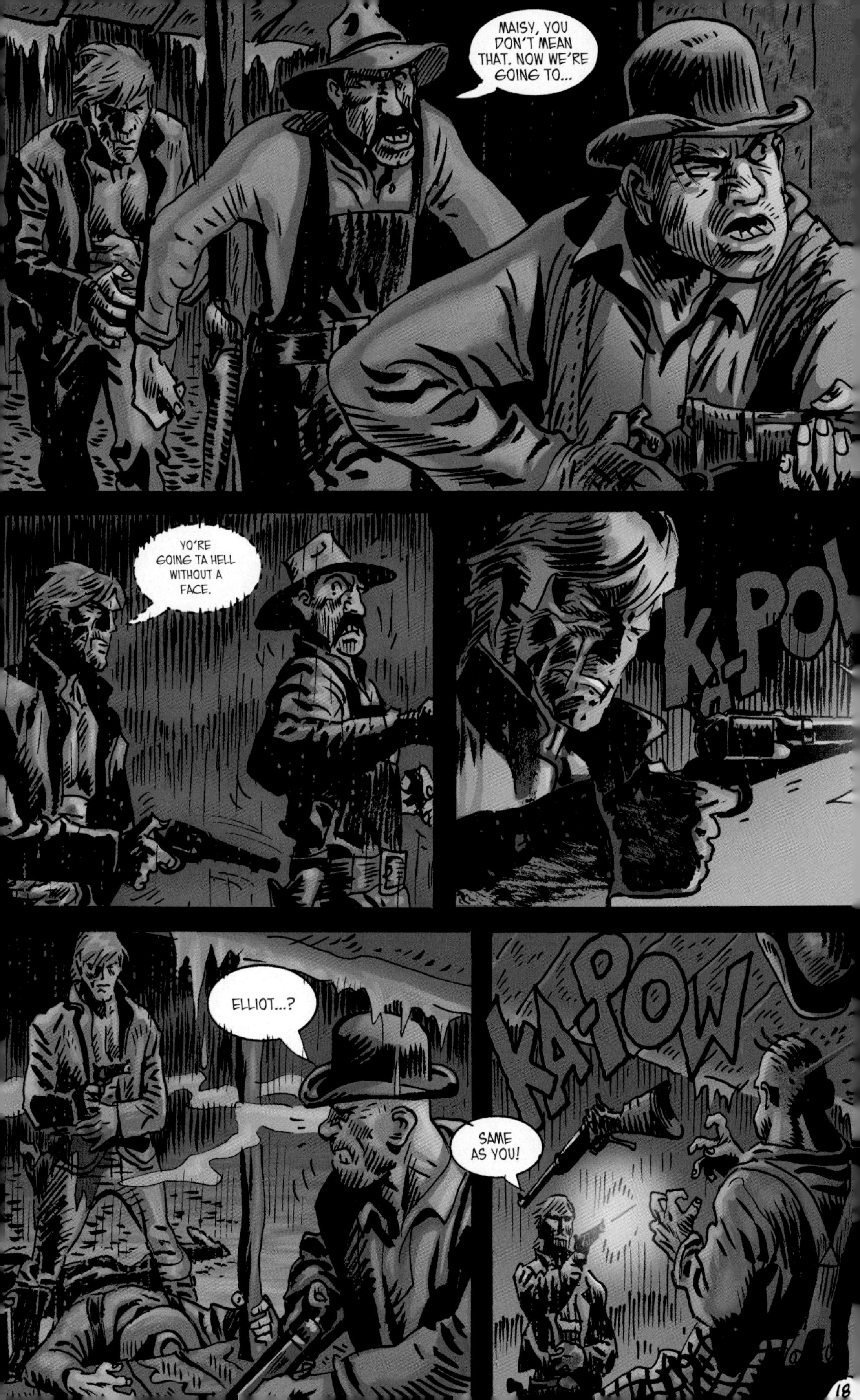
MAISY, YOU DON'T MEAN THAT. NOW WE'RE GOING TO...
YO'RE GOING TA HELL WITHOUT A FACE.
K-POW
ELLIOT...?
SAME AS YOU!
KA-POW

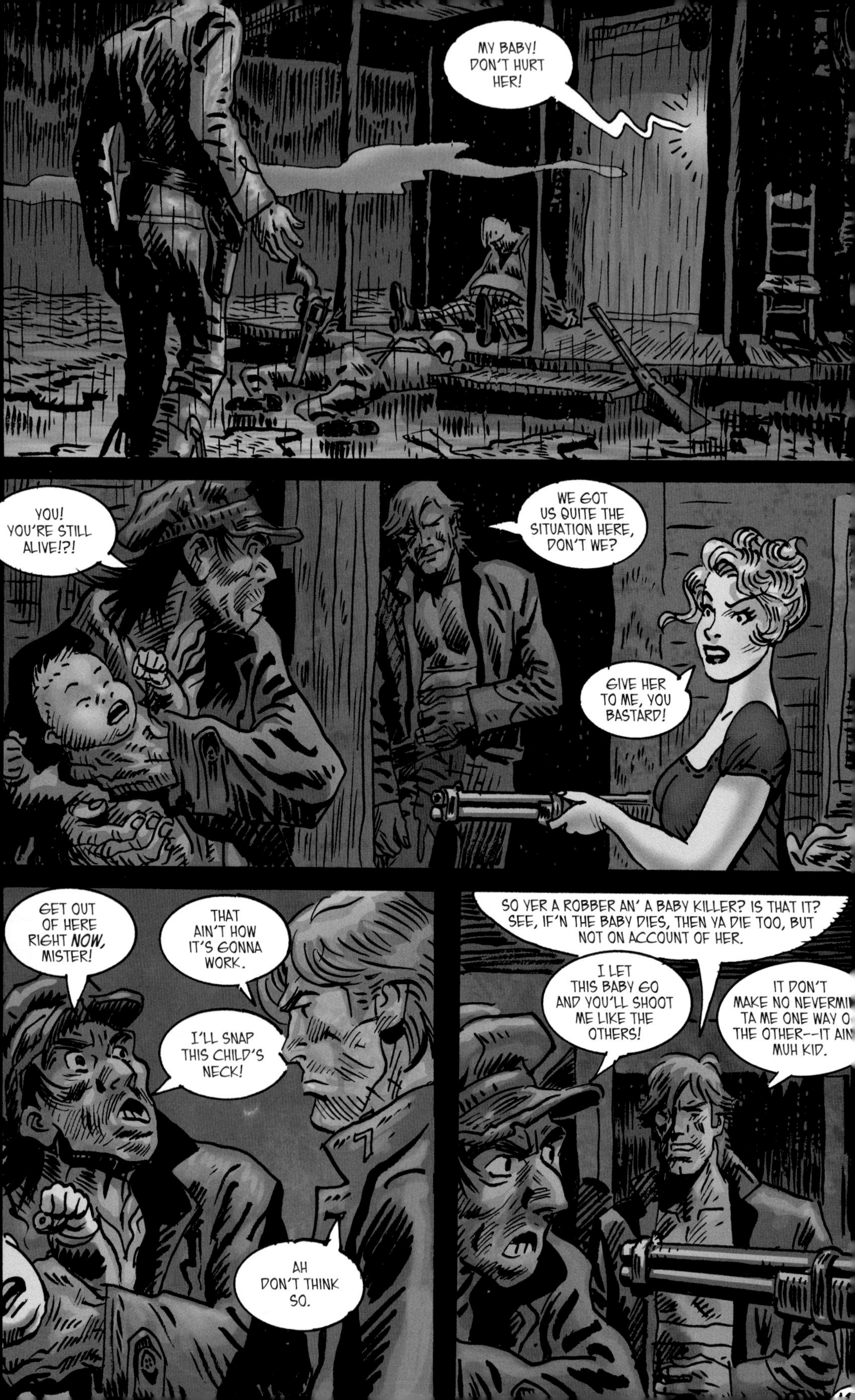
MY BABY! DON'T HURT HER!
YOU! YOU'RE STILL ALIVE!?!
WE GOT US QUITE THE SITUATION HERE, DON'T WE?
GIVE HER TO ME, YOU BASTARD!
GET OUT OF HERE RIGHT NOW, MISTER!
THAT AIN'T HOW IT'S GONNA WORK.
I'LL SNAP THIS CHILD'S NECK!
AH DON'T THINK SO.
SO YER A ROBBER AN' A BABY KILLER? IS THAT IT? SEE, IF'N THE BABY DIES, THEN YA DIE TOO, BUT NOT ON ACCOUNT OF HER.
I LET THIS BABY GO AND YOU'LL SHOOT ME LIKE THE OTHERS!
IT DON'T MAKE NO NEVERMI TA ME ONE WAY O THE OTHER--IT AIN MUH KID.

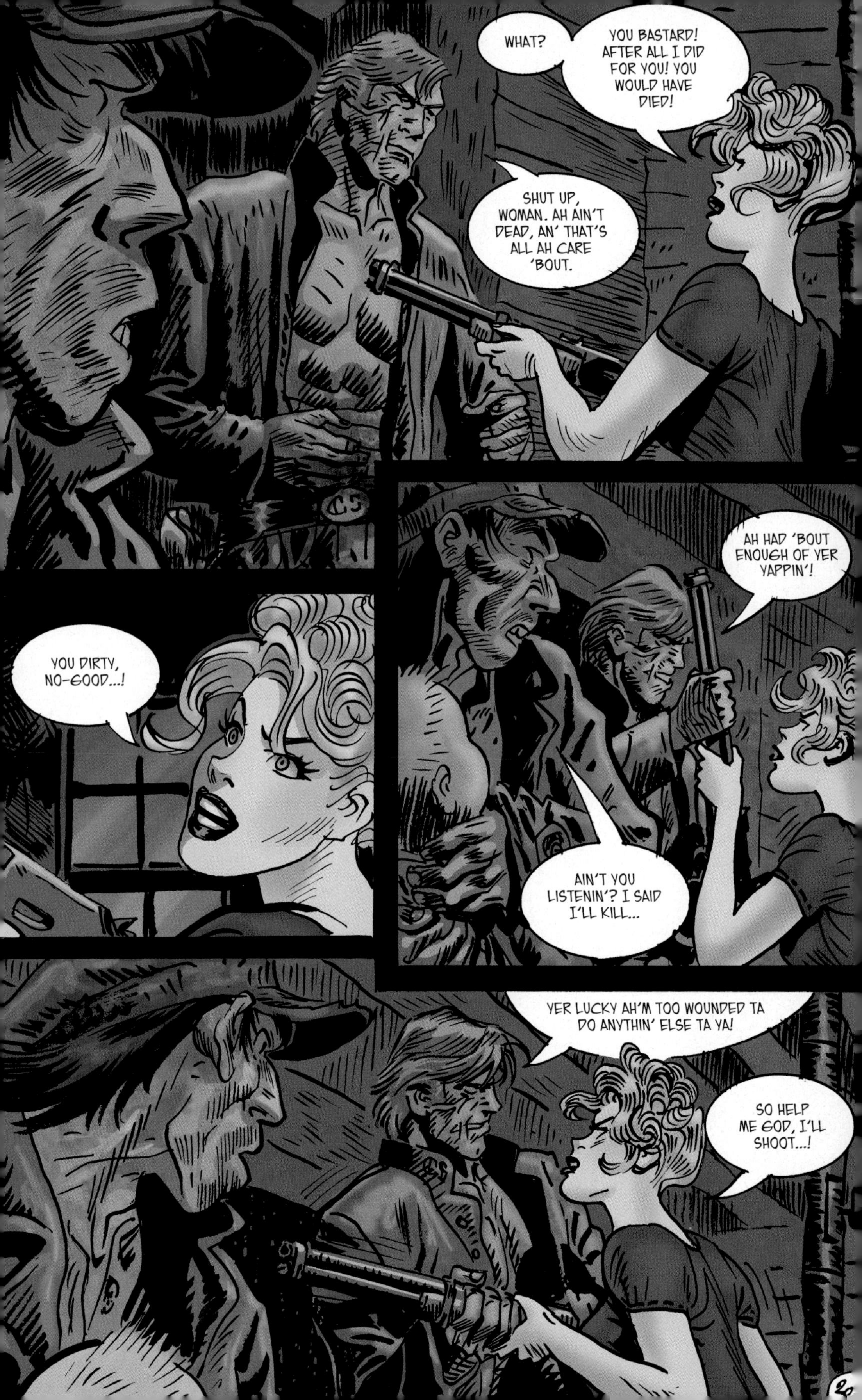
WHAT?
YOU BASTARD! AFTER ALL I DID FOR YOU! YOU WOULD HAVE DIED!
SHUT UP, WOMAN. AH AIN'T DEAD, AN' THAT'S ALL AH CARE 'BOUT.
YOU DIRTY, NO-GOOD...!
AH HAD 'BOUT ENOUGH OF YER YAPPIN'!
AIN'T YOU LISTENIN'? I SAID I'LL KILL...
YER LUCKY AH'M TOO WOUNDED TA DO ANYTHIN' ELSE TA YA!
SO HELP ME GOD, I'LL SHOOT...!

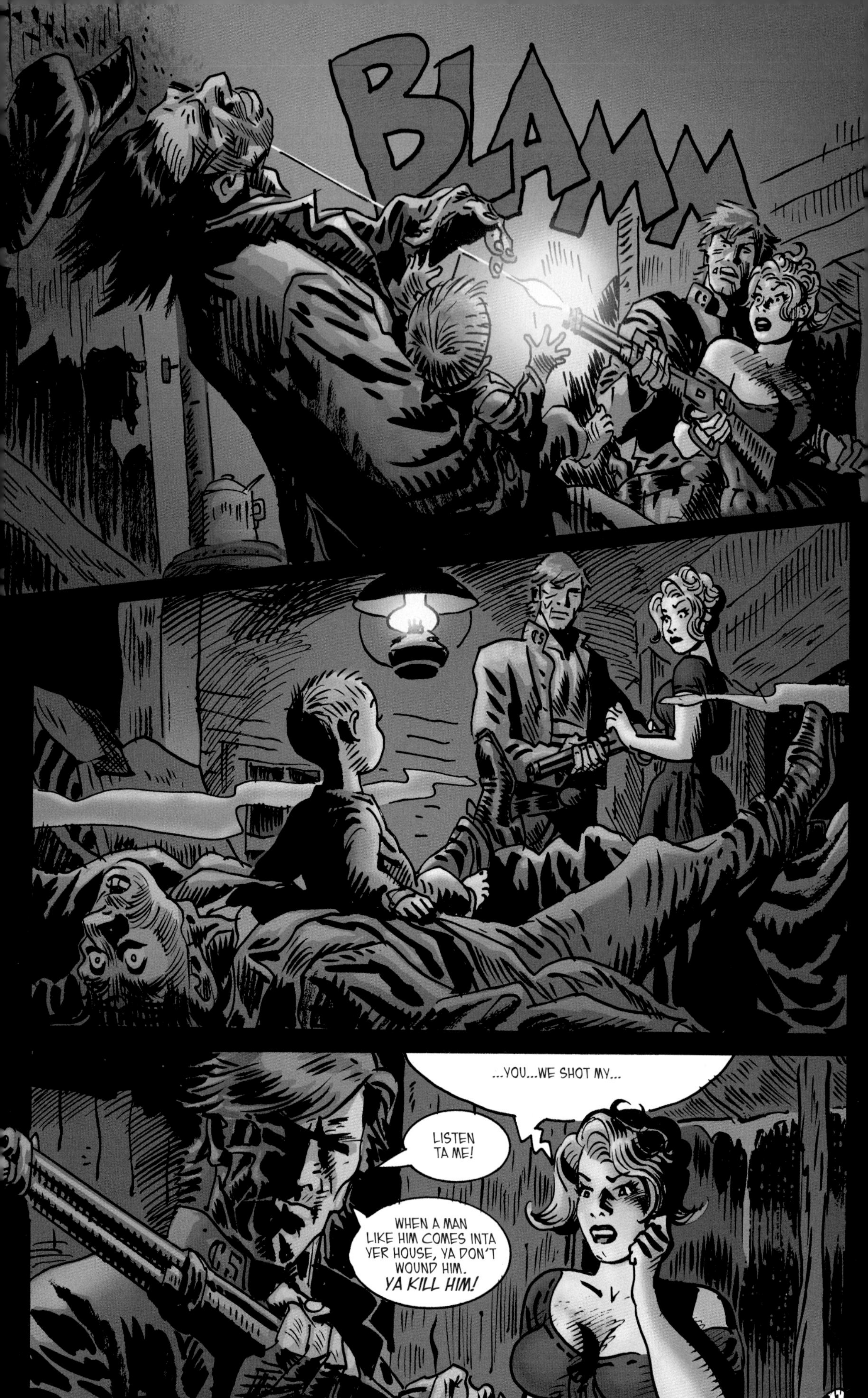
BLAMM
...YOU...WE SHOT MY...
LISTEN TA ME!
WHEN A MAN LIKE HIM COMES INTA YER HOUSE, YA DON'T WOUND HIM. YA KILL HIM!

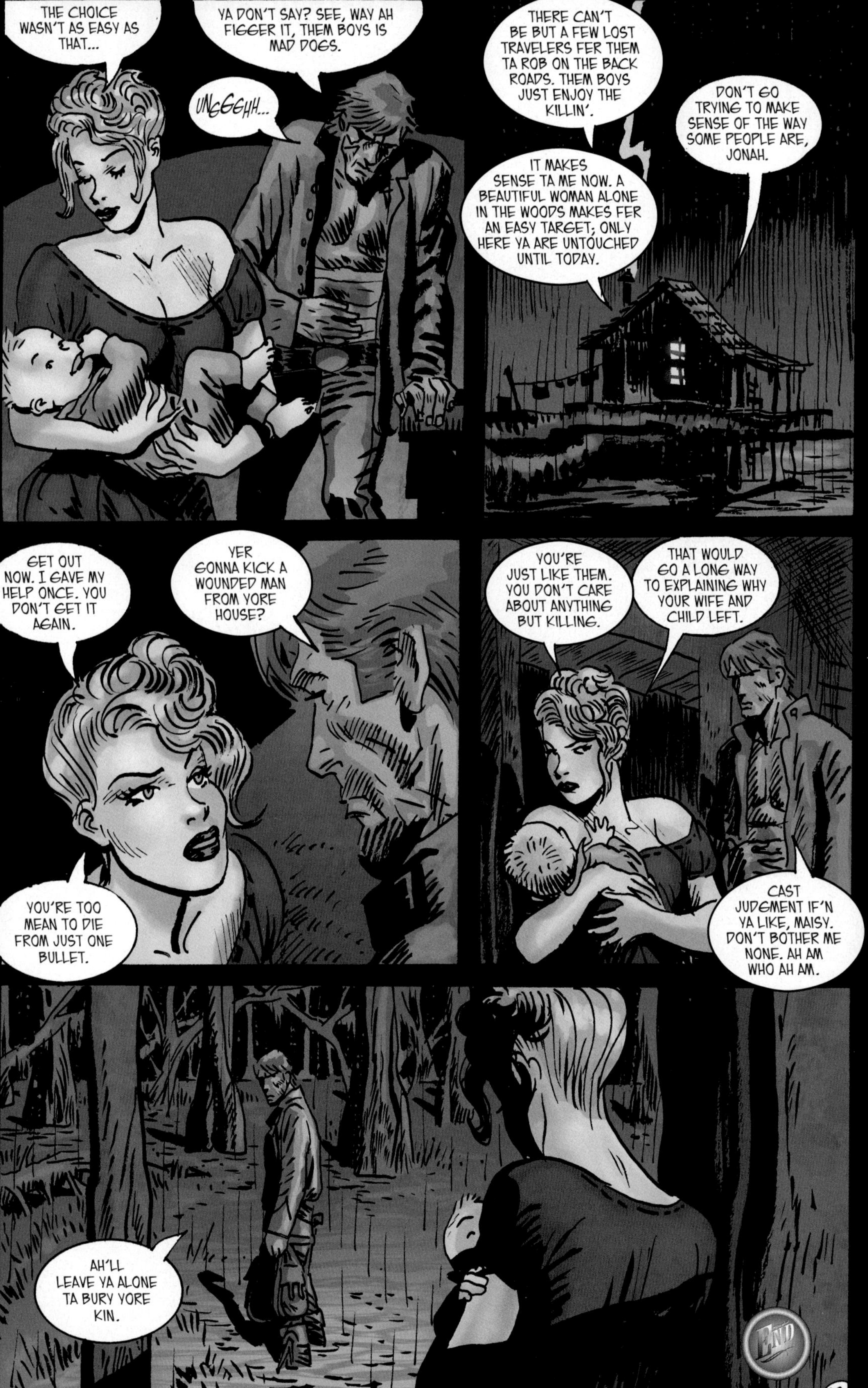
THE CHOICE WASN'T AS EASY AS THAT...
YA DON'T SAY? SEE, WAY AH FIGGER IT, THEM BOYS IS MAD DOGS.
UNGGGHH...
THERE CAN'T BE BUT A FEW LOST TRAVELERS FER THEM TA ROB ON THE BACK ROADS. THEM BOYS JUST ENJOY THE KILLIN'.
DON'T GO TRYING TO MAKE SENSE OF THE WAY SOME PEOPLE ARE, JONAH.
IT MAKES SENSE TA ME NOW. A BEAUTIFUL WOMAN ALONE IN THE WOODS MAKES FER AN EASY TARGET; ONLY HERE YA ARE UNTOUCHED UNTIL TODAY.
GET OUT NOW. I GAVE MY HELP ONCE. YOU DON'T GET IT AGAIN.
YER GONNA KICK A WOUNDED MAN FROM YORE HOUSE?
YOU'RE TOO MEAN TO DIE FROM JUST ONE BULLET.
YOU'RE JUST LIKE THEM. YOU DON'T CARE ABOUT ANYTHING BUT KILLING.
THAT WOULD GO A LONG WAY TO EXPLAINING WHY YOUR WIFE AND CHILD LEFT.
CAST JUDGMENT IF'N YA LIKE, MAISY. DON'T BOTHER ME NONE. AH AM WHO AH AM.
AH'LL LEAVE YA ALONE TA BURY YORE KIN.
END

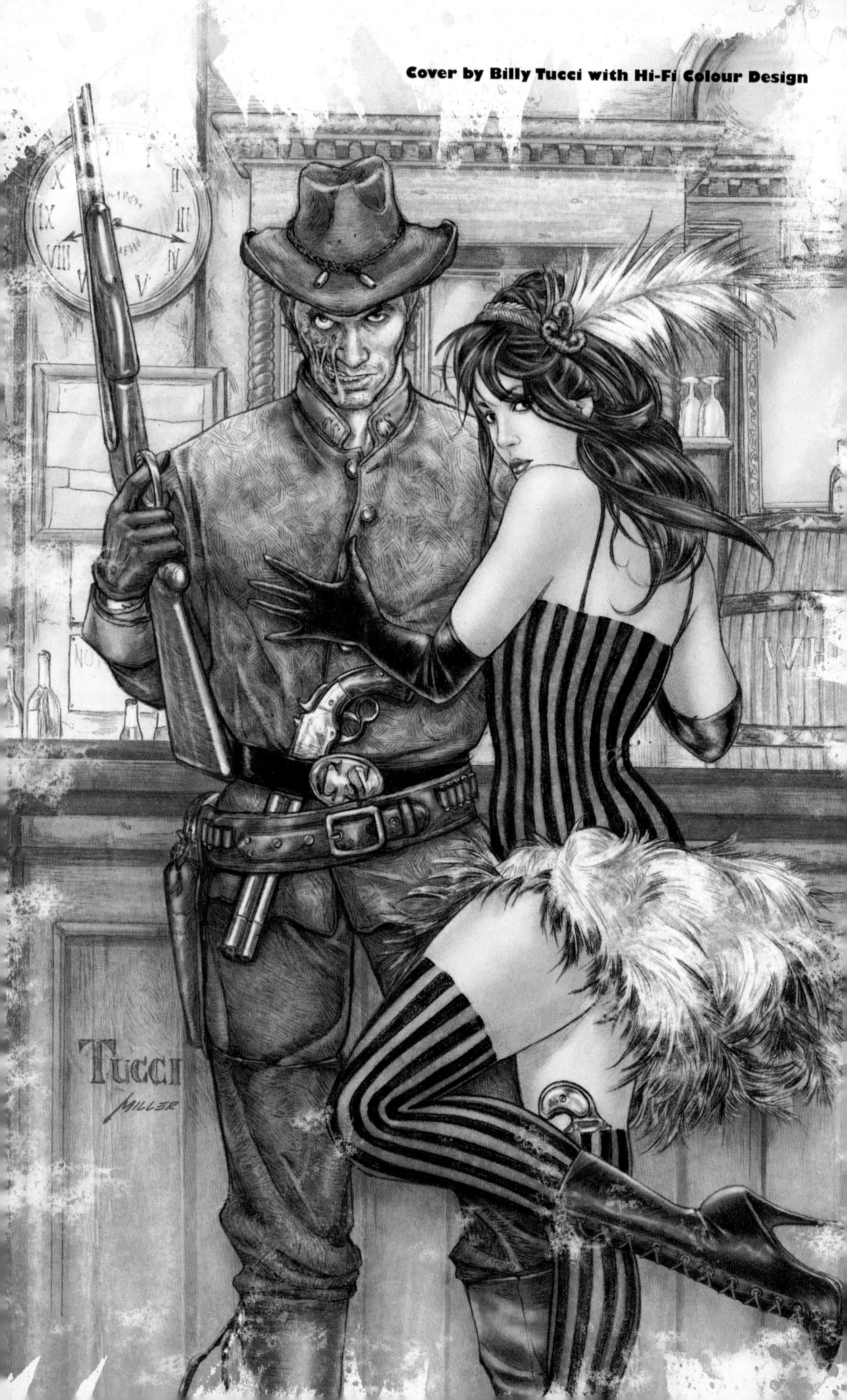
TUCCI
MILLER

Cover by Billy Tucci with Hi-Fi Colour Design

DANCE HALL GIRL

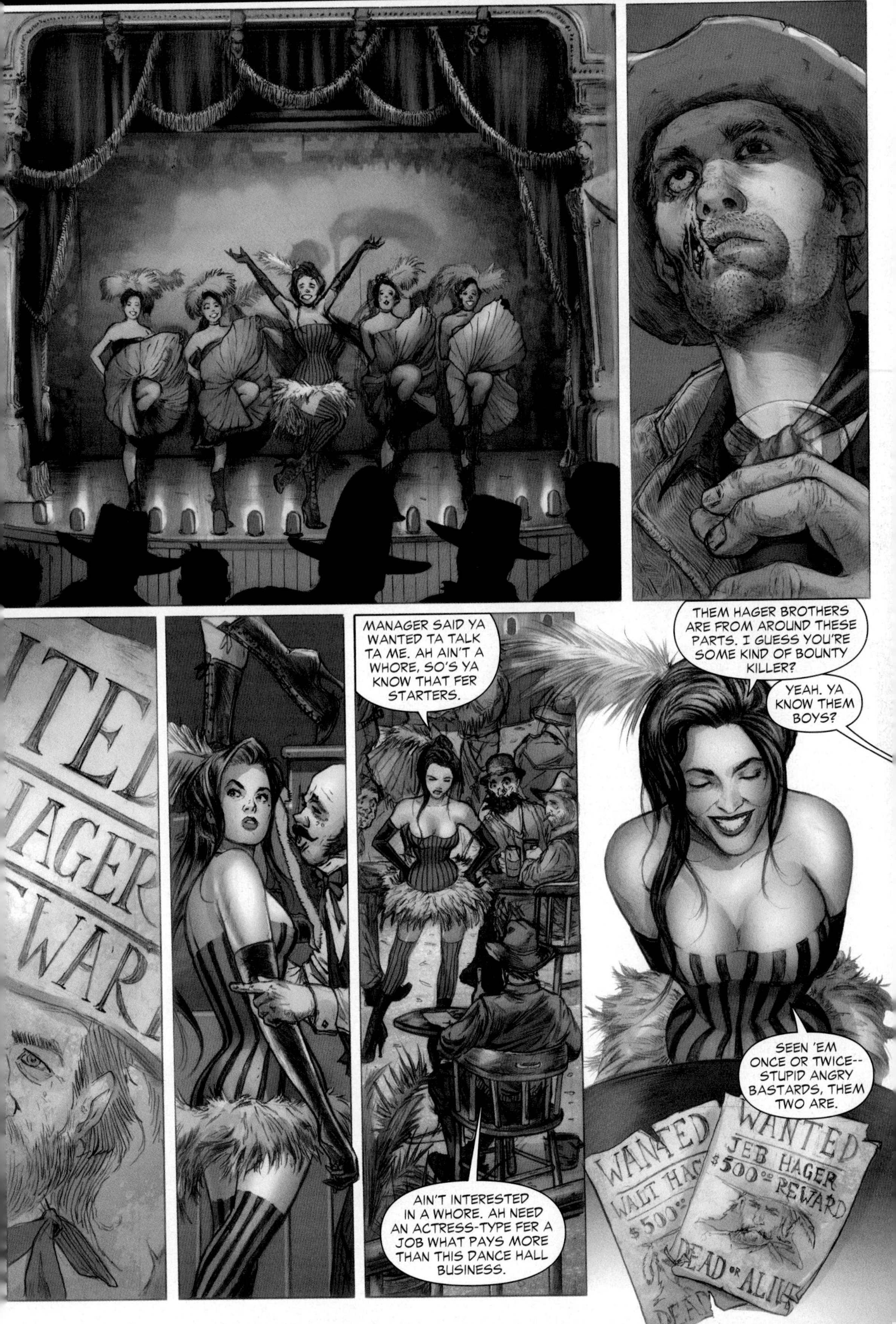

MANAGER SAID YA WANTED TA TALK TA ME. AH AIN'T A WHORE, SO'S YA KNOW THAT FER STARTERS.
AIN'T INTERESTED IN A WHORE. AH NEED AN ACTRESS-TYPE FER A JOB WHAT PAYS MORE THAN THIS DANCE HALL BUSINESS.
THEM HAGER BROTHERS ARE FROM AROUND THESE PARTS. I GUESS YOU'RE SOME KIND OF BOUNTY KILLER?
YEAH. YA KNOW THEM BOYS?
SEEN 'EM ONCE OR TWICE-- STUPID ANGRY BASTARDS, THEM TWO ARE.
WANTED
JEB HAGER
$500.00 REWARD
DEAD OR ALIVE

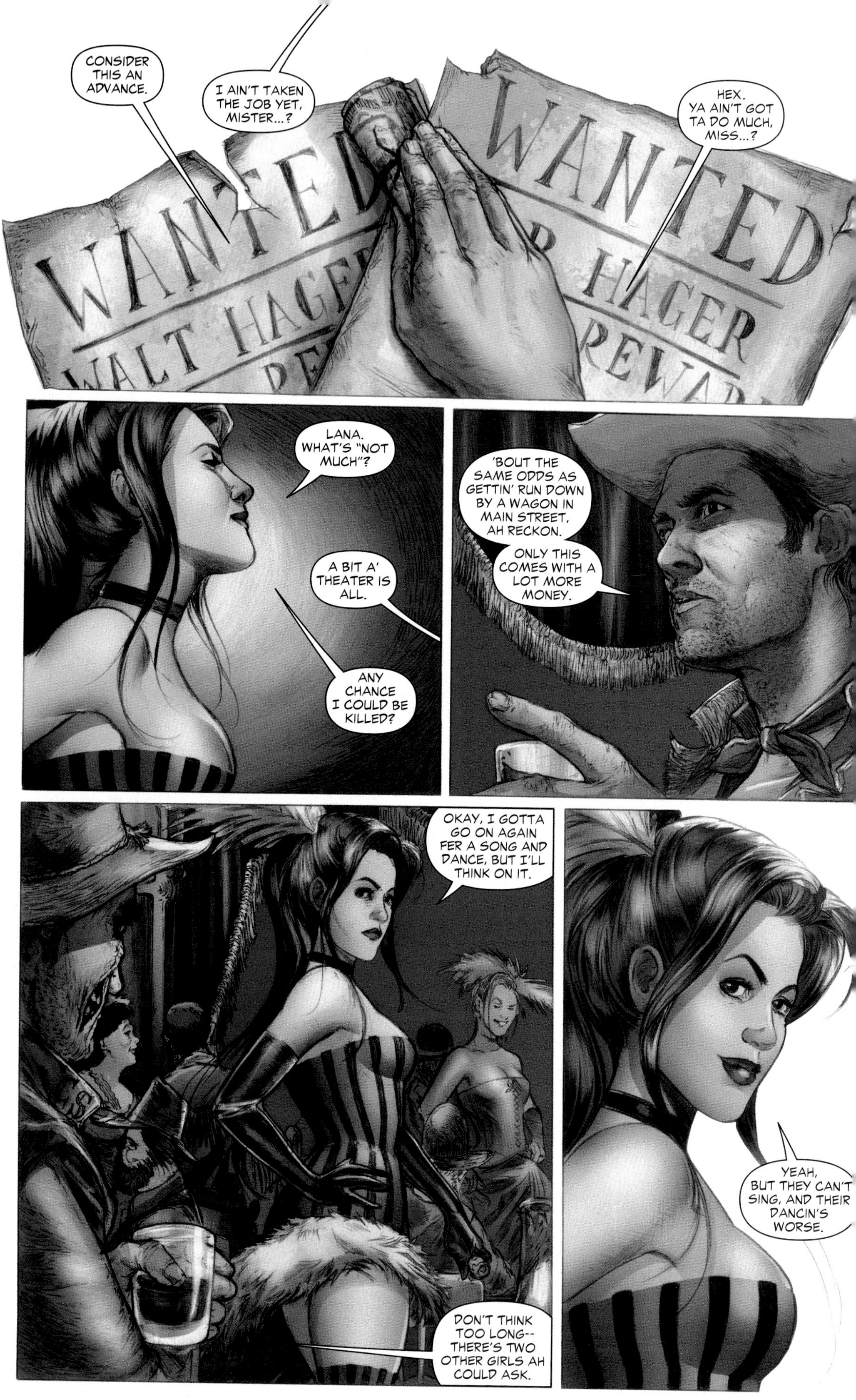
CONSIDER THIS AN ADVANCE.
I AIN'T TAKEN THE JOB YET, MISTER...?
HEX. YA AIN'T GOT TA DO MUCH, MISS...?
WANTED
WALT HAGER
WANTED
HAGER
LANA. WHAT'S "NOT MUCH"?
A BIT A' THEATER IS ALL.
ANY CHANCE I COULD BE KILLED?
'BOUT THE SAME ODDS AS GETTIN' RUN DOWN BY A WAGON IN MAIN STREET, AH RECKON.
ONLY THIS COMES WITH A LOT MORE MONEY.
OKAY, I GOTTA GO ON AGAIN FER A SONG AND DANCE, BUT I'LL THINK ON IT.
DON'T THINK TOO LONG-- THERE'S TWO OTHER GIRLS AH COULD ASK.
YEAH, BUT THEY CAN'T SING, AND THEIR DANCIN'S WORSE.

DAY OF THE BIG SHOW

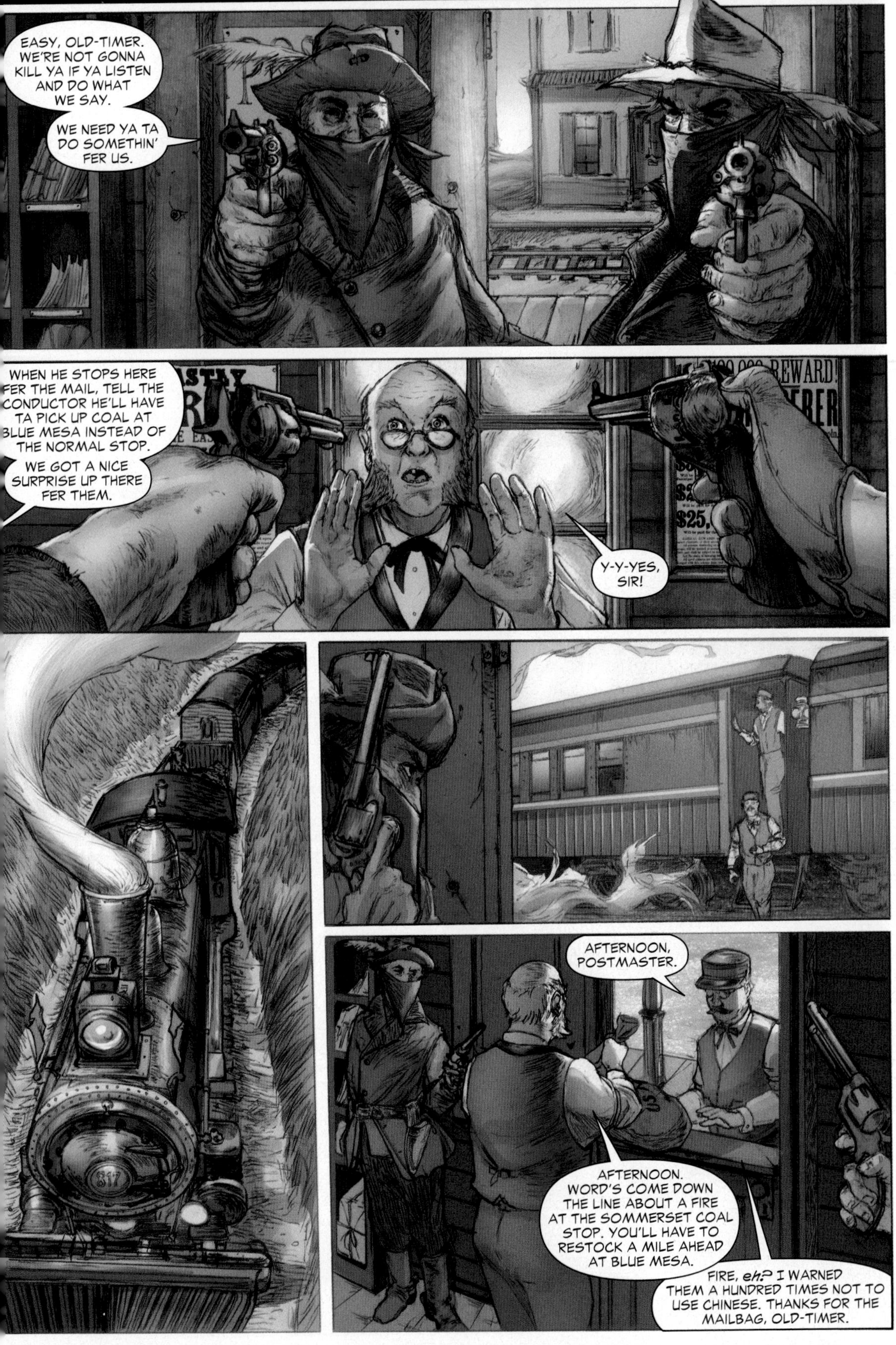
EASY, OLD-TIMER. WE'RE NOT GONNA KILL YA IF YA LISTEN AND DO WHAT WE SAY.
WE NEED YA TA DO SOMETHIN' FER US.
WHEN HE STOPS HERE FER THE MAIL, TELL THE CONDUCTOR HE'LL HAVE TA PICK UP COAL AT BLUE MESA INSTEAD OF THE NORMAL STOP.
WE GOT A NICE SURPRISE UP THERE FER THEM.
REWARD!
Y-Y-YES, SIR!
AFTERNOON, POSTMASTER.
AFTERNOON. WORD'S COME DOWN THE LINE ABOUT A FIRE AT THE SOMMERSET COAL STOP. YOU'LL HAVE TO RESTOCK A MILE AHEAD AT BLUE MESA.
FIRE, *eh?* I WARNED THEM A HUNDRED TIMES NOT TO USE CHINESE. THANKS FOR THE MAILBAG, OLD-TIMER.

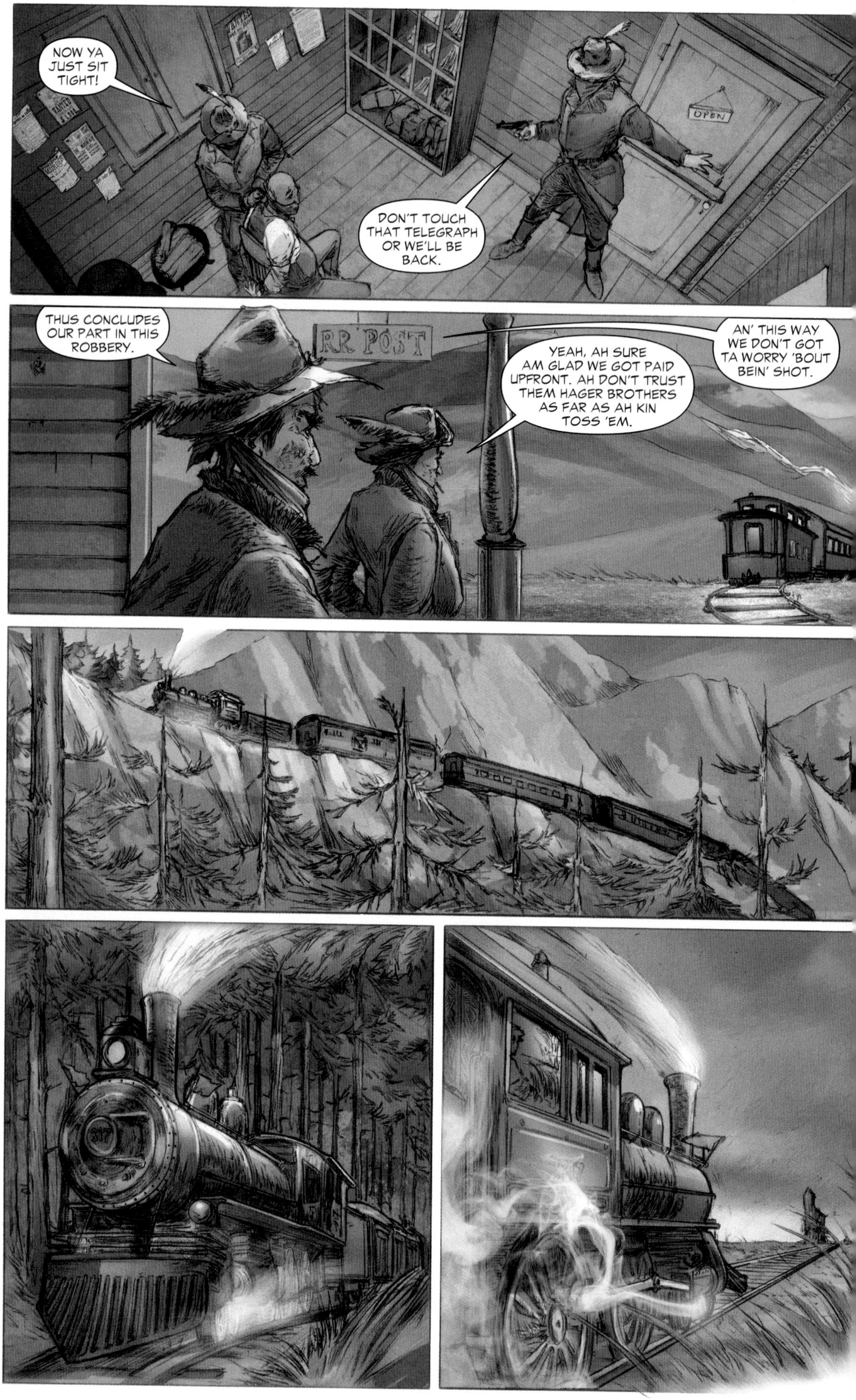
NOW YA JUST SIT TIGHT!
DON'T TOUCH THAT TELEGRAPH OR WE'LL BE BACK.
OPEN
RR POST
THUS CONCLUDES OUR PART IN THIS ROBBERY.
AN' THIS WAY WE DON'T GOT TA WORRY 'BOUT BEIN' SHOT.
YEAH, AH SURE AM GLAD WE GOT PAID UPFRONT. AH DON'T TRUST THEM HAGER BROTHERS AS FAR AS AH KIN TOSS 'EM.

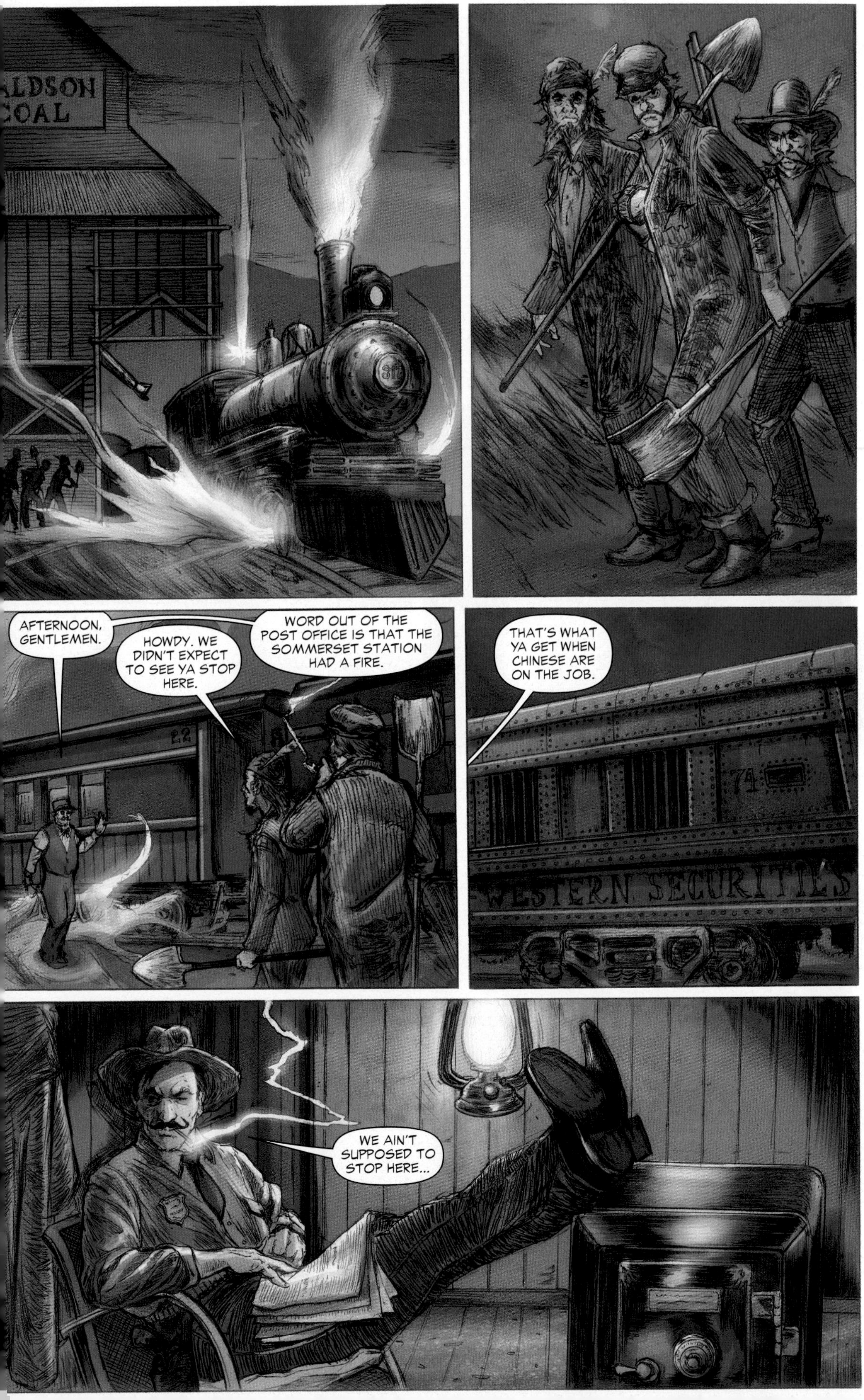

ALDSON
COAL
AFTERNOON, GENTLEMEN.
HOWDY. WE DIDN'T EXPECT TO SEE YA STOP HERE.
WORD OUT OF THE POST OFFICE IS THAT THE SOMMERSET STATION HAD A FIRE.
THAT'S WHAT YA GET WHEN CHINESE ARE ON THE JOB.
WESTERN SECURITIES
WE AIN'T SUPPOSED TO STOP HERE...

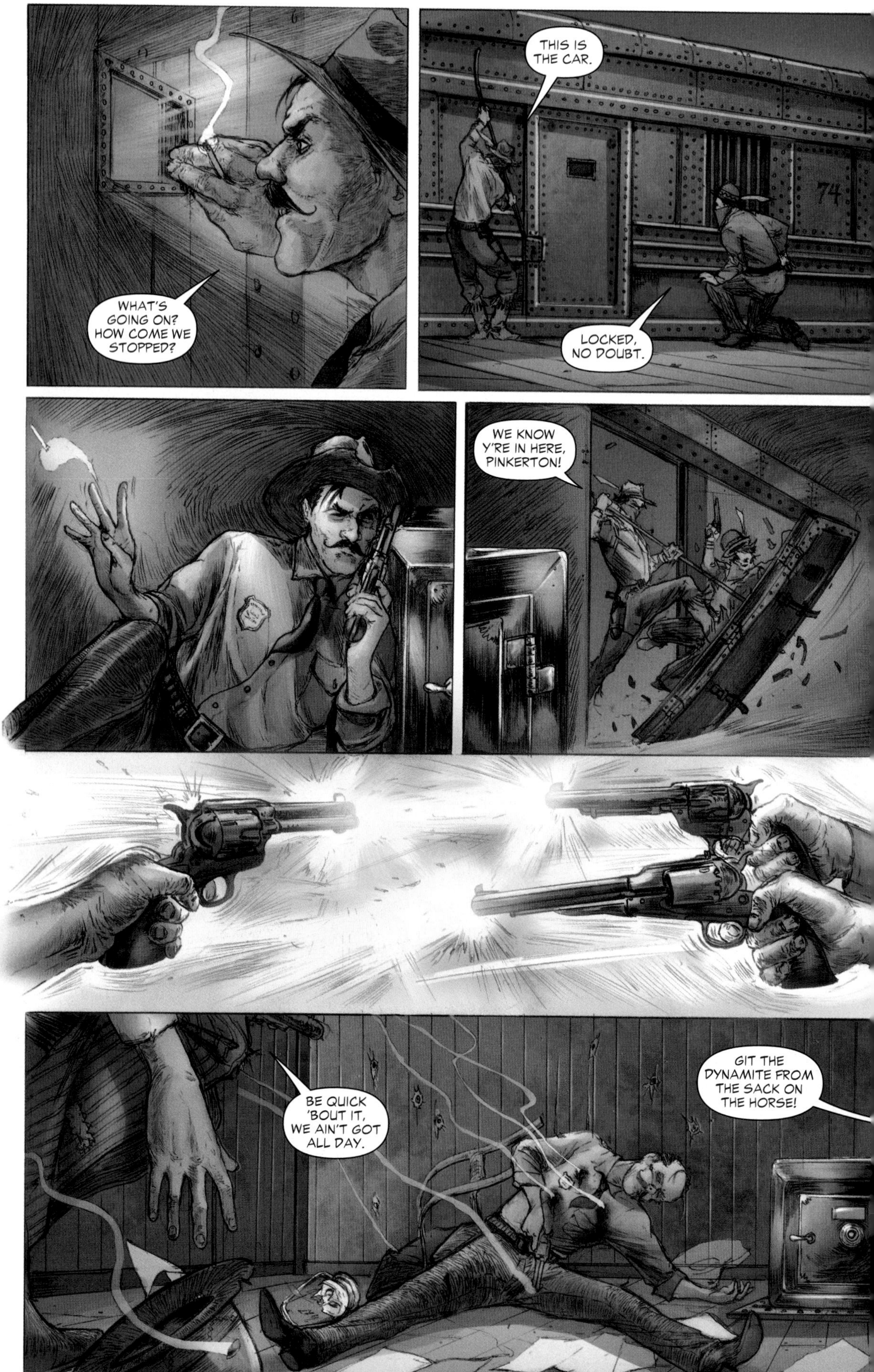
WHAT'S GOING ON? HOW COME WE STOPPED?
THIS IS THE CAR.
LOCKED, NO DOUBT.
WE KNOW Y'RE IN HERE, PINKERTON!
BE QUICK 'BOUT IT, WE AIN'T GOT ALL DAY.
GIT THE DYNAMITE FROM THE SACK ON THE HORSE!

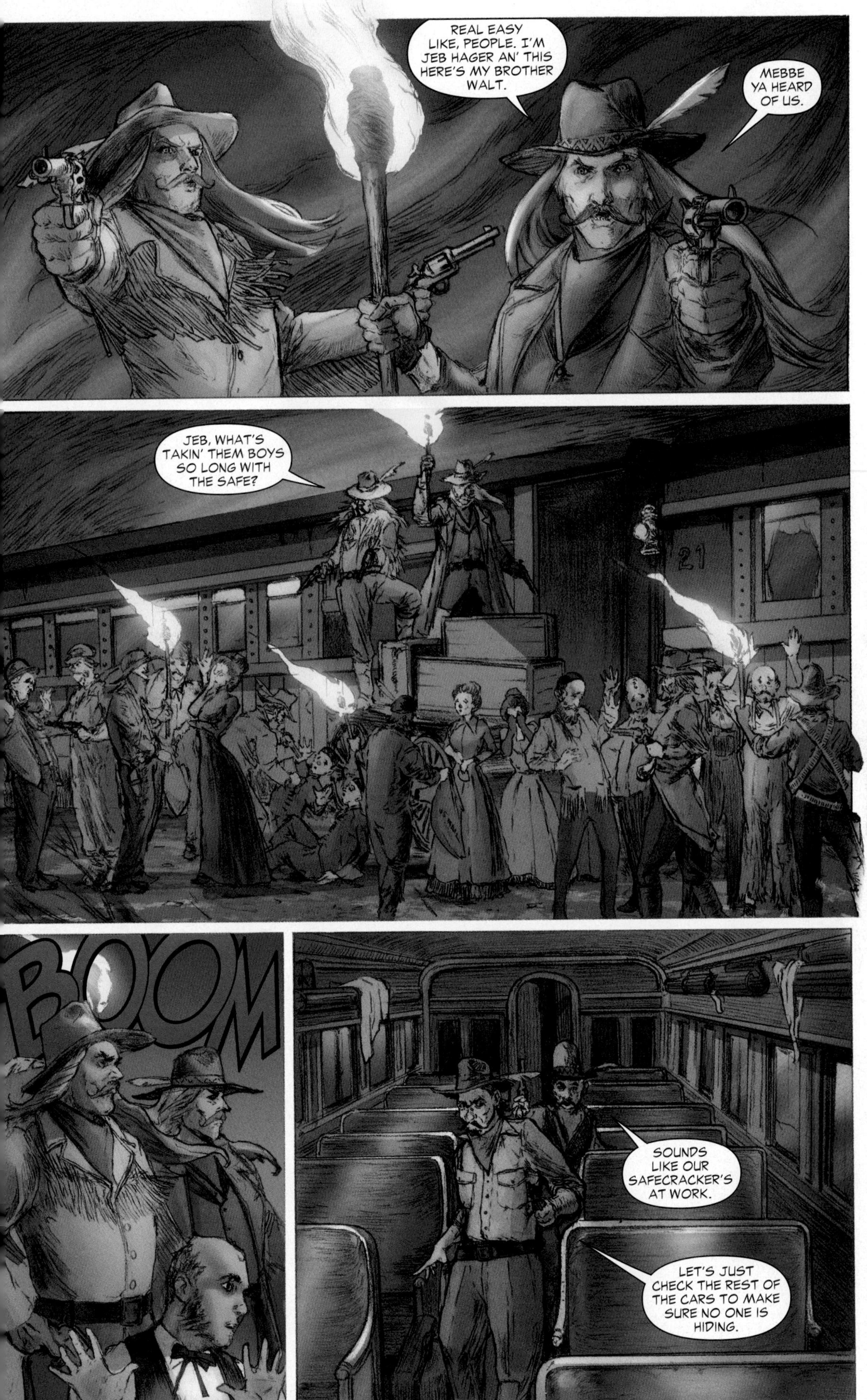
REAL EASY LIKE, PEOPLE. I'M JEB HAGER AN' THIS HERE'S MY BROTHER WALT.
MEBBE YA HEARD OF US.
JEB, WHAT'S TAKIN' THEM BOYS SO LONG WITH THE SAFE?
21
BOOM
SOUNDS LIKE OUR SAFECRACKER'S AT WORK.
LET'S JUST CHECK THE REST OF THE CARS TO MAKE SURE NO ONE IS HIDING.

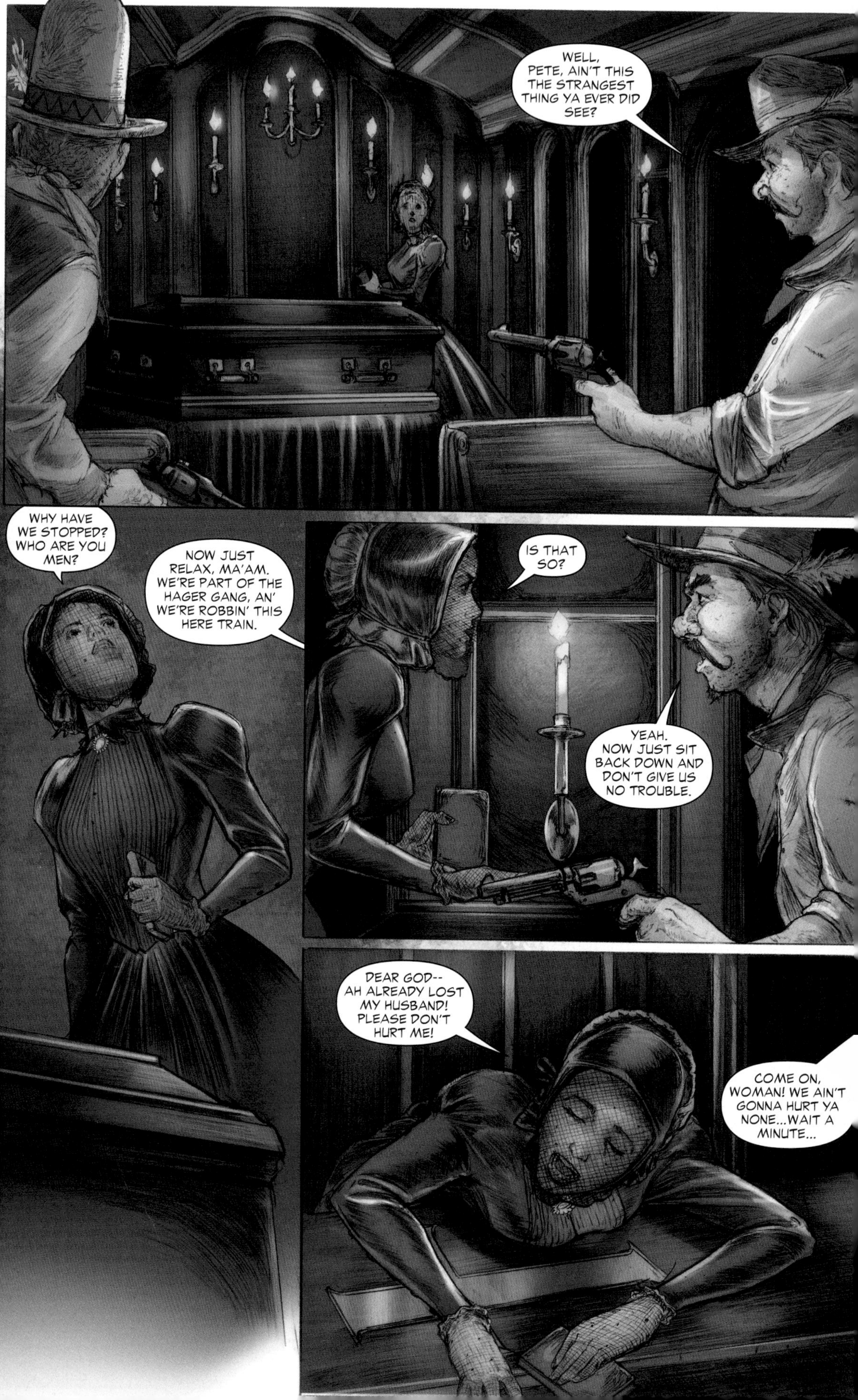
WELL, PETE, AIN'T THIS THE STRANGEST THING YA EVER DID SEE?
WHY HAVE WE STOPPED? WHO ARE YOU MEN?
NOW JUST RELAX, MA'AM. WE'RE PART OF THE HAGER GANG, AN' WE'RE ROBBIN' THIS HERE TRAIN.
IS THAT SO?
YEAH. NOW JUST SIT BACK DOWN AND DON'T GIVE US NO TROUBLE.
DEAR GOD-- AH ALREADY LOST MY HUSBAND! PLEASE DON'T HURT ME!
COME ON, WOMAN! WE AIN'T GONNA HURT YA NONE...WAIT A MINUTE...

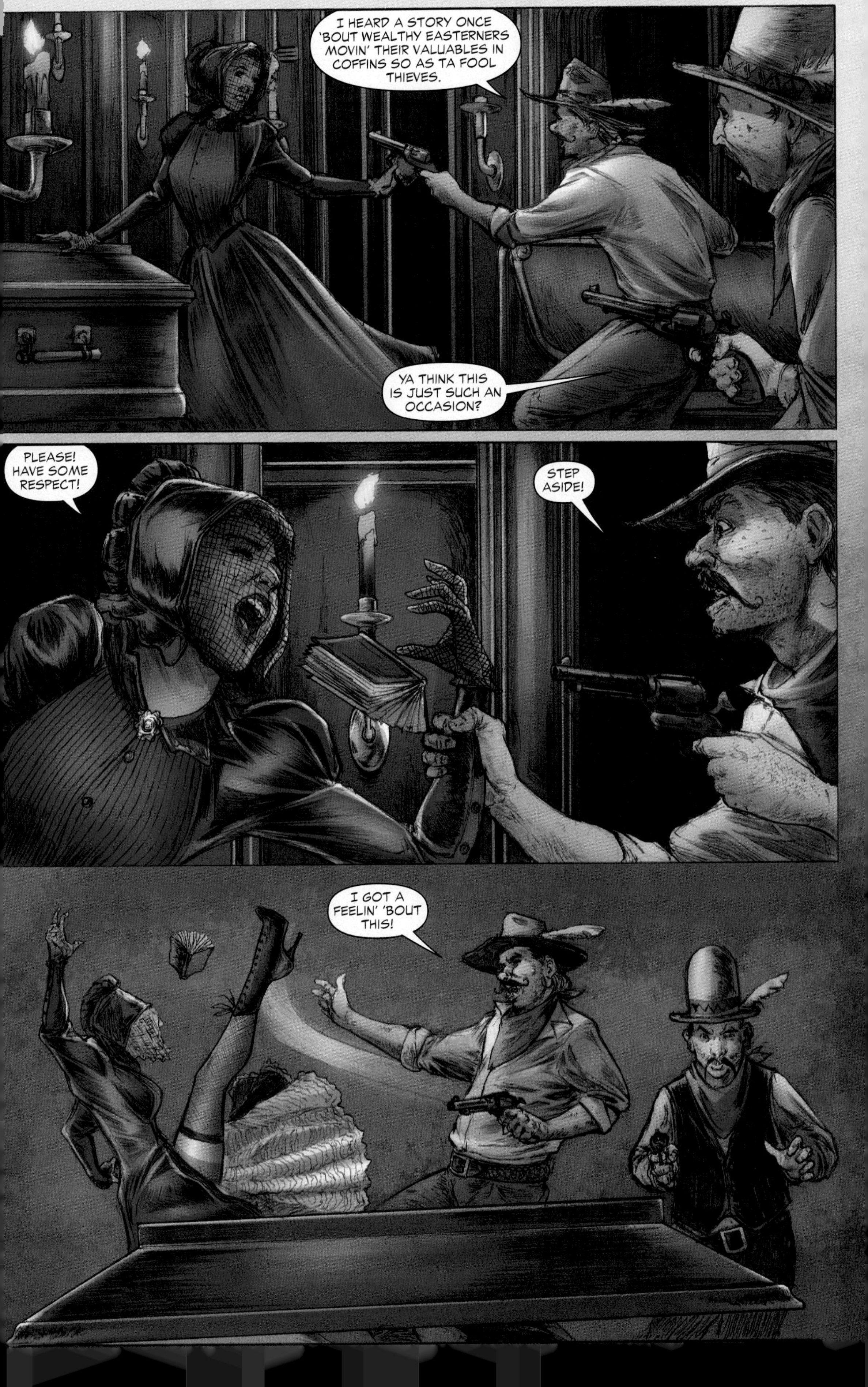
I HEARD A STORY ONCE 'BOUT WEALTHY EASTERNERS MOVIN' THEIR VALUABLES IN COFFINS SO AS TA FOOL THIEVES.
YA THINK THIS IS JUST SUCH AN OCCASION?
PLEASE! HAVE SOME RESPECT!
STEP ASIDE!
I GOT A FEELIN' 'BOUT THIS!

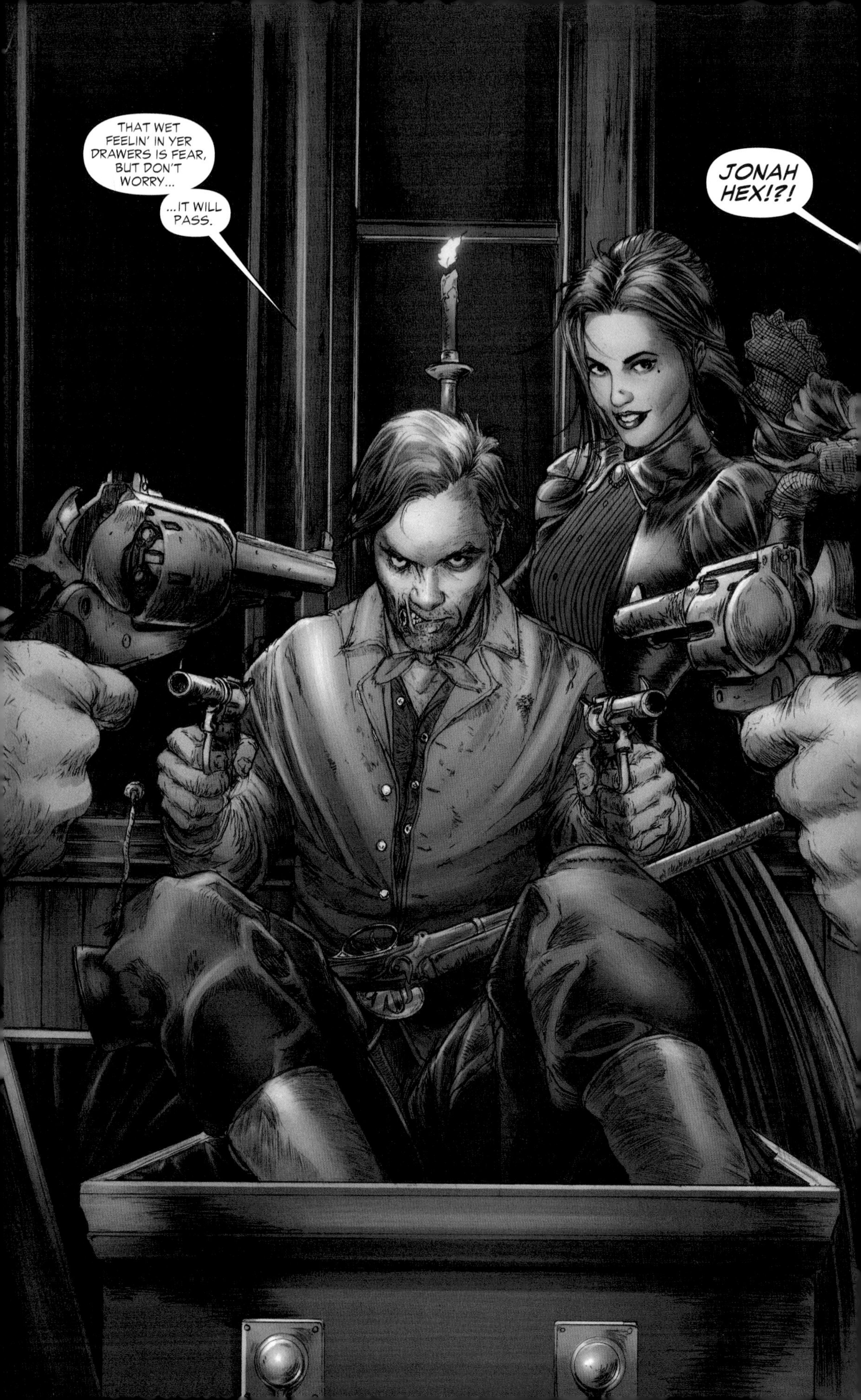
THAT WET FEELIN' IN YER DRAWERS IS FEAR, BUT DON'T WORRY...
...IT WILL PASS.
JONAH HEX!?!

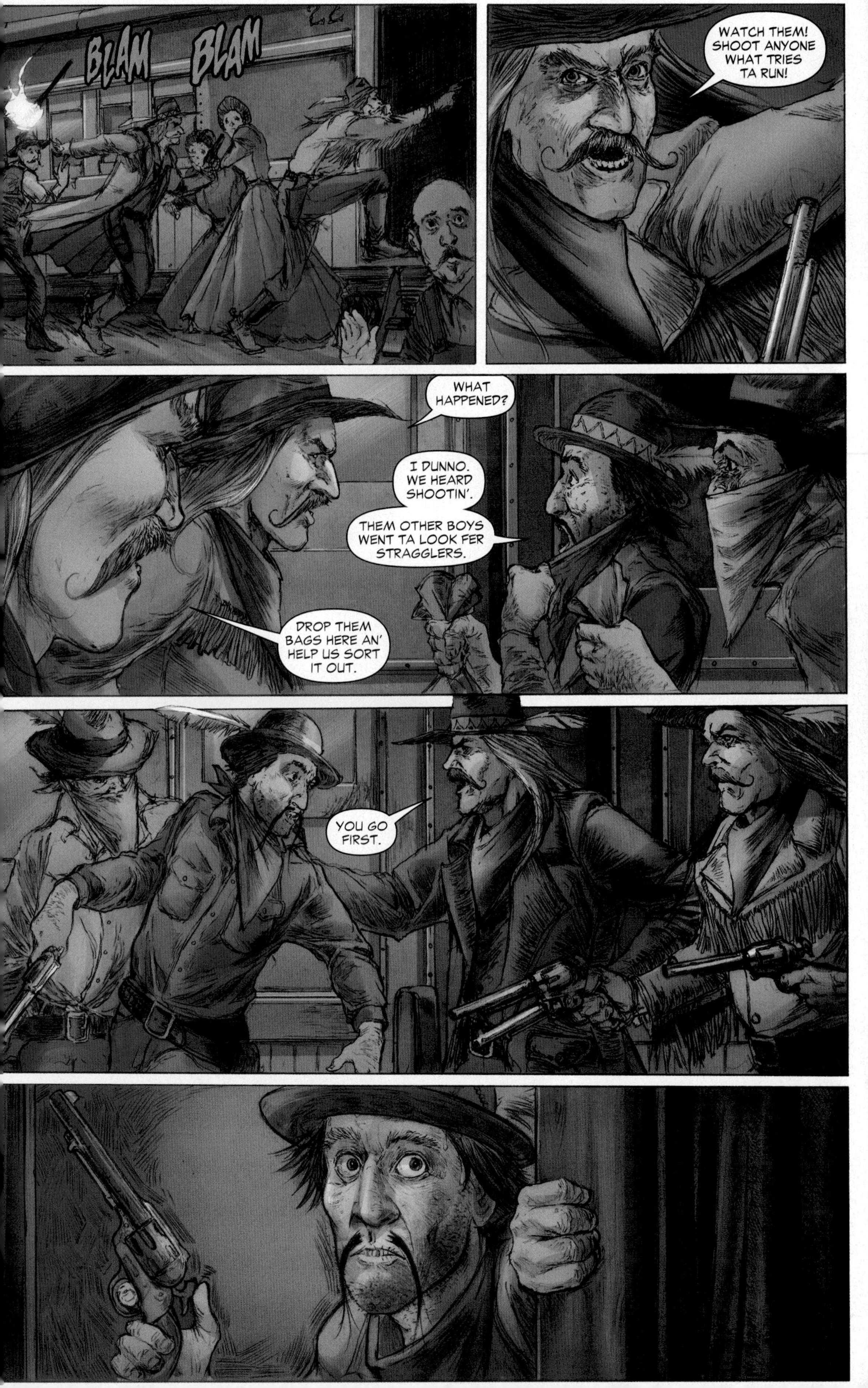
BLAM
BLAM
WATCH THEM! SHOOT ANYONE WHAT TRIES TA RUN!
WHAT HAPPENED?
I DUNNO. WE HEARD SHOOTIN'.
THEM OTHER BOYS WENT TA LOOK FER STRAGGLERS.
DROP THEM BAGS HERE AN' HELP US SORT IT OUT.
YOU GO FIRST.

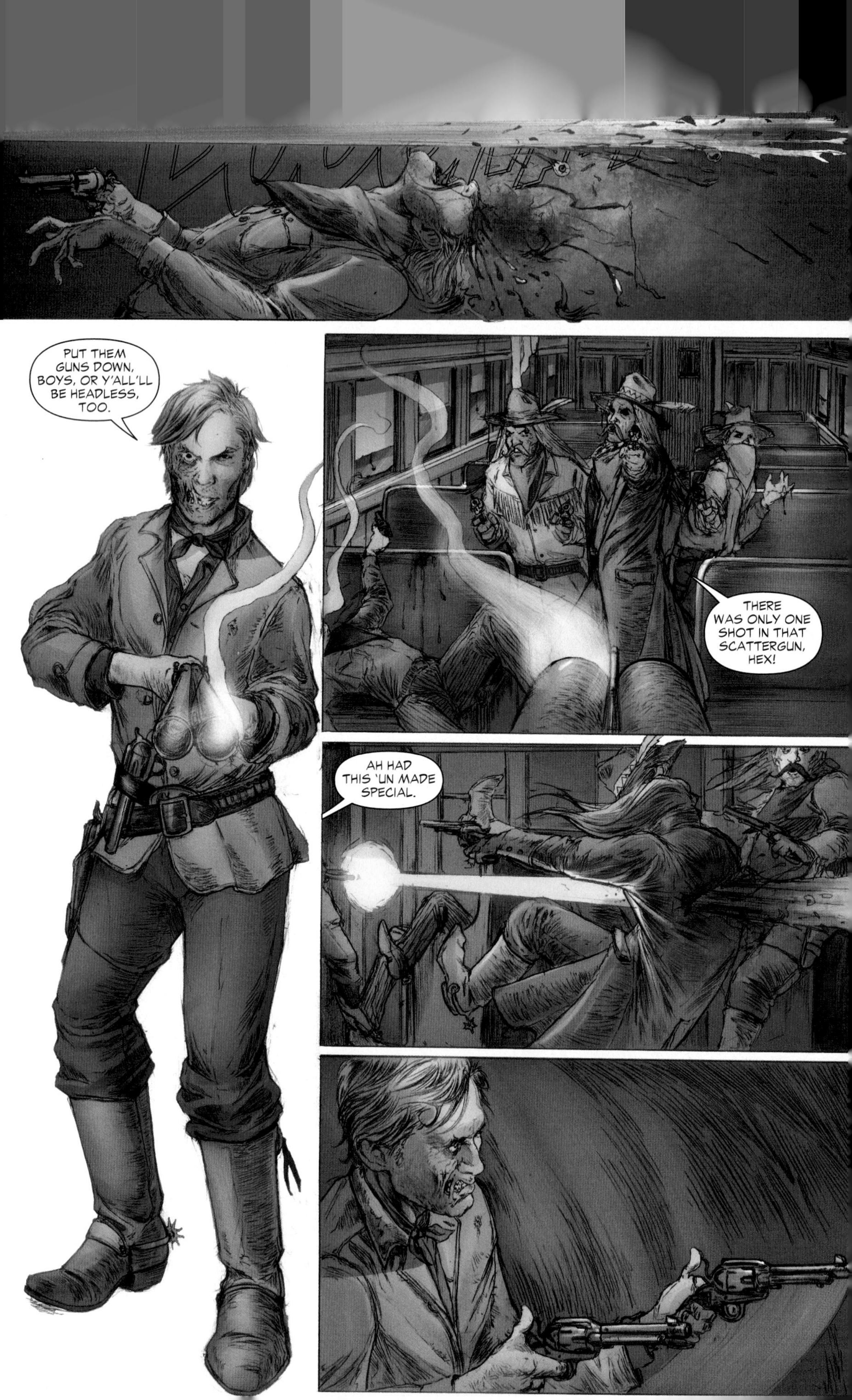
PUT THEM GUNS DOWN, BOYS, OR Y'ALL'LL BE HEADLESS, TOO.
THERE WAS ONLY ONE SHOT IN THAT SCATTERGUN, HEX!
AH HAD THIS 'UN MADE SPECIAL.

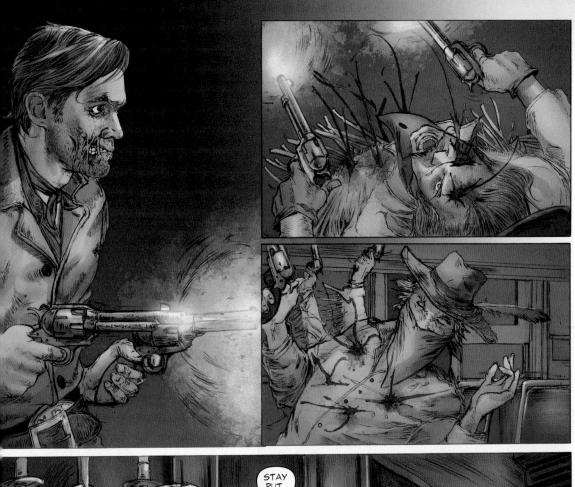

STAY PUT.

YES, SIR.

GET DOWN ON THE GROUND!

JEB? WALT? WHAT'S GOIN' ON?

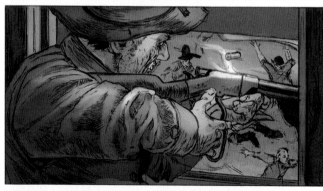

I'LL SHOOT HER IN TH--

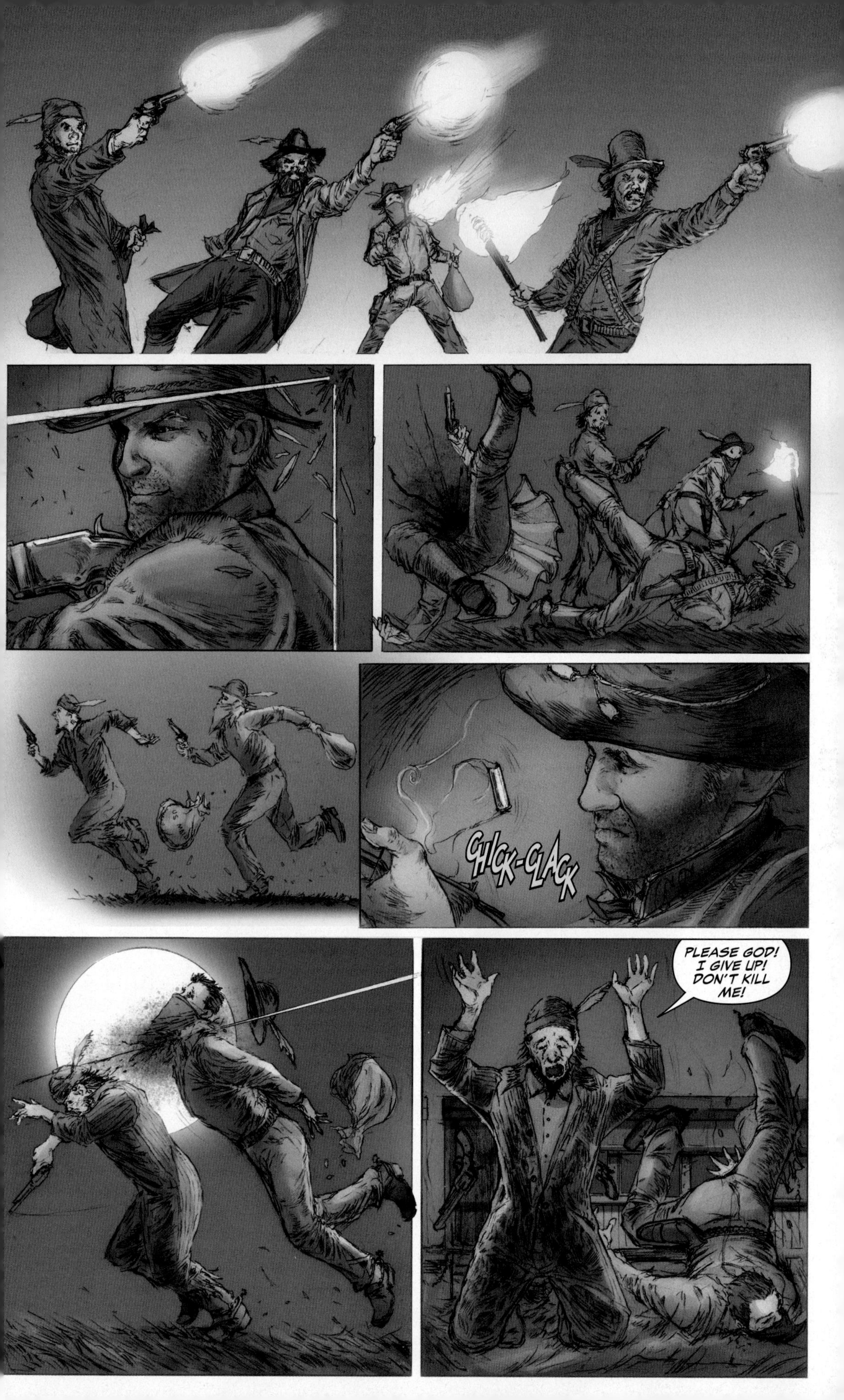
CHICK-CLACK
PLEASE GOD! I GIVE UP! DON'T KILL ME!

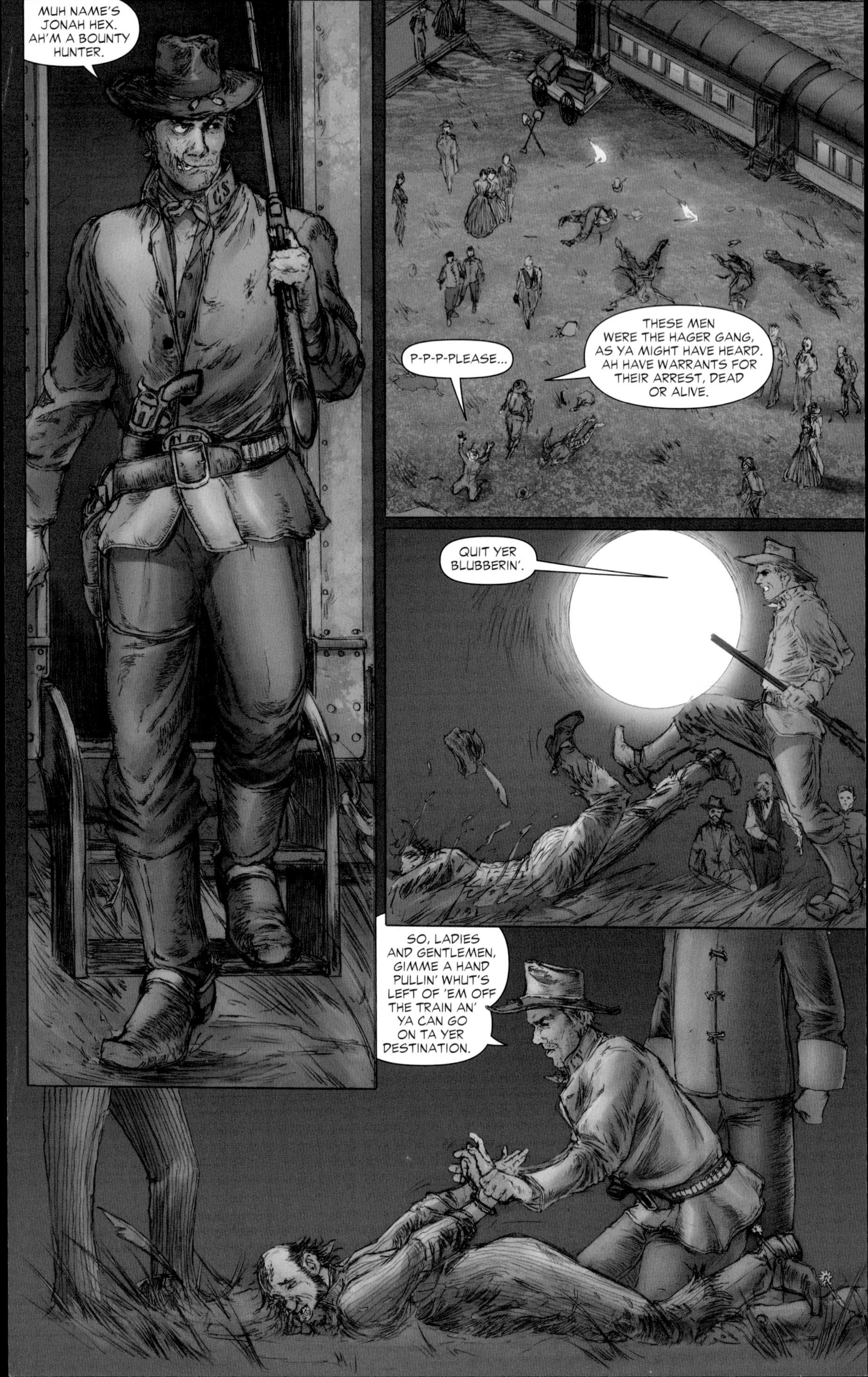
MUH NAME'S JONAH HEX. AH'M A BOUNTY HUNTER.
P-P-P-PLEASE...
THESE MEN WERE THE HAGER GANG, AS YA MIGHT HAVE HEARD. AH HAVE WARRANTS FOR THEIR ARREST, DEAD OR ALIVE.
QUIT YER BLUBBERIN'.
SO, LADIES AND GENTLEMEN, GIMME A HAND PULLIN' WHUT'S LEFT OF 'EM OFF THE TRAIN AN' YA CAN GO ON TA YER DESTINATION.

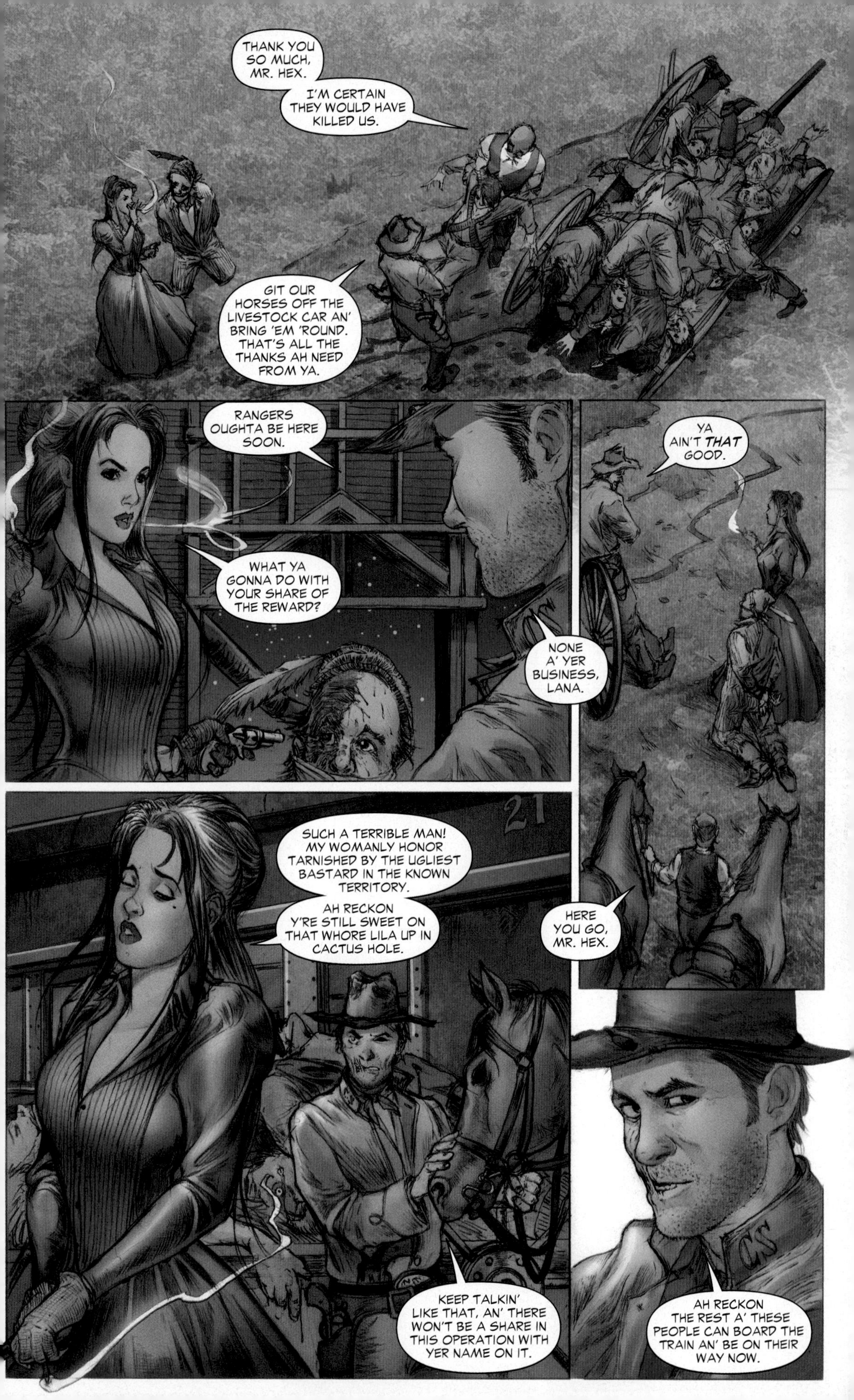
THANK YOU SO MUCH, MR. HEX.
I'M CERTAIN THEY WOULD HAVE KILLED US.
GIT OUR HORSES OFF THE LIVESTOCK CAR AN' BRING 'EM 'ROUND. THAT'S ALL THE THANKS AH NEED FROM YA.
RANGERS OUGHTA BE HERE SOON.
WHAT YA GONNA DO WITH YOUR SHARE OF THE REWARD?
NONE A' YER BUSINESS, LANA.
YA AIN'T *THAT* GOOD.
HERE YOU GO, MR. HEX.
SUCH A TERRIBLE MAN! MY WOMANLY HONOR TARNISHED BY THE UGLIEST BASTARD IN THE KNOWN TERRITORY.
AH RECKON Y'RE STILL SWEET ON THAT WHORE LILA UP IN CACTUS HOLE.
KEEP TALKIN' LIKE THAT, AN' THERE WON'T BE A SHARE IN THIS OPERATION WITH YER NAME ON IT.
AH RECKON THE REST A' THESE PEOPLE CAN BOARD THE TRAIN AN' BE ON THEIR WAY NOW.

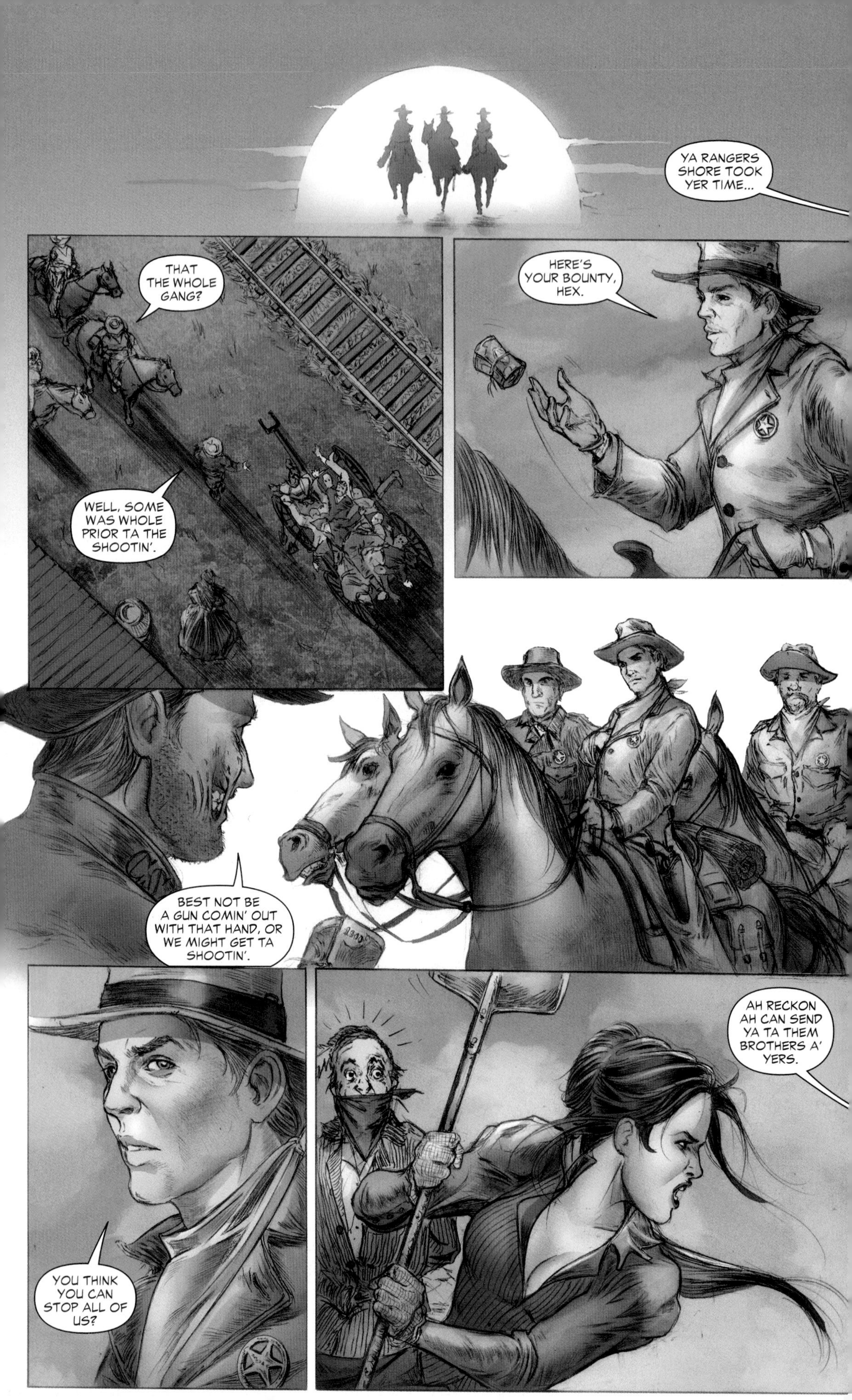
YA RANGERS SHORE TOOK YER TIME...
THAT THE WHOLE GANG?
WELL, SOME WAS WHOLE PRIOR TA THE SHOOTIN'.
HERE'S YOUR BOUNTY, HEX.
BEST NOT BE A GUN COMIN' OUT WITH THAT HAND, OR WE MIGHT GET TA SHOOTIN'.
YOU THINK YOU CAN STOP ALL OF US?
AH RECKON AH CAN SEND YA TA THEM BROTHERS A' YERS.

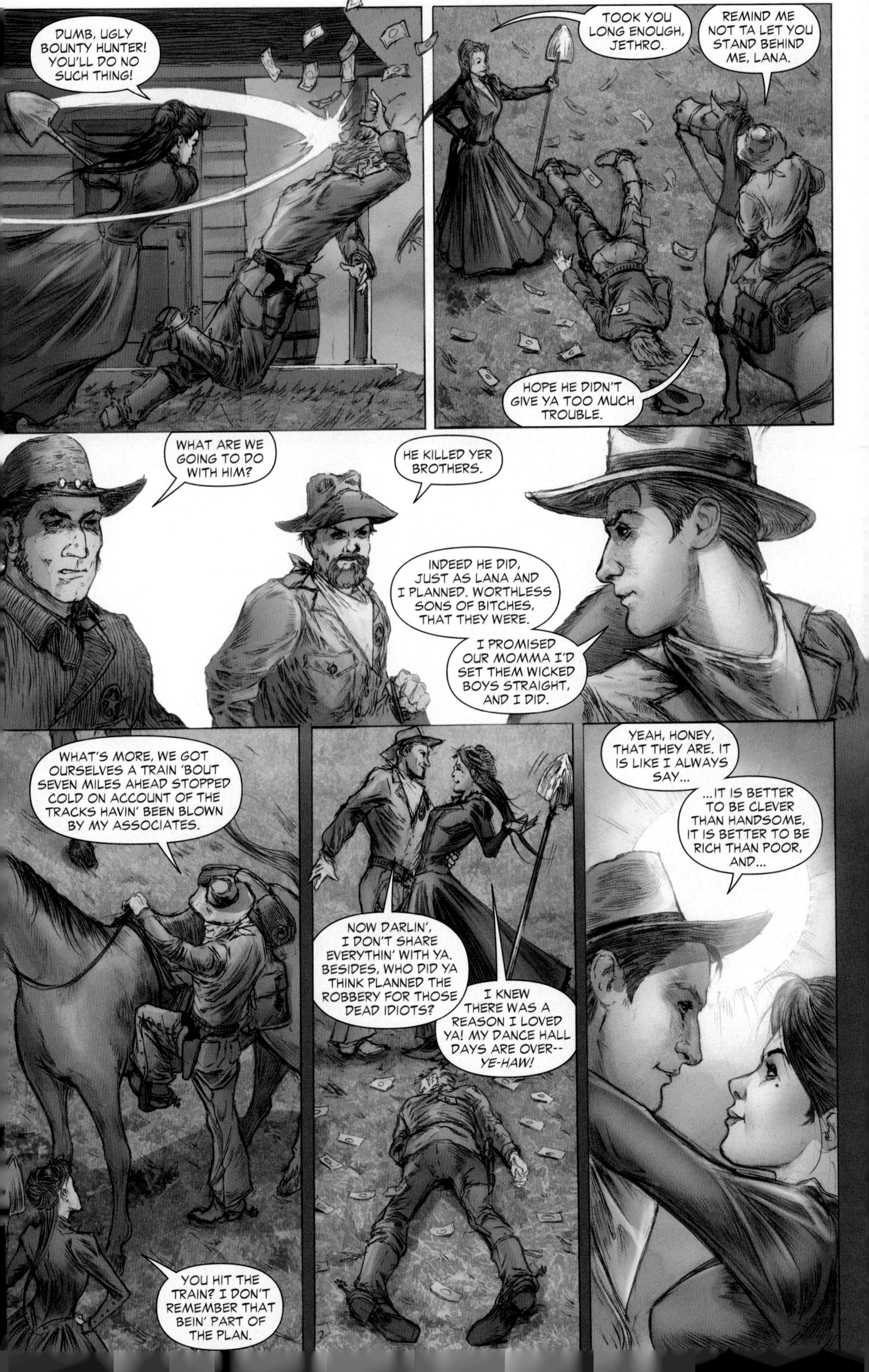
DUMB, UGLY BOUNTY HUNTER! YOU'LL DO NO SUCH THING!
TOOK YOU LONG ENOUGH, JETHRO.
REMIND ME NOT TA LET YOU STAND BEHIND ME, LANA.
HOPE HE DIDN'T GIVE YA TOO MUCH TROUBLE.
WHAT ARE WE GOING TO DO WITH HIM?
HE KILLED YER BROTHERS.
INDEED HE DID, JUST AS LANA AND I PLANNED. WORTHLESS SONS OF BITCHES, THAT THEY WERE.
I PROMISED OUR MOMMA I'D SET THEM WICKED BOYS STRAIGHT, AND I DID.
WHAT'S MORE, WE GOT OURSELVES A TRAIN 'BOUT SEVEN MILES AHEAD STOPPED COLD ON ACCOUNT OF THE TRACKS HAVIN' BEEN BLOWN BY MY ASSOCIATES.
YOU HIT THE TRAIN? I DON'T REMEMBER THAT BEIN' PART OF THE PLAN.
NOW DARLIN', I DON'T SHARE EVERYTHIN' WITH YA. BESIDES, WHO DID YA THINK PLANNED THE ROBBERY FOR THOSE DEAD IDIOTS?
I KNEW THERE WAS A REASON I LOVED YA! MY DANCE HALL DAYS ARE OVER-- YE-HAW!
YEAH, HONEY, THAT THEY ARE. IT IS LIKE I ALWAYS SAY...
...IT IS BETTER TO BE CLEVER THAN HANDSOME, IT IS BETTER TO BE RICH THAN POOR, AND...

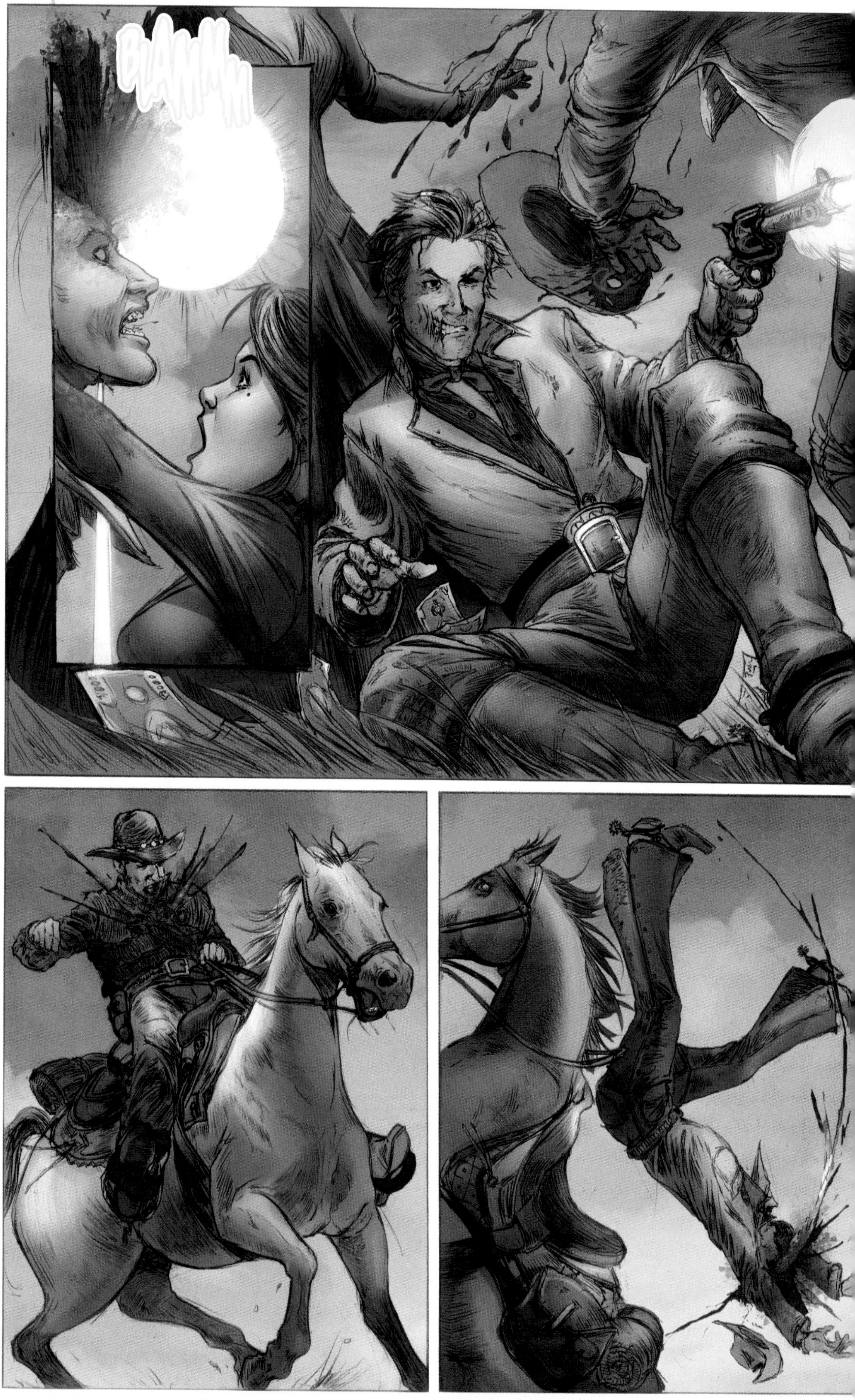
BLAMMM

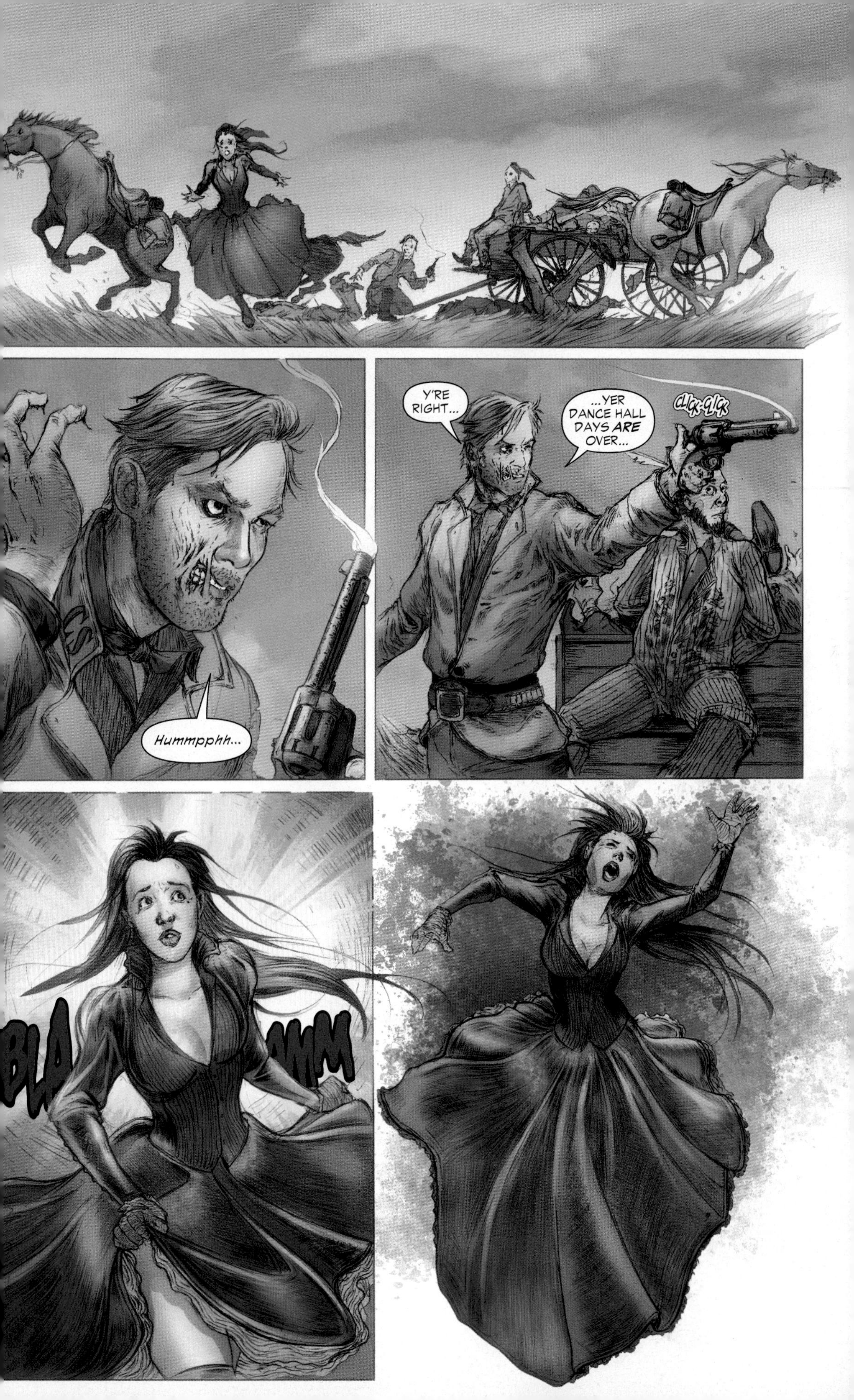
Hummmpphh...
Y'RE RIGHT...
...YER DANCE HALL DAYS ARE OVER...
CLICK-CLICK
BLA
AMM

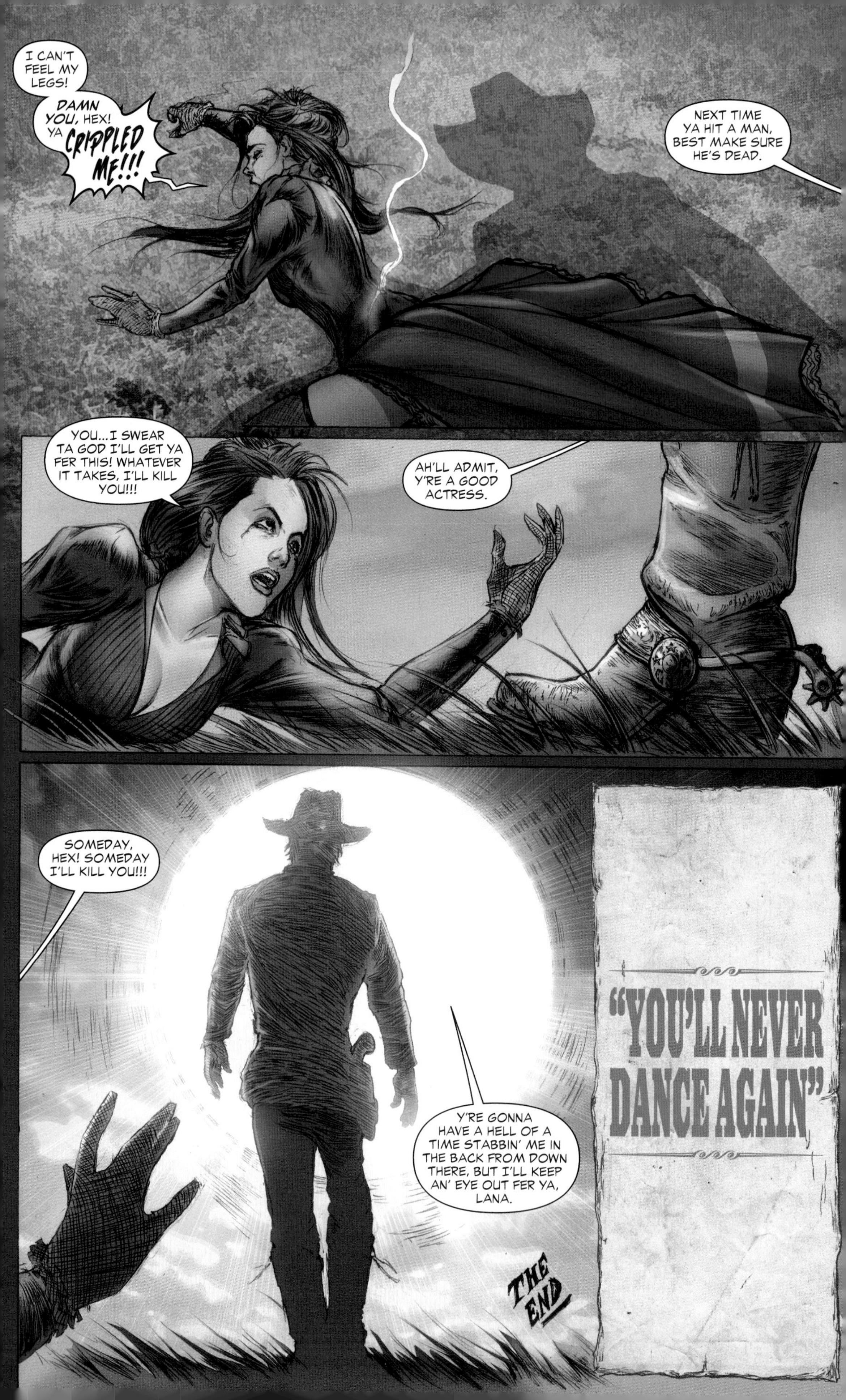
I CAN'T FEEL MY LEGS!
DAMN YOU, HEX! YA CRIPPLED ME!!!
NEXT TIME YA HIT A MAN, BEST MAKE SURE HE'S DEAD.
YOU...I SWEAR TA GOD I'LL GET YA FER THIS! WHATEVER IT TAKES, I'LL KILL YOU!!!
AH'LL ADMIT, Y'RE A GOOD ACTRESS.
SOMEDAY, HEX! SOMEDAY I'LL KILL YOU!!!
Y'RE GONNA HAVE A HELL OF A TIME STABBIN' ME IN THE BACK FROM DOWN THERE, BUT I'LL KEEP AN' EYE OUT FER YA, LANA.
"YOU'LL NEVER DANCE AGAIN"
THE END

Cover by Jordi Bernet with Rob Schwager

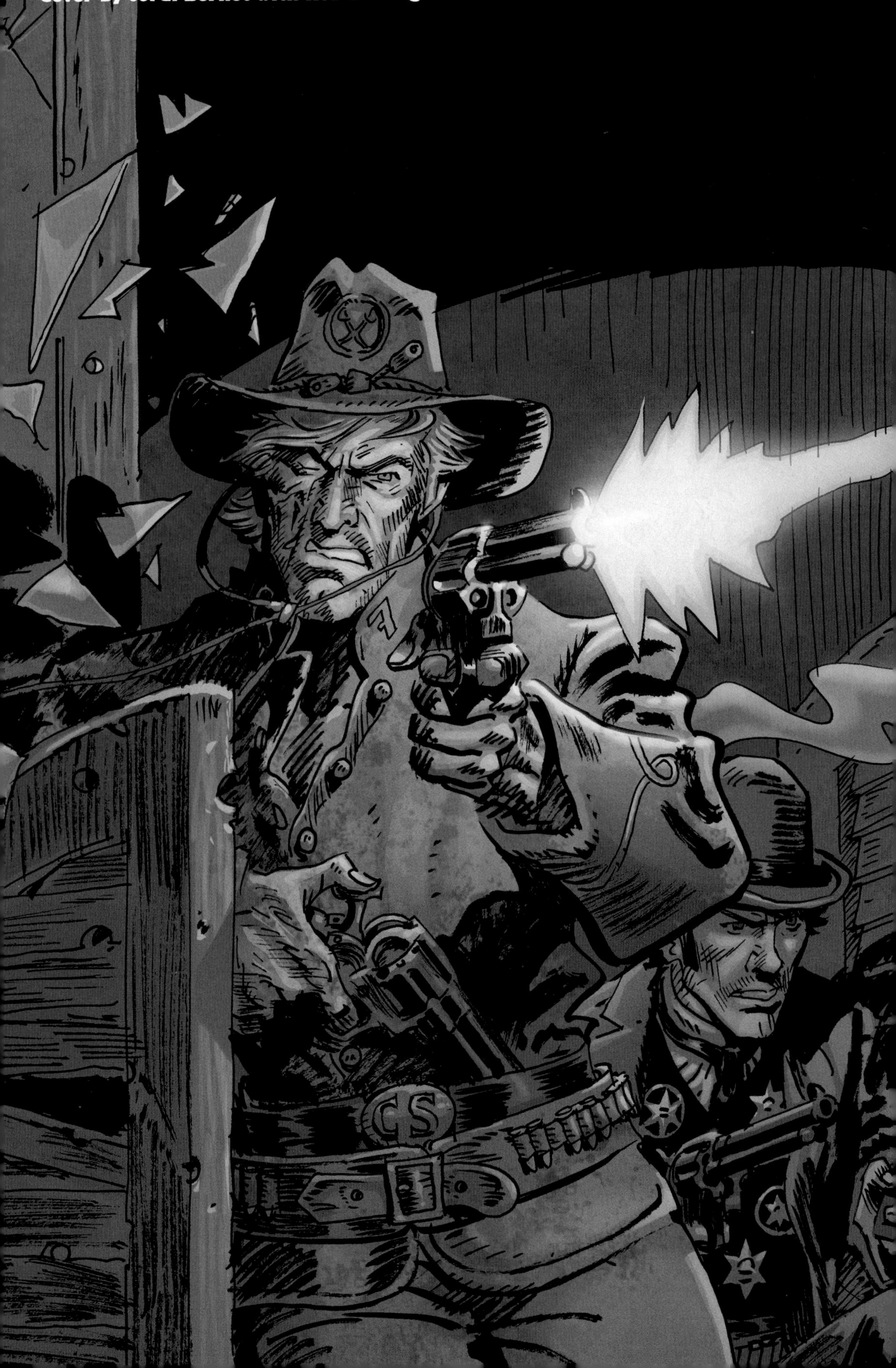

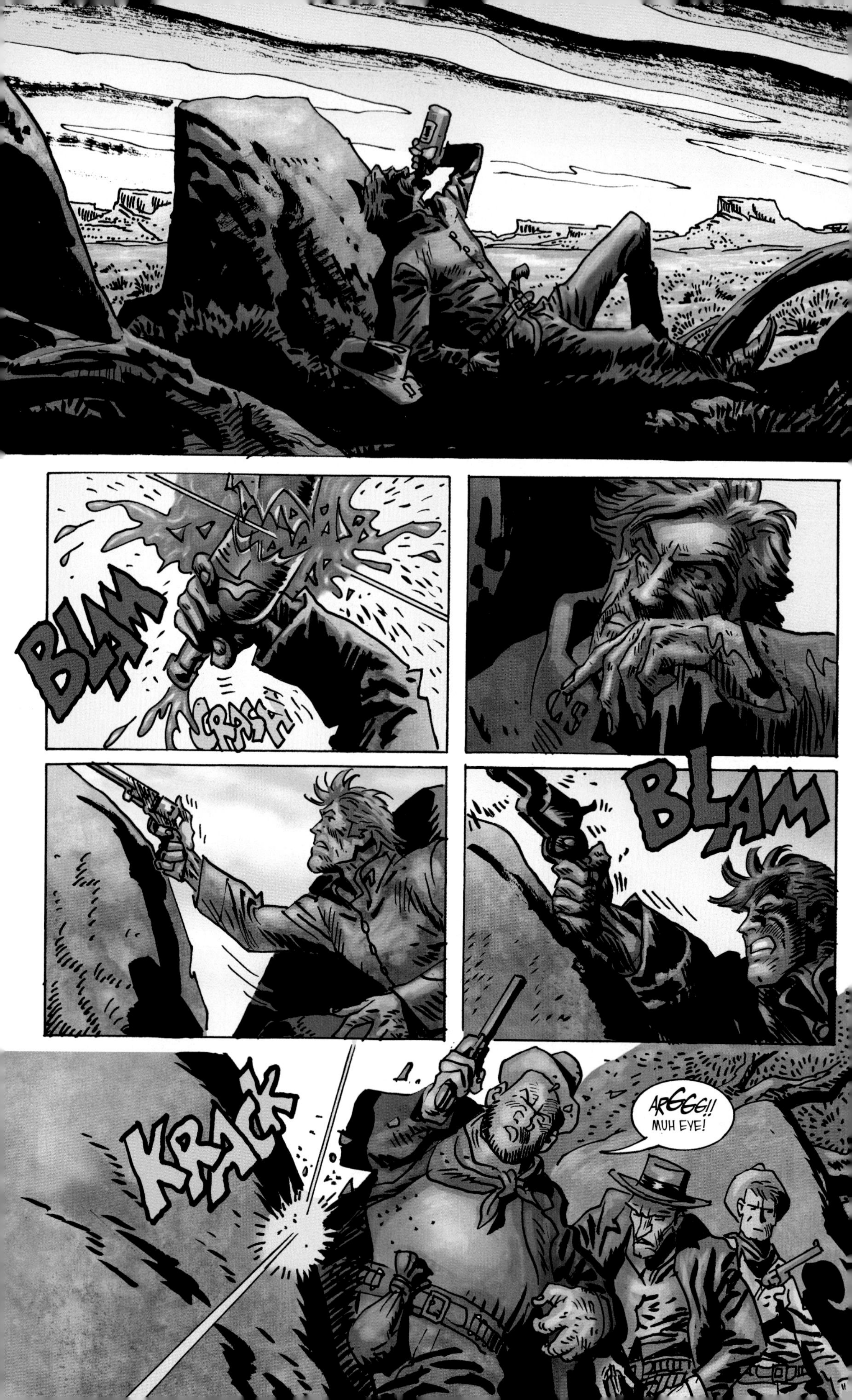
BLAM
CRASH
BLAM
KRACK
ARGGG!! MUH EYE!

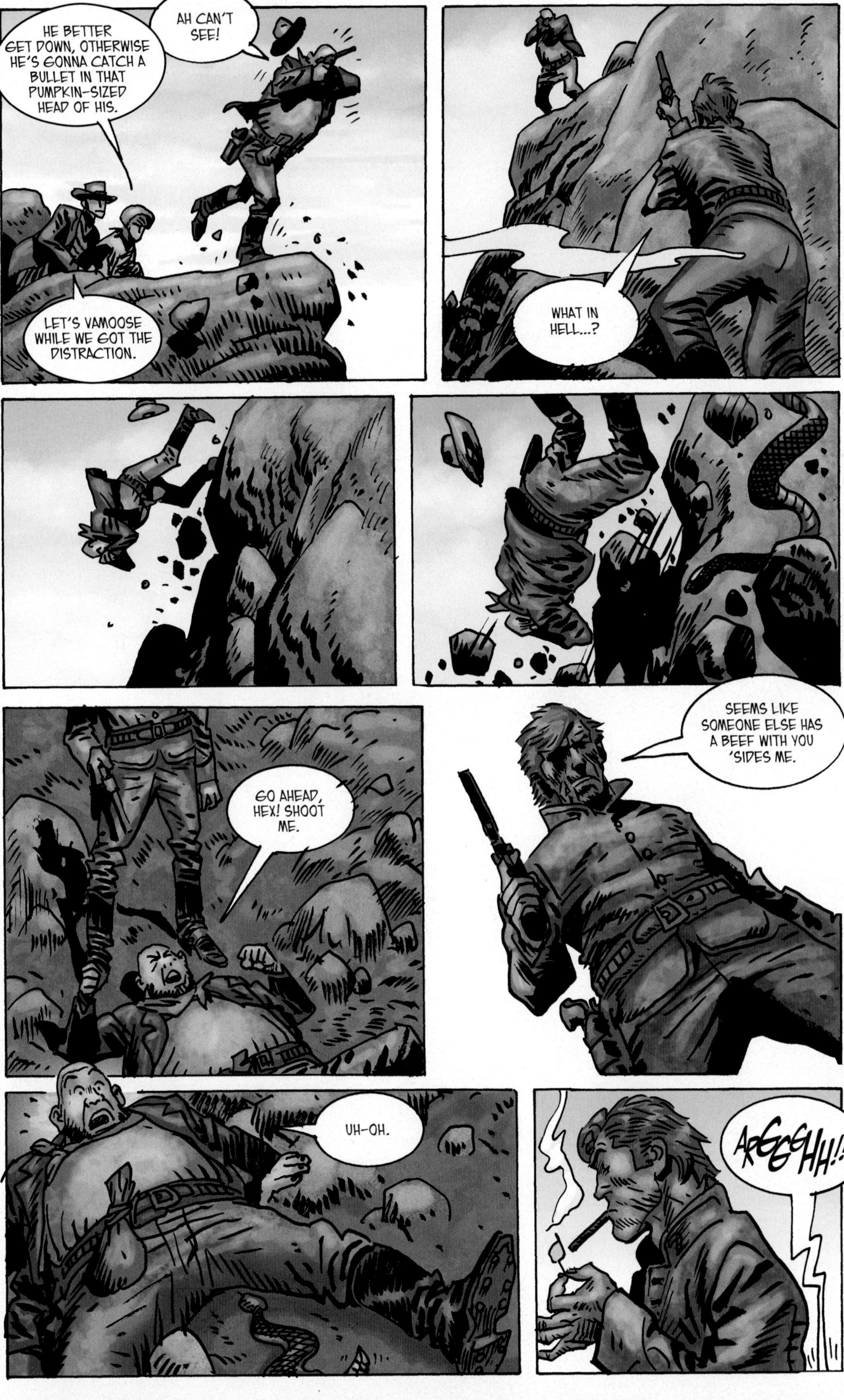
HE BETTER GET DOWN, OTHERWISE HE'S GONNA CATCH A BULLET IN THAT PUMPKIN-SIZED HEAD OF HIS.
AH CAN'T SEE!
LET'S VAMOOSE WHILE WE GOT THE DISTRACTION.
WHAT IN HELL...?
GO AHEAD, HEX! SHOOT ME.
SEEMS LIKE SOMEONE ELSE HAS A BEEF WITH YOU 'SIDES ME.
UH-OH.
ARGGGHH!!

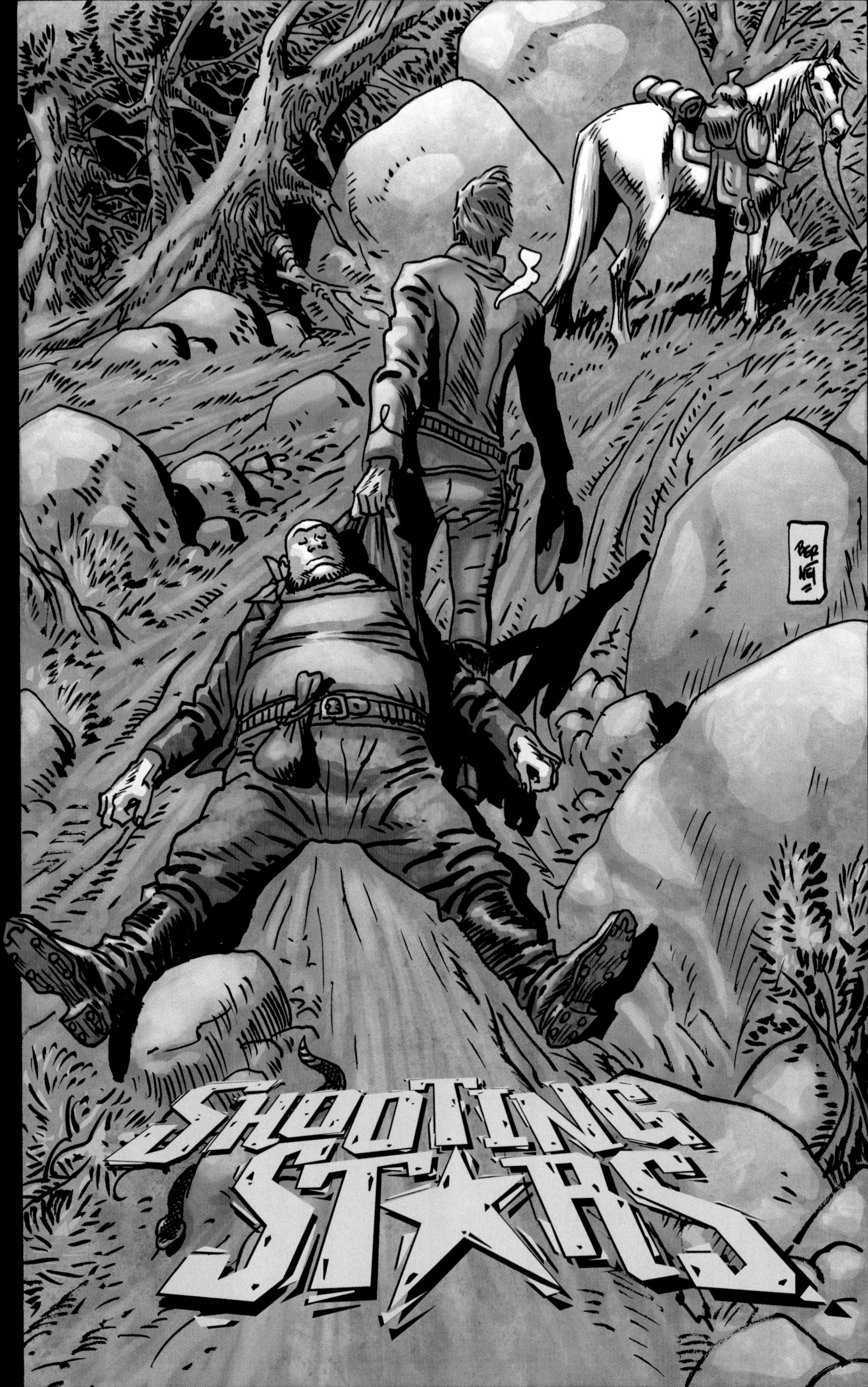
SHOOTING STARS

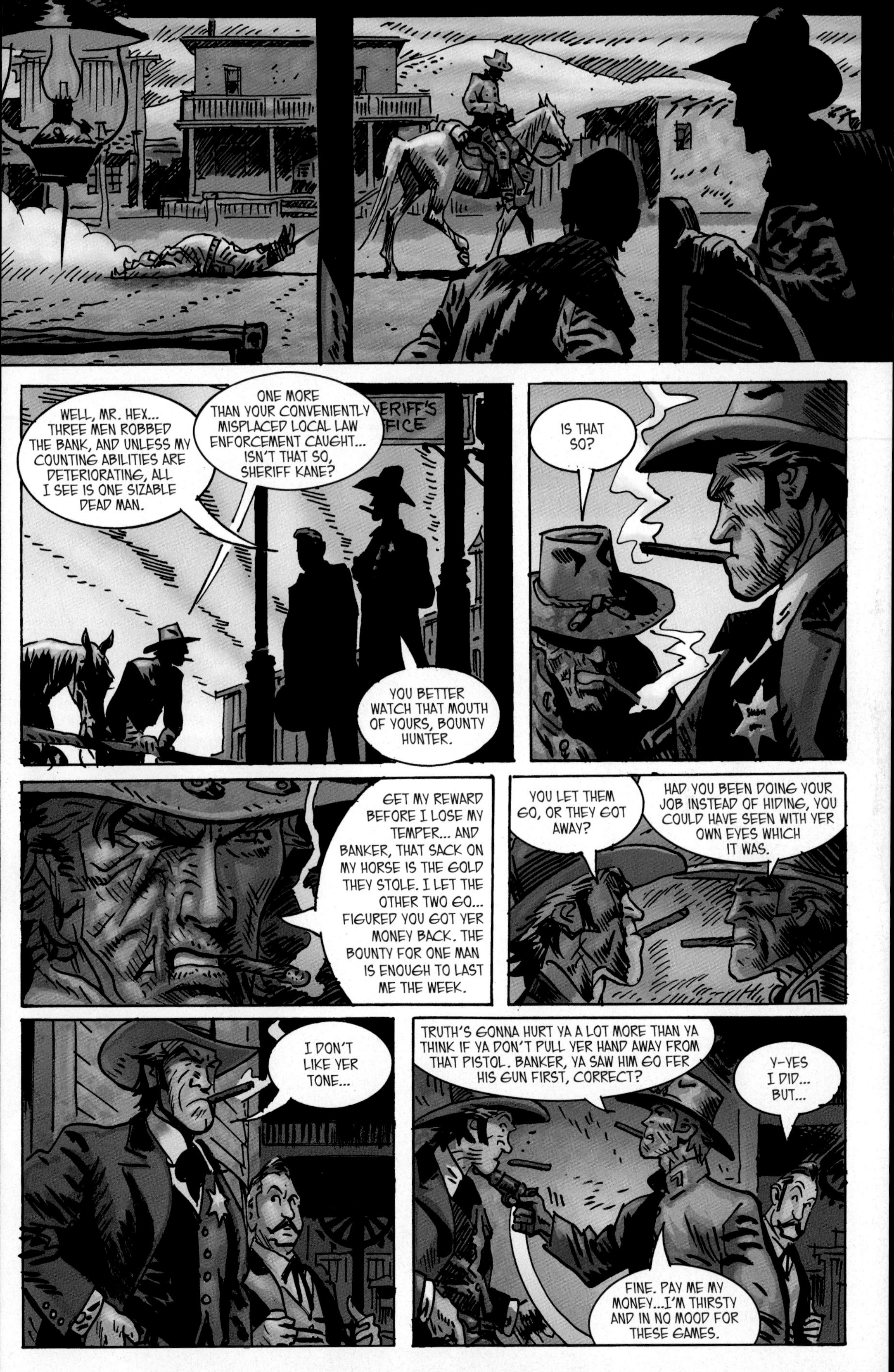
SHERIFF'S OFFICE
WELL, MR. HEX... THREE MEN ROBBED THE BANK, AND UNLESS MY COUNTING ABILITIES ARE DETERIORATING, ALL I SEE IS ONE SIZABLE DEAD MAN.
ONE MORE THAN YOUR CONVENIENTLY MISPLACED LOCAL LAW ENFORCEMENT CAUGHT... ISN'T THAT SO, SHERIFF KANE?
YOU BETTER WATCH THAT MOUTH OF YOURS, BOUNTY HUNTER.
IS THAT SO?
GET MY REWARD BEFORE I LOSE MY TEMPER... AND BANKER, THAT SACK ON MY HORSE IS THE GOLD THEY STOLE. I LET THE OTHER TWO GO... FIGURED YOU GOT YER MONEY BACK. THE BOUNTY FOR ONE MAN IS ENOUGH TO LAST ME THE WEEK.
YOU LET THEM GO, OR THEY GOT AWAY?
HAD YOU BEEN DOING YOUR JOB INSTEAD OF HIDING, YOU COULD HAVE SEEN WITH YER OWN EYES WHICH IT WAS.
I DON'T LIKE YER TONE...
TRUTH'S GONNA HURT YA A LOT MORE THAN YA THINK IF YA DON'T PULL YER HAND AWAY FROM THAT PISTOL. BANKER, YA SAW HIM GO FER HIS GUN FIRST, CORRECT?
Y-YES I DID... BUT...
FINE. PAY ME MY MONEY...I'M THIRSTY AND IN NO MOOD FOR THESE GAMES.

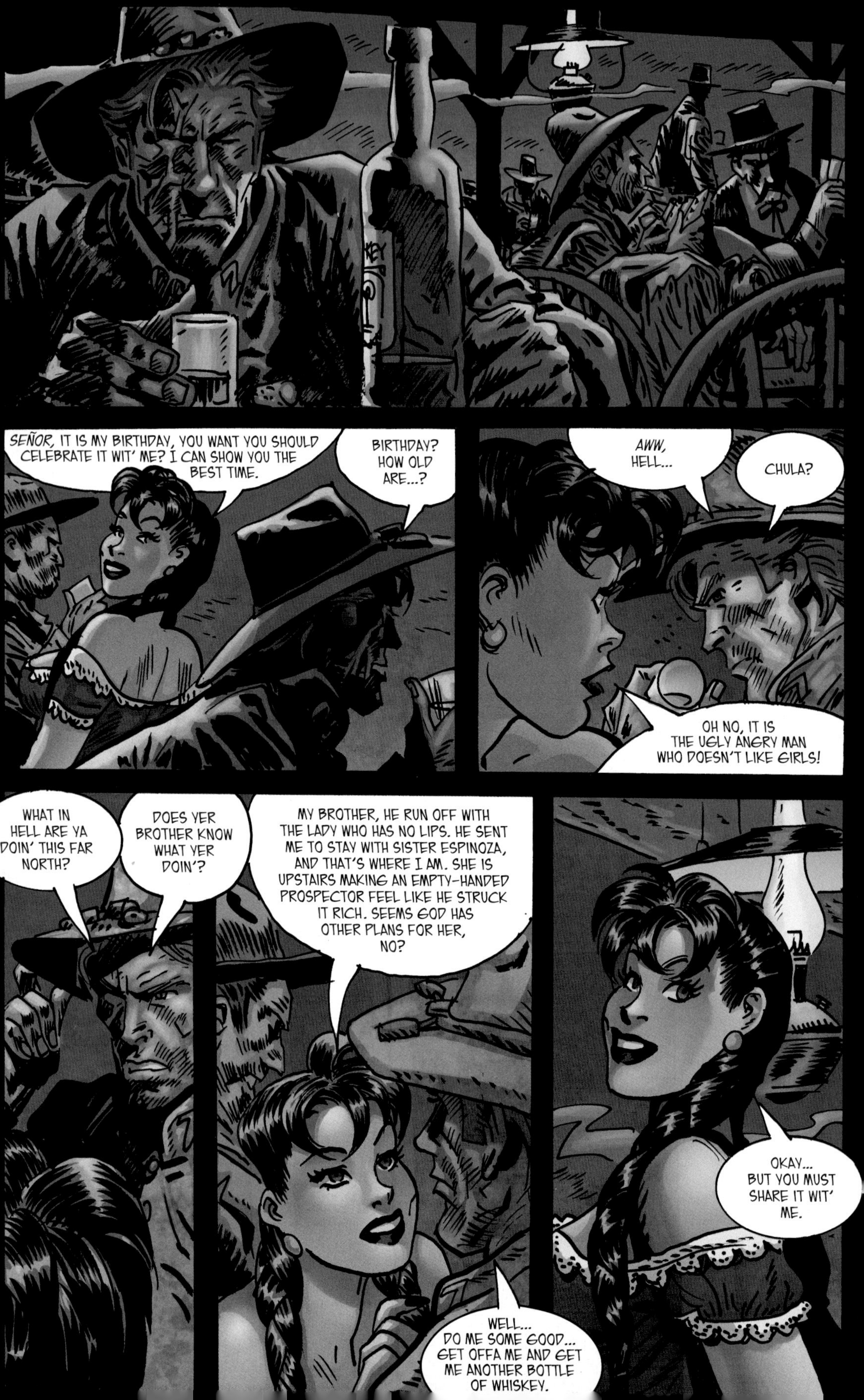
SEÑOR, IT IS MY BIRTHDAY, YOU WANT YOU SHOULD CELEBRATE IT WIT' ME? I CAN SHOW YOU THE BEST TIME.
BIRTHDAY? HOW OLD ARE...?
AWW, HELL...
CHULA?
OH NO, IT IS THE UGLY ANGRY MAN WHO DOESN'T LIKE GIRLS!
WHAT IN HELL ARE YA DOIN' THIS FAR NORTH?
DOES YER BROTHER KNOW WHAT YER DOIN'?
MY BROTHER, HE RUN OFF WITH THE LADY WHO HAS NO LIPS. HE SENT ME TO STAY WITH SISTER ESPINOZA, AND THAT'S WHERE I AM. SHE IS UPSTAIRS MAKING AN EMPTY-HANDED PROSPECTOR FEEL LIKE HE STRUCK IT RICH. SEEMS GOD HAS OTHER PLANS FOR HER, NO?
WELL... DO ME SOME GOOD... GET OFFA ME AND GET ME ANOTHER BOTTLE OF WHISKEY.
OKAY... BUT YOU MUST SHARE IT WIT' ME.

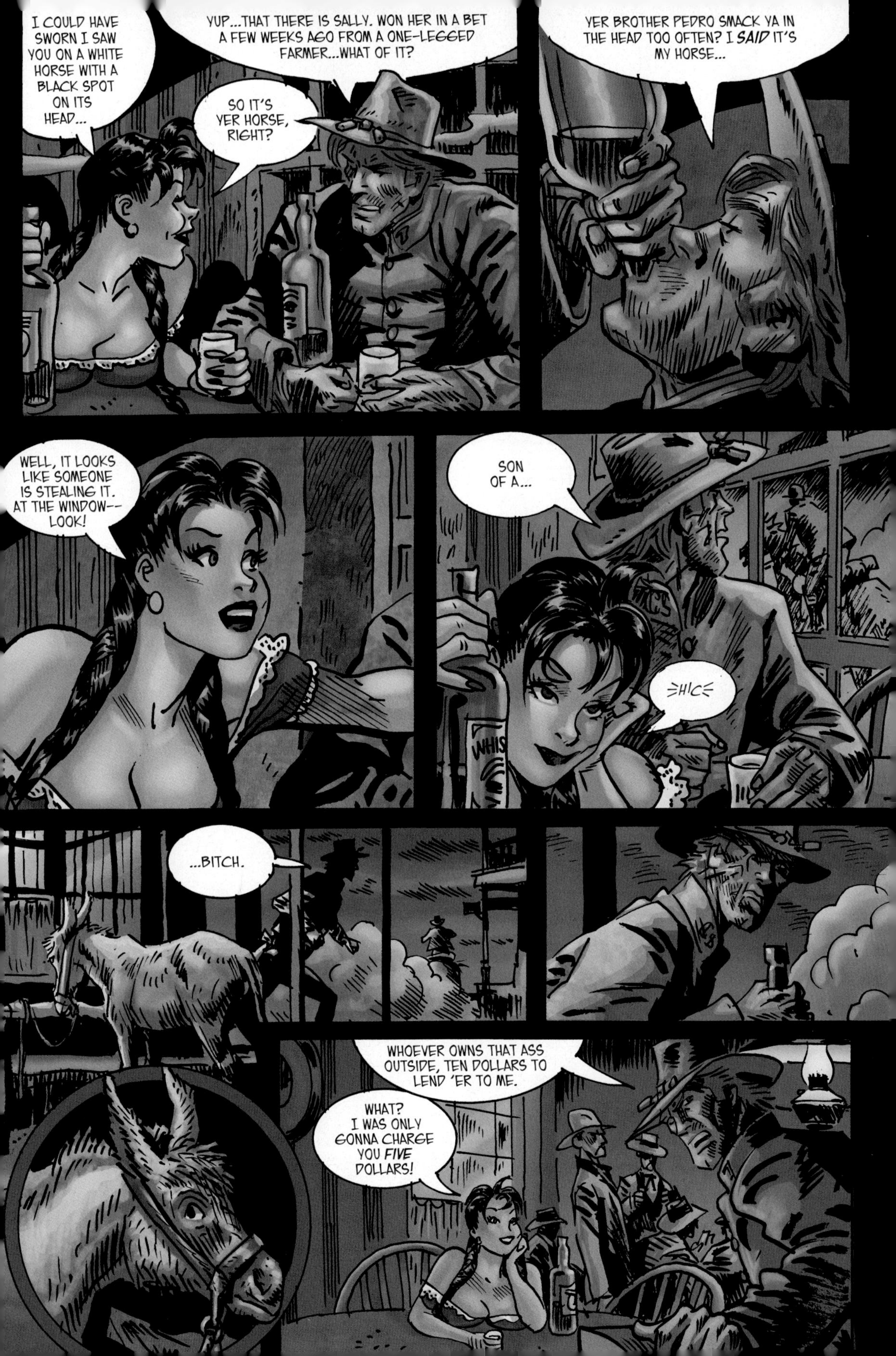
I COULD HAVE SWORN I SAW YOU ON A WHITE HORSE WITH A BLACK SPOT ON ITS HEAD...
YUP...THAT THERE IS SALLY. WON HER IN A BET A FEW WEEKS AGO FROM A ONE-LEGGED FARMER...WHAT OF IT?
SO IT'S YER HORSE, RIGHT?
YER BROTHER PEDRO SMACK YA IN THE HEAD TOO OFTEN? I *SAID* IT'S MY HORSE...
WELL, IT LOOKS LIKE SOMEONE IS STEALING IT. AT THE WINDOW-- LOOK!
SON OF A...
HIC
...BITCH.
WHOEVER OWNS THAT ASS OUTSIDE, TEN DOLLARS TO LEND 'ER TO ME.
WHAT? I WAS ONLY GONNA CHARGE YOU *FIVE* DOLLARS!

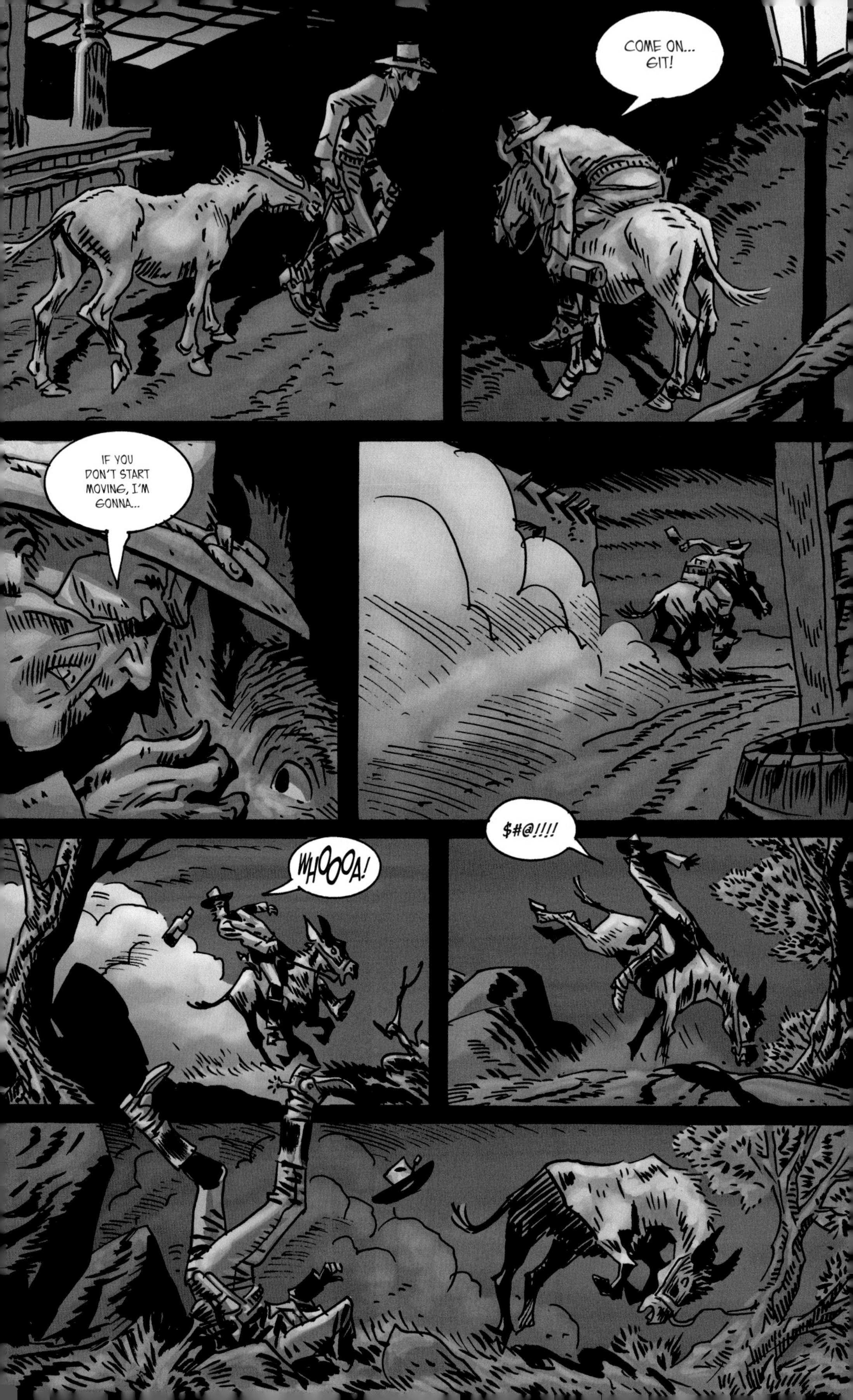
COME ON... GIT!
IF YOU DON'T START MOVING, I'M GONNA..
WHOOOA!
$#@!!!!

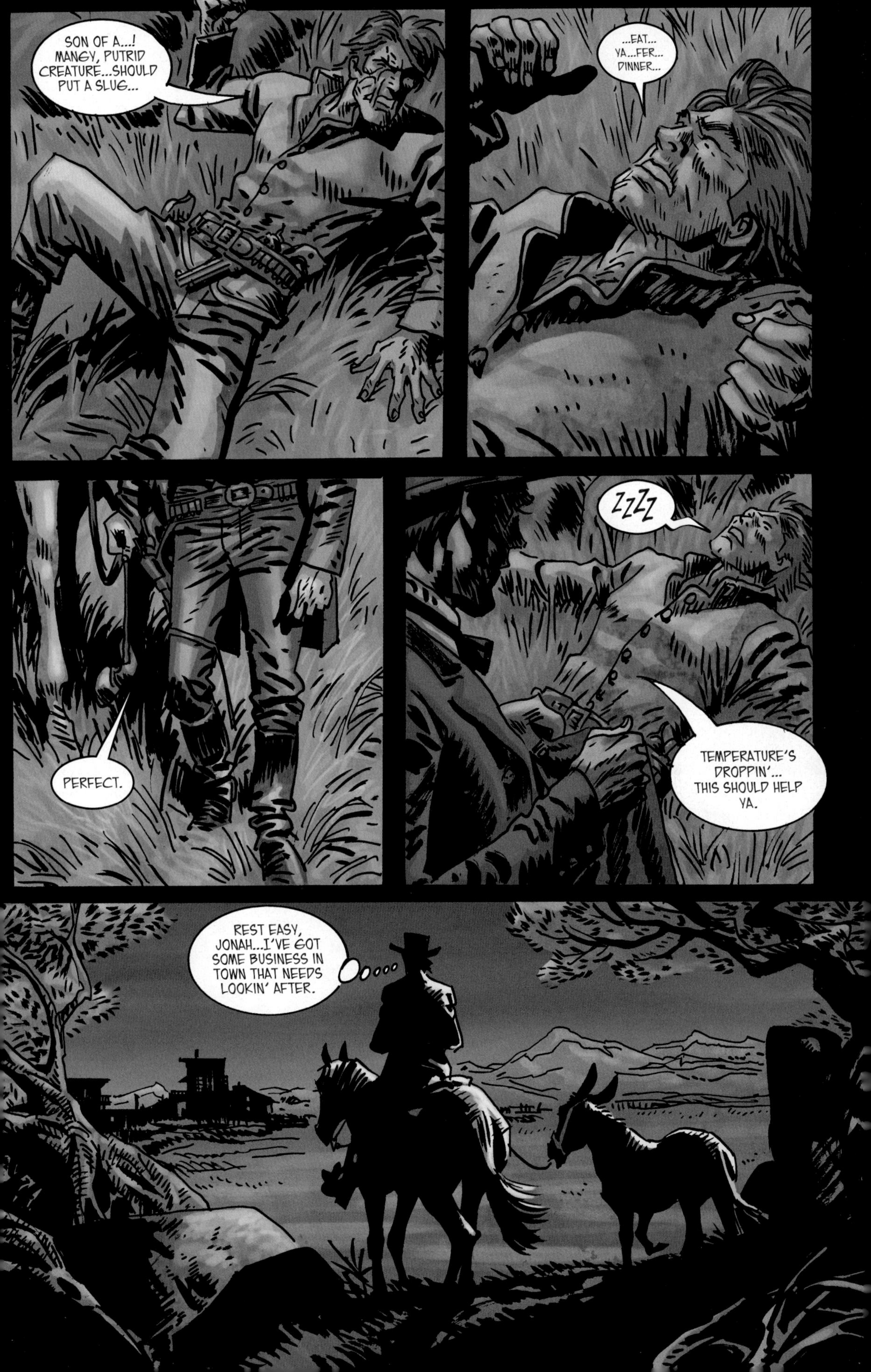
SON OF A...! MANGY, PUTRID CREATURE...SHOULD PUT A SLUG...
...EAT... YA...FER... DINNER...
PERFECT.
ZZZZ
TEMPERATURE'S DROPPIN'... THIS SHOULD HELP YA.
REST EASY, JONAH...I'VE GOT SOME BUSINESS IN TOWN THAT NEEDS LOOKIN' AFTER.

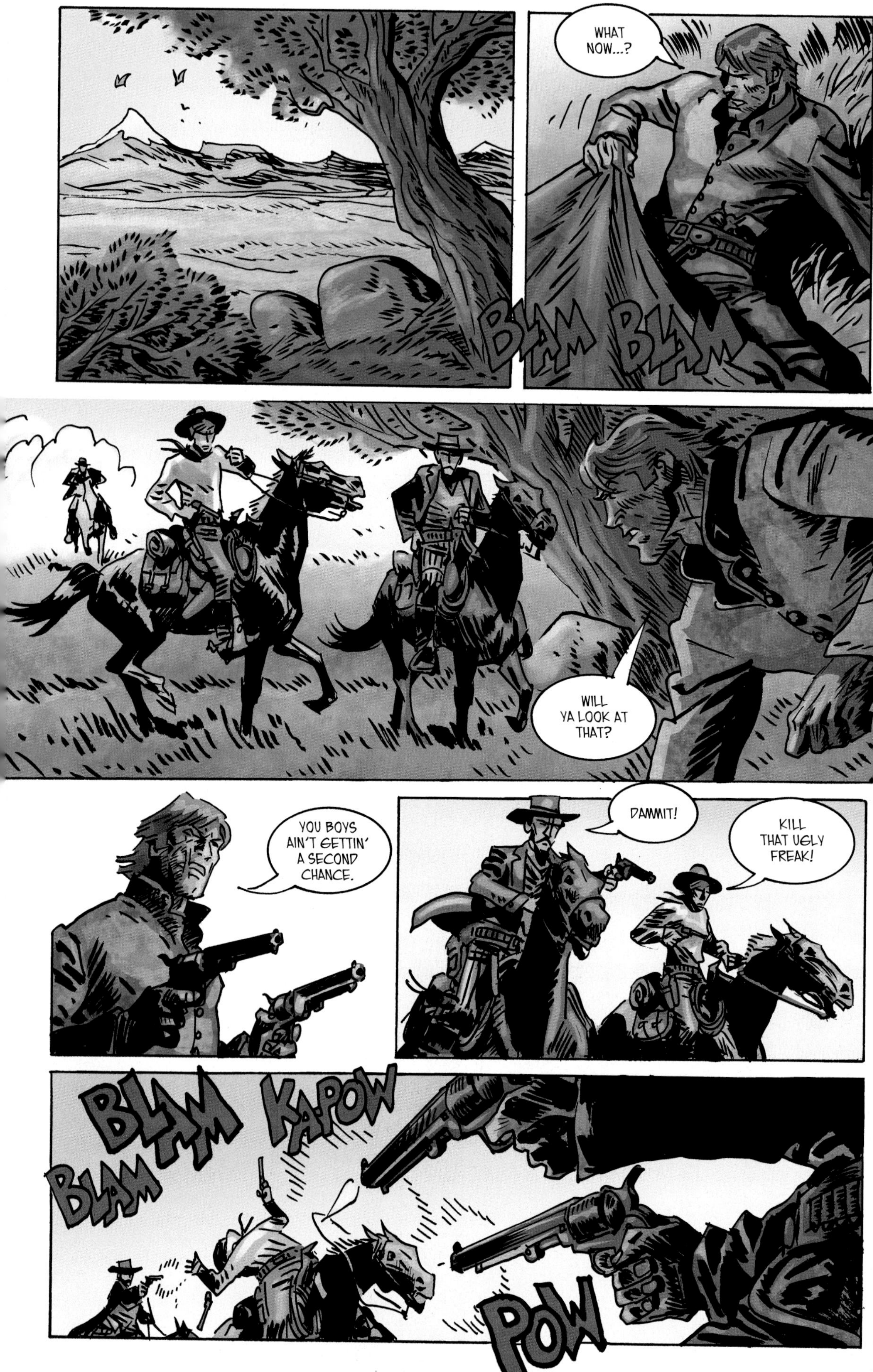
WHAT NOW...?
BLAM BLAM
WILL YA LOOK AT THAT?
YOU BOYS AIN'T GETTIN' A SECOND CHANCE.
DAMMIT!
KILL THAT UGLY FREAK!
BLAM BLAM KAPOW
BLAM
POW

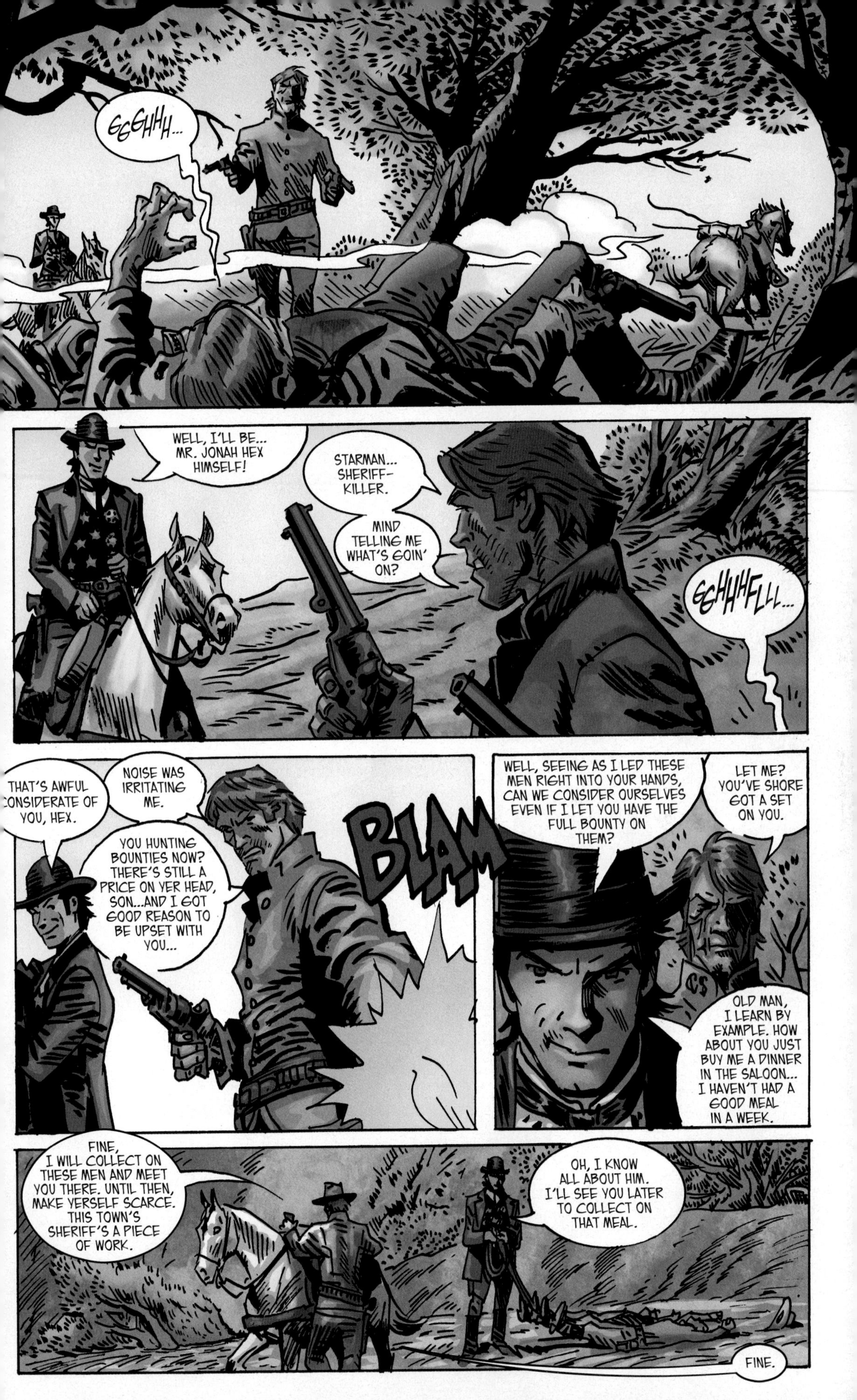
SSGHHH...
WELL, I'LL BE... MR. JONAH HEX HIMSELF!
STARMAN... SHERIFF-KILLER.
MIND TELLING ME WHAT'S GOIN' ON?
SSGHHFLLL...
THAT'S AWFUL CONSIDERATE OF YOU, HEX.
NOISE WAS IRRITATING ME.
YOU HUNTING BOUNTIES NOW? THERE'S STILL A PRICE ON YER HEAD, SON...AND I GOT GOOD REASON TO BE UPSET WITH YOU...
BLAM
WELL, SEEING AS I LED THESE MEN RIGHT INTO YOUR HANDS, CAN WE CONSIDER OURSELVES EVEN IF I LET YOU HAVE THE FULL BOUNTY ON THEM?
LET ME? YOU'VE SHORE GOT A SET ON YOU.
OLD MAN, I LEARN BY EXAMPLE. HOW ABOUT YOU JUST BUY ME A DINNER IN THE SALOON... I HAVEN'T HAD A GOOD MEAL IN A WEEK.
FINE, I WILL COLLECT ON THESE MEN AND MEET YOU THERE. UNTIL THEN, MAKE YERSELF SCARCE. THIS TOWN'S SHERIFF'S A PIECE OF WORK.
OH, I KNOW ALL ABOUT HIM. I'LL SEE YOU LATER TO COLLECT ON THAT MEAL.
FINE.

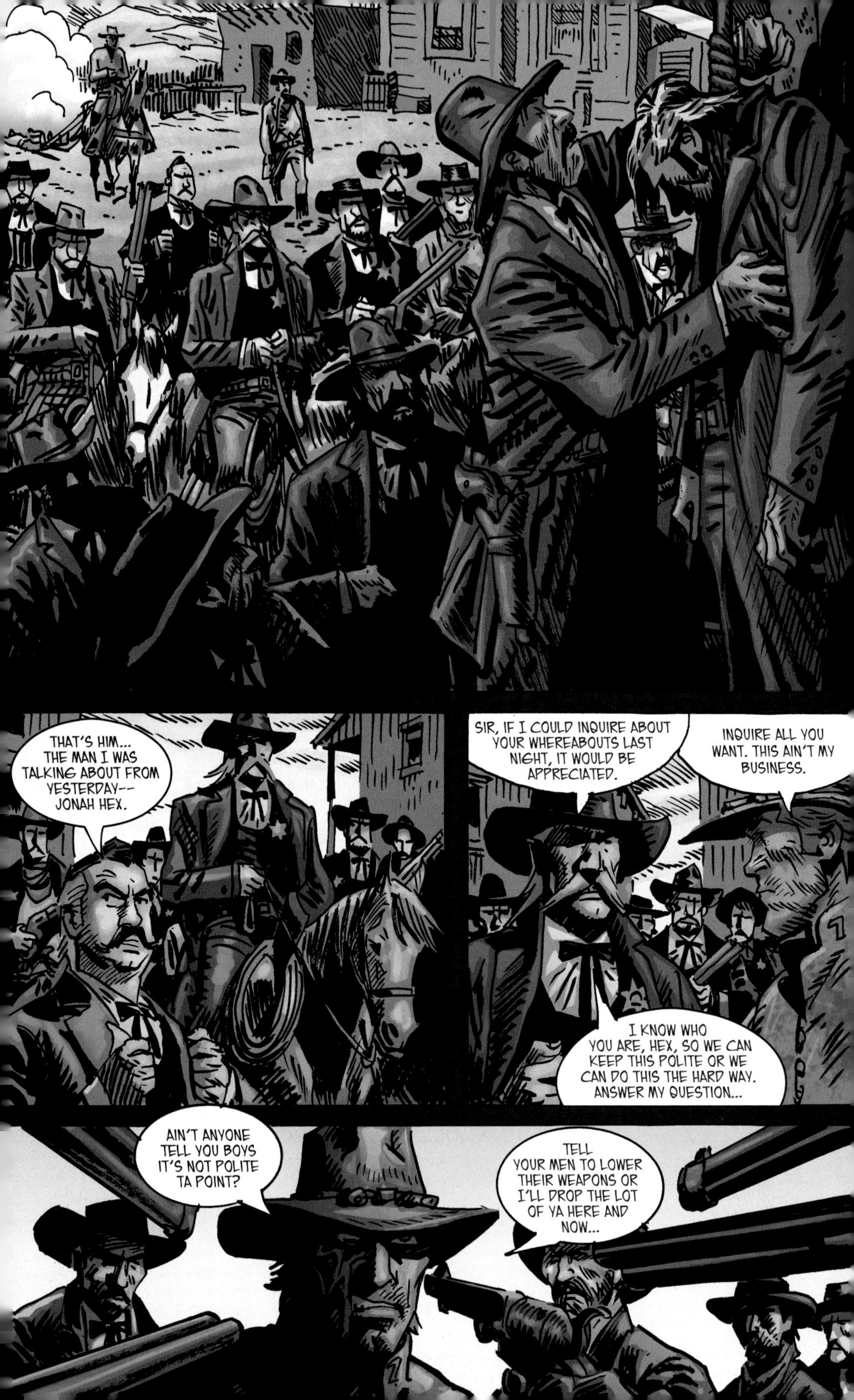
THAT'S HIM... THE MAN I WAS TALKING ABOUT FROM YESTERDAY-- JONAH HEX.
SIR, IF I COULD INQUIRE ABOUT YOUR WHEREABOUTS LAST NIGHT, IT WOULD BE APPRECIATED.
INQUIRE ALL YOU WANT. THIS AIN'T MY BUSINESS.
I KNOW WHO YOU ARE, HEX, SO WE CAN KEEP THIS POLITE OR WE CAN DO THIS THE HARD WAY. ANSWER MY QUESTION...
AIN'T ANYONE TELL YOU BOYS IT'S NOT POLITE TA POINT?
TELL YOUR MEN TO LOWER THEIR WEAPONS OR I'LL DROP THE LOT OF YA HERE AND NOW...

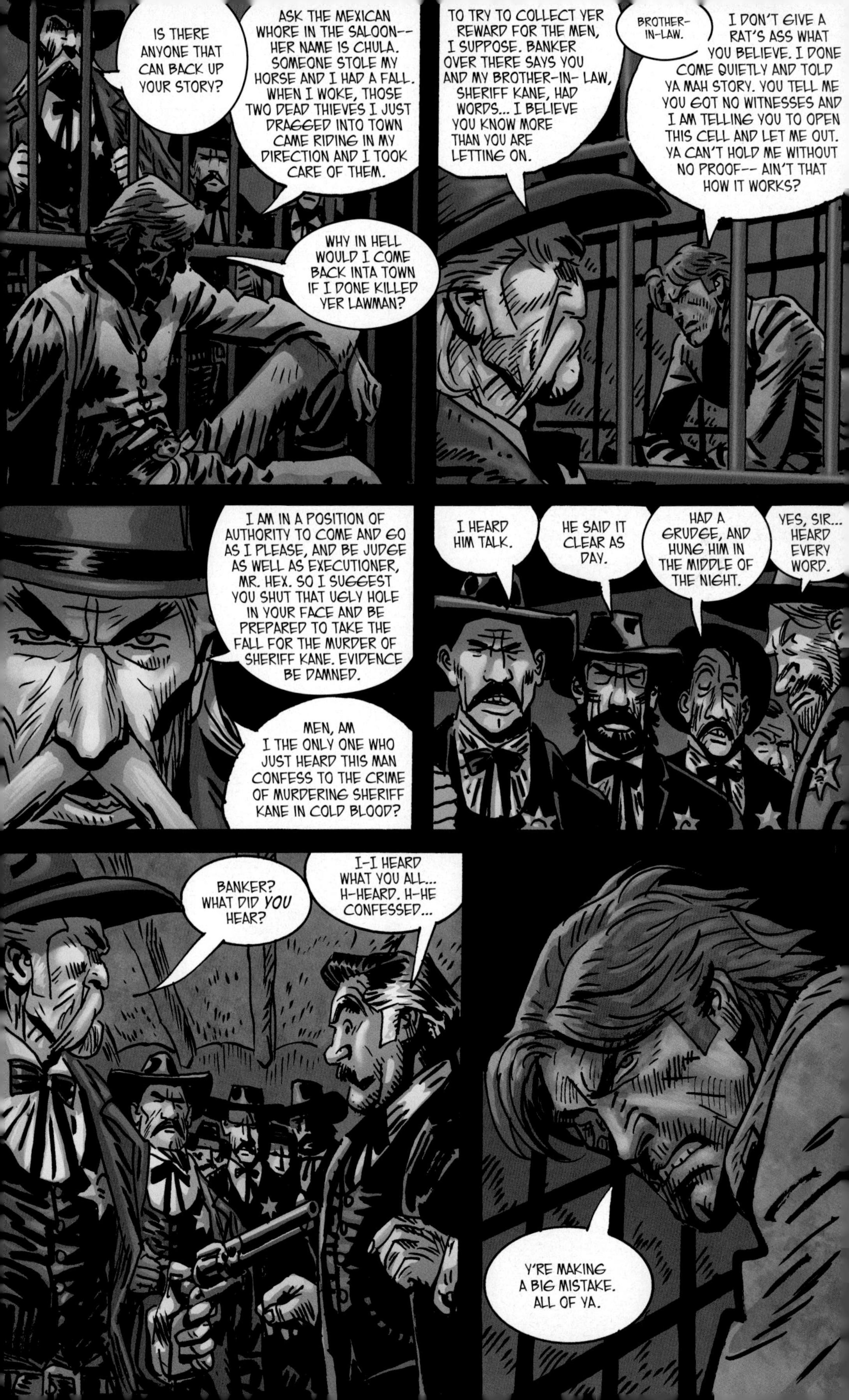
IS THERE ANYONE THAT CAN BACK UP YOUR STORY?
ASK THE MEXICAN WHORE IN THE SALOON-- HER NAME IS CHULA. SOMEONE STOLE MY HORSE AND I HAD A FALL. WHEN I WOKE, THOSE TWO DEAD THIEVES I JUST DRAGGED INTO TOWN CAME RIDING IN MY DIRECTION AND I TOOK CARE OF THEM.
WHY IN HELL WOULD I COME BACK INTA TOWN IF I DONE KILLED YER LAWMAN?
TO TRY TO COLLECT YER REWARD FOR THE MEN, I SUPPOSE. BANKER OVER THERE SAYS YOU AND MY BROTHER-IN- LAW, SHERIFF KANE, HAD WORDS... I BELIEVE YOU KNOW MORE THAN YOU ARE LETTING ON.
BROTHER-IN-LAW.
I DON'T GIVE A RAT'S ASS WHAT YOU BELIEVE. I DONE COME QUIETLY AND TOLD YA MAH STORY. YOU TELL ME YOU GOT NO WITNESSES AND I AM TELLING YOU TO OPEN THIS CELL AND LET ME OUT. YA CAN'T HOLD ME WITHOUT NO PROOF-- AIN'T THAT HOW IT WORKS?
I AM IN A POSITION OF AUTHORITY TO COME AND GO AS I PLEASE, AND BE JUDGE AS WELL AS EXECUTIONER, MR. HEX. SO I SUGGEST YOU SHUT THAT UGLY HOLE IN YOUR FACE AND BE PREPARED TO TAKE THE FALL FOR THE MURDER OF SHERIFF KANE. EVIDENCE BE DAMNED.
MEN, AM I THE ONLY ONE WHO JUST HEARD THIS MAN CONFESS TO THE CRIME OF MURDERING SHERIFF KANE IN COLD BLOOD?
I HEARD HIM TALK.
HE SAID IT CLEAR AS DAY.
HAD A GRUDGE, AND HUNG HIM IN THE MIDDLE OF THE NIGHT.
YES, SIR... HEARD EVERY WORD.
BANKER? WHAT DID *YOU* HEAR?
I-I HEARD WHAT YOU ALL... H-HEARD. H-HE CONFESSED...
Y'RE MAKING A BIG MISTAKE. ALL OF YA.

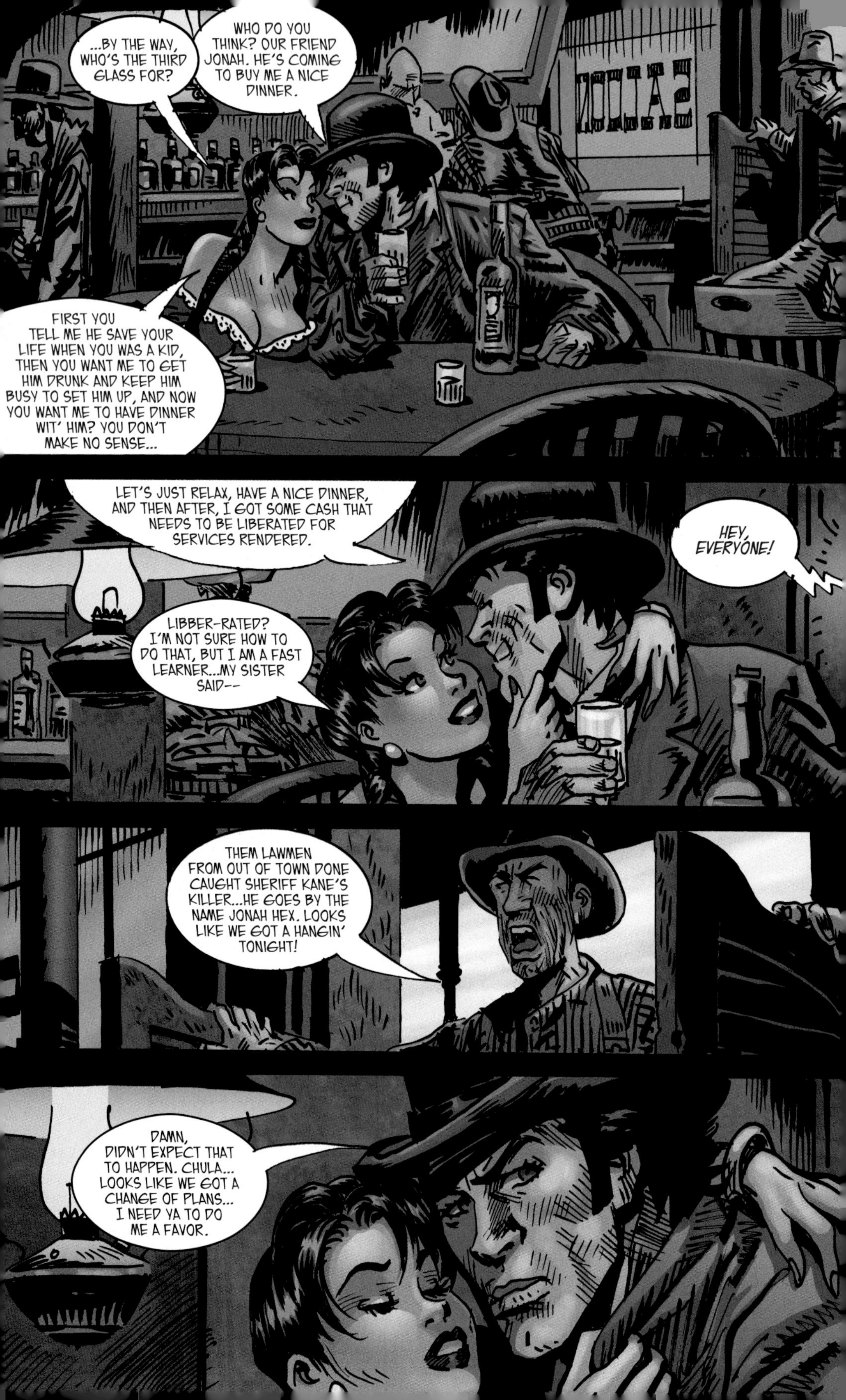
...BY THE WAY, WHO'S THE THIRD GLASS FOR?
WHO DO YOU THINK? OUR FRIEND JONAH. HE'S COMING TO BUY ME A NICE DINNER.
SALOON
FIRST YOU TELL ME HE SAVE YOUR LIFE WHEN YOU WAS A KID, THEN YOU WANT ME TO GET HIM DRUNK AND KEEP HIM BUSY TO SET HIM UP, AND NOW YOU WANT ME TO HAVE DINNER WIT' HIM? YOU DON'T MAKE NO SENSE...
LET'S JUST RELAX, HAVE A NICE DINNER, AND THEN AFTER, I GOT SOME CASH THAT NEEDS TO BE LIBERATED FOR SERVICES RENDERED.
HEY, EVERYONE!
LIBBER-RATED? I'M NOT SURE HOW TO DO THAT, BUT I AM A FAST LEARNER...MY SISTER SAID--
THEM LAWMEN FROM OUT OF TOWN DONE CAUGHT SHERIFF KANE'S KILLER...HE GOES BY THE NAME JONAH HEX. LOOKS LIKE WE GOT A HANGIN' TONIGHT!
DAMN, DIDN'T EXPECT THAT TO HAPPEN. CHULA... LOOKS LIKE WE GOT A CHANGE OF PLANS... I NEED YA TO DO ME A FAVOR.

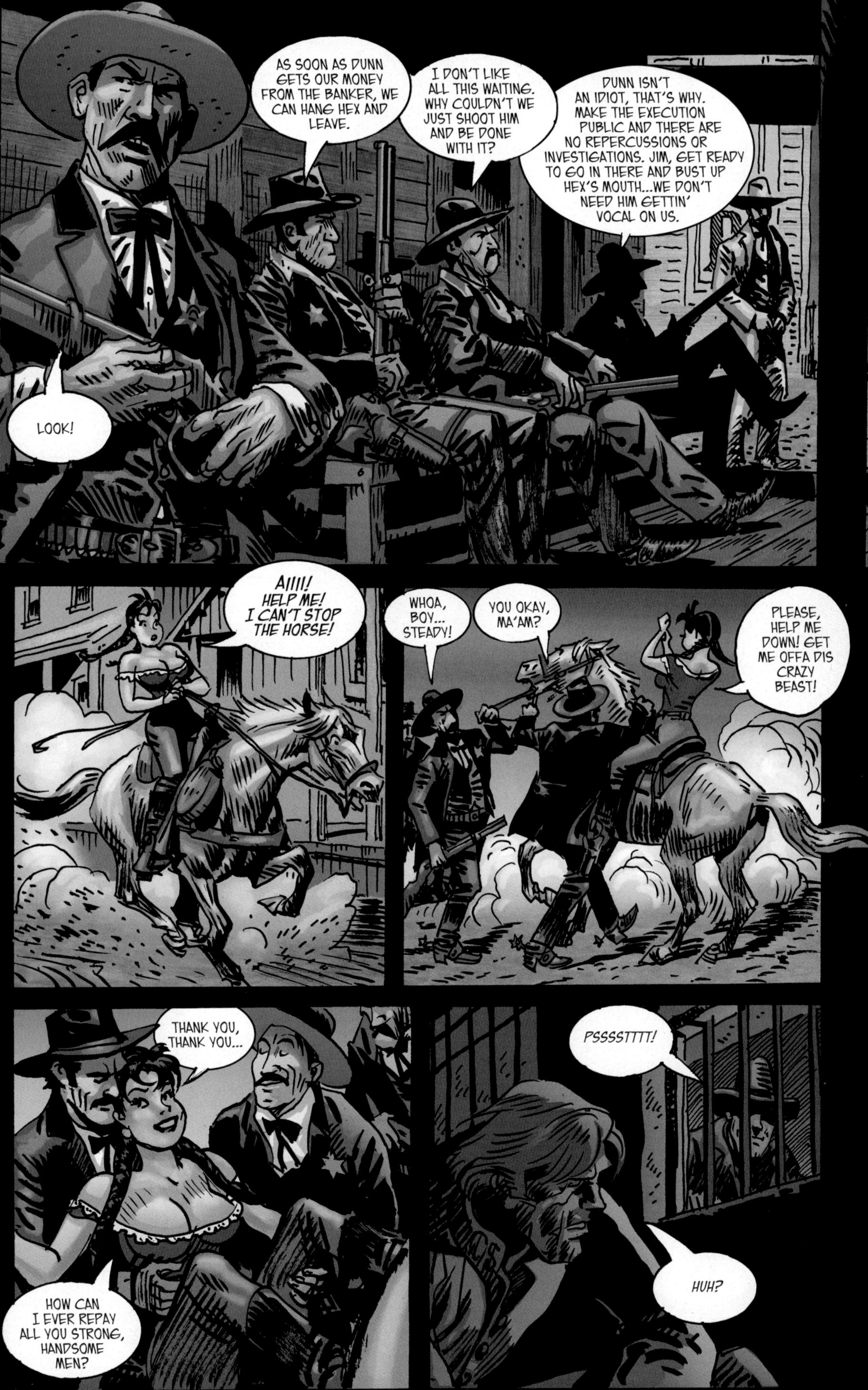
AS SOON AS DUNN GETS OUR MONEY FROM THE BANKER, WE CAN HANG HEX AND LEAVE.
I DON'T LIKE ALL THIS WAITING. WHY COULDN'T WE JUST SHOOT HIM AND BE DONE WITH IT?
DUNN ISN'T AN IDIOT, THAT'S WHY. MAKE THE EXECUTION PUBLIC AND THERE ARE NO REPERCUSSIONS OR INVESTIGATIONS. JIM, GET READY TO GO IN THERE AND BUST UP HEX'S MOUTH...WE DON'T NEED HIM GETTIN' VOCAL ON US.
LOOK!
AIIII! HELP ME! I CAN'T STOP THE HORSE!
WHOA, BOY... STEADY!
YOU OKAY, MA'AM?
PLEASE, HELP ME DOWN! GET ME OFFA DIS CRAZY BEAST!
THANK YOU, THANK YOU...
HOW CAN I EVER REPAY ALL YOU STRONG, HANDSOME MEN?
PSSSSTTTT!
HUH?

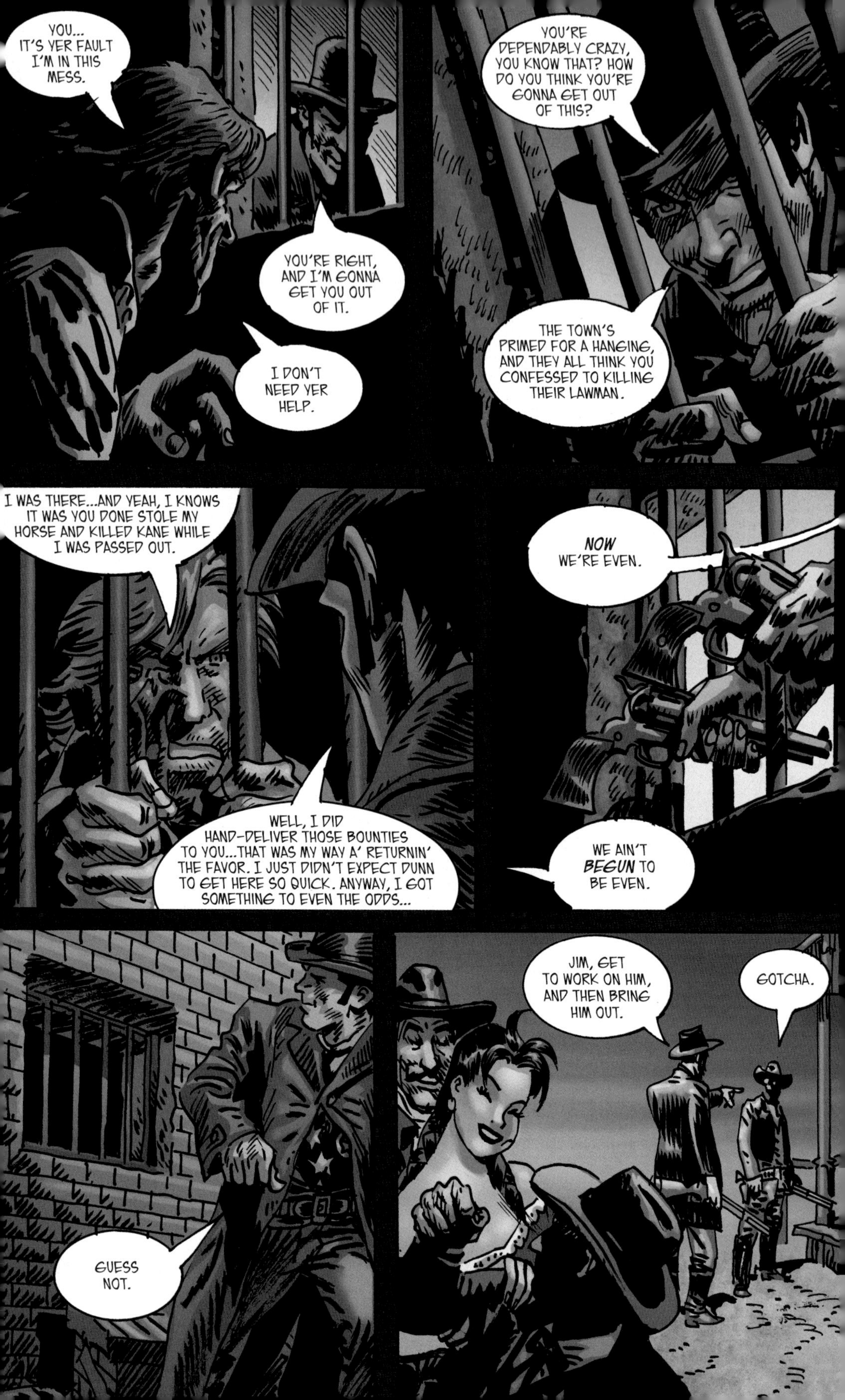
YOU... IT'S YER FAULT I'M IN THIS MESS.
YOU'RE RIGHT, AND I'M GONNA GET YOU OUT OF IT.
I DON'T NEED YER HELP.
YOU'RE DEPENDABLY CRAZY, YOU KNOW THAT? HOW DO YOU THINK YOU'RE GONNA GET OUT OF THIS?
THE TOWN'S PRIMED FOR A HANGING, AND THEY ALL THINK YOU CONFESSED TO KILLING THEIR LAWMAN.
I WAS THERE...AND YEAH, I KNOWS IT WAS YOU DONE STOLE MY HORSE AND KILLED KANE WHILE I WAS PASSED OUT.
WELL, I DID HAND-DELIVER THOSE BOUNTIES TO YOU...THAT WAS MY WAY A' RETURNIN' THE FAVOR. I JUST DIDN'T EXPECT DUNN TO GET HERE SO QUICK. ANYWAY, I GOT SOMETHING TO EVEN THE ODDS...
NOW WE'RE EVEN.
WE AIN'T BEGUN TO BE EVEN.
GUESS NOT.
JIM, GET TO WORK ON HIM, AND THEN BRING HIM OUT.
GOTCHA.

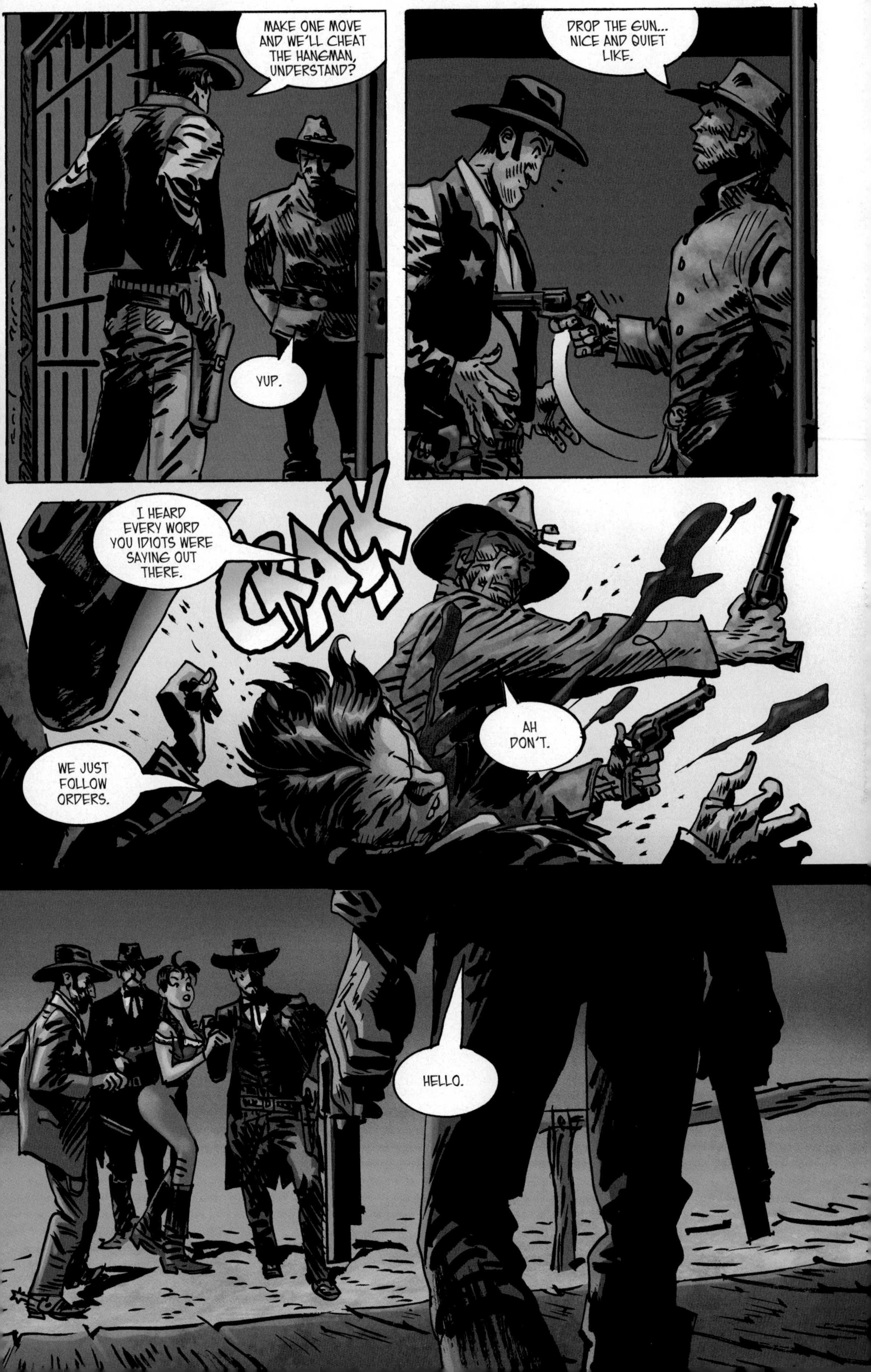
MAKE ONE MOVE AND WE'LL CHEAT THE HANGMAN, UNDERSTAND?
YUP.
DROP THE GUN... NICE AND QUIET LIKE.
CRACK
I HEARD EVERY WORD YOU IDIOTS WERE SAYING OUT THERE.
WE JUST FOLLOW ORDERS.
AH DON'T.
HELLO.

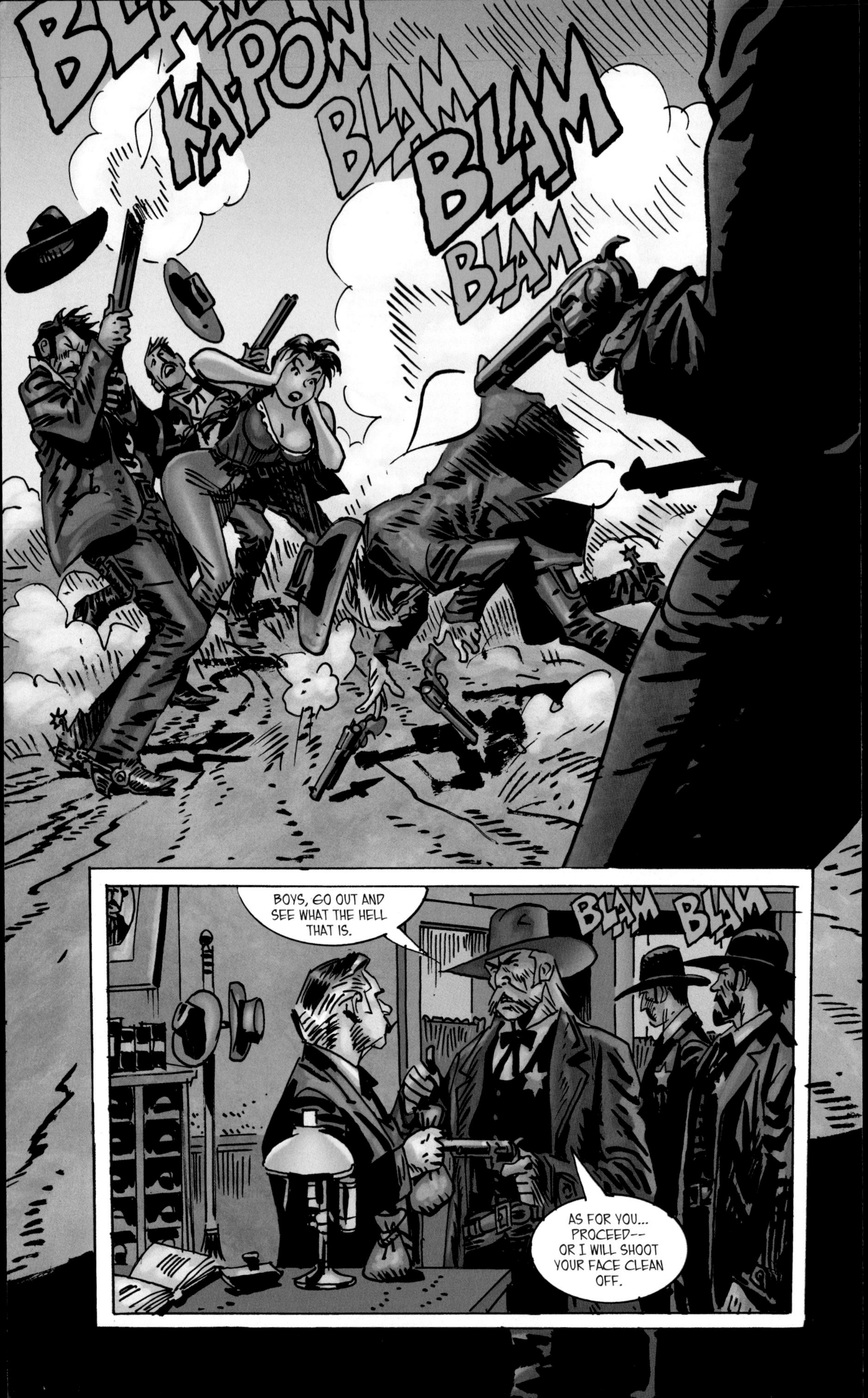
KA-POW
BLAM
BLAM
BLAM
BOYS, GO OUT AND SEE WHAT THE HELL THAT IS.
BLAM BLAM
AS FOR YOU... PROCEED-- OR I WILL SHOOT YOUR FACE CLEAN OFF.

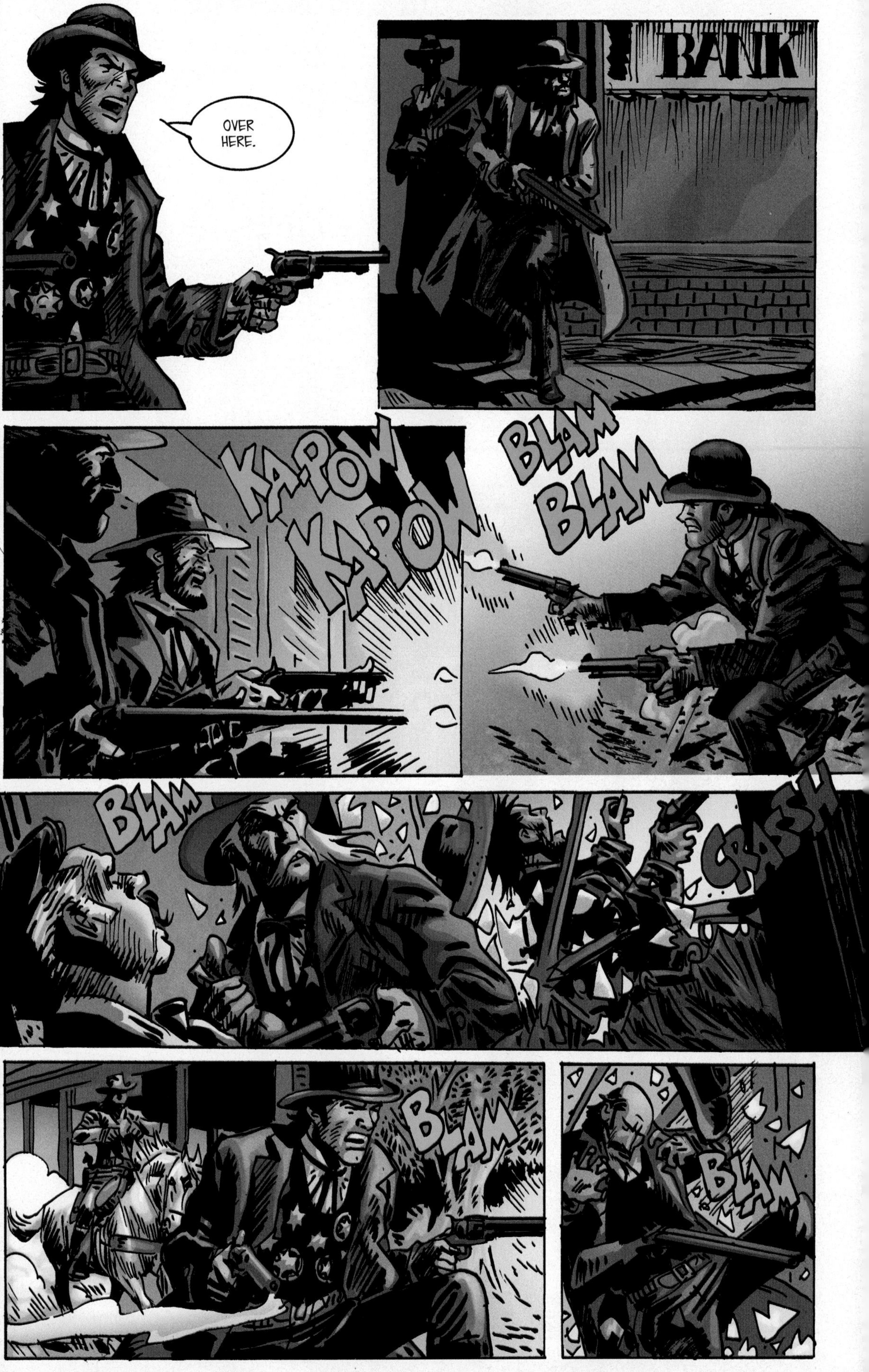
OVER HERE.
BANK
KAPOW
KAPOW
BLAM
BLAM
BLAM
CRASH
BLAM
BLAM

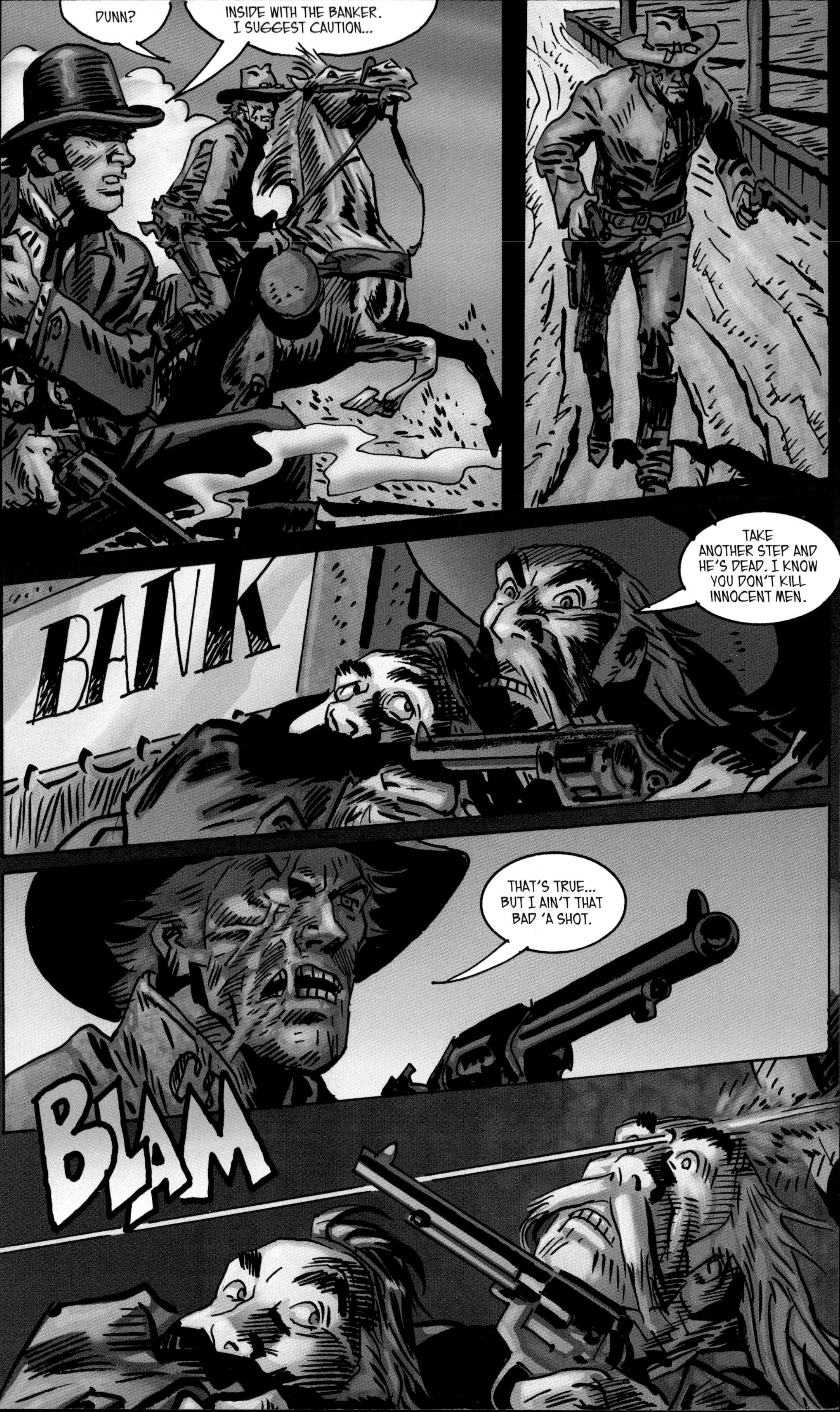
DUNN?
INSIDE WITH THE BANKER. I SUGGEST CAUTION...
BANK
TAKE ANOTHER STEP AND HE'S DEAD. I KNOW YOU DON'T KILL INNOCENT MEN.
THAT'S TRUE... BUT I AIN'T THAT BAD 'A SHOT.
BLAM

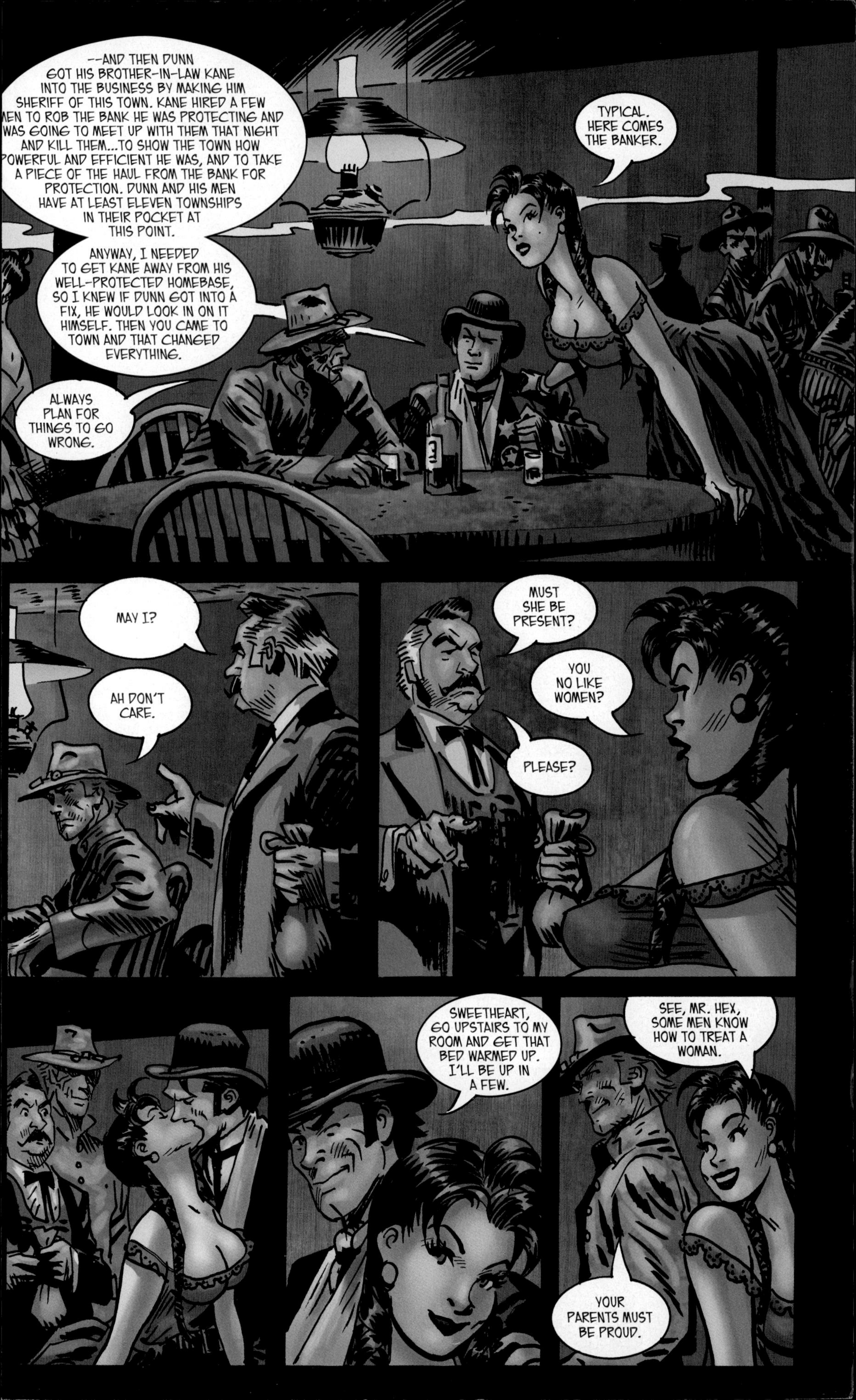
--AND THEN DUNN GOT HIS BROTHER-IN-LAW KANE INTO THE BUSINESS BY MAKING HIM SHERIFF OF THIS TOWN. KANE HIRED A FEW MEN TO ROB THE BANK HE WAS PROTECTING AND WAS GOING TO MEET UP WITH THEM THAT NIGHT AND KILL THEM...TO SHOW THE TOWN HOW POWERFUL AND EFFICIENT HE WAS, AND TO TAKE A PIECE OF THE HAUL FROM THE BANK FOR PROTECTION. DUNN AND HIS MEN HAVE AT LEAST ELEVEN TOWNSHIPS IN THEIR POCKET AT THIS POINT.
ANYWAY, I NEEDED TO GET KANE AWAY FROM HIS WELL-PROTECTED HOMEBASE, SO I KNEW IF DUNN GOT INTO A FIX, HE WOULD LOOK IN ON IT HIMSELF. THEN YOU CAME TO TOWN AND THAT CHANGED EVERYTHING.
ALWAYS PLAN FOR THINGS TO GO WRONG.
TYPICAL. HERE COMES THE BANKER.
MAY I?
AH DON'T CARE.
MUST SHE BE PRESENT?
YOU NO LIKE WOMEN?
PLEASE?
SWEETHEART, GO UPSTAIRS TO MY ROOM AND GET THAT BED WARMED UP. I'LL BE UP IN A FEW.
SEE, MR. HEX, SOME MEN KNOW HOW TO TREAT A WOMAN.
YOUR PARENTS MUST BE PROUD.

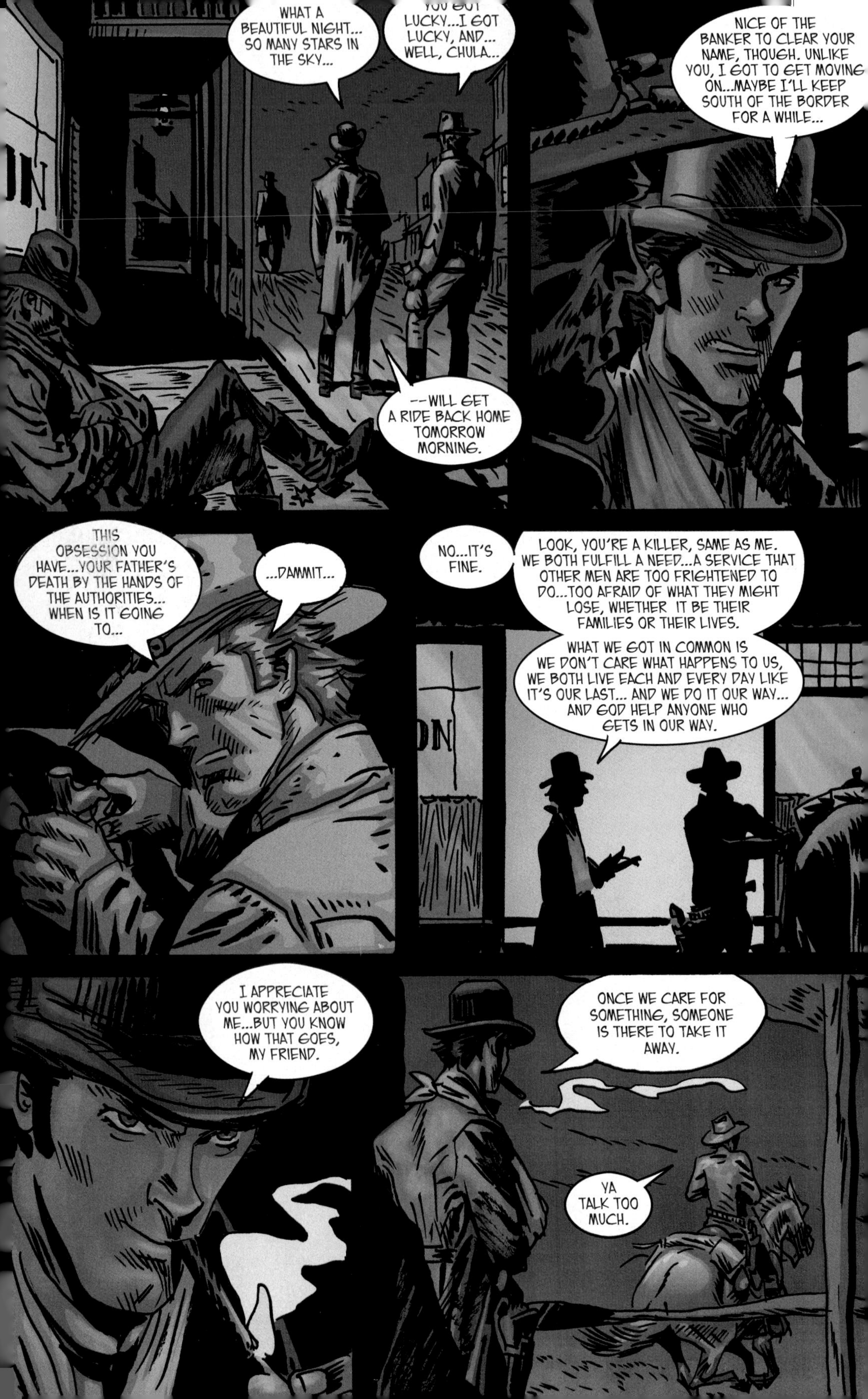
WHAT A BEAUTIFUL NIGHT... SO MANY STARS IN THE SKY...
YOU GOT LUCKY...I GOT LUCKY, AND... WELL, CHULA...
--WILL GET A RIDE BACK HOME TOMORROW MORNING.
NICE OF THE BANKER TO CLEAR YOUR NAME, THOUGH. UNLIKE YOU, I GOT TO GET MOVING ON...MAYBE I'LL KEEP SOUTH OF THE BORDER FOR A WHILE...
THIS OBSESSION YOU HAVE...YOUR FATHER'S DEATH BY THE HANDS OF THE AUTHORITIES... WHEN IS IT GOING TO...
...DAMMIT...
NO...IT'S FINE.
LOOK, YOU'RE A KILLER, SAME AS ME. WE BOTH FULFILL A NEED...A SERVICE THAT OTHER MEN ARE TOO FRIGHTENED TO DO...TOO AFRAID OF WHAT THEY MIGHT LOSE, WHETHER IT BE THEIR FAMILIES OR THEIR LIVES.
WHAT WE GOT IN COMMON IS WE DON'T CARE WHAT HAPPENS TO US, WE BOTH LIVE EACH AND EVERY DAY LIKE IT'S OUR LAST... AND WE DO IT OUR WAY... AND GOD HELP ANYONE WHO GETS IN OUR WAY.
I APPRECIATE YOU WORRYING ABOUT ME...BUT YOU KNOW HOW THAT GOES, MY FRIEND.
ONCE WE CARE FOR SOMETHING, SOMEONE IS THERE TO TAKE IT AWAY.
YA TALK TOO MUCH.

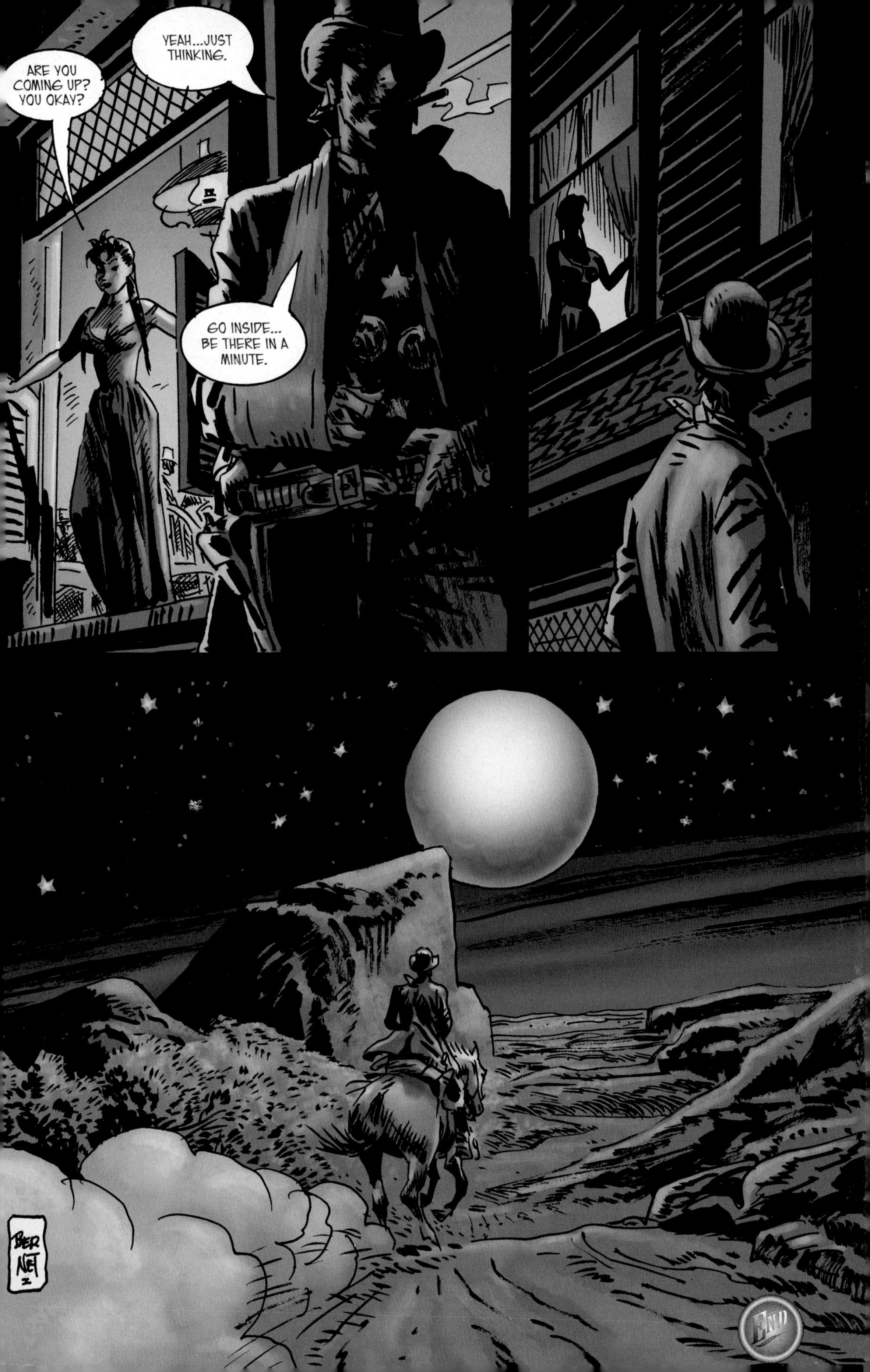
ARE YOU COMING UP? YOU OKAY?
YEAH...JUST THINKING.
GO INSIDE... BE THERE IN A MINUTE.
BER NET Z
END

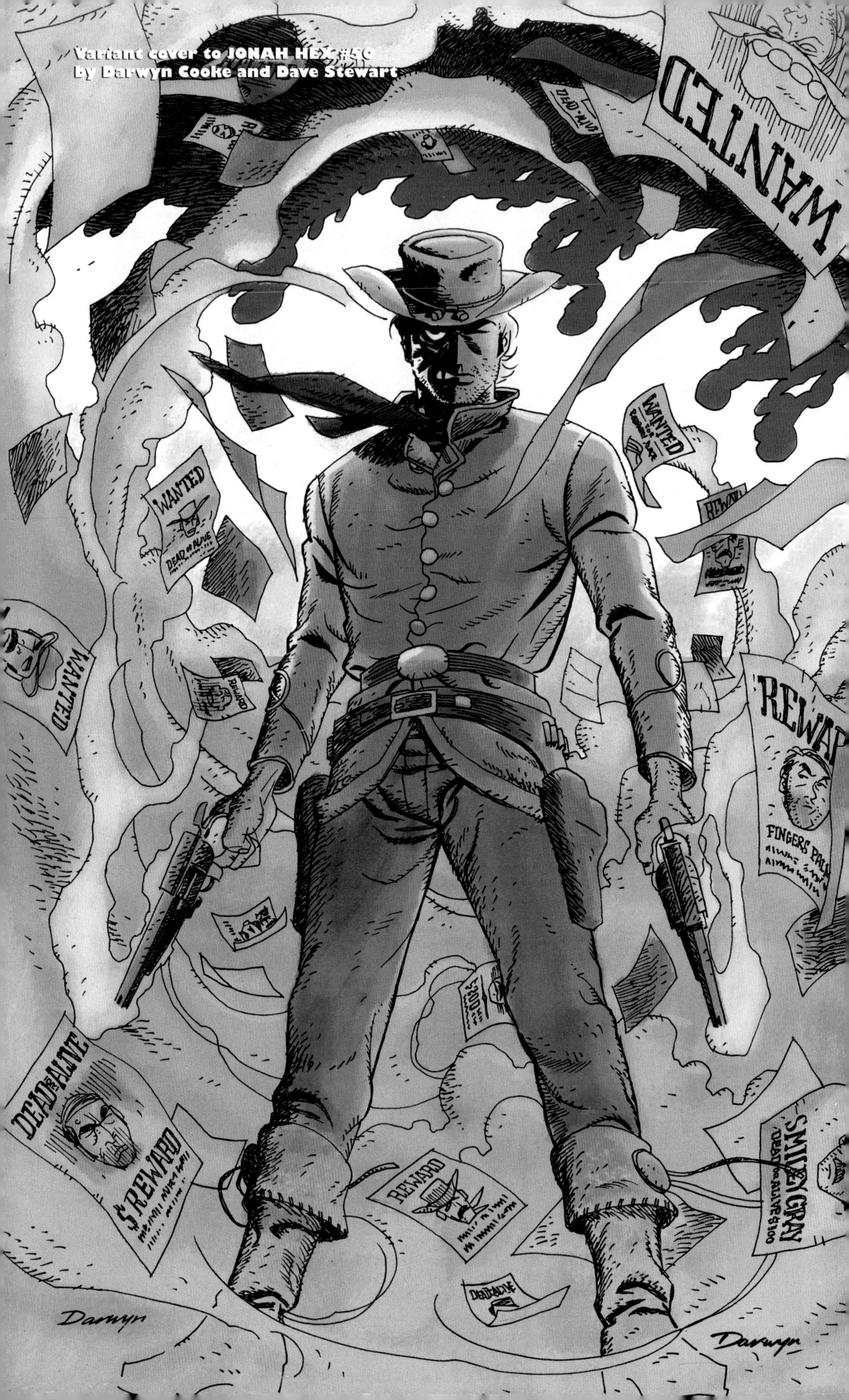
WANTED
WANTED
DEAD OR ALIVE
WANTED
REWARD
REWARD
FINGERS PAL
DEAD OR ALIVE
$REWARD
REWARD
SMILEY GRAY
DEAD OR ALIVE $100
Darwyn
Darwyn
Variant cover to JONAH HEX #50
by Darwyn Cooke and Dave Stewart